The Judiciary—Selection, Compensation, Ethics, and Discipline

The Judiciary—Selection, Compensation, Ethics, and Discipline

MARVIN COMISKY AND
PHILIP C. PATTERSON
WITH THE ASSISTANCE OF WILLIAM E. TAYLOR, III

Q QUORUM BOOKS

NEW YORK · WESTPORT, CONNECTICUT · LONDON

Library of Congress Cataloging-in-Publication Data

Comisky, Marvin.
 The judiciary—selection, compensation, ethics,
and discipline.

 Includes index.
 1. Judges—United States. 2. Judges—United States—
Discipline.   I. Patterson, Philip C.   II. Taylor,
William E.   III. Title.
KF8775.C65   1987   347.73'14   86–619
                       347.30714

 ISBN 0–89930–168–1 (lib. bdg. : alk. paper)

Library of Congress Catalog Card Number: 86–619
ISBN: 0–89930–168–1

First published in 1987 by Quorum Books

Greenwood Press, Inc.
88 Post Road West, Westport, Connecticut 06881

Printed in the United States of America

The paper used in this book complies with the
Permanent Paper Standard issued by the National
Information Standards Organization (Z39.48–1984).

10 9 8 7 6 5 4 3 2 1

Contents

1

Introduction

My friends are judges. Some of my former partners are judges. My classmates are judges. My contemporaries are judges. My social companions are judges. My clients are judges.

I respect judges.

I view judges as the bulwark of our administration of justice. They are the foundation for the preservation of the Bill of Rights and other constitutional guarantees—at the state as well as the federal level.

I have had the pleasure and honor of representing judges in varied issues: their compensation, their seniority, their pension rights. I have participated often at various levels of government—legislative and executive—in creating additional judicial offices. I have labored in the intricate and complex issue of selection of lawyers to fill judicial vacancies, both by executive appointment and by public election. I participated as general counsel in the limited Pennsylvania Constitutional Convention of 1967–68, where a cardinal issue was the establishment of a Supreme Court overview of all courts (unified state court system) and an intimate and detailed view of the selection-election process. I have represented judges in disciplinary proceedings, where I found the present procedures inadequate in concept and in execution.

My representation of judges, I hasten to add, has always been pro bono. I felt a lawyer's obligation to assist judges, when requested, without compensation because of the inadequacy of judicial compensation.

Judges preside over a myriad of issues—civil, equitable, criminal, bankruptcy, and reorganization—simple, complex, protracted. They cannot "pass the buck." The public little realizes the magnitude of their collective effort.

Day in and day out they perform. The media notes the occurrence of an occasional failure in the system but rarely comments on the multitude—literally thousands—of daily dispositions that satisfy the due process requirement and enforce our system of justice.

By reason of my many contacts with the judiciary in these varied fields of activity, I have become conscious of the need for a collection of relevant information dealing with the judiciary.

I have found an absence of such a text.

In drafting this volume, I have singularly abstained from policy decisions. If one occurs, it is by inadvertence in a text of this size.

We have attempted to gather relevant material in a single compilation of matters of major importance to the judiciary. This we hope will assist the legislative and executive bodies, and perhaps also the judiciary itself in determining recommendations and procedures in the various areas of concern.

Accordingly, we have dealt only with selected areas; much remains either for a supplementary edition or for others. We have dealt with judicial selection, judicial compensation, disqualification and removal, political activity, judicial discipline, removal of judges, and civil and criminal liability.

It is customary and proper to acknowledge the efforts of those who participated in this text. Philip C. Patterson, Esquire, now retired, came out of retirement to act as co-author. His duties also encompassed those of reporter and researcher. My extraordinary and capable editor is a practicing partner, William E. Taylor, III, who gave exhaustively of his time and effort to revise the text into more readable material. This work is in very large part attributable to their combined efforts. William H. Roberts, another partner, assisted in securing the publisher. Still another partner, Goncer Krestal, gave me comfort and advice through our long association. Finally, I publicly thank all my partners at Blank, Rome, Comisky & McCauley who sustained me in support of the publication.

I trust it will be as meaningful as we intend.

2

Judicial Selection

2.1 HISTORY OF JUDICIAL SELECTION IN ENGLAND AND IN THE UNITED STATES

In England prior to 1700, judges were deemed crown agents. They were selected and appointed by the king, acting through the chancellor, and were subject to instantaneous and arbitrary removal by the king.[1] The Act of Settlement, passed in 1700 after the English Revolution of 1688 and the ouster of James II, gave the English judiciary tenure "during good behavior" and provided that a judge could not be removed except by action of both houses of Parliament.[2] A 1761 statute provided for continued judicial tenure after the monarch's death.[3]

The English reforms of 1700 and 1761 did not, however, extend to the American colonies. Until the American Revolution, colonial judges were selected and appointed by the king, and, as was complained of in the Declaration of Independence,[4] were "dependent on his will alone, for the tenure of his offices, and the amount and payment of their salaries."[5]

Following the American Revolution, eight of the original thirteen states bestowed the power to select judges upon one or both houses of the legislature;[6] two of the states vested joint appointive power in the governor and the Council;[7] while the remaining three states gave appointive power to the governor, conditioned on the consent of the council.[8] The U.S. Constitution gave the power to appoint judges to the president of the United States, subject to confirmation by the U.S. Senate, and gave federal judges tenure "during good behavior."[9]

The failure to provide for popular election of judges at either the federal or state level has been ascribed to the founding fathers' belief that the electorate at large was not capable of evaluating the professional qualifications of prospective judges.[10] Commencing in the first half of the nineteenth century, however, the egalitarian philosophy engendered by the Jacksonian revolution resulted in many states opting in favor of popular election of judges, coupled with short terms of office.[11]

Dissatisfaction with partisan popular election, fostered by a belief that politicians had been able to acquire undue control over the selection and tenure of judges, arose between 1870 and 1930. Consequently, a considerable number of the elective states provided for nonpartisan rather than partisan judicial election.[12] Dissatisfaction with nonpartisan election, too, soon developed. The parties still selected the candidates, but, because candidates lacked indentifying party labels, the voters were even more uninformed about the candidates and their qualifications than they were in partisan elections.[13]

This dissatisfaction resulted in a movement within the legal profession to fashion a system in which judges would be selected by an elected official, such as a supreme court justice or governor, from a list of candidates nominated by an independent nonpartisan nominating commission composed principally of lawyers and laymen.[14] This system was originally proposed in 1914 by Albert M. Kales, a law professor and director of research for the American Judicature Society,[15] and endorsed by the American Bar Association in 1937.[16] Missouri, in 1940,[17] became the first state to actually adopt such a plan; since then, a large number of states[18] have followed suit. This type of plan is generally referred to as a "merit plan," a "Missouri plan," or a "merit selection plan."[19]

In the plan originally proposed by Professor Kales, the chief justice of the state supreme court was to select and appoint judges from among the nominees designated by a judicial conference.[20] In the plan endorsed by the American Bar Association and adopted by Missouri, the governor made the appointments and the nominations were presented by a nominating commission.[21] A feature of Professor Kales' plan, retained in Missouri and many other merit selection states, requires that an incumbent appointed under the plan run in a noncompetitive retention election following expiration of an initial probationary term and each subsequent term.[22]

In the ensuing sections of this chapter, the current status of each of the major methods of judicial selection will be reviewed. This will encompass how a judicial position is filled at the outset of a term of office ("initial selection"), how selections are made during a term of office to fill vacancies, either temporarily ("temporary vacancy selection") or until the end of the term ("final vacancy selection"), and noncompetitive retention elections.[23]

2.2 LEGISLATIVE APPOINTMENT OF JUDGES

Following the American Revolution, eight of the original thirteen states conferred the power to select judges upon one or both houses of the legislature,[24] but only Rhode Island,[25] South Carolina,[26] and Virginia[27] still employ this method. The legislature's power extends to all courts of record in Virginia and South Carolina, other than the probate courts in South Carolina, but solely to the supreme court in Rhode Island.[28] Both houses of the legislature participate in the selection process, apparently by a joint vote of both houses in Rhode Island and South Carolina, and by a separate majority vote of each house in Virginia.[29]

In each of these three states, the legislature has the power to make initial selection when an incumbent's term of office has expired or is about to expire, and also vacancy selection, viz. to fill a judicial office that has become vacant during an ongoing term of office.[30]

Although the legislative body has the final vote, the actual task of selecting potential nominees, investigating and reporting on their qualifications, and submitting the names of recommended candidates is done by legislative committees.[31]

The legislative selection of judges has been criticized on the ground that few legislators are competent to pass upon the qualifications of judicial candidates, that legislators are too apt to be politically motivated in selecting for judicial candidates, that judges selected in this manner are overly obligated to legislators voting for them, and that legislators seeking to be appointed as judges are apt to be beneficiaries of this system.[32]

2.3 EXECUTIVE APPOINTMENT OF JUDGES

In many states, where either partisan election or nonpartisan election is the primary method of selecting major court judges,[33] some form of executive appointment is used as a temporary vacancy selection device[34] pending an election to fill the vacancy permanently.[35] In most instances, these temporary gubernatorial appointments are not subject to legislative confirmation.[36] Since gubernatorial appointments of this type are a mere adjunct of elective selection, the states that utilize popular election for all or for most of their major courts must be considered elective rather than appointive states.

Most of the states that utilize gubernatorial appointment for final vacancy selection[37] also utilize it as a method of initially filling the office.[38] Only a few states utilize gubernatorial appointment solely as a device for final vacancy selection and not as a means of initial selection.[39]

The states and federal jurisdictions that utilize gubernatorial or presidential selection as a device for initial (as well as final vacancy) selection break down into three broad categories: those that require confirmation by the senate or legislature;[40] those that require confirmation by some nonlegislative body such as a council[41] or commission;[42] and those that give the governor power to make interim appointments without legislative confirmation when the legislature is not in session, to expire at a designated point of time after the legislature has reconvened.[43]

Although the applicable constitutional and statutory provisions generally do not detail the procedures to be followed by the legislature in considering gubernatorial appointments, the pertinent provisions in certain states, e.g., Connecticut and Maine, require that the gubernatorial nomination be referred to a joint legislative committee (Connecticut) or a legislative committee in each house (Maine) for review and recommendation.[44]

New Jersey's constitution specifies that gubernatorial judicial nominations shall not be sent to the senate for confirmation until the governor gives seven days public notice of the proposed appointment.[45] This requirement increases the likelihood that members of the bar or public will supply useful information to the legislature concerning the nominee.

The legislative veto has, at best, a negative value, since, if a governor is unwilling to select the most highly qualified candidate irrespective of partisan political considerations, the negative sanction of a legislative veto will probably not cause the governor to alter his approach. Executive selection of judges also has been criticized on the ground that it leaves the governor free to rely entirely upon his political advisers and does not require input from either the minority party or leaders of the bar. Critics of executive appointment have pointed out that the typical chief executive is subject to political pressures based on partisan considerations, and is also apt to expect a *quid pro quo* from his appointees. Finally, it has been argued that a governor's day-by-day experience in administering the affairs of the state has little to do with problems a judge is likely to encounter.[46]

In recognition of their own limitations in locating and choosing the best candidates, a number of governors have voluntarily issued executive orders adopting a voluntary merit selection plan similar to the Missouri plan.[47] Some voluntary plans have been adopted for both initial and final vacancy selection[48] and, in other instances, these plans relate only to temporary vacancy selection,[49] pending an election[50] to fill the office for the remainder of the unexpired term or pending expiration of the unexpired term when its duration has been deemed too brief to make an election worthwhile.[51]

2.4 JUDICIAL APPOINTMENT OF JUDGES

Judicial appointment of judges, the selection of judges by other judges or courts, is rare in this country.[52] Even for temporary vacancy selection, judicial appointment is presently used for major court judges only in Illinois and Louisiana.[53] On the other hand, judicial appointment frequently has been used as a method of initial and final vacancy selection of members of the minor judiciary, such as magistrates,[54] court commissioners,[55] and judges of courts of limited or specialized jurisdiction.[56] Additionally, it has been used as a method of initial and final vacancy selection for associate judges,[57] special judges,[58] and substitute judges.[59]

One of the earliest of the merit selection proposals, made by Hewlett H.

Hall at a symposium on judicial selection in 1909, advocated that the state supreme court make the nominations and that the governor be required to make an appointment from the supreme court's list of nominees, subject to confirmation by the senate.[60] Similarly, Professor Albert M. Kales, director of drafting of the American Judicature Society, in 1914 advocated that at least every other appointment to fill a judicial vacancy be made by an elected chief justice from standing eligibility lists submitted by a judicial council composed of judges.[61] In 1961, Herbert Harley, founder and first secretary of the Society proposed that this selection method be used for every appointment, rather than for every other appointment.[62]

During the next few years, merit selection proposals were made providing for appointments by the governor rather than the chief justice from lists of nominees submitted by either the state supreme court[63] or a panel of judges.[64]

During the years that elapsed between these proposals and the adoption of merit selections plans by Missouri and a number of other states, writers on the subject and, ultimately, the drafters of the merit selection plans that actually went into effect gradually modified the merit selection concept, first by adding lawyers to the nominating group, next by adding laymen to the group, and, eventually, by reducing the number of judges to a single judge, usually a chief justice or presiding judge.[65]

2.5 PARTISAN ELECTION OF JUDGES

The trend away from partisan election of judges began during the latter part of the nineteenth century. Seven states, Alabama, Arkansas, Mississippi, New Mexico, North Carolina, Texas, and West Virginia, still utilize partisan election as their sole method of finally selecting judges for all appellate courts and trial courts of general jurisdiction. In these states, partisan elections are utilized not only for initial selection and final vacancy selection, but also for determining whether to retain sitting judges for a new term.[66] Alabama uses a commission plan with respect to two of its counties, Jefferson County and Madison County.[67]

Two more jurisdictions, Illinois and Pennsylvania, employ partisan election for initial selection and final vacancy selection of judges for all their appellate courts and trial courts of general jurisdiction, but hold noncompetitive retention elections for judges who have been previously elected to office.[68]

Reliance on elections in Mississippi, New Mexico, North Carolina, Pennsylvania, and West Virginia is somewhat lessened by the use of gubernatorial appointments to fill temporary vacancies under voluntary commission plans adopted by the governors of these states.[69]

Finally, Indiana, Kansas, Louisiana, Missouri, New York, and Tennessee use partisan elections for all types of final judicial selection (initial selection, final vacancy selection, and retention determination) for some major courts[70] but a commission plan for others.[71] In addition, in a number of states, judges of various courts of specialized or limited jurisdiction are, at least initially, chosen by partisan election.[72]

As a general rule, partisan judicial elections coincide with general elections in even-numbered years.[73] On the theory that this practice created an undue tendency for voters to vote along party lines, the Pennsylvania constitution was amended in 1909 to require that judges be elected at "the municipal election next preceding the commencement of their respective terms of office."[74] These elections are held in odd-numbered years in Pennsylvania,[75] whereas general elections are held in even-numbered years.[76]

In states employing partisan elections, candidates for judicial office are generally nominated in partisan primaries or conventions.[77] The use of partisan primaries to nominate judicial candidates to run in partisan elections has been criticized on the ground that party leaders control the choice of delegates to the nominating conventions and, therefore, in effect also control the nominating conventions.[78]

An alternative method of securing nomination for judicial office is through nominating petitions, signed by a legally mandated number of qualified voters.[79] Since the required number of signatures is apt to be quite large,[80] this method can be cumbersome and onerous.

The principal arguments offered by proponents of partisan election are: (a) that judges make policy and, therefore, should be directly chosen by, and accountable to, the people who will be subject to or affected by those policies; (b) that partisan election is an open method of selection;[81] and (c) that identification of a judicial candidate's party affiliation provides voters with a clue as to his probable ideology.[82]

The principal arguments against partisan election are: (a) the voters generally lack knowledge of the candidates' qualifications and, perhaps for that reason, are generally relatively indifferent to the outcome of the judicial elections;[83] (b) the voters are not competent to evaluate the candidates' qualifications;[84] (c) each political party's nominees are generally selected by its political leaders, who are apt to select them for reasons of political expediency, rather than for reasons of comparative merit;[85] (d) the successful candidates are apt to feel unduly obligated to the political leaders who selected them and to the contributors to their campaign funds;[86] (e) many highly qualified potential candidates are apt to be deterred from seeking judicial office, by reason of the cost, time-consuming nature, and often demeaning quality of their campaigns;[87] (f) the necessity of periodically seeking re-election, especially when coupled with shortness of tenure, discourages many from sacrificing their law practices in order to run for judicial office;[88] (g) the political leaders who generally select the candidates are hardly the best qualified persons to select or seek out the best candidates;[89] (h) voters in judicial elections have a tendency to be influenced by factors irrelevant to the candidates' judicial qualifications, such as political party affiliation, familiarity of name, geographical location, and place on ballot;[90] and (i) even in elective states, most sitting judges owe their original accession to the bench to appointment to fill a vacancy, rather than to election,[91] and it has been inferred from statistics that incumbent judges have strong advantages over nonincumbent opponents in judicial elections.[92]

2.6 NONPARTISAN ELECTION OF JUDGES

With minor exceptions, eleven states, Georgia, Idaho, Kentucky, Louisiana, Michigan, Minnesota, North Dakota, Ohio, Oregon, Washington, and Wisconsin, utilize nonpartisan election for initial selection, final vacancy selection, and retention selection of all appellate and trial court judges.[93] A constitutional, statutory, or voluntary commission plan is, however, utilized in some of these states for temporary vacancy selection.[94]

Seven other states, California, Florida, Montana, Nevada, Oklahoma, South Dakota, and Utah, utilize nonpartisan election for some types of selection or for some major courts.[95] In these same states, a commission plan is used in lieu of nonpartisan election for other types of selection or for other major courts.[96] Except in Nevada, judges appointed pursuant to a commission plan in these states are accorded the right to run in a noncompetitive retention election. In Montana and Utah this privilege is, however, limited to instances where the judge is unopposed.[97]

In the great majority of the states that select judges in nonpartisan elections, e.g., Florida, Montana, Oregon, and Wisconsin, primary elections (or nominating conventions) are also nonpartisan, at least in the sense that the candidates' political party affiliations are not permitted to appear on the ballot.[98] Conversely, Ohio has partisan primaries followed by nonpartisan general elections.[99] Arizona employed this system before it adopted merit selection in 1974,[100] and Michigan has nonpartisan elections preceded by partisan nominating conventions.[101]

In addition to primary elections and nominating conventions, several states, e.g., Ohio and Montana, use nominating petitions as a means of selecting candidates in nonpartisan elections.[102]

A prohibition against placing candidates' party affiliations on the ballot does not necessarily ensure against this information being distributed by other means. Although judicial candidates and political parties in Florida are not permitted to identify the candidates' parties in non-partisan judicial elections,[103] political parties in other states have done so.[104] This practice tends to nullify, at least partially, the insulation from partisan politics supposedly provided by the prohibition against party identification on election ballots.

Nonpartisan elections have been criticized on numerous grounds. Nonpartisan elections are said to not address the problems of lack of voter knowledge concerning the candidates' qualifications or of voter inability to evaluate those qualifications.[105] Moreover, voters are likely to remain largely ignorant of the candidates' positions on the issues, since Canon 7 B (1)(c) of the American Bar Association's (ABA) widely adopted Code of Judicial Conduct[106] forbids candidates from making pledges or promises regarding conduct in office other than to promise faithful performance of the duties of the office. Judicial candidates are also forbidden to announce their views on disputed legal or political issues.[107]

It has also been argued that voters in nonpartisan competitive elections vote on the basis of irrelevant considerations such as the candidates' political affiliations, the possession of a well-known name, the location of the candidate's name on the ballot, or the candidate's television personality.[108] Moreover, inequality of financial resources appears even more telling in nonpartisan elections than in partisan elections.[109] Opponents of nonpartisan election maintain that these considerations and other largely irrelevant factors are much more determinative in nonpartisan judicial elections than the candidates' relative qualifications for the judgeship.[110]

2.7 THE COMMISSION PLAN FOR NOMINATING AND APPOINTING JUDGES

a. Preliminary Description of the Commission Plan

As it was originally conceived by Professor Kales in 1914, and as it has been adopted in many states since it was first endorsed by the American Bar Association in 1937 and adopted by the state of Missouri in 1940, the so-called commission plan has always had three key elements: (a) a nominating commission composed, at least in part, of judges and/or lawyers; (b) an elected appointing official, obligated to appoint judges from the commission's lists of nominees; and (c) a requirement that each judge appointed pursuant to the plan submit to a noncompetitive retention election prior to the expiration of a specified probationary period following his appointment and of each ensuing full term of office.[111]

b. The Courts Subject to the Various Commission Plans

Commission plans vary widely from state to state as to the courts encompassed by the plan. All appellate and major trial courts are subject to a constitutional or statutory commission plan in Alaska, Colorado, District of Columbia, Florida, Hawaii, Idaho, Iowa, Kentucky, Montana, Nebraska, Nevada, North Dakota, Oklahoma, South Dakota, Utah, Vermont, and Wyoming.[112] In addition, Delaware, Georgia, Maryland, Massachusetts, Minnesota, Mississippi, New Mexico, Pennsylvania, and West Virginia[113] have voluntary (and therefore revocable) commission plans, applicable to all appellate courts and trial courts of general jurisdiction.

States with a constitutional or statutory commission plan in effect for less than all of the state's major courts include Alabama, Arizona, Indiana, Kansas, Missouri, New York, and Tennessee; and a voluntary plan is in effect in New York with respect to Appellate Division Justices and in North Carolina with respect to superior court judges.[114]

c. The Nature of the Vacancies Filled by the Various Commission Plans

With a few exceptions, constitutional and statutory commission plans apply only to initial and final vacancy selection, and voluntary commission plans only to temporary vacancy selection.

Jurisdictions with constitutional or statutory commission plans applicable to initial and final vacancy selection for one or more courts include Alaska, Arizona, Colorado, District of Columbia, Florida (appellate courts), Hawaii, Indiana, Iowa, Kansas, Missouri, Montana, Nebraska, New York (Court of Appeals), Oklahoma, Tennessee, Utah, Vermont, and Wyoming,[115] Jurisdictions with voluntary commission plans applicable to initial and final vacancy selection include Delaware, Maryland, Massachusetts, and New York (Appellate Division of Supreme Court).[116]

Conversely, states with constitutional commission plans that are applicable only to temporary vacancy selection include Alabama (appellate courts and certain major trial courts), Florida (major trial courts), Idaho, Kentucky, and North Dakota;[117] and jurisdictions with voluntary commission plans that are applicable only to temporary vacancy selection include Georgia, Minnesota, Mississippi, New Mexico, North Carolina, Pennsylvania, and West Virginia.[118]

Nevada's supreme court commission plan applies solely to final vacancy selection, while its district court commission plan applies only to temporary vacancy selection. South Dakota's commission plan, for all its major courts, applies only to final vacancy selection and not to initial selection.[119]

In states with commission plans (whether constitutional, statutory, or voluntary) applicable only to temporary vacancy selection, initial selection, final vacancy selection, and retention determination are decided in competitive elections.[120] In Alabama, Mississippi, New Mexico, North Carolina, and Pennsylvania, the competitive elections are partisan, while in Florida (circuit and county courts only), Georgia, Idaho, Kentucky, Minnesota, and North Dakota, the competitive elections are nonpartisan.[121]

d. The Retention Features of the Various Commission Plans

In most states with the plans applicable to initial and final vacancy selection, retention of judges initially appointed under those plans is determined in noncompetitive elections, which are held both at the end of an initial probationary period and at the end of each ensuing term of office. These jurisdictions include Alaska, Arizona, Colorado, Florida, Indiana, Iowa, Kansas, Maryland, Missouri, Montana (if the incumbent is unopposed), Nebraska, Oklahoma, Tennessee, Utah (if the incumbent is unopposed), Vermont (election by legislature), and Wyoming.[122]

A few jurisdictions with commission plans for initial and final vacancy selection of major court judges do not, however, provide for noncompetitive retention elections for incumbent judges previously appointed under the commission plan. These states include Delaware (a voluntary commission plan state), the District of Columbia, Hawaii, Massachusetts, and New York (a constitutional plan as to the Court of Appeals and a voluntary plan as to the Appellate Division).[123] The District of Columbia grants automatic retention to incumbent judges who file timely declarations of candidacy and are found to be either exceptionally well qualified or well qualified by the Tenure Commission. Retention is, however, still dependent upon confirmation by the U.S. Senate.[124] In Massachusetts, a voluntary commission plan state, judges are granted lifetime tenure "during good behavior."[125] Retention is therefore not an issue.

Although noncompetitive retention elections were included in the original Kales merit selection proposal,[126] the American Judicature Society did not provide for them in its 1915 merit selection proposals on the ground that the public was "largely incompetent" to decide whether judges should be retained. The Society believed that the public had no way of ascertaining information on a judge's performance, was not qualified to appraise a judge's proficiency and standards, and was largely indifferent to judges' retention.[127] In its 1917 merit selection proposal, the Society again failed to endorse noncompetitive retention elections but did indicate that they would be preferable to competitive election.[128] The Society's apparent preference was for lifetime tenure during good behavior, as in the federal courts and Massachusetts.[129] Most commission plan proposals since 1917 have included noncompetitive retention elections. The proponents' motives in adopting this feature have probably been to confer security of tenure upon judges who had been selected on a merit selection basis, while pacifying the proponents of popular elections.[130]

e. Confirmation Requirements in Commission States

Only eight commission plan states require some form of additional confirmation. The District of Columbia, Hawaii, Maryland, Montana, New York, Pennsylvania, and Vermont require senate confirmation of appointees,[131] while Massachusetts (a voluntary plan state) requires confirmation by the Governor's Council.[132]

The lack of a confirmation requirement in most commission plans appears to minimize the likelihood of political pressure being brought to bear upon the governor and nominating commissions in making their selections.[133]

f. The Number of Commissions in the Various Jurisdictions with Commission Plans and the Extent to Which Different Courts in the Same Jurisdiction Are Subject to the Same Commission Plan or to Different Commission Plans

The number of separate nominating commissions in commission plan states differs widely.[134] At one end of the spectrum, twelve jurisdictions have a single commission for all courts to which a commission plan applies,[135] while two states have a single commission for major courts and a separate one for their minor courts.[136] Other jurisdictions have separate commissions for appellate courts and trial courts of general jurisdiction.[137] Most jurisdictions with multiple commissions nevertheless have only a single appellate court nominating commission,[138] although four of these states have two-tier appellate court systems.[139]

Other variations include a judicial nominating commission for each trial court but none for the appellate courts,[140] multiple commissions for appellate courts,[141] and a separate commission for each appellate position.[142]

g. The Composition of the Various Commissions

Commission plans vary considerably, both as to the numerical balance between lawyers and nonlawyers and as to whether the judiciary is represented on the commission. The typical commission is composed of a certain number of lawyers, a certain number of nonlawyers, and a single judge.[143] The next most prevalent type of commission consists of lawyers and nonlawyers but no judges.[144]

The most prevalent type of judicial nominating commission is composed of a designated number of lawyers, an equal number of nonlawyers, and a single judge. In ten jurisdictions, one or more nominating commissions fit this description.[145] In two of these jurisdictions, Kansas and Nebraska, however, the judge does not vote.[146]

Eight jurisdictions have one or more nominating commissions on which lawyers outnumber laymen, before adding any judicial member to the lawyers;[147] in six of these jurisdictions there is no judicial member.[148] In Idaho, although nonlawyers outnumber lawyers by one, there are two additional judicial members.[149] Georgia is the only state whose major court commission has no judicial members and an equal number of lawyers and nonlawyers.[150]

In Colorado, nonlawyers outnumber lawyers by one but after adding the judicial member, the numbers would be equal.[151] As with Nebraska, however, the judge is a nonvoting member.

In six jurisdictions, where some of the members can be either lawyers or nonlawyers at the appointer's option, the majority will vary with the nature of the appointments.[152] In Hawaii, where some of the members can be either lawyers or nonlawyers, nonlawyers will always be in the majority, since only four out of the nine members are permitted to be lawyers.[153]

Finally, on a number of commissions, the nonlawyers outnumber the lawyers even if the judicial members, if any, are counted as lawyers.[154] In several of these jurisdictions, there is no judicial member.[155]

h. The Appointers of the Judicial Nominating Commission's Members

The lawyers on most nominating commissions are elected by members of the bar.[156] In a given state, however, the lawyers making nominations may be drawn from the entire state or from a particular supreme court district, judicial district, congressional district, or grand division.[157]

Lawyers on nominating commissions are most commonly appointed by the board of governors of the state bar association.[158] Others responsible for appointing of lawyer members include the governor;[159] the president of the state bar association;[160] a triumvirate composed of the governor, the attorney general, and the chief justice;[161] and the state supreme court.[162] In some states, *ex officio* appointments are based on past or present positions in the state bar association.[163]

In all but a few commission states, the governor appoints the nonlawyer members.[164] Others who fill this role include the legislators from the area in which the court served by the commission has jurisdiction;[165] and a majority of the other members of the commission.[166]

In certain instances where particular appointees may be either lawyers or nonlawyers, the power to appoint has been vested in specified officials drawn from each major branch of government.[167] Similarly, in one state, where a certain number of members must be drawn from each house of the legislature, the power of appointment has been conferred upon the members of the appointee's house.[168]

Finally, under Pennsylvania's voluntary commission plan, the governor appoints all of the members of the commission, lawyers and nonlawyers alike.[169]

On many constitutional or statutory commissions, a designated judicial member serves on an *ex officio* basis (e.g., as chief or senior justice or judge of a designated court).[170] In several instances, a designated judge is required to elect between serving on an *ex officio* basis and naming another judge as a commission member.[171] In other states, the judicial members are appointed by a designated judge,[172] the members of a designated court,[173] or a judicial conference.[174] In at least one state, however, the governor also appoints the judicial members.[175]

The most significant difference between the voluntary commission plans and the constitutional and statutory commission plans appears to be the governor's power of appointment. The governor's appointive power under mandatory plans is generally limited to the nonlawyer members.[176] In contrast, the governor's appointive power under the Massachusetts, Pennsylvania, Rhode Island, and West Virginia voluntary commission plans generally, but not always, applies to all of the commission members.[177] Similarly, while a judicial member of a constitutional or statutory commission is generally designated by law as its chairman,[178] the governor generally (but not in New Mexico and North Carolina) selects the chairperson of a voluntary commission.[179]

Generally speaking, appointments to nominating commissions do not require legislative confirmation,[180] but a few plans do require legislative confirmation of all nonjudicial members[181] or of the nonlawyer members.[182]

i. The Persons or Entities Empowered to Select and Appoint Judges from Among the Nominating Commissions' Nominees

Virtually all the major court merit selection plans, whether constitutional, statutory, or voluntary, designate the governor as the final appointing authority.[183] Although the governor's appointments are not subject to confirmation by the state senate or legislature under most plans,[184] confirmation is required in a few instances.[185]

Another limitation on the governor's authority in a number of the merit selection jurisdictions is a proviso that, if, by a specified deadline (generally thirty to sixty days), the governor has not appointed one of the commission's nominees, an alternative appointing authority, usually the chief justice of the highest appellate court,[186] and occasionally the nominating commission itself,[187] shall make the appointment from the list of nominees previously presented to the governor. A number of merit selection states do not, however, incorporate this feature.[188]

j. The Maximum and Minimum Number of Nominees Required to Be Nominated by the Commissions

Most commission plans either require that the commission nominate a specified number of nominees or specify both a maximum and a minimum number of nominees.[189]

k. Restrictions Imposed upon the Proportionate Political Make-up of Various Nominating Commissions to Make Them Bipartisan in Nature

A number of commission plans have restrictions designed to ensure a reasonable balance between the major political parties to give the committees a bipartisan cast. This type of provision is found in Arizona, Colorado, Idaho, Kentucky, Nebraska, New York, Utah, and Vermont.[190]

There are two types of provisions imposing bipartisanship requirements on commission membership. One type, employed in Arizona, Kentucky, New York, Vermont, and the Utah trial judge plan, applies the requirement separately to each class of members chosen by a particular appointing authority. This type of restriction does not necessitate coordinated compliance by the different appointing authorities.[191] The other type of restriction, found in Colorado, Idaho, Nebraska, and the Utah supreme court justice plan, applies in general to all the members chosen by different appointing authorities. This, of course, necessitates coordinated compliance by those authorities.[192]

l. Restrictions Prohibiting Members of Nominating Commissions from Holding, Seeking , or Securing Governmental, Political, or Judicial Offices

To depoliticize the judicial nominating process in commission plan states and to eliminate conflicts of interest, restrictions have been included in many plans prohibiting commission members, other than incumbent judges,[193] from either holding or being elected or appointed to public office.[194] Other plans also extend the prohibition to political party office[195] or to judicial office.[196] In the case of judicial office most, but not all, of the restrictions bind commission members for a specified period after they have ceased to be members.[197] Some, but not all, plans also prohibit commission members from serving two consecutive terms.[198]

Some of the prohibitions against accession by a member to the bench appear to apply to all judicial offices within the state.[199] Others appear to apply only to the courts for which the commission makes nominations.[200]

m. Confidentiality Restrictions Imposed upon Nominating Commissions and the Governors and Other Appointing Authorities to Whom the Commissions Submit Their Nominations

It has been argued that the names of the candidates or nominees considered either by the commission in deciding whom to nominate or by the governor in deciding which nominee to appoint should be made public. Proponents of this view contend that it would be helpful for the public to be able to give the commission or the governor factual information and opinions concerning the candidates or nominees.[201] The opposing argument has been that the prospect of public knowledge of their candidacies, the commission's evaluation of their qualifications, and their possible rejection as candidates would deter many highly qualified potential candidates from even submitting themselves for consideration[202] and might encourage unqualified persons to enter their names to obtain public notice.[203]

A majority of the commission plan states have opted for confidentiality as to candidates not yet passed on by the commission or who have been passed on and rejected by the commission.[204] Only a few states have a contrary rule.[205] Conversely, a majority of the states have chosen to publicize the names of commission nominees before the governor makes his final selection.[206] A few states, however, withhold the nominees' names and disclose only the final appointees' names.[207]

The states that withhold the names of applicants other than nominees have accorded similar treatment to the applicants' answers to commission questionnaires[208] and to communications concerning applicants by or between commissioners or other persons.[209] These communications have been protected against disclosure even in states that require that the names of applicants be publicized at the commission stage.[210] Similarly, even some of the states that require public disclosure of the nominees' names prohibit disclosure of the evaluations of the nominees' judicial qualifications.[211] Other such states, however, require public disclosure of the evaluations.[212]

Access to confidential commission files concerning a disappointed candidate has even been denied to the candidate, on the ground that granting access would tend to defer the free flow of information, particularly adverse comments to the commission.[213]

Finally, in certain states the commissioners vote by secret ballot,[214] while in others the vote is by oral roll call.[215]

2.8 NONCOMPETITIVE RETENTION ELECTIONS

Noncompetitive retention election originated as an adjunct to merit selection and, with the exception of Illinois, California, and Pennsylvania,[216] has been adopted by only those states that have had commission plans and then solely as to judges appointed under the commission plan.[217] Illinois has no commission plan, being a partisan election state for purposes of initial and final vacancy selection.[218] Pennsylvania, although it employs a voluntary commission plan for purposes of temporary vacancy selection,[219] utilizes partisan election for purposes of initial selection and final vacancy selection and confers a retention election privilege only upon elected judges.[220] Illinois and Pennsylvania thus require appointed judges first to win a partisan election before becoming eligible for subsequent retention elections. Lastly, California's judicial selection system for its appellate courts (and for such of its general jurisdiction trial courts as hereafter adopt the same system) is an executive appointment system rather than a commission plan system. Even though the governor's appointments are subject to confirmation by a three-man committee composed of the attorney general, chief supreme court justice, and a senior presiding intermediate appellate court justice, the committee has nothing to do with the process of nominating or selecting anyone for any of the judicial offices in question until after the governor has made his appointment.[221] Appointees to the California supreme court of appeals have the right to seek retention in noncompetitive retention elections, both at the next general election after the judge's appointment and at the general election next preceding each subsequent term of office.[222]

Treating the period between appointment and the initial noncompetitive retention election as the probationary period (even though a probationer's term of office generally does not expire until a few weeks after the election even if he is defeated),[223] the probationary period for appointees ranges from zero years in Montana and Utah; thirty days in Tennessee; one year in Florida, Iowa, Kansas, Maryland, Missouri, Oklahoma, and Wyoming; two years in Arizona, Colorado, and Indiana; three years in Alaska, Nebraska, and South Dakota; and the remainder of the predecessor's unexpired term of office in Vermont.[224]

In all of the foregoing states, an appointee who successfully weathers the noncompetitive retention election at the end of his probationary period has a further noncompetitive retention election privilege at the end of each full term of office,[225] provided he complies with the particular state's pre-election requirements, such as filing a declaration of candidacy.[226]

Under the typical noncompetitive retention election system, the procedures are as follows: At the general election immediately preceding the expiration of an incumbent judge's term of office, whether the term of office be a probationary term of office or a regular full term of office, the incumbent judge is permitted to run for a new term of office in an election in which he has no opponent. The sole question put to the voters is whether the incumbent judge should be retained in office. The judge is retained in office if a majority votes to retain him.[227] Conversely, his office becomes vacant and he is not retained for a new term of office if a majority votes against retention.[228] To run in a noncompetitive retention election, the incumbent judge is generally required to file a declaration of candidacy within a specified minimum number of days prior to the election[229] and, in some cases, no earlier than a specified maximum number of days before that election.[230]

NOTES TO §2.1

1. Nelson, Variations on a Theme—Selection and Tenure of Judges, 36 So. Cal. L. Rev. 4, 13–14 (1962) (hereinafter cited as *Variations on a Theme*); Winters, Selection of Judges—An Historical Introduction, 44 Tex. L. Rev. 1081, 1081 (1966) (hereinafter cited as *Historical Introduction*); Comment, Selecting Judges in the States; A Brief History and Analysis, 9 No. Ky. L. Rev. 459, 461 (1982) (hereinafter cited as *Brief History*).

2. See *Variations on a Theme*, supra note 1, at 13; *Brief History*, supra note 1, at 461

3. See *Variations on a Theme*, supra note 1, at 13.

4. Declaration of Independence, Ninth Specification.

5. *See* Berkson, Judicial Selection in the United States: A Special Report, 64 Judicature 176, 176 (1980); Davidow, Judicial Selection: The Search for Quality and Effectiveness, 31 Case W. Res. 409, 411–412 (1981); *Variations on a Theme, supra* note 1, at 13–14; *Historical Introduction, supra* note 1, at 1081; *Brief History supra* note 1 at 461.

6. Connecticut, Delaware, Georgia, New Jersey, North Carolina, Rhode Island, South Carolina, and Virginia. *See* Vanderbilt, The Challenge of Law Reform 14 (1955); *Variations on a Theme, supra* note 1, at 14. In Delaware, the power of selection was held jointly by the legislature and the governor. *See* Seiler, Judicial Selection in New Jersey, 5 Seton Hall L. Rev. 721, 728 and n. 30 (1974); Note, Judicial Selection in the States: A Critical Study with Proposals for Reform, 4 Hofstra L. Rev. 267, 277, and nn. 28, 30 (1976) (hereinafter cited as *A Critical Study*).

7. New Hampshire and Pennsylvania. *See* Seiler, *supra* note 6, at 728 and nn. 28–29; *A Critical Study, supra* note 6, at 277 and n. 29.

8. Maryland, Massachusetts, and New York. *See A Critical Study supra* note 6, at 277 and n. 29.

9. U.S. Const. art. II, §2(2), and art. III, §1. *See Variations on a Theme, supra* note 1, at 14.

10. *See* Vanderbilt, *supra* note 6, at 15.

11. *See* Davidow, *supra* note 5, at 412; Elliott, Judicial Selection and Tenure, 3 Wayne L. Rev. 175, 175 (1957); *Variations on a Theme, supra* note 1, at 15–17; *Historical Introduction, supra* note 1, at 1082–1083; *Brief History, supra* note 1, at 461–462.

12. *See* Berkson, *supra* note 5, at 177; *Variations on a Theme, supra* note 1, at 19; *Historical Introduction, supra* note 1, at 1083. Concerning Ohio, *see* Heggs, Merit Selection of the Ohio Judiciary: An Analysis of S.J.R. 6 and a Proposal for Implementation, 28 Case W. Res. 628, 634–635 (1978); Milligan, The Proposed Changes in the Selection and Tenure of Judges in Ohio, 4 Ohio St. L.J. 157 (1938). Several states even abandoned partisan election in favor of legislative selection. E.g., Va. Const. art. VI, §§1, 7, 10 (1864). *See Historical Introduction, supra* note 1, at 1083. Mississippi switched from partisan election to gubernatorial selection. *See* Miss. Const. art. VI, §§2, 3, 11 (1868). *But see* Miss. Const. art. 6, §§145–145B, 153; and Miss. Code Ann. §§9–7–1, 23–3–63, 23–5–235, 23–5–239, 23–5–243 (reverting to partisan elective system).

13. *See* Berkson *supra* note 5, at 177; *Historical Introduction, supra* note 1, at 1083.

14. *See Historical Introduction, supra* note 1, at 1083–1087.

15. *Id.* at 1084.

16. 23 A.B.A.J. 102–108 (1937).

17. Mo. Const. art. 5, §29(a) (1945). *See Historical Introduction, supra* note 1, at 1084–1085. For a brief description of merit selection plans, *see infra* §2.7(a).

18. *See* Berkson, *supra* note 5, at 177, 178; Davidow, *supra* note 5, at 413–416; *Historical Introduction, supra* note 1, at 1085–1087.

19. *See Brief History, supra* note 1, at 462.

20. *See* Kales, Unpopular Government in the United States, 239, 245–247, 249–250 (Chicago: Chicago University Press, 1914). *See* Davidow, *supra* note 5, at 413, n. 18.

21. *See* Davidow, *supra* note 5, at 413, nn. 18–20.

22. *See* Berkson, *supra* note 5, at 177–178; *Historical Introduction, supra* note 1, at 1084–1085; and *Brief History, supra* note 1 at 462–463. *See also* §§2.7(d) and 2.8.

23. Because the methods used in the fifty states to select judges of appellate courts and trial or *nisi prius* courts of general jurisdiction (hereinafter referred to as "major courts") are particularly apt to be different from those used to select judges of courts of specialized or limited jurisdiction (hereinafter referred to as "non-major courts"), the discussion in this chapter will generally be confined to the methods utilized in selecting major court judges. For summaries of the methods of selection of judges of non–major courts, see Berkson, Beller, and Grimaldi, Judicial Selection in the United States: A Compendium of Provisions (Am. Jud. Soc. 1980) (hereinafter cited as *Compendium*), at 49–179.

NOTES to §2.2

24. *See* §2.1, *supra* n.6, and the accompanying text.

25. R.I. Const. art. 10. §§4, 5 (supreme court justices are elected by legislature); R.I. Gen. Laws §§8–1.1 to 8–1.1–9 (same). *But compare* R.I. Gen. Laws §§8–2–3, 8–8–5, 8–8–9, 8–10–11 (superior court, district court, and family court judges are appointed by governor, subject to confirmation by senate).

26. S.C. Const. art. V, §§3, 9 and 14; S.C. Code §§14–3–10, 14–3–40, 14–8–20 (Supp.), 14–8–60 (Supp.). Cf. S.C. Code §§14–21–330, 20–7–1370 (family court judges appointed by governor upon recommendation of a majority of legislators elected in area served by court). *Compare* S.C. Code §§7–13–30, 14–23–30 (partisan election of probate judges).

27. Va. Const. art. VI, §7; Va. Code §§17.120, 17.122.1, 16.1–69.9, 16.1–69.9–2, 16.1–69.9–4.

28. *See supra* notes 25–27.

29. *See supra* notes 25–27.

30. R.I. Const. art. 10, §5; S.C. Const. art. V, §14; S.C. Code §§14–3–40, 14–8–60; Va. Const. art. 6, §7; and Va. Code §§17–120, 17–122.1, 16.1–69.9–2, 16.1–69.9–4. Judges elected by the legislature to fill a vacancy of this type serve for a full term in Virginia, Va. Const. art. VI, §7; for life during good behavior in Rhode Island (the tenure conferred on initial selectees), R.I. Const. art. 10, §§4, 5; but only for the predecessor's unexpired term in South Carolina, S.C. Code §§14–3–40 (supreme court justices), 14–8–60 (Court of Appeals judges). Pending the holding of a legislative election to fill a vacancy, a power of temporary appointment has been conferred upon the legislature acting "in grand committee" in Rhode Island, R.I. Const. art. 10, §5, and upon the governor in South Carolina, S.C. Code §14–8–60 (Court of Appeals vacancies). In the case of South Carolina Supreme Court vacancies involving an unexpired term that does not exceed one year, the governor is empowered to fill the office for the rest of the unexpired term, S.C. Code §14–3–40.

31. R.I. Gen. Laws §§8–1.1–2 through 8–1.1–9. Although the applicable South Carolina and Virginia statutes do not contain similar provisions, it appears likely that similar procedures are followed in those states.

32. *See* Note, Analysis of Methods of Judicial Selection and Tenure, 6 Suffolk L. Rev. 955, 962 (1972) (hereinafter cited as *Analysis of Methods*), in which the first

two of these criticisms were made; and Culver, Politics and the California Plan for Choosing Appellate Judges, 66 Judicature 151, 160 (1982), and Sheldon, Judicial Recruitment: What Ought to Be and What Is, 51 Judicature 386 (1968), in which the third of these criticisms was made.

NOTES to §2.3

33. The term "major court judges" is intended to refer particularly to judges of appellate courts and trial courts of general jurisdiction. *See supra* note 23.

34. E.g., Ariz. Const. art. 6, §12; Ark. Const. amend. 29, §§1, 4; Cal. Const. art. 6, §16(c); Ind. Const. art. 5, §18; Mich. Const. art. VI, §23; N.M. Const. art. V, §§5, 4; N.M. Stat. Ann. §34–5–4; N.Y. Const. art. 6, §21; Ohio Const. art. IV, §13; Ohio Rev. Code Ann. §107.08; Ore. Const. art. V, §16, and art. VII, §1; Tenn. Code Ann. §17–1–301(a); Wash. Const. art. IV, §§3, 5; Wash. Rev. Code Ann. §§2.04.100 (Supp.), 2.06.080 (Supp.), 2.08.120; W. Va. Const. art. 8, §7; W. Va. Code §3–10–3; Wis. Const. art. 7, §9; Wis. Stat. Ann. §8.50(4) (f).

35. When the contemplated election is deemed too close to the time of expiration of the predecessor's term of office to make an election worthwhile, the appointee is, in some instances, permitted to hold the office until expiration of the predecessor's term. E.g. Ohio Const. art. IV, §13; W. Va. Const. art. 8, §7. *See infra* note 51, and the accompanying text. *A fortiori*, the appointment is apt to be for the unexpired term when that term expires on or before the date of the next general election. E.g., Ark. Const. amend. 29, §§1, 4. For purposes of analysis in this treatise, a jurisdiction that utilizes some type of election as its method of judicial selection of judges of a particular court for purposes of final vacancy selection is classified as an elective state with respect to final vacancy selection of judges for that court, notwithstanding the fact that its appointments to fill vacancies occurring near the end of the predecessor's term are filled by appointments lasting until the expiration of that term.

36. In all of the instances cited in note 34, *supra*, the appointment was not subject to confirmation by the senate or legislature. Occasionally, however, a gubernatorial appointment for temporary vacancy selection purposes is subject to confirmation by the senate or legislature. E.g., N.J. Stat. Ann. §§2A:5–7 (Surrogate Courts); Tex. Const. art. 5, §§4, 28. *Compare* N.D. Cent. Code §40–18–03 (appointment of municipal court judge by mayor subject to confirmation by municipality's governing body).

37. *See infra* notes 39 and 50.

38. *See infra* notes 39–43, and the accompanying text. This discussion applies not only to states in which the governor makes his appointments without the assistance of a commission plan, but also to states in which a commission plan (whether nonvoluntary or voluntary) is in effect.

39. Examples of use of gubernatorial appointment as a device solely for final vacancy selection and not for initial selection are few and far between. One such example is found in Md. Const. art. IV, §40 (gubernatorial appointment to fill orphans' court vacancy for predecessor's unexpired term, subject to senate confirmation; initial selection by partisan election).

40. Examples are: U.S. Const. art. II, §2 (U.S. Senate confirmation as to presidential appointments); Del. Const. art. IV, §63, 30 (senate confirmation), Del. Code Ann. tit. 10, §§906, 1303, 1702 (senate confirmation); N.J. Const. art. 6, §6,

¶1 (Supp.), 3 (Supp.) (confirmation by senate); P.R. Const. art. V, §8 (Puerto Rico senate confirmation); R.I. Gen. Laws §§8–2–2, 8–8–7, 8–10–11 (senate confirmation). *Cf.* Conn. Const. art. 5, §§2, 3 (governor to "nominate" and legislature to "appoint").

41. *Cf.* Mass. Const. pt. 2, c.2, §1, art. 9, and Mass. Exec. Order No. 114 (all judicial officers; governor assisted by nominating commission under voluntary merit plan; confirmation by nine-man governor's council, elected by legislature, required); N.H. Const. pt. 2, arts. 46, 60 ("all judicial officers" nominated and appointed both by governor and by five-member executive council elected by people of state).

42. *Compare* Cal. Const. art. 6, §16 (Supreme Court and Courts of Appeal, plus all Superior Courts adopting plan; confirmation by three-member commission required; appointment is solely for temporary vacancy selection purposes).

43. E.g., Conn. Gen. Stat. §4–19.

44. E.g., Conn. Gen. Stat. §2–40, and Conn. Const. art. 5, §§2, 3; Me. Const. art. V, pt. 1, §8.

45. N.J. Const. art. 6, §6, ¶1.

46. See, *Analysis of Methods supra* note 32, at 957–958.

47. *See infra* notes 113 and (as to New York's appellate division) 114, and the accompanying text.

48. *See infra* note 116, and the accompanying text.

49. *See infra* note 118, and the accompanying text.

50. Initial selection and final vacancy selection in all appellate and major trial courts are accomplished by partisan election in Mississippi, New Mexico, North Carolina, Pennsylvania, and West Virginia and by nonpartisan election in Georgia and Minnesota. *See infra* notes 66 and 68, and the accompanying text, as to partisan election in all of the above states other than Georgia and Minnesota; and *see infra* note 93, and the accompanying text, as to nonpartisan election in Georgia and Minnesota.

51. E.g., N.C. Const. art. IV, §19; W.Va. Const. art. 8, §7; W.Va. Code §3–10–3. *See supra* note 35, and the accompanying text.

NOTES TO §2.4

52. *See Compendium, supra* note 23, at 119–179.

53. Ill. Const. art. 6, §12(c) (Supreme, Appellate, and Circuit Courts); La. Const. art. 5, §22(B) (all judges).

54. E.g., Alaska Stat. §22.15.170(c); N.C. Gen. Stat. §7A–171; S.D. Comp. Laws Ann. §§16–12A–4, 4.1; Va. Code §§19.2–35, 19.2–38.

55. E.g., La. Rev. Stat. Ann. §13: 1347(C), (D); Mo. Ann. Stat. §§478.265 to 267 (Supp.); Wyo. Stat. §5–3–301.

56. E.g., Hawaii Rev. Stat. §604–2 (district court, family court, and other judges); Ga. Code Ann. §15–11–3(b) (1) (juvenile court judges). *Compare* Tex. Const. art. 5, §§15, 28 (County Judges judicially appointed for temporary vacancy selection purposes and elected for all other purposes).

57. E.g., I11, Const. art. 6, §8, (Associate Circuit Court Judges)

58, E.g , Okla Const. art 7, §9(h) (special judges of district court).

59. E.g., Va. Code §16.1–69.21 (substitute district judges). *Cf.* Ga. Code Ann.

§15–11–63 (judge *pro tempore* of juvenile court, pending return of absent or disqualified judge).

60. Report of the 26th Annual Session of the Georgia Bar Association at 225, 226 (1909).

61. *See* Kales, *supra* note 20, at 250–251; Model State-Wide Judicature Act, drafted by Kales, Am. Jud. Soc'y. Bull. 7-A (1914); Model Court for a Metropolitan District, also drafted by Kales, Am. Jud. Soc'y Bull. 4-A (1914); Kales, Methods of Selecting and Retiring Judges in a Metropolitan District, 52 Annals 1, 8 (1914). *See also Historical Introduction, supra* note 1 at 1084; Winters, The Merit Plan for Judicial Selection and Tenure—Its Historical Development, 7 Duquesne L. Rev. 61, 65–67 (1968) (hereinafter cited as *Merit Plan Historical Development*).

62. Harley, Taking Judges Out of Politics, 64 Annals 184, 193 (1916).

63. In 1920, Amos C. Miller advocated, and the Illinois Constitutional Convention of 1922 approved, a merit selection plan, under which the governor would be required to appoint judges in Cook County, Illinois, from a list of four nominees submitted to him by the state supreme court with respect to the specific judicial office to be filled, rather than from a standing eligible list such as that proposed by Kales. 4 Am. Jud. Soc'y Bull. 31 (1920); 5 Am. Jud. Soc'y. Bull. 50–52 (1921); 6 Am. Jud. Soc'y Bull. 5 (1922).

64. At a Louisiana Constitutional Convention held contemporaneously with the proposals referred to in note 63, the Louisiana State Bar Association proposed a plan under which the governor would make judicial appointments from nominations submitted by a body composed of twelve judges, named the Supreme Judicial Council. The Special Committee on Judiciary Ordinance of the New Constitution, Rep. La. Bar Ass'n. at 20–21 (1920); 5 Am. Jud. Soc'y. Bull. at 19–25 (1921).

65. *See Merit Plan Historical Development, supra* note 61, at 68–73; *Variations on a Theme, supra* note 1, at 34–37; *A Critical Study, supra* note 6, app. at 326–353 (detailed descriptions of judicial nominating commissions).

NOTES to §2.5

66. Ala. Const. amend. 328, art. VI, §6.13; Ala. Code §§12–2–1, 17–2–6, 17–2–7, 12–3–2, 12–3–3; Ark. Const. art. 7, §§6, 13, 17; Ark. Stat. Ann. §§22–200(b), 22–326.3, 22–409, 22–1202 (Supp.); Miss. Const. art. 6, §§145–145B, 153; Miss. Code Ann. §§9–5–1, 9–7–1, 9–9–5, 23–5–235, 23–5–239, 23–5–243, 23–5–247; N.M. Const. art. VI, §§4, 12, 28; N.C. Const. art. IV, §§16, 19; N.C. Gen. Stat. §§7A–10, 7A–16, 163–9; Tex. Const. art. 5, §§2, 4, 6, 7, 28; Tex. Rev. Civ. Stat. Ann. (Supp.) arts. 1715, 1801, 1813(a), 1884; Tex. Rev. Civ. Stat. Ann. art. 1926; W. Va. Const. art.. 8, §§2, 5, 7; W. Va. Code §§3–1–16, 3–1–17, 3–10–3, 51–2–1(d). *See also* Berkson, *supra* note 5, at 179–185, Tables 1–3. For a very minor and technical exception to the generality of the statement in the text accompanying this footnote, *see supra* note 35. It will be noted that, whenever an incumbent judge is a candidate in a partisan or nonpartisan election at the end of a term, the concepts of initial selection and retention selection overlap.

67. Ala. Const. amend. 83, 110, 334.

68. Ill. Const. art. 6, §12; Pa. Const. Art. 5, §§13, 15; 42 Pa. Cons. Stat. Ann. §§3131–3133, 4164. In one respect, Illinois and Pennsylvania differ; whereas a simple majority of those voting on the retention question is sufficient for retention in

Pennsylvania, a three-fifths majority is necessary in Illinois. Ill. Const. art. 6, §12; Pa. Const. art. 5, §15; Pa. Cons. Stat. Ann. §3153.

69. *See infra* note 113.

70. *See* Ind. Code §33–4–4–1 (most circuit judges); Kan. Const. art. 3, §6, and Kan. Stat. §20–2902 (district courts not adopting commission plan); La. Const. art. 5, §22; Mo. Ann. Stat. §478.010 (most circuit judges); N.Y. Const. art. 6, §6 (justices of New York Supreme Court); Tenn Const. art. 6, §§3 (supreme court judges), 4 (judges of circuit, chancery, and inferior courts). *Compare* Tenn. Code Ann. §§16–3–101, 16–4–102, 16–5–103, 16–15–202, 17–1–103, 17–4–101 to 116 (judges of all courts of record other than intermediate appellate courts).

71. Ind. Const. art. 7 §§9, 10; Ind. Code §§33.2.1–4–6 to 11 (appellate judges); Ind. Code §§3–5–5.1–31.1 to 44, 33–5–29.5–27 to 42 (superior court judges for certain counties); Kan. Const. art. 3, §2; Kan. Stat. §§20–327, 20–2901 to 2913 (district judges in districts adopting commission plan); Mo. Const. art. V, §§25(a) (appellate courts and judges of certain circuit courts), 25(b) (judges of circuit courts adopting commission plan); N.Y. Const. art. 6, §2(d) to (f) (Supp.) (judges of New York Court of Appeals); N.Y. Const. art. 6, §4(c) (gubernatorial appointment of justices of Appellate Division of New York Supreme Court from justices of trial division of latter court), as supplemented by N.Y. Exec. Order No. 4, Feb. 24, 1975 (voluntary commission plan as to Appellate Division justices); Tenn. Code Ann. §§17–4–101 to 17–4–101 to 17–4–116 (intermediate appellate judges).

72. For a few illustrative examples, *see* Ariz. Const. art. 6, §32; Ariz. Rev. Stat. §22–111 (justices of peace); Ark. Const. art. VII, §29; Ark. Stat. Ann. §§17–3601(a) (1), 17–3602 (county court); Ark. Const. art. 7, §38; Ark. Stat. Ann. §17–3601(b) (1), 17–3602 (justices of peace); Conn. Const. art. V, §4; Ind. Code Ann. §§33–8–2–3 (St. Joseph County probate court), 33–10, 5–4–2 (county courts); Md. Const. art. IV, §40 (Orphans' Courts); N.J. Stat. Ann. §§2A.5–1, 2A:5–7 (Surrogate Courts); S.C. Code §14–23–1020 (probate courts); Tex. Const. art. 5, §§5, 7, 15, 16 (family district court judges and county court judges); W. Va. Code §50–1–1 (magistrates); W. Va. Const. art. 9, §10 (county commissioners). *See also* Berkson, *supra* note 5, Tables 4 and 5, at 186–193.

73. E.g., Ala. Const. amend. 328, §6.14; Ark. Const. amend. 29, §4; Miss. Code Ann. §23–5–247; N.M. Const. art. XX, §4; N.M. Stat. Ann. §34–5–4; N.C. Const. art. IV, §19; Tex. Const. art. 5, §§4, 28.

74. Pa. Const. art. V, §13(a). *See* Kauffman, Judicial Selection in Pennsylvania: A Proposal, 27 Vill. L. Rev. 1163, 1168, n. 22 (1982).

75. Pa. Const. art. VII, §3.

76. Pa. Const. art. VII, §2.

77. *See* Adamany and Dubois, Electing State Judges, Wis. L. Rev. 731, 737 (1976).

78. *See* Kaminsky, Available Compromises for Continued Judicial Selection Reform, 53 St. Johns L. Rev. 466, 489, n. 110 (1979).

79. E.g., Ohio Rev. Code Ann. §3513.257. *See* Heggs, *supra* note 12, at 647, n. 113.

80. E.g., *see* Heggs, *supra* note 12, at 647, n. 113.

81. *See* Costikyan, Behind Closed Doors: Politics in the Public Interest 173–210 (1966); Adamany and Dubois, *supra* note 77 at 777–778; Harding, The Case for Partisan Election of Judges, 55 A.B.A. J. 1162, 1163–1164 (1969); Burnett,

Observations on the Direct-Election Method of Judicial Selection, 44 Tex. L. Rev. 1098, 1098 (1966); Mullinax, Judicial Revisions—An Argument against the Merit Plan for Judicial Selection and Tenure, 5 Tex. Tech. L. Rev. 21, 25, 29, 34 (1973); Roth, Why I Am against the California Merit Plan, the Missouri Plan—Or Any Reasonable Facsimile Thereof, 42 Cal. S.B.J. 346 (1967); Spence, Should Judges Be Selected by Merit Plan? No, 40 Fla. B.J. 1147–1152 (1973); Comment, Judicial Selection in New York: A Need for Change, III Fordham Urban L.J. 605, 618 (1975) (hereinafter cited as *A Need For Change*).

82. *See* Adamany and Dubois, *supra* note 77, at 777–778.

83. *See* Kauffman, *supra* note 74, at 1166–1167; Warden, The Case for Merit Selection, 8 Student L. 32, 34 (1979); Ellis, Court Reform in New York State: An Overview for 1975, 3 Hofstra L. Rev. 663, 669–670 (1975); *A Critical Study, supra* note 6, at 294–295, and nn. 95, 98, 100; *A Need for Change, supra* note 81, at 618; Note, Judicial Selection and Tenure: The Merit Plan in Ohio, 42. U. Cincinn. L. Rev. 205, 266–267, n. 54 (1973) (hereinafter cited as *Merit Plan in Ohio*); New York Times, The Judicial Election Farce, October 1982, at A–18.

84. *See* Laski, The Technique of Judicial Appointment, 24 Mich. L. Rev. 529, 531 (1926); *A Critical Study, supra* note 6, at 294–295; *A Need for Change, supra* note 81, at 618.

85. *See* Wicker, Proceedings of the Sixth Annual Institute of Local Government 14 (1947); *A Critical Study, supra* note 6, at 289–290; *A Need for Change, supra* note 1, at 619; Geller, A Judge Goes Courting, Philadelphia Inquirer Magazine, Nov. 13, 1983, 12, 14, 28–29. A recent successful candidate stated that victory in the primary elections hinged on persuading ward leaders to place the candidate's name on sample ballots. *Id.* at 12. Also, it has been said that political leaders select the delegates to judicial nominating conventions, that the delegates vote as instructed by the leaders, and, therefore, that the leaders determine who is nominated at the conventions. *See* Kaminsky, *supra* note 78, at 487.

86. *See A Critical Study, supra* note 6, at 292.

87. *See A Need for Change, supra* note 81, at 619–620.

88. *See* Vanderbilt, Impasses in Justice, 1956 Wash. U.L.Q. 267, 275; *A Critical Study, supra* note 6, at 289.

89. *Cf. supra* note 51, and the accompanying text (governor not well qualified to select judges); Allard, Application of the Missouri Court Plan to Judicial Selection and Tenure, 15 Buffalo L. Rev. 378, 378–384 (1966) (elected judges are in most instances picked by political leaders).

90. *See* Kaufman, *supra* note 74, at 1167; *Cf. Merit Plan in Ohio, supra* note 83, at 268–269 (discussing nonpartisan elections).

91. *See* Allard, *supra* note 89, at 383; Kaminsky, *supra* note 78, at 468–469; Melone, Political Realities and Democratic Ideals: Accession and Competition in a State Judicial System, 54 N.D. L. Rev. 187, 192–198 (1977); Parks, Judicial Selection—The Tennessee Experience, 7 Memphis St. U.L. Rev. 615, 629, and n. 84 (1977); *A Need for Change, supra* note 81, at 617.

92. Melone, *supra* note 91, at 193. Often, moreover, incumbents are reelected in uncontested elections. E.g., *see* Note, Judicial Selection in North Dakota—Is Constitutional Revision Necessary, 18 N.D.L. Rev. 327, 333 (1972). Also, meaningful electoral competition is frequently eliminated by bipartisan endorsement of candidates in judicial elections. E.g., *see* Kaminsky, *supra* note 78, at 489.

NOTES to §2.6

93. Ga. Const. art. 6, §7, ¶1; Idaho Const. art. 4, §6, art. 5, §§6, 11; Idaho Const. art. 6, §7; Idaho Code §§1–201 (Supp.), 1–702, 1–2404(b) and (f), 34–615, 34–616, 34–905, 59–914; Ky. Const. §§117, 152; La. Const. art. 5, §§4, 9, 22; La. Rev. Stat. Ann. §§13.312.1 to 13.312.3, 13.321; Mich. Const. art. 6, §§2, 8, 11, 12, 23; Mich. Comp. Laws §§600.203, 600.303, 600.8204 (Supp.), 168.699; Minn. Const. art. 6, §8; Minn. Stat. Ann. §487.03(2) and (5); N.D. Const. art. VI, §§7, 9, 13; N.D. Cent. Code §§27.05–02, 16.1–11–08, 16.1–06–08; Ohio Const. art. IV, §§6(A); Ohio Rev. Code Ann. §§2503.02, 2503.03, 3505.04 (Supp.); Ore. Const. art. VII, §1; Ore. Rev. Stat., §§249.072, 249.205, 249.088(2), 254.125, 254.135; Wash. Const. art. IV, §§3, 5, 30; Wash. Rev. Code Ann. §§2.04.071 (Supp.), 2.04.100 (Supp.), 2.06.070 (Supp.), 2.06,075 (Supp.), 2.06.080 (Supp.), 2.08.069, 2.08.070, 29.21.070 (Supp.); Wis. Const. art. 7, §§4, 5, 7, 9; Wis. Stat. §§752.04, 5.60(1). *See Compendium, supra* note 23, at 94, 135, 137, 144–145, 170–171, 176.

94. Ga. Exec. Order, April 28, 1975 (voluntary commission plan); Idaho Const. art. IV, §6; Idaho Const. art. V, §19; Idaho Code §§1–2101, 1–2102(3); Ky. Const. §118; Minn. Exec. Order No. 79–23 (voluntary commission plan); N.D. Const. art. 6, §13; N.D. Cent. Code §§27–25–01 through 27–25–09. *See* Vandenberg, Voluntary Merit Selection: Its History and Current Status, 66 Judicature 265, 266–267, Table 1 (1983); *Compendium, supra* note 23, at 104 (vacancies in Michigan temporarily filled by gubernatorial appointment from nominees recommended by bar committee); notes 48–51, *supra*, and the accompanying text.

95. Cal. Const. art. 6, §16; Fla. Const. arts. 5, 10, §11(a); Fla. Stat. §§105.011(2), 105.041(3); Mont. Const. art. VII, §8; Mont. Rev. Code Ann. §§3–2–101, 3–5–201, 13–14–111 to 13–14–118, 13–14–211 to 13–14–213; Nev. Const. art. 6, §§3, 5, 20; Nev. Rev. Stat. §§2.030, 2.040, 293.195 to 293.197, 293.200; Okla. Const. art. 7, §§3, 9; Okla. Const. art. 7-B, §§2, 4; Okla. Stat. Ann. tit. 20, §§30.9 to 30.10; Okla. Stat. Ann. tit. 51, §§10(a) (Supp.), 15; S.D. Const. art. V, §7; S.D. Comp. Laws §§16–1–2, 16–6–3; Utah Code Ann. §§20–1–7.7 and .8. *See Compendium supra* note 23, at 60, 71, 114, 118, 140–141, 155–156, 164; and Thompson, Selection of Judges of the California Court of Appeal, 40 Cal. St. B. J. 381, 381 (1973) ("As a matter of legal theory, California trial judges are selected on a nonpartisan ballot").

96. *See infra* note 112 as to all of the seven states just enumerated except California, and the accompanying text; and see also Cal. Const. art. 6, §§7, 16.

97. *See infra* note 122, and Cal. Const. art. 6, §16, and the accompanying text.

98. E.g., Fla. Stat. Ann. §§105.011, 105.041(3), 105.071(1) and (2); Mont, Rev. Code Ann. §13–14–115 to 116; Ore. Rev. Code §254.125; Wis. Stat. §§5.58 (1973) (non-partisan judicial primaries), 5.60(1) (a) (nonpartisan judicial ballots in spring elections). *See* Adamany and Dubois, *supra* note 77, at 738, n. 36, and the accompanying text.

99. *See* Adamany and Dubois, *supra* note 77, at 739 and 740; Kaminsky, *supra* note 78, at 192, n. 124; *The Merit Plan in Ohio, supra* note 83, at 268.

100. Ariz. Const. art. 6, §§4, 12 (1960). *See* Comment, Judicial Selection and Tenure—A Merit Selection Plan for Arizona, 9 Ariz. L. Rev. 297, 298 (1967); *see also* Ariz. Const. art. IV, §§36–40 (merit selection adopted in 1974).

101. *See* Adamany and Dubois, *supra* note 77, at 739.

102. E.g., Ohio Rev. Code Ann. §§3505.04, 3513.257; Mont. Rev. Code Ann. §13–14–113. *See also* Heggs, *supra* note 12, at 647–648, n. 113, and the accompanying text.

103. Fla. Stat. Ann. §§105.071 (1) to (2), 105.09.

104. *See* Kaminsky, *supra* note 78, at 492, n. 124.

105. *Id.*, at 490–493 (and law review articles cited); The Dictatorship of Irrelevancy, 48 Judicature 124 (1964); Clark, Pro-Commentary on Proposal for Selection and Tenure of Judges, 30 Ohio Bar Ass'n. 916, 918 (1957).

106. *See* Cameron, The Inherent Power of a State's Highest Court to Discipline the Judiciary, 54 Chi-Kent L. Rev. 1, 52–53 (1977); and Comment, Ethical Conduct in a Judicial Campaign: Is Campaigning an Ethical Activity? 57 Wash. L. Rev. 119, 121, n. 7 (1981) (hereinafter cited as *Ethical Conduct*), and the accompanying text.

107. Canon 7(B) (1)(c) of ABA Code of Judicial Conduct. *See Ethical Conduct, supra* note 106, at 134–138.

108. *See A Need for Change, supra* note 81, at 620, n. 73; Editorial, 48 J. Am. Jud. Soc. 124, 125 (1964).

109. *See* Editorial, *supra* note 108, at 125.

110. *Id.*

NOTE to §2.7(a)

111. *See supra* notes 14–22, and the accompanying text.

NOTES to §2.7(b)

112. Alaska Const. art. IV, §§5–8; Alaska Stat. §§22.05.080, 22.05.100, 22.07.060, 22.070, 22.10.100, 22.10.150, 22.15.170, 15.35.030 to 15.35.140; Colo. Const. art. VI, §§20(1), 24, 25; District of Columbia Self-Government and Governmental Reorganization Act §§433, 434; Fla. Const. art. 5, §§10, 11, 20(c); Hawaii Const. art. VI, §3; Idaho Const. art. 5, §10; Idaho Const. art. 6, §7; Idaho Code §§1–2101, 1–2102, 34–615, 34–616, 34–905; Iowa Const. art. 5, §§15–17; Iowa Code §§46.20 to 46.24; Ky. Const. §§117, 118, 152; Mont. Const. art. VII, §8; Mont. Rev. Code Ann. §§3–1–1001 to 3–1–1014, 3–2–101, 3-5-201, 13–14–212; Neb. Const. art. V, §21; Neb. Rev. Stat. §§24–801 to 24–818; Nev. Const. art. 6, §§3, 5, 20; Nev. Rev. Stats. §§2.030, 2.040, 293.195 to 293.197, 293.200; N.D. Const. art. VI, §§7, 13; N.D. Cent. Code §§27–05–02, 27–25–01 to 27–25–08; Okla. Const. art. 7-B, §§1–5; Okla. Const. art. 7, §§3, 9; Okla. Stat. Ann. tit. 20, §§30.9 to 30.12; Okla. Stat. Ann. tit. 51, §§10(a), 13, 15; S.D. Const. art. V, §7; S.D. Comp. Laws Ann. §§12–9–2, 12–9–12, 12–16–11, 12–2–2, 16–1–2, 16–6–3; Utah Code Ann. §§20–1–7.1 to 20–1–7.7; Vt. Const. ch. II, §§32–34; Vt. Stat. Ann. tit. 4, §§601–604, 607, 608, 471, 444; Wyo. Const. art. 5, §4; Wyo. Stat. §22–6–125.

113. Del. Exec. Order No. 4 (1977); Ga. Exec. Order of Apr. 28, 1975; Md. Exec. Order of Dec. 18, 1974; Md. Court of Appeals Order of Jan. 6, 1975; Mass. Exec. Order of Jan. 1979; Minn. Exec. Order No. 79–23 (1979); N.C. Exec. Order No. 12 (July 28, 1977); Pa. Exec. Order Nos. 1973–5 and 1980–18. *See* Vandenberg, *supra* note 94, at 266–269, Table 1, as to Mississippi, New Mexico, and West Virginia. Voluntary commission plans were formerly adopted, and were thereafter rescinded in Ohio and Wisconsin. *Id.* at 267.

114. Ala. Const. amend. Nos. 83, 110, 328 (§6.14), 334 (all appellate courts and some circuit courts); Ariz. Const. art. 6, §§30, 36A–36E, 37–40, and Ariz. Rev. Stat. Ann. §§12–101, 12–120.01, 12–120.02 (all appellate courts and most Circuit Courts); Ind. Const. art. 7, §§9–11; Ind. Const. art. 5, §18, and Ind. Code §33–5–5.1–31 to 43. 1 (Supp.), 33–5–29.5–27 to 40, 33–5–40–33 to 47 (all appellate courts, and some Superior Courts); Kan. Const. art. 3, §2 and Kan. Stat. §§20–2901 through 20–2913 (supreme court and most district courts); Mo. Const. art. V, §§25(a), 25(c) (i), 25(d), 25(g), 27(19), 27(23) (all appellate courts and some circuit courts); N.Y. Const. art. 6, §2, and N.Y. Judic. Law §§61-68 (Court of Appeals); N.Y. Const. art. 6, §4; N.Y. Judic. Law §71; N.Y. Exec. Order No. 5 (Feb. 24, 1975), and N.Y. Exec. Order No. 10 (April 11, 1975) (voluntary plan re Appellate Division Justices, who must be selected from Supreme Court Trial Division Justices); Tenn. Code Ann. §§17–4–112 to 116 (intermediate appellate court judges). *See also* Vandenberg, *supra* note 94, 66 Judicature at 266-269 as to North Carolina.

NOTES to §2.7(c)

115. *See supra* notes 112 and 114, and the accompanying text.
116. *See supra* notes 113 and 114. *See also* Vandenberg, *supra* note 94, at 266–267.
117. *See supra* notes 112 and 114.
118. *See* note 113. *See* Vandenberg, *supra* note 94, at 267, 269, Tables 1 and 2, with particular reference to Mississippi, New Mexico, and West Virginia.
119. *See Supra* note 112.
120. *See infra* note 121.
121. *See supra* notes 112–114 and notes 66–68, and 93–97.

NOTES to §2.7(d)

122. Alaska Const. art. IV, §6; Alaska Stat. §§22.05.100, 22.07.060, 22.10.150; Alaska Stat. §§,15.35.030 through 15.35.110; Ariz. Const. art. 6, §38; Colo. Const. art. 6, §§20(1), 25; Fla. Const. art. 5, §10(a) (appellate judges); Ind. Const. art. 7, §11 (appellate judges); Ind. Code §§33–5–29.5–27, 41–42, and §33–5–40–47 (superior court judges of Lake and St. Joseph Counties); Iowa Const. art. 5, §17; Iowa Code §§46.20 to 24; Kan. Const. art. 3, §5(c) (supreme court justices); Kan. Stat. §20–2908 (judges of district courts adopting commission plan); Md. Const. art. IV, §§5(A)(c) to (e) (appellate judges); Mo. Const. art. 5, §25(c)(1) and (2) (appellate judges and judges of circuit courts adopting commission plan); Mont. Const. art. VII, §§8(2) and (3), and Mont. Rev. Code Ann. §§13–14–211 to 213 (noncompetitive retention election is granted only if incumbent is unopposed); Neb. Const. art. V, §21(3); Neb. Rev. Stat. §§24–814 through 24–818; Okla. Const. art. 7-B, §§1, 2, 5 (judges of supreme court and court of criminal appeals); S.D. Const. art. VI, §7; Tenn. Code Ann. §§17–4–114 through 17–4–116 (intermediate appellate judges); Utah Code Ann. §20–1–7.7 (same as Montana); Vt. Const. ch. II, §32, and Vt. Stat. Ann. tit. 4, §§4(c) and (d), and 71(b) and (c) (retention election held by legislature); Wyo. Const. art. 5, §4(g) and (h); Wyo. Stat. §22–6–125, But compare Ind. Code §22 C 3.1 to 15.1 (supp) (Allen County superior court judges, commission plan for final vacancy selection, but no noncompetitive retention election privilege.

123. Del. Const. art. IV, §3; Del. Code Ann. tit. 10, §1303; Del. Exec. Order No. 4 (1977); District of Columbia Self-Government and Governmental Reorganization Act §433(c); Mass. Const. pt. 2, ch. 2, §1, art. IX; Mass. Exec. Order of Jan. 1979; Hawaii Const. art. VI, §3; N.Y. Const. art. 6, §§2, 4; N.Y. Judic. Law (McKinney's Consol. Stat.) §71; N.Y. Exec. Order No. 5 (Feb. 24, 1975). *See Compendium, supra* note 23, at 68, 69–70, 77, 103, 128–129.

124. *See supra* note 123.

125. *See supra* note 123.

126. *See* Kales, *supra* note 20, ch. 17 and p. 239.

127. *See* Am. Jud. Soc'y Bull. 4-A (April 1915) at 91–92. *See also* Carbon and Berkson, Judicial Retention Elections in the United States, Amer. Jud. Soc'y. Bull. 3, nn. 19–21 (1980), and the accompanying text.

128. Am. Jud. Soc'y, Bull. 7-A (March 1917). *See also* Carbon and Berkson *supra* note 127, at 3, nn. 22–25 and the accompanying text.

129. *Id.*

130. *See* Carbon and Berkson, *supra* note 127, at 4–6.

NOTES to §2.7(e)

131. *See* District of Columbia Self-Government and Governmental Reorganization Act (Supp.) §§433(a), 434(d) (i); Hawaii Const. art. VI, §3; Md. Const. art. IV, §5A, and Md. Exec. Order of Dec. 18, 1974 (appellate judges); Mont. Const. art. VII, §8, and Mont. Rev. Code Ann. §3–1013; N.Y. Const. art. 6, §§2(e) and (f) (only Court of Appeals appointments and not Appellate Division appointments); Pa. Const. art. 5, §§13 (b) and (c) (two-thirds vote required); Pa. Exec. Orders 1973–5 and 1980–18; Vt. Const. ch. II, §32.

132. Mass. Const. pt. 2, ch. 2, §1, art. IX; Mass. Exec. Order of January 1979.

133. *See* Geller, A Judge Goes Courting, The Philadelphia Inquirer Magazine, November 13, 1983, at p. 29.

NOTES to §2.7(f)

134. *See A Critical Study, supra* note 6, Appendix V, at 327–341; Ashman and Alfini, The Key to Judicial Selection: The Nominating Process (1974), Table I, at 27–37; Vandenberg, *supra* note 94, Table 2, at 269; *Compendium, supra* note 23, Tables 1 and 2, at 10–11, and summaries, at 49–55, 63–65, 68–80, 84–93, 100–104, 107–120, 125–136, 140–143, 147–148, 151–158, 164–167, 173–175, 178–179.

135. Alaska, Delaware, District of Columbia, Georgia, Hawaii, Massachusetts, Minnesota, Montana, South Dakota, Vermont, W. Virginia, and Wyoming: *See A Critical Study. supra* note 6, Appendix I, at 326, 330, 334–336, 340–341; Ashman and Alfini, *supra* note 134, at 27, 29, 34, 36–37; Vandenberg, *supra* note 94, Table 2, at 269; *Compendium, supra* note 23, at 51, 68–69, 73–74, 77–78, 103, 107, 154, 156–157, 173, 178. Alaska, Georgia, Hawaii, Idaho, Massachusetts, Minnesota, New Mexico, and Tennessee have two–tier appellate court systems, and, in the case of Delaware, Montana, Nevada, South Dakota, Vermont, and Wyoming, each has a single appellate court. *Id.*

136. Georgia and Idaho: *See* Ashman and Alfini, *supra* note 134 at 29–30; and *Compendium, supra* note 23, at 73–76, 79–80.

137. E.g., Utah. See Ashman and Alfini, *supra* note 134, at 37, and *Compendium*, *supra* note 23, at 164–165.

138. Indiana, Iowa, Kansas, Kentucky, Maryland, Missouri, Nevada, and North Dakota. *See A Critical Study*, *supra* note 6, at 331–335; Ashman and Alfini, *supra* note 134, at 30–33; Vandenberg, *supra* note 94, Table 2, at 269, as to Maryland; Kentucky Const. §118(a); Nev. Const. art. 6, §20; N.D. Cent. Code §27–25–02. In Nevada and North Dakota, there is a permanent committee that makes appellate court nominations and, when enlarged by addition of temporary members, it makes district court nominations.

139. E.g., Indiana, Kentucky, Missouri and Maryland. *See supra* note 134.

140. E.g., Minnesota and North Carolina. *See* Vandenberg, *supra* note 94, Table 1, at 267, and Table 2, at 269.

141. E.g., New York. *See Compendium*, *supra* note 23, at 128–131; Vandenberg, *supra* note 94, Table 1, at 266–267, and Table 2, at 269, and, also the text at 268–269 (separate commissions for highest appellate court, each division of its intermediate appellate court, and each of certain specialized or inferior courts).

142. E.g., Nebraska. *See A Critical Study*, *supra* note 6, at 336; Ashman and Alfini, *supra* note 134, at 34 (separate commissions for each supreme court justice, each district court, and each county court; and other commissions).

NOTES to §2.7(g)

143. E.g., Alabama, Alaska, Arizona, Colorado, District of Columbia, Indiana, Iowa (two judges), Missouri, Montana, Nebraska, Utah, Wyoming. *See A Critical Study*, *supra* note 6, at 326–329, 331–333, 335–337, 340–341, and Ashman and Alfini, *supra* note 134, at 27–34, 37.

144. E.g., Florida, Kansas, Oklahoma, Pennsylvania, Tennessee, and New York City. *See A Critical Study*, *supra* note 6, at 329, 333, 338–340; Ashman and Alfini, *supra* note 134, at 29, 32, 35–36; and Pa. Exec. Order No. 1980–18 (Sept. 3, 1980), §§7.113, 7.134.

145. *See* Ala. Const. amend. nos. 83, 328, §6.14, and 334; Alaska Const. art. IV, §8; Ind. Const. art. 7, §9, and Ind. Code §§33–2.1–4–1 and 2, 33–5–29.5–29 to 31; Iowa Const. art. 5, §16 (flexible number of gubernatorial appointees, equal number elected by bar, and one judge); Kan. Const. art. 3, §2(f); Kan. Stat. §20–2903; Mo. Const. art. 5, §25(d); Neb. Const. art. V, §21(4) (judicial member not entitled to vote); Nev. Const. art. 6, §20; N.D. Cent. Code §27–25–02 (supreme court nominating committee); Wyo. Const. art. 5, §4(c).

146. *See supra* note 145.

147. Delaware, Kentucky, Mississippi, New Mexico, North Carolina, Pennsylvania, South Dakota, West Virginia. *See* Dela. Exec. Order No. 4 (1977); N.C. Exec. Order No. 12 (July 28, 1977) (trial court nominating commission); Pa. Exec. Order 1980–18 (Sept. 3, 1980), §7.113 (appellate court nominating commission); S.D. Const. art. VI, §9; S.D. Comp. Laws §16–1A–2. *See* Vandenberg, *supra*, note 94, Table 3, at 270–271, as to Mississippi, New Mexico, and W. Virginia.

148. Delaware, Mississippi, New Mexico, North Carolina, Pennsylvania, W. Virginia. *See supra* note 147.

149. Idaho Code §§1–2101, 1–2102.

150. Ga. Exec. Order of April 28, 1975; and *see* Vandenberg, *supra* note 94, Tables 2 and 3, at 269–270.

151. Colo. Const. art. VI, §§24(2), (3).

152. *See* District of Columbia Self-Government Reorganization Act, §434(b) (4); Fla. Const. art. 5, §§11, 20(f); Md. Exec. Order No. 01.01.1979.08 (June 8, 1979); N.Y. Const. art. 6, §2(d) (1); N.Y. Exec. Order No.5 (February 24, 1975); N.Y. City Exec. Order No. 10 (April 11, 1978); N.D. Const. art. VI, §13; N.D. Cent. Code §§27–25–01, 27–25–02 (trial court nominating commissions); Tenn. Code Ann. §17–4–102. *See* Vandenberg, *supra* note 94, Tables 2 and 3, at 269–270, and nn. 3, 5; Ashman and Alfini, *supra* note 134, at 35; and *A Critical Study*, *supra* note 6, at 337.

153. Hawaii Const. art. VI, §3.

154. *See* Ariz. Const. art. 6, §36(A); Ariz. Const. art. 6, §36(B) (judicial member is entitled to vote only in the event of a tie); Ky. Const. §118(2); Mass. Exec. Order, Jan. 1979; Minn. Exec. Order No. 79–23; Mont. Rev. Code Ann. §3–1–1001; Okla. Const. art. 7-B, §§1, 3; Okla. Stat. Ann. tit. 20, §30.10; Okla. Stat. Ann. tit. 4, §51, §10(a); Vt. Stat. Ann. tit. 4, §601. *See also* Vandenberg, *supra* note 94, Tables 2 and 3, at 269–270. *Compare A Critical Study*, *supra* note 6, at 334, as to Massachusetts.

155. Minnesota, Oklahoma, and Vermont. *See supra* note 154.

NOTES to §2.7(h)

156. E.g., *see* Ala. Const. amend. nos. 83, 328, §6.14 and 334; Ind. Const. art. 7, §9; Kan. Const. art. 3, §§2(f) and (g); Kan. Stat. §20–2904; Md. Exec. Order No. 01.01.1979.08 (June 8, 1979), §§1(a)(37), 2(a)(3); Mo. Const. art. 5, §25(d), and Mo. S. Ct. R. 10.02; Neb. Const. art. V, §21(4), and Neb. Rev. Stat. §§24–803, 806, 808; Okla. Const. art. 7-B, §3(a) (2); Tenn. Code Ann. §17–4–102; Vt. Stat. Ann. tit. 4, §601; Wyo. Const. art. 5, §4(c).

157. In states with two-tier appellate systems, such as Indiana, Missouri, Oklahoma, or Tennessee, each lawyer member of an appellate nominating commission is generally drawn from and elected by lawyer residents of one of the court of appeals districts (e.g., Indiana and Missouri), congressional districts (e.g., Oklahoma), or other areas (Tennessee). *See supra* note 156. On the other hand, in the case of single-tier appellate systems, although each lawyer member of some supreme court nominating commissions is drawn from and elected by lawyers from one of the supreme court districts of the state (e.g., Nebraska), lawyer members of other supreme court nominating commissions are elected by members of the bar of the entire state (e.g., Vermont and Wyoming). *See supra* note 156. Also, in the case of trial court nominating commissions, the lawyers electing the lawyer members are generally required to be residents of the judicial district, circuit, or county over which the court in question has jurisdiction (e.g., Alabama, Indiana, Missouri, Nebraska). *See supra* note 156. When, however, a single commission handles all supreme court and major trial court nominations in the state, as is more apt to be the case when the state is relatively small than when it is relatively large, the lawyer members are at times elected by the entire state bar (e.g., Vermont and Wyoming). *See supra* note 156.

158. E.g., Alaska Const. art. IV, §8; Ariz. Const. art. 6, §§36(A) 36(B); Fla. Const. art. 5, §20(5); Idaho Code §1–2101; Nev. Const. art. 6, §20.

159. E.g., *see* Pa. Exec. Order No. 1980–18 (Sept. 13, 1980), §7.113.

160. E.g., *see* S.D. Const. art. V, §§7, 9; and S.D. Comp. Laws Ann. §16–1A–2.

161. E.g., *see* Colo. Const. art. V, §24(4).

162. E.g., *see* Mont. Rev. Code Ann. §3–1–1001.

163. E.g., *see* Ga. Exec. Order of April 28, 1975; Vandenberg, *supra* note 94, at 270, nn. 1 and 2.

164. E.g., Alaska, Colorado, Kansas, Missouri, Montana, Nebraska, Nevada, Oklahoma, Pennsylvania, South Dakota, Tennessee, Utah and Vermont. *See supra* notes 156, and 158–163. The Pennsylvania plan is unique, since both the lawyer members and the nonlawyer members are chosen by the governor. *See supra* note 159.

165. E.g., *see* Ala. Const. amend. nos. 83, 110, 328 (§6.14), and 334.

166. E.g., Fla. Const. art. 5, §20(5)(c).

167. E.g., *see* District of Columbia Self-Government and Governmental Reorganization Act §434(b)(4); N.Y. Const. art. 6, §2(d)(1) (Court of Appeals); N.Y. Exec. Order No. 5 (Feb. 24, 1975) (Appellate Division). *See A Critical Study, supra* note 6, Appellate V., at 337.

168. Vt. Stat. Ann. §601(b). The remaining commission members are three lawyers elected by lawyers residing in the state. *Id.*, §601(b) (4).

169. *See supra* note 159.

170. E.g., *see* Alaska Const. art. IV, §8; Ariz. art. 6, §§36(A), 36B; Idaho Code §1–2101; Iowa Const. art. 5, §16; Mo. Const. art. 5, §25(d) (circuit judicial commission); Utah Code Ann. §20–1–7–3.

171. E.g., *see* Ind. Const. art. 7, §9, and Nev. Const. art. 6, §§20(3)(a).

172. E.g., *see* District of Columbia Self-Government and Self-Reorganization Act §434(b)(4)(E).

173. E.g., *see* Ala. Const. amend. nos. 83, 328 (§6.14), 334; Mont. Rev. Code Ann. §3–1–1001; Mo. Const. art. 5, §25(d) (appellate judicial commission).

174. S.D. Comp. Laws Ann. §16–1A–2.

175. Neb. Const. art. V, §21(4) (a supreme court judge designated by the governor; not entitled to vote).

176. *See supra* notes 156, 158–163, 167–172, and the accompanying text.

177. E.g., *see* Mass. Exec. Order of Jan. 1979; Pa. Exec. Order No. 1980–18 (Sept. 3, 1980). *See* Vandenberg, *supra* note 94, Table 3, at 270–271, as to Rhode Island and West Virginia.

178. E.g., Alaska, Const. art. IV, §8; Ariz Const. art. 6, §§36A, 36B; Colo. Const. art VII, §§24(2) and (3); Idaho Const. art. 5, §19; Idaho Code §§1–2101; Ind. Const. art. VI, §9; Iowa Const. art. 5, §16; Neb. Const. art. V, §21(4) (not entitled to vote); Utah Code Ann. §20–1–7–6; Wyo. Const. art. 5, §4. *Cf.* Mont. Rev. Code Ann. §3–1–1–1001 (district judge, elected by district judges); Nev. Const. art. 3, §2(f) (silent as to chairman). *Contra*: Kan. Const. art. 3, §2(f) (attorney, chosen by bar members); S.D. Comp. Laws Ann. §16–1A–2 (elected by members from among them).

179. E.g., *see* Ga. Exec. Order of April 28, 1975· Md Exec. Order III III 1970.00 (June 8, 1970), Mass, Exec. Order of Jan. 1979; Minn. Exec. Order No. 79–23; N.1. Exec. Order No. 5 (Feb. 24, 1975); Pa. Exec. Order No. 1980–18 (Sept.

3, 1980); and Vandenberg, *supra* note 94, Table 3, at 270–271, as to Mississippi, Rhode Island, and West Virginia.

180. *See supra* notes 156, 158–162, 165–168, and 174–175, except as to Alaska, Arizona and Idaho.

181. E.g., Ariz. Const. art. 6, §§36(A) (senate confirmation), §36(B) (same); Idaho Code §1–2101 (same).

182. Alaska Const. art. IV, §8 (confirmation by a majority of the legislature in joint session).

NOTES to §2.7(i)

183. E.g., Ala. Const. amend. nos. 83, 100, 328 (§6.14), 334; Alaska Const. art. IV, §5; Alaska Stat. §§22.05.080, 22.07.070, 22.10.100; Ariz. Const. art. 6, §37; Colo. Const. art. VI, §20; Del. Exec. Order No. 4 (1977) (voluntary plan); D.C. Self–Government and Governmental Reorganization Act §§433, 434 (president is appointing authority); Fla. Const. art. 5, §11 (Supp.); Hawaii Const. art. VI, §3; Ga. Exec. Order of April 28, 1975 (voluntary plan); Idaho Code §1–2102; Ind. Const. art. 7, §10; Iowa Const. art. 5, §15; Kan. Const. art. 3, §2(d); Kan. Stat. §§20–2909 to 2911; Ky. Const. §118; Md. Exec. Order No. 01.01.1979 (June 8, 1979), §6 (voluntary plan); Mass. Exec. Order of Jan. 1979 (voluntary plan); Minn. Exec. Order No. 79–23 (1979) (voluntary plan); Mo. Const. art. 5, §25(a); Mont. Rev. Code Ann. §§3–1–1010 and 1011; Neb. Const. art. V, §21(1); Nev. Const. art. 6, §20(1); N.Y. Const. art. 6, §§2(e) and (f), and N.Y. Judic. Law §63 (New York Court of Appeals); N.Y. Exec. Order No. 5 (February 24, 1975) (voluntary plan for appellate division); N.C. Exec. Order No. 12 (July 28, 1977) (voluntary plan); N.D. Const. art. VI, §13; N.D. Cent. Code §§27–25–03 to 04; Okla. Const. art. 7-B, §4; Pa. Exec. Order 1980–18 (Sept. 3, 1980) (10 Pa. B. 4180), §7.116(e) (voluntary plan); S.D. Const. art. VI, §7; Tenn. Code Ann. §§17–4–109(e), 112, 113; Utah Code Ann. §20–1–7.6; Vt. Stat. Ann. §§602–603; Wyo. Const. art. 5, §4(b); Wyo. Stat. §5–5–111. In addition to the seven voluntary plans cited above, other voluntary plans in which the governor is the appointing authority are in effect in Mississippi, New Mexico, Rhode Island, and West Virginia. *See* Vandenberg, *supra* note 94, Tables 1 and 2, at 266–267, 269.

184. *See supra* note 183 as to all jurisdictions cited in that note other than Delaware, District of Columbia, Hawaii, Maryland, Massachusetts, Montana, New York, Utah, and Vermont.

185. E.g., Delaware, District of Columbia, Hawaii, Maryland, Montana, New York (Court of appeals and appellate division), Utah, and Vermont. *See supra* note 183. *Cf.* Mass. Const. pt. 2, ch. 2, sec. 1, art. IX, and Mass. Exec. Order of Jan. 1979 (confirmation by governor's council required).

186. E.g., Alabama, Arizona, Colorado, Indiana, Iowa, Kansas, Kentucky, Montana, Nebraska, Oklahoma, Utah and Wyoming. *See supra* note 183. The ABA Model Merit Selection Plan contains such a provision. *See* Kauffman, *supra* note 74, at 1172–1173, n. 46, as to the ABA plan, and Ashman and Alfini, *supra* note 134, at 99–100, 117 (as to the Alabama plan). *But see* Nelson, Maintaining an Independent Judiciary, Cal. State B J (Mar.-Apr. 1979), 78, 83 (sole appointing authority should be a judge or court); and notes 61 62, *supra* (original Kales and Harley recommendations: sole appointing authority should be chief justice).

187. District of Columbia Self-Government and Reorganization Act §434(d); Hawaii Const. art. VI, §3; Mo. Const. art. 5, §25(a).

188. E.g., Alaska, Florida, Idaho, New York, North Dakota, Tennessee, Utah, Vermont, and Wyoming. *See supra* note 184. *Cf.* Nev. Const. art. 6, §20(8) (governor failing to make appointment by deadline is prohibited from making any other appointment to public office until he has appointed a judge from the commission's list of nominees).

NOTE to §2.7(j)

189. The required numbers of commission nominees in various commission plan states, including any required minimum or maximum numbers, are as follows (terms "appellate" and "trial" preceding required numbers respectively refer to an appellate court nominating commission and a trial court nominating commission; two numbers separated by a hyphen constitute a required minimum number and a required maximum number): Alabama (3), Alaska (2 or more), Arizona (min. of 3), Colorado (appellate court, 3; trial court. 2), Delaware (3), District of Columbia (3), Florida (appellate, 3; trial, minimum of 3), Georgia (maximum of 5), Idaho (2–4), Indiana (3), Iowa (appellate, 3; trial, 2), Kansas (appellate, 3; trial, 2–3), Kentucky (3), Massachusetts (all qualified applicants), Maryland (appellate, 5–7; trial, maximum of 7), Minnesota (3–5), Mississippi (supreme court, 5; trial, 3), Missouri (3), Montana (3–5), Nebraska (minimum of 2), New Mexico (all "highly qualified" applicants), Nevada (3), New York (Court of Appeals: chief justice, 7; associate justice, 3–5), North Carolina (3–5), North Dakota (2–7), Oklahoma (3), Pennsylvania (5), R.I. (3), Tennessee (3), Utah (3), Vermont (as many as commission deems qualified), West Virginia (not indicated), Wyoming (3). *See supra* note 184; and Vandenberg, *supra* note 94, Table 4, at 272. *See also Merit Plan in Ohio, supra* note 83, at 273. *Cf.* Ashman and Alfini, *supra* note 134, at 149–150.

NOTES to §2.7(k)

190. *See* Ariz. Const. art. VI, §§36A, 36B; Colo. Const. art. VI, §24; Idaho Code §1–2101; Ky. Const. §118(2); Neb. Rev. Stat. §§24–803(2) and (3); N.Y. Const. art. 6, §2(d)(1); Utah Code Ann. §20–1–7.3; Vt. Stat. Ann. tit. 4, §601. *Compare* Iowa Const. art. 5, §16 (members "shall be chosen without regard to political affiliation").

191. *See supra* note 190.

192. *See supra* note 190.

NOTES to §2.7(l)

193. Incumbent judges are generally exempted from these restrictions. E.g., Ala. Const. amend. 83, and 334; Mo. Const. art. 5, §25(d). *Cf.* N.Y. Const. art. 6, §2(d)(1) (exempting former judges).

194. E.g., Ala. Const. amend. 83, 334; Alaska Const. art. IV, §8; Ariz. Const. art. VI, §11(1); Hawaii Const. art. VI, §1, Idaho Code §1–2101; Ind. Const. art. VII, §9; Iowa Const. art. 5, §16; Kan. Const. art. 3, §2(f)(4); Md. Exec. Order

01.01.1979.08 (June 8, 1979); §§1(a)(2), 2(a)(2); Mo. Const. art. 5, §25(d); N.Y. Const. art. 6, §2(d)(1); Okla. Const. art. 7-B, §3(f); Wyo. Const. art. 5, §4(d). *See* Ashman and Alfini, *supra* note 134, at 73–75, and particularly Table X, at 74.

195. E.g., the plans in Alabama, Colorado, Hawaii, Indiana, Kansas, Maryland, Missouri, New York, Oklahoma and Wyoming. *See supra* note 194. *See also* Kan. Stat. §20–2906.

196. E.g., the plans in Alabama, Colorado, Hawaii, Indiana, Kansas, Maryland, New York, North Dakota, Oklahoma, Utah and Wyoming. *See supra* note 195; Md. Exec. Order 01.01.1979.08 (June 8, 1979), §§1(d), 2(d); N.D. Cent. Code §27–25–07; Utah Code §20–1–7(6)(1)(b); and Wyo. Const. art. 5, §4(d). *See also* Ashman and Alfini, *supra* note 134, at 73–74, and Table X, at 74.

197. The time periods specified include, for example, six months in Kansas and Utah; one year in New York and Wyoming; three years in Colorado, Hawaii, and Indiana; and five years in Oklahoma. *See supra* note 194 and 196.

198. E.g., Ala. amend. 83, 334; Colo. Const. art. VI, §24(4); Ind. Code §§33–2.1–4–5; Iowa Const. art. 5, §16; Okla. Stat. Ann. art. 7-B, §3(h). *Cf.* Ind. Code §33–5–29.5–34 (prohibiting more than two successive terms), and Neb. Rev. Stat. §24–803(3) (prohibiting service for more than eight consecutive years or reappointment after serving for six years).

199. E.g., the plans in Hawaii, Indiana, New York, and Wyoming. *See supra* note 194.

200. E.g., the plans in Colorado, Kansas, Maryland, North Dakota, and Oklahoma. *See supra* notes 194 (except as to North Dakota) and 197 (as to North Dakota).

NOTES to §2.7(m)

201. *See* Heggs, *supra* note 12, at 673–674.

202. *See A Critical Study, supra* note 6, at 397; Mo. S. Ct. Rules Re Non-Partisan Judicial Commissions, R.10.28 (hereinafter cited as "Mo. S. Ct. R.10.28"); *Merit Plan in Ohio, supra* note 2–83, at 272–273.

203. Mo. S. Ct. R.10.28, *supra* note 202.

204. E.g., Colorado, Florida, Idaho (at commission's discretion), Indiana, Iowa, Kansas, Maryland, Nebraska, New York City, Ohio, Oklahoma, Pennsylvania, Utah, Vermont, and Wyoming. *See* Ashman and Alfini, *supra* note 134, Table III, at 56 as to the states just listed. *See also* Md. Exec. Order 01.01.1979.08 (June 8, 1979), §5; Pa. Exec. Order 1980–18, September 3, 1980, §§7.117(a), 7.138(a); N.Y. Judic. Law art. 3-A, §66(3); Mo. S. Ct. R.10.28, *supra* note 202; Vt. Stat. Ann. §602(c); City of Denver Charter §A13–8–14(3). Cf. Rules of Proc. for Judic. Nomin. Comm. on Maricopa Co., Ariz., Super Ct. Appts., RR. 6(e), 10.

205. E.g., Alabama, Alaska, Missouri, Montana and Tennessee. *See* Ashman and Alfini, *supra* note 134, Table III, at 56, 109–110. Mont. Rev. Code Ann. §24–810 requires the chairperson of the commission to call a public hearing and, at least two days prior thereto, to release to the public "the names of lawyers who have signified in writing their willingness to serve as a judge if nominated and appointed to such judgeship," and that "any member of the public shall be entitled to attend the public hearing to express, either orally or in writing, his or her views concerning candidates." Also, Mont. Rev. Code Ann. §§ 1–1007(2) provides that the proceedings of the commission and the related documents shall be open to the public "except

when the demands of individual privacy clearly outweigh the merits of public exposure."

206. E.g., Florida, Idaho (at commission's discretion), Indiana, Iowa, Kansas, Maryland, Montana (at discretion of governor), Nebraska, Oklahoma, Pennsylvania, and Utah. *See* Ind. Code §33–3.1–4–7(c) (names of nominees may be publicly disclosed); N.Y. Judic. Law §63(3) (requires release of commission's report concerning nominees); Mont. Rev. Stat. Ann. §3–1–1007. *See* Ashman and Alfini, *supra* note 134, Table III, at 55, as to the other states just listed (other than New York).

207. E.g., United States (U.S. circ. Judge Nomin. Comm.), Colorado, Ohio, Vermont and Wyoming. *See* Vt. Stat. Ann. §603; Ashman and Alfini, *supra* note 134, Table III, at 56, as to the states just listed; Berkson, Carbon, and Neff, A Study of the U.S. Circuit Judge Nominating Committee, 63 Judicature 104, 112 (1979).

208. E.g., Md. Exec. Order 01.01.1979.08 (June 8, 1979), §5.

209. E.g., cf. Ariz. Rules of Proc. for Judic. Nomin. Comm. on Maricopa Co. Super. Ct. Appts., R.3(d); Uniform Rules of Proc. for Judic. Nomin. Comm. on Pima Co. [Ariz.] Super. Ct. and Appell. Ct. Appts. R.3(d).

210. E.g., Mont. Rev. Stats. Ann. §24.812.

211. E.g., Ind. Code §33–2.1–4–7(c); Pa. Exec. Order No. 1980–18 (Sept. 3, 1980) (10 Pa. B. 4180) §§7.117(a), 7.138(a).

212. E.g., Md. Exec. Order 01.01.1979.08 (June 8, 1979), §4(d).

213. E.g.,in re Baumgarten, N.Y.L.J. (Oct. 27, 1978), at 55, col. 2.

214. E.g., Missouri Supreme Court Rules on Nonpartisan Judicial Nominating Commissions, S. Ct. R.10.29.

215. Neb. Rev. Stat. Ann. §24–809.

NOTES to §2.8

216. *See infra* notes 218–222, and the accompanying text.

217. *See supra* note 122, and the accompanying text.

218. Ill. Const. art. 6, 12; Ill. Rev. Stat. §7A–1.

219. *See* Pa. Exec. Order No. 1980–18 (Sept. 3, 1980).

220. *See* Pa. Const. art. 5, §15(b); 42 Pa. Consol. St. Ann. §§3131(b), 3132(c) and (d), 3153.

221. *See* Cal. Const. art. 6, §16.

222. Cal. Const. art. 6, §16(c).

223. *See infra* note 224.

224. *See* Alaska Const. art. IV, §6; Ind. Const. art. 7, §11; Iowa Const. art. 5, §17; Mont. Const. art. VII, §8; Neb. Const. art. V, §21(3); Okla. Const. art. 7-B, §5; Vt. Stat. Ann. tit. 4, §604; Wyo. Stat. §§5.114.12 and .17. See *supra* note 122 as to Arizona, Colorado, Kansas, Maryland, Missouri and South Dakota. *See also Merit Plan in Ohio, supra* note 83, at 271.

225. *See* note 122 *supra*, and the accompanying text.

226. *See infra* notes 229 and 230, and the accompanying text.

227. *See supra* notes 122 and 217–222, and the accompanying text. *See also* Carbon and Berkson, Judicial Retention Elections in the United States (Am. Jud. Soc. 1980), at 70–75, app A). In Illinois, a three-fifths majority is necessary for retention. Ill. Const. art. 6, §11(d).

228. *See supra* notes 122 and 218–222, and the accompanying text.

229. E.g., Alaska Stat. Ann. §§15.35.040, 15.35.055, 15.35.070; Ariz. Const. art. 6, §38; Colo. Const. art. VI, §25; Ill. Const. art. 6, §12(d); Iowa Code §§46.16, 46.24; Kan. Const. art. 3, §2(e); Kan. Stat. §2908; Mo. Const. art. 5, §25(c)(1); Okla. Const. art. 7-B, §2; Tenn. Code Ann. §§17-4-114 through 17-4-116; Utah Code Ann. §20-1-7.7; Vt. Stat. Ann. tit. 4, §§4(c), 71(b).

230. E.g., Ariz. Const. art. 6, §38; Colo. Const. art. VI, §25.

3

Judicial Compensation

3.1 AUTHORITY AND DUTY TO DETERMINE JUDICIAL COMPENSATION

As a general rule, the constitution in each American jurisdiction invests the legislature with both the authority and the duty to determine judges' compensation.[1] These provisions either expressly so provide or provide that judges shall be compensated as provided by law. At any specific point in time, judicial salaries have generally been set by statutes enacted when the legislature increased existing salaries.[2] Under the statutes it has been held that the delegation by the legislature to the judiciary of the power to determine judicial salaries is unconstitutional.[3]

In some states, the legislature receives recommendations on judicial compensation from a commission on compensation.[4] These recommendations take two forms: those that are binding if not rejected or modified by the legislature within a specified period of time[5] and those that are purely advisory in nature and not even conditionally binding.[6] In a number of other states, judicial salaries are automatically increased or decreased by formulas tied to changes in the cost of living, changes in population, changes in the average compensation of state employees, or other objective criteria.[7]

3.2 METHODS OF DETERMINING JUDICIAL COMPENSATION

There are three principal methods of determining judicial salaries: (a) by the legislature,[8] (b) by a compensation commission,[9] and (c) by automatic salary adjustments based on objective criteria.[10]

The factors that should be considered either by the legislature or by a compensation commission in determining judicial salaries and fringe benefits include: (a) the earnings or salaries of lawyers in the jurisdiction, corporate executives, federal judges, and judges in other jurisdictions; (b) the retirement and fringe benefits received by federal judges and judges in other jurisdictions, lawyers, and corporate executives; (c) increases in the cost of living during statistically significant periods ending in the present; (d) the rate of increase in earnings or salaries of lawyers in the jurisdiction, corporate executives, federal judges, and judges in other jurisdictions; and (e) unfavorable aspects of the judgeship, such as the shortness or insecurity of tenure, high cost of living in the locale, or unsatisfactory living conditions in that area.[11]

The most succinct and comprehensive comparisons of judicial compensation in the various states are now being published by the National Center for State Courts and are titled "Survey of Judicial Salaries."[12] Similar studies were previously published by the American Judicature Society.[13]

3.3 AUTOMATIC COST-OF-LIVING SALARY ADJUSTMENTS

Statutes providing for automatic adjustments in judicial salaries based upon changes in the cost of living or other objective criteria have been enacted by the federal government, California, Kentucky, and Tennessee.[14] These cost-of-living adjustment statutes are commonly referred to as "COLA statutes."

The federal COLA statute provides for automatic yearly salary increases for federal judges, various other top-level federal officials, and members of Congress based on increases in salaries of comparable nongovernment executives and employees.[15]

When first enacted in 1964, the California COLA statute provided for automatic increases in judicial salaries every fourth year, based on the percentage increase in per capita personal income in the state as reported by the U.S. Department of Commerce.[16] In 1968, the statute was amended to provide for annual increases based upon increases in the consumer price index reported by the California Department of Industrial Relations.[17] In 1979, it was further amended to provide for annual increases in judicial salaries based upon the average percentage increase in state employee salaries.[18]

The Kentucky COLA statute, enacted in 1981 and applicable to all appellate judges, circuit judges, and district judges, provides for automatic increases or decreases based upon the annual increase or decrease in the Consumer Price Index, with the proviso that the salary increases shall not exceed 5 percent in any one year.[19] A similar Kentucky statute applies to county judges and justices of the peace.[20] The Tennessee COLA statute likewise provides for annual increases or decreases in judicial salaries, based on the percentages of increase or decrease in the average Consumer Price Index.[21] A similar statute was enacted in Wisconsin in 1975, but was repealed in 1977.[22]

Finally, in Massachusetts, whenever there is a 3 percent increase in the average cost of living, the director of personnel and standardization is required by statute to recommend legislation for a corresponding increase in judicial salaries.[23] When there is a cost increase of less than 3 percent, the director may, but is not required to, recommend legislation for a corresponding judicial salary increase.[24] He may also recommend decreases corresponding to decreases in the average cost of living, except that any such decrease may not lower any judicial salary below the level in effect on December 31, 1969.[25] The statute does not specify whether the average cost of living referred to is that in effect on December 31, 1969.[26]

Maryland has a similar statute, under which the secretary of personnel may, but is not required to, recommend cost–of–living increases in judicial salaries. These recommendations are made as part of salary plans that he is required to prepare and submit to the governor and that, to become effective, must be approved by the governor and implemented by the legislature.[27] The secretary does, however, have authority to provide for automatic judicial salary increases based on cost–of–living increases.[28]

Automatic cost–of–living adjustment statutes have been advocated as the ideal solution to the problem of keeping judicial salaries abreast of increases in the cost of living. Proponents contend that the statutes make judicial lobbying for salary increases unnecessary, that they make judges more independent, and that they save the judicial time and expense that necessarily attend lobbying.[29] The need for such legislation is corroborated by many studies and surveys on judicial compensation that show a significant gap between the cost of living and judicial salaries.[30]

The current federal and California statutes entitling judges to percentage increases equivalent to those granted to other state employees have counterparts in other states, predicated for example, upon the average percentage increases accorded to state employees generally[31] or the percentage increases awarded to a designated grade of classified employees.[32]

3.4 JUDICIAL COMPENSATION COMMISSIONS

The widespread adoption of judicial selection commissions has been paralleled by that of judicial compensation commissions, empowered to investigate and make recommendations on judicial salaries. Jurisdictions with commissions created pursuant to a constitutional provision or statute include the United States and nineteen states: Alabama, Arizona, Colorado, Connecticut, Florida, Georgia, Illinois, Iowa, Louisiana, Massachusetts, Maryland, Michigan, Montana, New York, Rhode Island, South Dakota, Utah,

Vermont, and Washington.[33] Ohio and Pennsylvania formerly had compensation commissions.[34] In all but Alabama and Maryland, the commission's jurisdiction encompasses all state officials, not just judges.[35]

States in which the commission's recommendations are conditionally binding, i.e., become automatically effective to the extent not rejected or altered by the legislature within a specified period of time, include Alabama, Maryland, Michigan and Rhode Island[36] and formerly included Pennsylvania.[37]

The federal and Arizona compensation commission statutes are unique in that each combines advisory commission recommendations with conditionally binding recommendations by the chief executive. The federal Commission on Executive, Legislative, and Judicial Salaries submits its recommendations to the president of the United States, who submits his own recommendations to Congress. Those recommendations become effective at a specified time unless Congress enacts a statute establishing different rates of pay or one House adopts a resolution specifically disapproving of all or part of the recommendations.[38] The federal statute is carefully drawn to ensure that partial alteration or rejection of the president's recommendations will not prevent the remainder from going into effect.[39] The Arizona statute is substantially identical to the federal statute.[40]

Turning to the states, the former Pennsylvania statute expressly provided that the commission's recommendations would be effective to the extent not altered or rejected by the legislature.[41] The existing Alabama, Maryland, and Michigan statutes, although not explicit on this point, also may be so construed.'[42] A "one-house veto" suffices to nullify a salary recommendation by the federal commission,[43] but, in Alabama, Maryland, and Michigan, a rejection must be by a joint resolution passed by both houses of the legislature.[44] This was also the case under the repealed Pennsylvania statute.

The one-house veto provision in the federal compensation commission statute was sustained by the court of claims in *Atkins v. United States*,[45] as not in violation of the bicameral and presentment clauses of the U.S. Constitution which require legislation to be enacted jointly by the Senate and House and be presented to the president for signature or veto.[46] The questions presented by *Atkins* are inapplicable in Arizona, Colorado, Connecticut, Florida, Illinois, Iowa, Louisiana, Massachusetts, Montana, New York, South Dakota, Utah, and Washington, where the compensation commission's recommendations are advisory only and do not become law unless they are affirmatively enacted by the legislature.[47]

Although the members of several compensation commissions are appointed solely by the governor, one or more of the members of most commissions are chosen by each of several different appointers. Typically, these include the governor, the president or majority leader of the state house of representatives, the chief justice of the state supreme court and, occasionally, the minority leaders of the senate and house.[48] Almost invariably, the statute provides that vacancies shall be filled by the same person who made the original appointment.[49] The compensation commission statutes in a few states, including Arizona, Florida, Illinois, South Dakota, and Utah, contain provisions designed to ensure at least a degree of bipartisanship on the commission.[50]

A number of compensation commission statutes contain eligibility restrictions, rendering varying types of public, state, or local officers or employees ineligible for commission membership.[51] Several other compensation commission statutes contain restrictions forbidding commission members to hold public office or political party office.[52] Also, at least one compensation commission statute renders its members ineligible for a state judicial office both while they are members and for a specified time period thereafter.[53]

The terms of office of compensation commission members vary in length: two years in Arizona, Illinois, Pennsylvania, Rhode Island, and South Dakota; three years in New York; four years in Alabama, Colorado, Connecticut, Georgia, Montana and Utah; five years in Iowa; and six years in Maryland.[54] Almost invariably, a member appointed to fill a vacancy serves until the end of his predecessor's unexpired term, rather than for a full new term.[55]

With the exception of the Alabama compensation commission statute, none of the compensation commission statutes confers subpoena power on the compensation commission.[56] The Alabama statute, by contrast, empowers each member of the commission to administer oaths, take testimony, subpoena witnesses, and require the production of records or documents deemed to be material or pertinent to any subject within the scope of the commission's studies and investigations.[57] Similar subpoena powers have been granted to the New York Permanent Commission on Public Employee Pension and Retirement Systems.[58]

3.5 CONSTITUTIONAL AND OTHER PROHIBITIONS AGAINST DECREASES IN JUDICIAL COMPENSATION

The federal Constitution, many state constitutions, and several state statutes prohibit a reduction of a judge's compensation while in office.[59] Practically all of these clauses apply specifically and solely to judges, rather than to public officials in general.[60] The federal antidiminishment provision, in article III, section 1 of the U.S. Constitution, provides: "The judges, both of the Supreme and inferior courts, shall hold their offices during good behavior, and shall, at stated times, receive for their services, a compensation, which shall not be diminished during their continuance in office." A typical state antidiminishment provision is found in section 5, article 6 of the Minnesota Constitution, which provides. "The compensation of all judges shall be prescribed by the legislature and shall not be diminished during their term of office."

Since a federal judge's tenure is "during good behavior," rather than for a definite term, the federal antidiminishment provision's use of the term "during their continuance in office" is more appropriate than a reference to a judge's term of office. Since few state judges serve for indefinite terms, most constitutional antidiminishment provisions refer to the applicable time period as the judge's term of office,[61] meaning the existing term of office and not subsequently commencing terms of office.[62] Other antidiminishment provisions refer to the term of office for which the judge was elected,[63] undoubtedly also solely meaning the judge's existing term.[64] Still other antidiminishment provisions refer to a judge's continuance in office.[65] Although it is less clear that these provisions refer only to the existing term and not to subsequent terms, these provisions should nevertheless be similarly construed.

In three states, Alaska, Michigan, and Pennsylvania, the restriction on decreases in compensation is expressly inapplicable to decreases applying across the board to all salaried state officals.[66] The rationale behind this exception was undoubtedly that, since antidiminishment clauses were adopted to prevent legislatures from undermining the independence of judges by punitive attacks on their economic welfare,[67] it appeared unlikely that nondiscriminatory reductions applicable to all state officers would be aimed at, or severe enough to impair seriously, judicial independence. This argument, however, has not sufficed to preclude judicial salary cuts from being held invalid under constitutional provisions not containing the express exception just mentioned, even though they were part of general salary cuts to counteract the effects of the Great Depression.[68]

A few antidiminishment clauses prohibit both decreases and increases in compensation. Provisions of this type are found in Idaho, Iowa, Kentucky, Mississippi, Nebraska, Tennessee, Washington, Wisconsin, and Wyoming.[69] Decisions construing these provisions have precedential value in cases involving either increases or decreases in compensation.

The courts are divided on the question whether antidiminishment and anti-increase provisions apply to a judge appointed to fill a vacancy after a salary increase or decrease. A number of cases can be found supporting each of these conflicting views.[70]

Perhaps the most interesting questions under the antidiminishment statutes have arisen in cases where judges have contended that the acknowledged failure of judicial salaries to keep abreast of the cost of living constitutes an impermissible decrease in real compensation. This contention was partially, but not entirely, rejected by the Federal Court of Claims in *Atkins v. United States*.[71] The court held that the federal antidiminishment clause can be violated by indirect diminution as well as direct diminution of judicial compensation, but that "the indirect diminution . . . must be of a character discriminatory against judges and must work in a manner to attack their independence as judges." Therefore, according to the court, a failure to keep judicial salaries abreast of inflation does not per se violate the antidiminishment clauses; and violation occurs only when it can be established that the failure to increase salaries is discriminatory, intentional or grossly negligent, and "ineluctably operating to punish the judges *qua* judges, or to drive them from office."

The *Atkins* court held such a showing had not been made. While inflation in the United States had been high and had serious effects, it had not reached the proportions found in certain European and South American nations, and it did not, in any way, resemble the hyperinflation suffered by Weimar Germany in the early 1920s. The court also noted that, while a few federal judges had resigned for financial reasons, there had been no mass exodus. Plaintiff's claim that there had been a discriminatory attack upon judges was further weakened by the fact that the salary freeze had included not only federal judges but also the top level civil servants and, to a lesser extent, Congress itself. The court concluded that the failure to grant salary increases to judges and other top-level officers and legislators had been motivated not by a desire to attack judicial independence but by political considerations, namely, a fear of public displeasure if increases were granted. Since there had been no showing of discrimination against judges, or of an attack on judicial independence, the federal antidiminishment provision had not been violated.

Aggrieved federal judges suffered another setback in *United States v. Will*.[72] In *Will*, congressional nullification of automatic cost-of-living salary increases was held not to violate the federal antidiminishment provision. Although the enactment of the statutory formula had preceded the commencement of the current terms of office and executive branch determinations of entitlement to increases had preceded nullification, the nullification had occurred before the increases had ripened into accrued payment obligations. Therefore, held the court, there would be a violation only when current accrual commenced before nullification.

The U.S. Supreme Court's ruling in *Will* is inconsistent with decisions by the Delaware Supreme Court in *Stiffel v. Malarkey*[73] and by the California Supreme Court in *Olson v. Cory*[74] ("*Olson v. Cory I*"), in which statutes revoking (*Stiffel*) or placing a ceiling on (*Olson v. Cory I*) automatic salary increases before they began to accrue were held violative of the Delaware and California antidiminution provisions, article IV, section 4 of the Delaware Constitution and article II, section 4 of the California Constitution. In *Olson v. Cory I*, the limiting statute was also held to violate the state and federal constitutional prohibitions against the impairment of contracts.[75] In applying the impairment of contracts clause of the federal Constitution, the California Supreme Court arrived at a conclusion directly contrary to that of the Delaware Supreme Court in *Grant v. Nellius*,[76] where a statute revoking a cost-of-living increase before it began to accrue was held not to violate that clause.

Following the *Stiffel* decision, an amendment to the antidiminution provision of the Delaware Constitution, article XV, section 4, was enacted,[77] overruling *Stiffel*. Article XV, section 4, as amended, provides:

No law shall extend the term of any public officer or diminish his salary or emoluments after his election or appointment. The term "salary or emoluments" refers to those provided during term in office, *not increases scheduled by statute for a future date and not yet received by the officer* [emphasis added].

Subsequent to the 1980 decision in *Olson v. Cory I*, the antidiminution provision of the California Constitution was likewise amended to overrule *Olsen v. Cory I*. Article III, section 4, was amended to read:

(a) Except as provided in subdivision (b), salaries of elected state officers may not be reduced during their term of office. Laws that set these salaries areappropriations.
(b) Beginning on January 1, 1981, the base salary of a judge of a court of record shall equal the annual salary payable as of July 1, 1980, for that office had the judge been elected in 1978. *The Legislature* may prescribe increases in those salaries during a term of office, and it *may terminate prospective increases in those salaries at any time during a term of office, but it shall not reduce the salary of a judge during a term of office below the highest level paid during that term of office.* Laws setting the salaries of judges shall not constitute an obligation of contract pursuant to Section 9 of Article 1 or any other provision of law [emphasis added].

In a 1982 decision, also titled *Olson v. Cory* ("*Olson v. Cory II*"),[78] the California Supreme Court of Appeals held that even though the amendment had eliminated the objections under the California Constitution to legislation limiting cost-of-living salary increases, the statute still violated article I, section 10 of the U.S. Constitution.

Given the Delaware Supreme Court's decision in *Grant v. Nellius*[79] that the federal impairment of contract clause was not violated by repeal of a statute providing for automatic cost-of-living salary increases, it would appear that unless and until successfully challenged in a federal court under the federal impairment of contract clause, the Delaware constitutional amendment overruling *Stiffel* would be sustained by the Delaware courts. It remains to be seen whether other state supreme courts, unconstrained by limiting language such as that contained in the Delaware and California constitutional amendments, will follow *Will* or the contrary decisions in *Stiffel* and *Olson v. Cory I*.

A final effort by judges to secure redress in the courts, this time on the theory that the legislative failure to grant cost-of-living increases to judges violated an implied constitutional requirement that judicial salaries be "adequate," was rejected by the Pennsylvania Supreme Court in *Klinger v. Barbieri*.[80] Prior to this decision, the Pennsylvania Supreme Court, in *Glancey v. Casey*[81] had established the principle that there is an implied constitutional requirement in Pennsylvania that the legislature provide "adequate salaries" for judges. Adequate salaries were defined by the court to be "compensation adequate in amount and commensurate with the duties and responsibilities of the judges involved." The complaining judges in *Kremer* contended that failure to provide cost-of-living salary increases sufficient to prevent a considerable inflationary reduction of real earnings caused their salaries to be constitutionally inadequate.[82] The court rejected this interpretation of *Glancey*, and held that the inadequacy of judicial compensation can be established only by proof of a resulting impairment of the judicial system, and that proof of financial hardship to judges and their inability to meet their personal needs was insufficient to establish the necessary impairment.[83] More specifically, proof of a 55.7 percent increase in prices since 1972, contrasted with a 12.5 percent increase in common pleas judges' salaries during the same period, proof of the inadequacy of judges' compensation compared with that of lawyers in private practice and federal district court judges, and proof of resignations for economic reasons and of the unwillingness of qualified lawyers (not named) to seek or accept judicial office, were held insufficient to establish that the judicial system had been impaired.

Kentucky has an express constitutional provision mandating adequate judicial compensation.[84] That provision, and a constitutional provision imposing dollar ceilings on judges' salaries, were construed by the Kentucky Supreme Court (then known as the Kentucky Court of Appeals) in 1962 in *Matthews v. Allen*[85] as permitting the legislature to enact cost–of-living adjustments to the dollar ceilings.[86] The same court nevertheless held in 1965 in *Meade County v. Neafus*[87] that when the legislature has not adjusted the constitutional salary maximums, the courts are powerless to increase salaries to adjust for changes in purchasing power. The court made it clear that there is no implied constitutional requirement in Kentucky that judicial salaries be adjusted for changes in the cost of living:[88]

We did not say, nor intend to say, in the Matthews v. Allen case, as construed by the trial court, that the salaries of all officers were automatically geared to the price of living index or the value of the dollar. Or that any or all officers in the state could go into court and ask the court to adjust their compensation based on the price of living index or the value of the dollar in the community.

It must be concluded from *Kremer* that, at least in Pennsylvania, mass resignations would have to be shown to establish inadequacy of salaries. In the light of *Atkins* and *Will*, it is probable that even if the U.S. Supreme Court were to hold that adequate judicial salaries are constitutionally mandated, the Pennsylvania Supreme Court would still apply its requirement that a showing of resulting impairment of the proper functioning of the judicial system is necessary to establish the inadequacy of judicial salaries.

There is, however, much to be said for a contrary conclusion, which would remove, in part, the issue of judicial salary increases from the political arena and would require automatic minimum increases that would narrow the difference between the earnings of practicing lawyers and judges.

Another recurring issue under antidiminishment provisions is whether passage of a nondiscriminatory income tax during a judge's term of office violates constitutional antidiminution provisions. The federal view was, at one time, that such a tax did violate the antidiminution clause in the federal Constitution,[89] but that position has since then been reversed.[90] The state courts are divided on this question,[91] but the recent trend is to uphold the constitutionality of the tax.[92] Similarly, adoption of a mandatory contributory retirement plan has been upheld as not involving an impermissible salary decrease.[93]

Retired judges are generally held entitled to protection under antidiminishment provisions.[94]

3.6 CONSTITUTIONAL PROHIBITIONS AGAINST INCREASES IN JUDICIAL COMPENSATION

A considerable number of state constitutions once contained provisions prohibiting salary increases for incumbent judges.[95] Opposition to these provisions, on the ground that they unfairly discriminated in favor of newer judges and against older and more experienced judges, has resulted in the repeal of most of these provisions.[96] Anti-increase provisions are, however, still in effect in a few states, including Idaho, Iowa, Kentucky, Mississippi, Nebraska, Oklahoma, Tennessee, Wisconsin, and Wyoming.[97]

Perhaps the most interesting, and certainly the most important, of the problems that have arisen under the anti-increase provisions has been the question of whether an automatic salary increase, going into effect during a judge's term of office pursuant to a statutory formula enacted prior to the commencement of that term, can inure to the benefit of that judge without violating an anti-increase provision. As might be expected, given the contrast between *Will* and cases such as *Stiffel*, *Olson v. Cory I*, and *Olson v. Cory II*,[98] the decisions on this question vary,[99] but the trend is running in favor of constitutionality.[100] In *Stiffel*,[101] the Delaware Supreme Court specifically stated that an automatic cost-of-living salary increase pursuant to a statutory formula enacted before the commencement of a judge's term is validly available to the judge, notwithstanding an applicable constitutional anti-increase provision. Citing decisions sustaining changes in public officers' salaries established during the same term of office, pursuant to a pre-term statutory formula for salary revisions based on population changes, the court explained:[102]

there is a species of formula which has been tested over several decades in several other states whose constitutions forbid increases as well as decreases, and it has generally been held that arithmetical applications of a pre-legislated formula, resulting in changes in the numbers of annual dollars, are not constitutionally forbidden in the eyes of the law, provided the formula itself remains unchanged.

In the most recent decision on this question, *Overton County v. State ex. rel. Hale*, [103] the Tennessee supreme court held that an automatic salary increase did not violate the anti-increase provision. The court pointed out: (a) that the rationale underlying anti-increase and antidecrease provisions is that they preserve judicial independence by insulating judges from legislative punishment or reward for their decisions; (b) that, in prohibiting increases or decreases of judges' salaries "during the time for which they are elected," the intention was to prohibit legislative action during their term of office to increase or diminish the judges compensation; and (c) that, in the case of salary changes automatically resulting from changes in the Consumer Price Index, pursuant to a statutory formula enacted before the judges' term of office, the legislature has no power over the amount of the indexed salary change and, therefore, no power over the judges.

Further exceptions to the application of constitutional anti-increase provisions include salary increases to compensate judges for assuming new and additional duties beyond the scope of their offices, [104] bona fide reimbursement for expenses, [105] fringe benefits granted after induction into office, [106] the setting of a salary for a new position [107] or a previously uncompensated position, [108] allowances for maintenance and upkeep, [109] and adoption of a retirement plan [110] or a plan for survivor's benefits. [111]

The constitutional anti-increase (and antidecrease) statute in Nebraska [112] contains an express exception providing that when members of a court have terms beginning and ending at different times, the compensation for all members may be increased or diminished at the beginning of any member's full term. This provision has been construed as permitting across–the–board increases for all judges on a court even if one or more of those members' terms of office commenced before the enactment of the salary increase, as long as the term of office of at least one member commenced after the salary increase. [113] A similar provision in Alabama provides that, as to judges of a court whose terms do not run concurrently, an increase or decrease in salary shall become effective as to all members immediately after the expiration of the term of office of the judge whose term first expires. [114]

Statutory salary increases held violative of a constitutional anti-increase provision when applied to judges whose terms of office began before the enactment of the statute also have been held severable and, therefore, validly applicable to judges whose terms began after the increase. [115]

Salary increases applicable to certain classes of judges and not others, such as salary increases applicable to judges of appellate courts and trial courts of general jurisdiction but not to judges of trial courts of limited jurisdiction, have been sustained in challenges on equal protection grounds. [116] Also, state constitutional provisions forbidding increases in sitting judges' salaries, which necessarily discriminate between sitting judges and judges whose terms begin after an increase, have been held not to violate the federal equal protection clause.[117] The courts that have adopted this view have reasoned that the provision is rationally related to the goal of preventing judges from utilizing their inherent influence and power to induce the legislature to grant them salary increases.[118]

In states whose constitutions contain an antidiminishment provision, but not an anti-increase provision, the courts have held that salary increases for incumbent judges, as well as future judges, were impliedly authorized.[119] *A fortiori*, increases have been held impliedly authorized when there was neither an anti-increase provision nor an antidecrease provision.[120]

3.7 PROHIBITIONS AGAINST REMUNERATION NOT AUTHORIZED BY LAW

The typical constitutional and statutory limitations on judicial remuneration[121] normally also provide that judges shall not receive any remuneration for judicial service other than the salary or compensation authorized by law.[122] In other states, the same result is arguably achieved by constitutional provisions that, although not expressly prohibiting other compensation, provide that judges shall receive such compensation as may be provided by law.[123]

The first-mentioned type of constitutional provision has been held not violated by a statute granting additional compensation to judges for additional judicial duties imposed upon them; the court deemed the additional compensation an increase in that salary authorized by law.[124] On the other hand, when the constitutional provision prohibits any nonsalary remuneration "for or on account of his office," extra compensation for work in a nonjudicial office (e.g., an insanity board) to which the judge was appointed by reason of his judicial status has been held violative of the provision.[125]

Finally, statutes granting expense allowances have been held not to infringe this type of constitutional provision.[126]

3.8 PROHIBITIONS AGAINST PAYMENT OF EXTRA COMPENSATION

A few state constitutions contain a provision prohibiting legislation authorizing extra compensation for any public officer or employee after services have been rendered. The principal interpretative issue raised by this type of provision has been whether legislation granting pensions to public officers or employees may be applied to public officers or employees who retired before the legislation was enacted. Cases holding that legislation granting pensions to employees who retired before its passage does not violate the extra compensation provision have reasoned that, while such pension legislation does not serve the public purpose of encouraging persons to become public officers and employees, it satisfies a moral obligation to reward the past public services. These decisions also hold that the constitutional prohibition only applies to persons still holding public office when the allegedly offending legislation is enacted and does not apply to former public employees.[127]

Cases taking a contrary view[128] have construed the term "extra compensation" as any compensation over and above that fixed by contract or by law when the services were rendered.[129] The New York court of appeals has taken the position that there is no moral obligation to establish a pension system for public officials or employees[130] and that the granting of a pension to a person not then in service is a mere gratuity.[131]

3.9 PROHIBITIONS AGAINST THE RECEIPT OF FEES BY JUDGES, JUSTICES OF THE PEACE, OR MAGISTRATES

Compensation consisting of, or derived from, fees or fines paid by the parties into the compensated judge's court, or based upon the volume of cases instituted before that judge, has been a subject of increasing controversy. Since judges of courts of limited jurisdiction ("minor court judges") have often been compensated in this manner,[132] these challenges have great importance to the lesser judiciary.

In 1927, in *Tumey v. Ohio*,[133] the U.S. Supreme Court dealt a body blow to the system of compensating the minor judiciary through the costs and fines paid by unsuccessful criminal defendants appearing before them. The Court held that this violated the due process clause of the Fourteenth Amendment, reasoning that the defendant's liberty or property could not be constitutionally subjected to the judgement of a court in which the judge had "a direct, personal substantial pecuniary interest in reaching a conclusion against him in his case."[134] In so holding, the Court analyzed the antecedent case law and concluded that the practice of compensating minor court judges out of fees or fines paid by convicted defendants in petty criminal cases had not become so imbedded in the general practice, either at common law or in this country generally, that it could be regarded as due process of law, "unless the costs usually imposed are so small that they may be properly ignored as within the maxim *de minimis non curat lex*."[135] Receipt by the judge in *Tumey* of costs, amounting to $12 in that specific Prohibition Act case, and aggregating $100 per year in cases of that type, was held substantial, rather than *de minimis*.

Later in its opinion, the Court enunciated an even stricter principle, saying:[136]

Every procedure which would offer a possible temptation to the average man as a judge to forget the burden of proof required to convict the defendant, or which might lead him not to hold the balance nice, clear and true between the State and the accused denies the latter due process of law.

Applying this principle, the Court held that the judge's interest, as mayor, in increasing the village revenues via criminal fines (half of which were payable to the village) created a potential bias sufficient to violate due process, separate and apart from his personal interest in his own fees.[137] This latter ruling was predicated upon the judge also being the mayor of the village, with the responsibility for both raising revenue and the village's general financial condition.[138] In a subsequent case, *Dugan v. Ohio*,[139] where the mayor had very limited executive authority compared to that of the city manager, a mayor-judge, who did not receive compensation derived from fees or costs paid by convicted defendants, was held not disqualifed merely because fines were paid to the municipality's treasury.

Finally, in 1972, in *Ward v. Village of Monroeville*,[140] the Court reaffirmed its pronouncement that the "possible temptation" for a mayor-judge to disregard the burden of proof required to convict the defendant violated due process.[141] The Court also held that when an unacceptable possibility of bias existed at the trial level, a right of appeal and trial *de novo* in a higher court do not render the potential trial court bias any less unconstitutional.[142]

In a leading post-*Ward* decision by the Fifth Circuit Court of Appeals, *Brown v. Vance*,[143] an unconstitutional potential for bias was held to exist even when a judge's compensation is based on fees payable irrespective of the result, when their aggregate amount is predicated upon the number of cases brought before him. The rationale was that prosecutors would favor conviction–prone judges over others and thus create an inherent temptation for all affected judges to become conviction prone.[144] The due process clause was held violated under such circumstances, even though there was both a right of jury trial in the proceeding before the minor court judge and a right of appeal and trial *de novo* in the court to which the appeal was taken. Prior to *Ward*, this type of potential bias had been held insufficient to violate due process,[145] particularly when there was a right to a jury trial in the minor court.[146]

Waiver represents one potential ground for sustaining convictions before justices of the peace whose compensation varies according to the number of actions brought before them. This ground was relied on in at least one post-*Tumey* state court decision, but has not yet been considered by the Supreme Court. In that decision, the defendant was offered, but rejected, a change of venue to a minor court where the judge was salaried and his compensation unrelated to the number of cases he heard.[147]

Commentators have variously categorized the principal fee systems as follows: (1) the system involved in the *Tumey* case in which the judge receives a bundled fees only on conviction of the defendant, has been called the "simple fee system"; (2) the system involved in *Brown*, under which each of two or more judges competing with each other receives a scheduled fee for each case regardless of the outcome, and, therefore, each is compensated according to how many cases he hears, has been called the "competitive fee system"; (3) a system under which the judge is paid a salary that, although not dependent on outcome, is payable solely out of a fund composed of fees and fines that have been imposed by him, has been referred to as the "salary fund fee system"; (4) a system under which judges are compensated, at least partially, by scheduled fees derived either from con-. victed defendants or, in case of an acquittal, from the applicable governmental unit, has been termed the "alternative fee system"; (5) the system just described, except that the judge's aggregate compensation from all cases is limited to a specified maximum figure, has been termed the "limited alternative fee system"; and (6) a system under which the judge is compensated by fees derived from a fund created and funded by fines and fees imposed by the same court in prior cases, has been called the "penalty fund fee system."[148]

The simple fee system is, of course, invalid under *Tumey*; and the competitive fee system is also invalid under the rationale of *Brown*, assuming, of course, that the U.S. Supreme Court would agree with *Brown*. The salary fund fee system appears to be invalid under the rationale employed in *Tumey*, *Ward*, and *Brown*. Finally, the validity of the alternative fee system, the limited alternative fee system, and the penalty fund system may well depend on whether circumstances create an appreciable, inherent temptation for the judge to convict or hold against the defendant. We would anticipate that each of those practices will be declared invalid.

Statutes have been enacted in a number of states abolishing or restricting the fee system, at least as to certain classes of judges.[149] Although there are slight variations, the prevailing theme is to prohibit judges from being compensated from fees.[150] Several of these provisions, moreover, specifically provide that the judge's compensation shall not depend on fees or other money received or the number of cases heard by the judge.[151] Although certain of these prohibitions expressly apply to justices of the peace or magistrates,[152] others are ambiguous since they refer simply to "judges" or to "justices" as well as "judges."[153] A number of them either expressly or clearly exempt or exclude justices of the peace.[154]

3.10 PROHIBITIONS AGAINST THE PRACTICE OF LAW BY JUDGES

At common law, there were several schools of thought on whether judges could or should practice law. The older and more traditional view was that the practice of law was not incompatible with the holding of judicial office, and was permissible when not prohibited by a statutory or constitutional provision.[155] This permissive view even permitted a judge to practice before another judge of his own court.[156] An intermediate view permitted judges to practice but only in courts other than their own.[157] Another common law variation prohibited members of the minor judiciary from practicing in any court of the county in which they sat.[158] Finally, in a growing number of jurisdictions, judges were entirely precluded from practicing law, despite the absence of any prohibitory statute.[159]

Today, with respect to major court judges, these common law cases are largely of academic interest only. The constitution or statute law of most states now expressly prohibits the practice of law by major court judges.[160] Although several of these prohibitions are limited to courtroom practice[161] or even practice in the judge's own court,[162] the great majority of them apply broadly to "the practice of law"[163] and, therefore, prohibit office practice as well as courtroom practice.[164]

Although some of the prohibitions against the practice of law by judges are expressly applicable only to judges of enumerated courts or judges of courts of record,[165] many merely apply to "judges" or "justices and judges," without indicating whether minor court judges are subject to the prohibition.[166]

Although a rarity, at least one jurisdiction expressly permits full-time major court judges who are attorneys to practice law when it does not conflict with their official duties, cause them to be absent from their courts, or delay performance of their official duties.[167]

The distinction between major court judges and minor court judges that, in some states, prohibits major court judges from practicing law, but permits minor court judges to do so, was sustained in 1940 by the Tennessee supreme court in *Reynolds v. Chumbley*[168] as not violating the equal protection clause of the federal Constitution.

Efforts by the organized bar to disbar or impose bar discipline upon sitting judges for violating restrictions forbidding them to practice law have met with resounding rebuffs from some courts, on the ground that such proceedings constitute an unwarranted invasion by the bar of the courts' jurisdiction to discipline their own members.[169] Such proceedings have also been characterized as constituting a threat to judicial independence.[170] These decisions have constituted applications of a broader rule existing in some states to the effect that jurisdiction is lacking in proceedings to disbar or impose bar discipline upon sitting judges by reason of judicial misconduct.[171] An even larger number of jurisdictions have rejected this broader rule, however, and have sustained jurisdiction in proceedings to disbar or impose bar discipline upon sitting judges for judicial misconduct.[172] In these latter states, the violation by a judge of a restriction prohibiting judges from practicing law is necessarily a basis for imposing bar discipline upon sitting judges.[173]

It also follows that regardless of whether jurisdiction to impose bar discipline upon sitting judges is recognized or denied in any particular jurisdiction, judges are subject to judicial discipline (as distinguished from bar discipline) and have been so disciplined for wrongfully practicing law.[174]

NOTES to §3.1

1. E.g., Ala. Const. amend. no. 328, §6.08(a); Alaska Const. art. IV, §13; Ariz. Const. art. 6, §13; Ark. Const. art. 7, §§10, 18; Cal. Const. art. 6, §19 (Supp.); Colo. Const. art. 6, §18; Del. Const. art. IV, §4; Fla. Const. art. 5, §14 (Supp.) ("the judiciary shall have no power to fix appropriations"); Ga. Const. art. 6, §7, ¶5; Idaho Const. art. 5, §§17, 27; Ill. Const. art. 6, §14; Iowa Const. art. 5, §9; Kan. Const. art. 3, §13; Ky. Const. §120; Me. Const. art. 6, §2; Md. Const. art. IV, §§14, 40; Mich. Const. art. 6, §§7, 18; Minn. Const. art. 6, §5; Miss. Const. art. 6, §166; Mo. Const. art. 5, §20; Mont. Const. art. VII, §7(1); Neb. Const. art. V, §13; Nev. Const. art. 6, §15; N.J. Const. art. 6, §6, ¶6; N.Y. Const. art. 6, §25a; N.C. Const. art. IV, §21; N.D. Const. art. VI, §§7, 9; Ohio Const. art. IV, §6(B); Okla. Const. art. 7, §11(a); Ore. Const. art. VII (amended), §1; Pa. Const. art. 5, §16(a); S.C. Const. art. V, §12; Tenn. Const. art. 6, §7; Tex. Const. art. 5, §§2 (Supp.), 4, 6 (Supp.), 7, 15; Utah Const. art. VIII, §12; Va. Const. art. VI, §9; Vt. Const. ch. II, §57; Wash. Const. art. 4, §§13, 14; W. Va. Const. art. 8, §7; Wis. Const. art. 7, §10(2) (Supp.); Wyo. Const. art. 5, §17.

2. E.g., Ala. Code §12–17–30; Alaska Stat. §§22.05.140, 22.07.090, 22.10.190; Ariz. Rev. Stat. Ann. (Supp.) §§12–106, 12–120.03, 12–128; Ark. Stat. Ann. (Supp.) §§22.140, 22.140.1, 22.140.4; Cal. Govt. Code §§68, 200–68,203 (Supp.); Colo. Rev. Stat. §13–30–103 to 104 (Supp.); Conn. Gen Stat. Ann. §51–47; Del. Code Ann. tit. 10 (Supp.), §§103, 304, 503; Ga. Code Ann. §§45–7–4(a)(18) to (20 (Supp.); Idaho code §59–502 (Supp.); Ind. Code Ann. §33–13–12–7 to 9; Ky. Rev. Stat. Ann. §64.485 (Supp.); Me. Rev. Stat. tit. 4 (Supp.) §§4, 102, 157 (Supp.); Md. H. Jt. Resol. 17 and S. Jt. Resol. 14 (1982); Mass. Gen. Laws ch. 211, §22 (Supp.); id., ch. 211A, §2 (Supp.); id, ch. 211B, §4 (Supp.); Minn. Stat. Ann. §15A.083 (Supp.); Miss. Code Ann. §25–3–35 and 36; Mo. Ann. Stat. (Supp.) §§477.130, 478.013, 478.018; Mont. Code Ann. §2–16–405; Neb. Rev. Stat. §§24–201.01, 24–301.01, 24–513; Nev. Rev. Stat. §§2.050, 3.030; N.H. Rev. Stat. Ann. §§94.1-a (Supp.) 94–2; N.J. Stat. Ann. §2A:1A–6 (Supp.), N.Y. Judic. Law art. 7-B, §§221 to 221-g; N.D. Cent. Code (Supp.) §§27–02–02, 27–05–03; Ohio Rev. Code Ann. §141.04 and 141.06; Ore. Rev. Stat. §§292.405 to 292.425; S.D. Comp. Laws §§16–1–3, 16–1–3.1, 16–6–5, 16–6–5.1; Va. Code (Supp.) §§16.1–69.44, 17–116.012; W. Va. Code §§51–1–10a, 51–2–13; Wis. Stat. Ann. §20.923.

3. E.g., *Colbert v. Bond*, 110 Tenn. 370, 75 S.W. 1061 (1903). See *Chambers v. Marcum*, 195 Tenn. 1, 5, 255 S.W.2d 1 (1953).

4. See §3.4 for description and discussion of state and federal compensation commissions. *See also* Connelly, Compensation Commissions: An American Judicature Society Research Report (1973), Preliminary Draft, for an analysis of the principal compensation commissions concerned in whole or in part with judicial salaries.

5. See *infra* notes 30–44, and the accompanying text.

6. *See infra* note 47, and the accompanying text.

7. *See infra* notes 14–32, 72–88, 98–103, and the accompanying text.

NOTES to §3.2

8. *See supra* notes 1 and 2, and the accompanying text.

9. *See infra* §3.4

10. *See infra* notes 14–32, 73–88, and 98–103, and the accompanying text.

11. *See* Winters, Judicial Compensation and Retirement (Amer. Judic. Soc., Address before National Conference on the Judiciary, Williamsburg Conference Center, Williamsburg, Va., March 13, 1971) 1, 16–18; Pericak, Maintaining a Fixed and Permanent Value for Judicial Salaries in Massachusetts, 16 Suffolk U. L. Rev. 1, 5–12, 36–39 (1982); The Model Judicial Article for State Constitutions §7 (1962) (judicial salaries shall not be less than highest salary paid to an officer of the executive branch of the state government).

12. E.g., *see* Surveys of Judicial Salaries, published by the National Center for State Courts for Nov. 1983 (vol. 9, no. 2), May 1983 (vol. 9, no. 1), Nov. 1982 (vol. 8, no. 3), May 1982 (vol. 8, no. 2), Jan. 1982 (vol. 8, no. 1), July 1980 (vol. 6, no. 2), Jan. 1980 (vol. 6, no. 1), and Sept. 1979 (vol. 5, no. 2).

13. E.g., *see* Chapin (compiler), Current Compensation Provisions, 58 Judicature (No. 4), 168–206 (Nov. 1974); McConnell (compiler), Judicial Salaries and Retirement Plans 1972, 56 Judicature 140–169 (Nov. 1972); Judicial Salaries and Retirement Plans in the United States, 54 Judicature (No. 5), 184–214 (Dec. 1970); Selig (compiler), 1968 Survey of Judicial Salaries in the United States, Amer. Jud. Soc. Bull. (1968); Winters, The Campaign for Adequate Judicial Compensation— A Progress Report and Challenge, and Summaries of Judicial Salaries and Retirement Plans, plus Appendices, 49 Judicature (No. 9) 163–195 (Feb. 1966); Judicial Salary Survey Supplement, 50 Judicature (No. 5), 172–173 (Jan. 1967).

NOTES TO §3.3

14. The Executive Salary Cost-of-Living Adjustment Act, U.S. Publ. L. No. 94–82, 89 Stat. 419 (1975); Cal. Govt. Code §68203; Ky. Rev. Stat. §§64.485(5), 64.527; Tenn. Code Ann. (Supp.) §§8–23–103, 16–15–205. *Compare* Md. Code Ann. §1–703(a) (judges to receive same percentage increases that are awarded to lowest step for highest grade for state employees whenever general salary increase is granted state employees).

15. *See supra* note 14.

16. Cal. Stat. 1964, 1st Ex. Sess., ch. 144, p. 418, §4.

17. Cal. Stat. 1969, ch. 1507, §1; Cal. Govt. Code §68203 (Supp. 1974).

18. Cal. Govt. Code §68203 (Supp. 1982).

19. Ky. Rev. Stat. Ann. §64.485(5).

20. Ky. Rev. Stat. Ann. §64.527.

21. Tenn. Code Ann. §8–23–103(b).

22. *See* Chapin, The Judicial Vanishing Act, 58 Judicature 159, 163 (1974).

23. Mass. Gen. Laws ch. 30, §46 (1973).

24. *Id. See* Comment, Compensation of the Federal Judiciary: A Reexamination, 8 U. Mich. J. of L. Rev. 594, 609, n. 96 (1975), and the accompanying text.

25. *See supra* note 24.

26. *Id.*

27. Md. Code art. 26, §47(a), art. 64A, §27 *et seq.*

28. Md. Code art. 64A, §30(a).

29. *See* Comment, *supra* note 24, at 608–611.

30. E.g., see Chapin at 160, 161–166; Pericak, *supra*, note 11, at 1–4, 6–17; Comment, *supra* note 24, at 595, 597–603, 608.

31. E.g., Colo. Rev. Stat. §13–30–104.

32. E.g., Md. Code Ann. §1–703(a).

NOTES TO §3.4

33. 2 U.S.C.A. §§351–361; Ala. Const. amend. no. 328, §609; Ala. Code §§12–10–1 through 12–10–5; Alaska Stat. §§3.923.010 to 130 (repealed 1980); Ariz. Const. art. 5, §13; Ariz. Rev. Stat. Ann. 3–8–1 to 11 (replacing §§41–1901 to 1904); Colo. Rev. Stat. §§2–3–801 to 806; Conn. Gen. Stat. §2–9a; Fla. Stat. Ann. §112.192; Ga. Code Ann. §§45–7–91 to 96; Ill. Ann. Stat. §§551–556; Iowa Code Ann. ch. 2A, §2A.1; La. Rev. Stat. Ann. §§42–1401 to 1405; Md. Cts. & Jud. Proc. Code Ann. §1–708; Mass. Gen. Laws Ann. tit. 6, §162; Mich. Comp. Laws Ann. §15.211 through 218; Mont. Rev. Code Ann. §§2–16–401 and 402; R.I. Gen. Laws §§36–4–16 to 36–4–16.4; S.D. Comp. Laws Ann. §§3–8–1.1 to 1.12; Utah Code Ann. §§67–8–1 to 6; and Wash. Rev. Code §4.03.028.

34. Ohio Rev. Code Ann. §§103.58 through 62 (Page 1978) (repealed 1979); Pa. Act of June 16, 1971, no. 8, §2, 46 P.S. §§5, 6; Pa. Stat. Ann. tit. 65 (Supp. 1985) app. at 49 (repealed 1973); Pa. Act of June 29, 1976, P.L. 452, no. 111, Pa. Stat. Ann. tit. 65, §364 (Supp. 1981).

35. *See supra* notes 33 and 34.

36. Ala. Const. amend. no. 328, §609(d); Md. Cts. & Jud. Prac. Code Ann. §1–708(d)(1); Mich. Const. art. 4, §12, and Mich. Comp. Laws Ann. §15.217; R.I. Gen. Laws §36–4–16.4.

37. *See supra* note 34.

38. 2 U.S.C.A. §359(1).

39. *Id.*

40. Ariz. Rev. Stat. §§41–1901 to 41–1904.

41. *See supra* note 34.

42. *See supra* note 36.

43. *See supra* note 38.

44. *See supra* note 33. A two-thirds majority of the members of each house is requisite to rejection of the commission's report in Michigan. *Id.*

45. 556 F. 2d 1028 (Ct. Cl. 1977).

46. U.S. Const. art. I, §1 (bicameral clause); U.S. Const. art. I, §7, cls. 2, 3 (presentment clauses).

47. *See supra* note 33. This was true, also, of the former Ohio Compensation Commission's recommendations. *See supra* note 34.

48. The following symbols will be used to identify the appointers: governor ("G"); lieutenant governor ("LG"); president of senate ("PS"); majority leader of senate ("MJLG"); minority leader of senate ("MNLS"); speaker of house ("SH"); majority leader of house ("MJLH"); minority leader of house ("MNLH"); gov-

erning body of state bar ("GBSB"); judges' association or associations ("JA"); supreme court ("SC"); chief justice of supreme court ("CJ"); president of United States ("P"); the other members ("OM"). Utilizing these symbols to identify the appointers, and an adjacent number to signify the number of members appointed by each of those appointers, the appointers and number of commission members appointed by each in the following states were as follows: 2 U.S.C. §352(1) (3 P, 2 PS, 2 SH, 2 CJ); Ala. Const. amend. no. 328, §6.09(a) (1 G, 1 PS, 1 SH, 2 GBSB); Ariz. Const. art. 5, §13, and Ariz. Rev. Stat. Ann. §41–1902A (2 G, 1 PS, 1 SH, 1 CJ); Colo. Rev. Stat. §2–3–803(2) (3 G, 2 PS, 2 SH, 2 CJ); Conn. Gen. Stat. §2–9(a) (3 G, 2 PS, 2 SH, 2 MNLS, 2 MNLH); Fla. Stat. Ann. §112.192 (1 G, 2 PS, 2 SH, 1 CJ); Ga. Code Ann. §45–7–91 (4 G, 2 LG, 2 SH, 4 SC); Ill. Ann. Stat. tit. 127, ¶551 (5 G); Iowa Code Ann. §2A.1 (5 G, 5 PS, 5 SH); La. Rev. Stat. Ann. §42–1401A (5 G, 1 CJ, 3 JA, 5 PS, 5 SH); Md. Cts. & Jud. Proc. & Code Ann. §1–708(b)(2) (7 G; 2, 2, and 1 being, respectively, from lists of nominees submitted by P, SH, and GBSB, and 2 being at large); Mass. Gen. Laws Ann. tit. 6, §162 (5 G); Mich. Const. art. 4, §12 (7 G); Mont. Code Ann. §2–16–401 (2 G, 2 SC, 1 MJLS, 1 MNLS, 1 SH, 1 MNLH); McKinney's Consol. Laws (N.Y.), Public Officers, §112.192 (5 G); Ohio Rev. Code Ann. §103.58 (9 G) (repealed 1979); Pa. Stat. Ann. tit. 46, §364 (repealed 1979) (2 G, 1 PS, 1 SH, 1 CJ); R.I. Gen. Laws §36–4–16 (2 SH, 2 MJLS, 3 court administrators); S.D. Comp. Laws §3–8–1.3 (2 G, 1 PS, 1 SH, 1 CJ); Utah Code Ann. §67–8–4 (1 G, 1 PS, 1 SH, 2 OM); Wash. Rev. Code §43.03.028 (president of each of 7 educational, business, bar, and labor associations).

49. For example, such provisions are found in Ala. Const. amend. no. 328, §609(b); Ariz. Rev. Stat. Ann. §3–8–1.4; Fla. Stat. Ann. §112.192(2); Ga. Code Ann. §45–7–91; Iowa Code Ann. §2A.2; La. Rev. Stat. Ann. §1401B; Mont. Code Ann. §2–16–401(3); S.D. Comp. Laws Ann. §3–8–1.4; Utah Code Ann. §67–8–4(3).

50. E.g., Ariz. Rev. Stat. Ann. §3–8–1.2; Fla. Stat. Ann. §112.192(4); Ill. Ann. Stat. §551; S.D. Comp. Laws Ann. §3–8–1.2; Utah Code Ann. §§67–8–4(1) and (3).

51. E.g., Ariz. Const. art. 5, §13 (persons not "from private life"); Ariz. Rev. Stat. Ann. §3–8–1.2 (members or employees of the legislative, judicial, or executive branches of the state government or its political subdivisions); Colo. Rev. Stat. §2–3–804(3) (elected or appointed officials or state employees); Conn. Gen. Stat. §2–9a (officials or employees of the state or any of its agencies or political subdivisions); Ga. Code Ann. §45–7–91 (state officers or employees); Iowa Code Ann. §2A.1 (similar to Connecticut statute); Md. Cts. & Jud. Proc. Ann. §1–708(b)(3) (similar to Connecticut statute; expressly disqualifies judges and former judges); Mont. Code Ann. §2–16–401(1)(a) (public officers, either elected or appointed); S.D Comp. Laws Ann. §3–8–1.2 (similar to Arizona statute); Utah Code Ann. §67–8–4(4) (similar to Arizona statute).

52. E.g., Ala. Const. amend. no. 328, §609(c); Ill. Ann. Stat. tit, 127, ¶551.

53. E.g., Ala. Const. amend. no. 328, §609(c).

54. *See supra* note 33.

55. E.g., Colo. Rev. Stat. §2–3–803(4)(a); Fla. Stat. Ann. §112.192(2); Ga. Code Ann. §45–7–91; Iowa Code Ann. §2A.2; La. Rev. Stat. Ann. §42–1401(B); Mich.

Comp. Laws Ann. §15.211; Ohio Rev. Code Ann. §103.58 (repealed); Utah Code Ann. §67–8–4(3).

56. *See supra* note 33.

57. Ala. Code §12–10–2.

58. McKinney's Consolidated Laws (N.Y.) art. 27, §802(4).

NOTES TO §3.5

59. E.g., U.S. Const. Art. III, §1; Ala. Const. amend. no. 328, §609(d); Alaska Const. art. IV, §13; Ariz. Const. art. VI, §33; Ark. Const. art. 7, §18; Cal. Const. art. 3, §4; Colo. Const. art. VI, §18; Del. Const. art. XV, §4,; Ga. Const. art. 6, §7, ¶5; Idaho Const. art. 5, §26; Ind. Const. art. 7, §19; Ill. Const. art. 6, §14; Iowa Const. art. 5, §9; Ky. Const. §§120, 235; La. Const. art. 5, §21, and La. Const. art. 10, §23; Me. Const. art. VI, §2; Md. Const. art. IV, §§14, 24; Md. Code Ann. §1–701; Mich. Const. art. 6, §18; Minn. Const. art. 6, §5; Miss. Const. art. 6, §166; Mo. Const. art. 5, §20; Mont. Const. art. VII, §7(1); Neb. Const. art. III, §15; N.J. Const. art. 6, §6, ¶6; N.Y. Const. art. 6, §25(a); Ohio Const. art. IV, §6(B); Okla. Const. art. 7, §11; Okla. Const. art. 23, §10; Ore. Const. art. VII, §1(a); Pa. Const. art. 5, §16(a); R.I. Const. art. 10, §6; S.C. Const. art. V, §12; Tenn. Const. art. 6, §7; Utah Const. art. VIII, §13; Utah Code Ann. §78–4–14 (Supp.); Va. Const. art. VI, §9; Va. Code §16.1–69.13; Wash. Const. art. 2, §25, and art. 3, §25; W. Va. Const. art. 8, §7; Wis. Const. art. 4, §26; Wyo. Const. art. 5, §17.

60. Of the provisions cited in note 59, *supra*, only the Idaho and Wisconsin provisions apply to public officers other than judges, and all of the rest apply solely to judges.

61. The Alabama, Alaska, Colorado, Delaware, Illinois, Kentucky, Minnesota, Michigan, Missouri, Montana, Nebraska, Ohio, South Carolina, Virginia, Washington, West Virginia, and Wisconsin provisions prohibiting diminishment of judicial salaries all refer to the applicable time period as the term or terms of office of the affected judges. *See supra* note 59.

62. *Cf. Bayless v. Knox County*, 199 Tenn. 268, 286 S.W. 2d 979 (1955) (prohibition against increasing or diminishing a judge's compensation "during the time for which they are elected" refers only to a judge's existing term, and not to a subsequent term; salary increase was involved); *Clark v. Logan County*, 138 Ky. 676, 128 S.W. 1079 (1910) (prohibition against changes in judicial compensation held applicable to salary increase only as applied to incumbent judge's existing term and not as applied to a new term commencing after his subsequent re–election).

63. These provisions are contained in the Iowa, New York, Oregon, Tennessee, Utah, Washington, and Wyoming Constitutions. *See supra* note 59.

64. *See supra* note 63, and the accompanying text.

65. These provisions are found in the Indiana, Maine, Maryland, Mississippi, and Rhode Island Constitutions. *See supra* note 59. Despite the use in these provisions of language identical to that in the corresponding federal provisions, all major court judges in Indiana, Maine, Maryland, and Mississippi serve for fixed terms rather than indefinite periods, and the same is true of supreme court judges in Rhode Island. Only trial court judges in Rhode Island serve, as do federal judges, during good behavior. *See Compendium, supra* note 23 (Chapter 2), at 103 and 149–150.

66. *See supra* note 59.

67. *See* Rosenn, The Constitutional Guaranty against Diminution of Judicial Compensation, 24 U.C.L.A. L. Rev. 308, 311–317 (1976); Fellman, The Diminution of Judicial Salaries, 24 Iowa L. Rev. 89, 89–93 (1938); Comment, *supra* note 24, at 603–608.

68. *Smith v. Thompson*, 219 Iowa 888, 894, 258 N.W. 190, 194–195 (1934); *People ex. rel. Lyle v. Chicago*, 360 Ill. 25, 195 N.E. 451 (1935); *Riley v. Carter*, 165 Okla. 262, 276–277, 25 P. 2d 666, 680 (1933); *Grimball v. Beattie*, 174 S.C. 422, 443–444, 177 S.E. 668, 677 (1934).

69. *See supra* note 59.

70. Cases holding that a salary increase or decrease granted to a public official (not necessarily a judicial officer) under such circumstances is valid include, *inter alia*, *Ballangee v. Board of County Comm'rs*, 66 Wyo. 390, 212 P. 2d71 (1949) (salary increase); *Gaines v. Horrigan*, 72 Tenn. 608 (1880) (salary decrease); *State ex. rel. Bashford v. Frear*, 138 Wis. 536, 120 N.W. 216 (1909) (salary increase); *State ex. rel. Jackson v. Porter*, 57 Mont. 343, 188 Pac. 375 (1920) (salary increase). Cases holding to the contrary include *State ex. rel. Hovey v. Clausen*, 117 Wash. 475, 201 Pac. 770 (1921) (salary increase); *Wilson v. Shaw*, 194 Iowa 28, 188 N.W. 940 (1922) (salary increase). For cases pro and con, *see* Ann. 166 A.L.R. 842–849 (1947).

71. *See supra* note 45, 556 F.2d at 1054.

72. 449 U.S. 200 (1980), *rev'g Will v. United States*, 478 F. Supp. 621 (N.D. Ill. 1979).

73. 384 A.2d 9 (Del. 1977). *But compare Grant v. Nellius*, 377 A. 2d 354 (Del. 1977) (legislative rescission of statute providing for automatic cost-of-living increases in salaries of state employees before they started to currently accrue held not violative either of contract clause in article I, §1(1) of federal Constitution or of due process clause in Fourteenth Amendment of federal Constitution and in article 1, §7 of Delaware Constitution.

74. 27 Cal.3d 532, 178 Cal. Rptr. 568, 636 P.2d 532 (In Bank 1980), *modifying* 27 Cal. 3d 203, 164 Cal. Rptr. 217, 609 P. 2d 991 (In Bank 1980).

75. U.S. Const. art. I, §10(1); Cal. Const. art. III, §4.

76. *See supra* note 73.

77. Del. Const. amend. to art. XV, §4, dated June 21, 1979.

78. 134 Cal. App. 3d 85, 184 Cal. Rptr. 325 (2d Dist. 1982), *cert. denied*, 459 U.S. 1172 (1983).

79. *See supra* notes 76 and 73, and the accompanying text.

80. 490 Pa. 444, 417 A. 2d 121 (1980) (2 dissents), *aff'g. per curiam* 411 A.2d 558 (Pa. Cmwlth. Ct. 1980).

81. 447 Pa. 77, 288 A. 2d 812 (1972).

82. *See supra* note 80.

83. *See supra* note 80.

84. Ky. Const. §120.

85. 360 S.W.2d 135 (Ky. 1962).

86. In so holding, the court referred to and relied, at least in part, upon the express constitutional requirement that judicial compensation be adequate.

87. 395 S.W.2d 573 (Ky. App. 1965).

88. *Id.* at 574.

89. *Evans v. Gore*, 253 U.S. 245 (1920) (invalidating income tax statute as applied

to federal judges whose term of office commenced prior to enactment of taxing statute); *Miles v. Graham*, 268 U.S. 501 (1925) (invalidating income tax statute even as to judge whose term of office did not commence until after enactment of taxing statute).

90. *O'Malley v. Woodrough*, 307 U.S. 277 (1939) (sustaining taxing statute as to judge whose term of office did not commence until after enactment of taxing statute). Although *Evans* is factually distinguishable from *O'Malley* by reason of the fact that the term of office of the judge sought to be taxed commenced after the enactment of the income tax statute sustained in *O'Malley* the reasoning in the *O'Malley* opinion appears to undermine the *Evans* holding.

91. State cases invalidating income tax statutes as applied to judges whose term of office commenced before enactment of the taxing statute include *Gordy v. Dennis*, 176 Md. 106, 5 A.2d 69 (1939); *Long v. Watts*, 183 N.C. 99, 110 S.E. 765, 22 A.L.R. 277 (1922); In re Taxation of Salaries of Judges, 131 N.C. 692, 42 S.E. 970 (1902); *New Orleans v. Lea*, 14 La. Ann. 194 (1859); and *Commonwealth ex. rel. Hepburn v. Mann*, 5 Watts & Serg, 403 (Pa. 1843), *overruling Comm'rs. of Northumberland Co. v. Chapman*, 2 Rawle 73 (Pa. 1829). Cases validating an income tax even as applied to judges taking office before the tax was enacted include *Black v. Graves*, 257 App. Div. 176, 12 N.Y.S.2d 785 (3d Dep't. 1939), *aff'd.*, 281 N.Y. 792, 24 N.E.2d 478 (1939); *Poorman v. State Board of Equalization*, 99 Mont. 543, 45 P.2d 307 (1935); *Taylor v. Gehner*, 329 Mo. 511, 45 S.W.2d 59, 82 A.L.R. 986 (In Banc 1931); *State ex. rel. Wickham v. Nygaard*, 159 Wis. 396, 150 N.W. 513 (1915). *Cf. duPont v. Green*, 195 Atl. 273 (Del. 1937) (validating Delaware income tax as applied to state's attorney general notwithstanding a constitutional provision forbidding the diminution of the salary of a "public officer"), *overruling Green v. duPont*, 7 W. W. Harr. 40, 180 Atl. 437 (Del. Super. 1935). For cases pro and con, see Annot., 82 A.L.R. 989–995 (1933).

92. *See supra* note 91, in which most of the more recent cases cited therein have sustained the constitutionality of such income taxation of incumbent judges.

93. E.g., *Booth v. United States*, 291 U.S. 339 (1934).

94. *People ex. rel. Judges Retirement System v. Wright*, 379 Ill. 328, 40 N.E.2d 719 (1942).

NOTES TO §3.6

95. *See* The Improvement of the Administration of Justice (ABA Judicial Administr. Div., 6th ed. 1981), 67 (hereinafter referred to as *Improvement of Administration of Justice*).

96. *Id. E.g., see* Wash. Const. amend. no. 54, in effect repealing Wash. Const. art. 4, §13.

97. E.g., *see* Idaho Const. art. 5, §27; Iowa Const. art. 5, §9; Ky. Const. §235 ("the salaries of public officers shall not be changed during the terms for which they were elected"); Miss. Const. art. 6, §166; Neb. Const. art. III, §15 (applies to "any public officer, including any officer whose compensation is fixed by the Legislature"); Okla. Const. art. 23, §10; Tenn. Const. art. 6, §7; Wis. Const. art. 4, §26 (applies to "public officers"); Wyo. Const. art. 5, §17; and *Improvement of Administration of Justice, supra* note 95, at 67.

98. *See supra* §3.5 and notes 72–79, and the accompanying text.

99. Illustrative cases sustaining constitutionality of formula increases in salaries of judges or other public officials, based on population changes or changes in assessed valuation, as against constitutional anti-increase provisions, include, e.g., *Yuma County v. Sturges*, 15 Ariz. 538, 140 P.504 (1917); *St. Joseph County v. Crowe*, 214 Ind. 437, 15 N.E. 903 (1938); *State ex. rel. Moss v. Hamilton*, 303 Mo. 302, 260 S.W. 466 (In Banc 1924); *State of Ohio ex. rel. Mack v. Guckenberger*, 139 Ohio St. 273, 39 N.E.2d 840, 845, 139 A.L.R. 728 (1942) (judge). *Cf. Delaware County v. Williams*, 38 Okla. 738, 135 p. 420 (1913) (prohibition against salary change after election or appointment or during term of office "unless by operation of law enacted prior to such election or appointment"); *Compare Brissenden v. Howlett*, 30 Ill. 2d 247, 195 N.E. 2d 625 (1964) (automatic decrease); *Drolte v. Board of County Comm'rs. of Ellis County*, 176 Okla. 622, 56 P.2d 800 (1936) (same). Examples of cases denying constitutionality include: *Shubat v. Montana*, 157 Mont. 143, 484 P.2d 278 (1971); *Commonwealth ex. rel. Woodring v. Walter*, 274 Pa. 553, 118 A. 510, 512 (1922); *Guthrie v. Board of Comm'rs. of Converse Co.*, 7 Wyo. 95, 50 P. 229 (1907). *Cf. Statee ex. rel. Maltbie v. Will*, 54 Wash. 453, 103 P. 479 (1909) (constitution required compensation to continue without change during entire term of office). *See* Annot., 139 A.L.R. 737–750 (1942).

100. Most of the more recent decisions have sustained such an automatic salary increase as constitutional. *See supra* note 99, and *infra* notes 101–103, and the accompanying text.

101. *See Stiffel, supra* note 73.

102. *Id.*, 384 A.2d at 16.

103. 588 S.W.2d 282 (Tenn. 1979).

104. E.g., *see Shannon v. Combs*, 273 Ky. 514, 117 S.W.2d 219 (1938); *Hopson v. Department of Revenue*, 298 Ky. 635, 183 S.W.2d 812 (1944). *See* Annot., 21 A.L.R. 256–260 (1922); Annot., 51 A.L.R. 1522–1523 (1927).

105. E.g., *Manning v. Sims*, 308 Ky. 587, 213 S.W.2d 577, 5 A.L.R.2d 1154 (1948). *See* Annot., 106 A.L.R. 779–788 (1937).

106. *See Dennis v. Rich*, 434 S.W.2d 632, 636 (Ky. 1968).

107. *Id.*, at 635–636.

108. *State ex. rel. Webb v. Brown*, 132 Tenn. 685, 179 S.W. 321 (1915).

109. E.g., *Cummings v. Smith*, 368 Ill. 94, 73 N.E.2d 69 (1938).

110. *People ex. rel. Judges Retirement System, supra* note 94; *DeWolf v. Bowley*, 355 Ill. 530, 189 N.E. 893 (1934).

111. *People ex. rel. McDavid v. Barrett*, 370 Ill. 478, 19 N.E.2d 356, 121 A.L.R. 1311 (1939).

112. Neb. Const. art. III, §19.

113. *Garrotto v. McManus*, 185 Neb. 644, 177 N.W.2d 570, (1970).

114. Ala. Const. amend. no. 92 (1952).

115. *Bayless v. Knox County*, 199 Tenn. 268, 286 S.W.2d 979 (1956).

116. *Ohio Municipal Judges Association v. Davis*, 411 U.S. 144 (1973), *rehearing denied*, 411 U.S. 959 (1973).

117. E.g., *Kavanagh v. Brown*, 206 F. Supp. 479 (E.D. Mich. 1962). *See* 48A C.J.S. §79b.

118. *See Kavanagh, supra* note 117, 206 F. Supp. at 185. *See also* 48A C.J.S. Judges, §79(a), at 673 (purpose of constitutional prohibition of increase in judicial

compensation is to remove temptation to favor individuals procuring legislative increases).

119. E.g., *Steiner v. Sullivan*, 74 Minn. 498, 77 N.W. 286 (1898); *Stone v. State ex. rel. Berney*, 20 Ala. App. 69, 101 So. 58, 59–60 (1924), *cert. denied sub nom Ex Parte Stone*, 211 Ala. 601, 101 So. 62 (1924).

120. *Jones v. Alexander*, 122 Tex. 328, 59 S.W.2d 1080, 1083 (Comm. of Apps. 1933); *Sevier v. Riley*, 198 Cal. 170, 244 P. 323 (1926); *State ex. rel. Devening v. Bartholomew*, 176 Ind. 182, 95 N.E. 417, 422 (1911).

NOTES to §3.7

121. *See supra* note 1 and the accompanying text; and §§3.8 and 3.9, *infra*.

122. E.g., *see* note 1 as to Alabama, Delaware, Florida, Kansas, Maine, and Missouri. *Accord.* Ind. Code Ann. §33–10.1–4–2 (city court judges); Md. Const. art. IV, §6; Mich. Comp. Laws Ann. §600.2513 (Supp.); Mo. Ann. Stat. (Supp.) §§477.130(2), 478.023; Ohio Rev. Code Ann. §141.13; Pa. Const. art. 5. §17(c); 42 Pa. Stat. Ann. §3303; W. Va. Const. art. 8, §10 (magistrates); Wis. Const. art. 7, §10.

123. E.g., Ariz. Const. art. 6, §32 (*pro tempore* judges); Kan. Const. art. 3, §12; Neb. Const. art. V, §13; Ore. Const. art. VII, §1.

124. E.g., *Tipton v. Sands*, 103 Mont. 1, 60 P.2d 662, 106 A.L.R. 474 (1936) (extra compensation deemed salary increase). *See* 46 Am. Jur.2d, Judges, §63.

125. E.g., *Burns v. Board of Devel. County Comm'rs.*, 39 S.D.426, 154 N.D. 1028 (1917).

126. E.g., *Manning, supra* note 105; *McCoy v. Handlin*, 35 S.D. 487, 153 N.W. 361 (1915) (upholding a statutory allowance to supreme court judges taking up residence at the state capital).

NOTES TO §3.8

127. E.g., *Bedford v. White*, 106 Colo. 439, 106 P.2d 469, 475–476 (1940); *Wright, supra* note 94, 40 N.E.2d, at 722–724. *Compare* notes 110 and 94, *supra*.

128. E.g., *State ex. rel. Sena v. Trujillo*, 46 N.M. 361, 129 P.2d 329 (1942); *Mahon v. Board of Education*, 171 N.Y. 263, 63 N.E. 1107 (1902).

129. E.g., *Mahon, supra* note 128, 63 N.E., at 1108.

130. E.g., *id.*

131. E.g., *id.*, 63 N.E., at 1109.

NOTES TO §3.9

132. *See* Comment, The Fee System Courts: Financial Interest of Judges and Due Process, 31 Wash. & Lee L. Rev. 474, 475, n. 8 (1974), and the accompanying text.

133. 273 U.S. 510 (1927).

134. *Id.*, at 523. *Accord.* *Bennett v. Cottingham*, 290 F. Supp. 759 (N.D. Ala. 1968), *aff'd mem.* 393 U.S. 317 (1969).

135. *See Tumey, supra note* 133, 273 U.S., at 531.

136. *Id.*, at 532.

137. *Id.*, at 532–535.

138. *Id.*, at 533.

139. 277 U.S. 61 (1928).

140. 409 U.S. 57 (1972).

141. *Id.*, at 60–61. Certain cases decided between *Tumey* and *Ward* had held lack of substantial, direct pecuniary interest was a defense even though the inherent temptation test laid down in *Ward* and *in dicta* in Tumey was apparently met. E.g., *Ex Parte Kelly*, 111 Tex. Crim. 54, 10 S.W.2d 728 (1928); *Ex. Parte Lewis*, 47 Okla. Crim. 72, 288 P. 354, 356 (1930); *People v. Cheever*, 370 Mich. 165, 121 N.W.2d 430 (1963).

142. *See Ward, supra* note 140, at 61–62. *Accord: Roberts v. Noel*, 296 S.W.2d 745, 748 (Ky. 1956) (pre–*Ward*). *Contra: Hill v. State*, 174 Ark. 886, 298 S.W. 321 (1929) (pre-Ward).

143. 637 F.2d 272 (5th Cir. 1981).

144. Id.

145. E.g., *Milikian v. Arent*, 300 F. Supp. 516 (N.D. Miss. 1969); *Ex Parte Lewis*, 47 Okla. Crim. 72, 288 P. 354 (1930); *Richardson v. State*, 109 Tex. Crim. 48, 4 S.W.2d 79 (1928); *Application of Borchert*, 57 Wash.2d 719, 359 P.2d 789 (En Banc 1961, 5–4 decision); *State ex. rel. Moats v. Janco*, 154 W. Va. 887, 180 S.E.2d 74 (1971).

146. E.g., *People v. Cheever*, 370 Mich. 116, 121 N.W.2d 430 (1963); *Ex Parte Steele*, 220 N.C. 685, 18 S.E.2d 132 (1942); *Borchert, supra* note 145. *Contra: Ex Parte v. Kelly*, 111 Tex. Crim. Rep. 54, 10 S.W.2d 728, 729 (1928) (right to jury trial does not negate potential injury due to justice of peace's right to control intro- duction of evidence).

147. *Borchert, supra* note 145.

148. *See* Reynolds, The Fee System Courts—Denial of Due Process, 17 Okla. L. Rev. 373, 376–377 (1964); Comment, The Fee System Courts: Financial Interest of Judges and Due Process, 31 Wash. & Lee L. Rev., 475–476 (1974).

149. Ala. Const. art. VI, §150; Ark. Const. art. 7, §§10, 18; Cal. Const. art. 6, §§15, 17; Ill. Const. art. 6, §14; Kan. Const. art. 3, §13; Md. Const. art IV, §6; Me. Const. art VI, §2; Mich. Const. art. 6, §17; Mo. Const. art. 5, §24; N.M. Const. art. VI, §30; N.D. Const. art. IV, §6; Ohio Const. art. IV, §6(B); Pa. Const. art. 5, §17(c); S.C. Const. art. V, §12; Tenn. Const. art. 6, §7; Wash. Const. art. 4, §13; W. Va. Const. art. 8, §10; Wis. Const. art. 7, §10.

150. *See* note 149 *supra.*

151. E.g., Mich. Const. art. 6, §17 (applies to judge's "salary"); Mo. Ann. Stat. §479.020(6) (Supp.) (municipal judges); N.D. Const. art. VI, §7 (applies to judge's "compensation").

152. E.g., Cal. Const. art. 6, §15; N.M. Const. art. VI, §29; Pa. Const. art. 5, §17(c).

153. E.g., Ark. Const. art. 7, §§10, 18; Me. Const. art. VI, §2; Mich. Const. art. 6, §17; N.D. Const. art. VI, §10. *Compare* People v. Mann, 97 N.Y. 532 (1885) (construing terms "judge or justice" in constitutional age limitation provision as inapplicable to justices of peace); and *People v. Carr*, 100 N.Y. 236, 3 N.E. 82 (1880) (similar holding as to surrogate).

154. Ala. Const. art. VI, §150 (article provision expressly applicable solely to judges of courts of record); S.C. Const. art. V, §12 (expressly applicable only to

supreme court justices and circuit court judges); Wash. Const. art. 4, §13 (expressly applies to all judicial officers "except court commissioners and unsalaried justices of the peace"); Wis. Const. art. 7, §10.

NOTES TO §3.10

155. E.g., *Kost v. Cox*, 317 F. Supp. 884 (W.D. Va. 1970) (substitute county judge permitted to practice in court of record); *Morton v. Detroit, B.C. & A.R. Co.*, 81 Mich, 423, 46 N.W. 111 (1890) (circuit judge permitted to practice in adjacent circuit; statute forbade such judge to practice in his own court); *Davis v. Sexton*, 211 Va. 410, 177 S.E.2d 524 (1970) (municipal court judge permitted to practice in circuit court; statute forbade such judge to practice in his own court). *See* Annot., 89 A.L.R.2d 886, 888–890.

156. E.g., *French v. Town of Waterbury*, 72 Conn. 435, 44 A. 740 (1899) (deputy judge).

157. E.g., *Young v. Grauman*, 278 Ky. 197, 128 S.W.2d 549 (1939) (justice of peace).

158. E.g., *In re Kenton County Bar Association*, 314 Ky. 664, 236 S.W. 2d 906 (1951) (judge of subordinate court).

159. E.g., *Bassi v. Langloss*, 22 Ill.2d 190, 174 N.E.2d 682, 89 A.L.R.2d 881 (1961); *Perry v. Bush*, 46 Fla. 242, 35 So. 225 (1903). *See* Ann. 89 A.L.R.2d 886, 887–890 (1963).

160. E.g., Ala. Const. amend. no. 328, §6.08(a); Alaska Const. art. IV, §14; Ariz. Const. art. 6, §28; Ark. Const. art. 7, §25; Cal. Const. art. 6, §17 (Supp.); Conn. Gen. Stat. §51–47(c); Colo. Const. art. 6, §18; Del. Code Ann. tit. 10, §1303(c); Fla. Const. art. 5, §13 (Supp.); Ill. Const. art. 6, §13(b); Hawaii Const. art. VI, §3; Kan. Const. art. 3, §13 (prohibition limited in terms to practice in any of the courts of the state); La. Const. art. 5, §24; Minn. Stat. Ann. §484.06; Mass. Gen. Laws Ann. ch. 211, §22 (Supp.); *id.*, ch. 212, §27 (repealed); *id.*, ch. 218, §77A (repealed); Miss. Code. Ann. §9–1–25; Mo. Const. art. 5, §20 (Supp.); Mo. Ann. Stat. (Supp.) §§476.290, 477.130, 478.013; Mont. Const. art. VII, §9(3); Neb. Const. art. IV, §14; N.Y. Const. art. 6, §20(b)(4); N.D. Const. art. VI, §10; Okla. Const. art. 7, §11(b); Pa. Const. art. 5, §16(a); S.C. Const. art. V, §12; S.D. Const. art. V, §10; Va. Const. art. VI, §11; Va. Code §17–3.1; W.Va. Const. art. 8, §7; Wyo. Const. art. 5, §25; V.I. Code tit. 4, ch. 17, §288(a). *Compare* 42 Pa. Stat. Ann. §§3304 ("no judge or district justice shall act as an agent for a person in the collection of a claim or judgment for money"), 3304(b) ("no judge or district justice shall receive any fee or emolument for performing the duties of an arbitrator").

161. E.g., Kan. Const. art. 3, §13; Mo. Ann. Stat. §476.290 (Supp.).

162. Conn. Gen. Stat. Ann. §51–40.

163. *See supra* note 160 as to Alaska, Arizona, California, Colorado, Delaware, Florida, Illinois, Louisana, Minnesota, Mississippi, Nebraska, Montana, New York, North Dakota, Oklahoma, Pennsylvania, Virginia, West Virginia, Wyoming, and Virgin Islands.

164. E.g., *see Bassi v. Langloss*, 22 Ill.2d 190, 174 N.E.2d 682, 89 A.L.R.2d at 885 (1961) ("the practice of law by an attorney during his tenure as county judge, in or out of court, directly or indirectly, is incompatible with his judicial responsibilities and duties and contrary to public policy" [emphasis added]). *Compare also*

People ex. rel. Institute of San Diego v. Merchants' Protective Corp., 209 Pac. 363, 189 Cal. 531 (1922).

165. E.g., *see supra* note 160 as to Alaska, Arkansas, Arizona, California, Colorado, Kansas, Louisiana, Mississippi, Missouri, Montana, New York, North Dakota, South Carolina, Virginia, West Virginia and Wyoming. *Compare* Mo. Ann. Stat. §§476. 290 (Supp.) (applies to any judge except a part-time municipal judge) and Okla. Const. art. 7, §11(b) (applies to "justices" and "judges", except those of municipal court).

166. E.g., *see supra* note 160 as to Alabama, Connecticut, Delaware, Florida, Hawaii, Illinois, Pennsylvania, and Virgin Islands.

167. E.g., Ind. Code Ann. §33–11.6–3–8.

168. 175 Tenn. 492, 135 S.W.2d 939 (1940) (stating following reasons for prohibiting major court judges from practicing law are inapplicable to minor court judges: (a) undue influence of attorney-judges over juries is inapplicable to minor court judges, since jury trials are unknown to minor courts, and (b) need for full-time major court judges due to onerousness of their duties, does not apply to minor court judges, since their duties are rather light).

169. E.g., *State Bar of California v. Superior Court in and for Los Angeles County*, 207 Cal. 323, 278 P. 432 (1929) (judge of court of record who was totally prohibited from practicing law); *Re Silkman*, 88 App. Div. 102, 84 N.Y. Supp. 1025 (2d Dep't 1903) (surrogate who was assumed to have been prohibited from practicing law in any court of record). *See* Ann. 17 A.L.R. 4th 829, 842–844 (1982).

170. *See Silkman, supra* note 169, 84 N.Y. Supp., at 1027.

171. *See infra* notes 28 (chapter 6) and 77 and 79 (Chapter 7), and the accompanying text. *See also* §§6.2(g) and 7.8.

172. *See infra* notes 28 (chapter 6) and 76 and 78 (chapter 7), and the accompanying text.

173. E.g., *In re Piper*, 534 P.2d 159, 165–166 (Ore. In Banc 1975) (reprimanding sitting circuit judges in bar discipline proceeding, as well as in judicial discipline proceeding, for wrongfully practicing law). *Cf. In re Sisemore*, 534 P.2d 167, 168 (Ore. 1975) (reprimanding sitting circuit judges in bar discipline proceedings for signing orders wrongfully presented by judge acting as attorney; latter was respondent judge in *Piper*). For decisions imposing bar discipline upon former judges for having wrongfully practiced law while judges, *see People v. Lindsey*, 86 Colo. 458, 283 P. 539 (1929) (disbarment) and *State v. Wiebusch*, 153 Neb. 583 45 N.W.2d 583 (1954).

174. E.g., *In re DiSabato*, 76 N.J. 46, 385 A.2d 234 (1978) (censure); *In re Piper*, 271 Or. 726, 534 P.2d 159 (In Banc 1975) (reprimand); *In re Van Susteren*, 82 Wis.2d 307, 262 N.W.2d 133 (1978) (reprimand).

4

Disqualification and Recusal

4.1 THE HISTORICAL DEVELOPMENT OF JUDICIAL DISQUALIFICATION

a. The Common Law

Historically, the principal grounds for disqualification have been (i) pecuniary interest, (ii) prior professional involvement in a proceeding or transaction, (iii) a family relationship with a party or attorney, and (iv) actual bias or prejudice against or in favor of one of the parties.

Although Bracton cited each of these four bases for disqualification in approximately 1250,[1] the only surviving ground for disqualification in seventeenth and eighteenth century England appears to have been pecuniary interest,[2] including both cases where the judge was a party[3] and cases where, although not a party, the judge had a pecuniary interest in the result.[4] Family relationship,[5] prior professional involvement,[6] and actual bias or prejudice[7] were, at this time, all rejected as grounds for disqualification.

Following the establishment of the American judicial systems, pecuniary interest was reaffirmed as a ground for disqualification.[8] The standards relating to the other grounds for judicial disqualification, except for actual bias, were soon liberalized. Family relationship was quickly deemed a disqualifying ground by most American courts,[9] although some still adhered to the contrary English view.[10] Likewise, prior professional involvement in a matter later coming before the judge was rapidly accepted by a majority of the American courts as a ground for disqualification,[11] despite several very early cases to the contrary.[12] With several exceptions,[13] however, the American decisions prior to 1900 overwhelmingly rejected actual bias or prejudice as a ground for judicial disqualification.[14] These decisions were often based on the noninclusion of actual bias or prejudice in the applicable disqualification statute.[15] At the turn of the century, however, a few courts adopted the view that, even at common law, actual bias or prejudice was a ground for disqualification.[16] In addition, certain courts have held that a biased judge's refusal to disqualify himself violates provisions in state constitutions guaranteeing impartial administration of justice,[17] trial by an impartial judge,[18] complete justice,[19] or the federal due process clause.[20]

b. The American Disqualification Statutes

At various times during the nineteenth and twentieth centuries, many states enacted statutes codifying and expanding the common law grounds for disqualification, *viz.*, pecuniary interest, family relationship, and prior professional involvement.[21] Although quite a few of these statutes did not provide for disqualification on the ground of bias,[22] a considerable number of them did specify prejudice or bias as a ground for disqualification.[23]

c. Peremptory Disqualification Statutes

The next significant development in judicial disqualification on the ground of prejudice was the enactment of statutes or rules of court entitling litigants to disqualify judges peremptorily, without proving prejudice or any other disqualifying ground. Some of these statutes or rules required that the movant file an affidavit averring both prejudice and underlying facts demonstrating prejudice. The sufficiency of the affidavit, but not the correctness of its factual averments, would then be subject to challenge and a final judicial determination.[24] In other states, the affidavit averring prejudice need not contain any supporting reasons or facts. In these jurisdictions, the affidavit is conclusive, both as to its factual averment of prejudice, and as to its legal sufficiency.[25] Finally, in a number of states, the movant need not even file an affidavit, but need only request or demand that the judge be changed.[26]

The peremptory disqualification statutes or rules generally contain limitations on the time within which the motion must be filed and on the number of peremptory changes available to each party or side. Although the timeliness requirements vary, they generally require the motion to be filed some time before trial.[27] Similarly, the great majority of the statutes permit only one peremptory change per party,[28] per side,[29] or per grouping of parties with common or nonadverse interests,[30] although several provide for two or three changes.[31]

d. The ABA-Sponsored Code of Judicial Conduct

The other major development in judicial disqualification has been the adoption, with minor variations, of the American Bar Association Code of

Judicial Conduct by the Supreme Courts of a large majority of the states. This Code was first adopted by the ABA House of Delegates on August 6, 1972.[32] Canons 3C and 3D of the Code pertain to judicial disqualifications and greatly enlarge the common law and statutory bases for disqualification previously in effect in most of the adopting states.[33] In addition to expanding the specific common law and statutory rules with respect to pecuniary interest, family relationship, and prior professional involvement, Canon 3C(1) of the Code not only adopts bias and prejudice as disqualifying grounds; but also expands this ground to include both the concept of actual bias and that of an appearance of bias, defined as circumstances where a judge's "impartiality might be reasonably questioned."

e. The Federal Disqualification Statutes

The final significant development in the law of disqualification was the passage in 1974 of a federal disqualification statute, 28 U.S.C. §455, predicated upon and taken, substantially verbatim, from Canon 3C of the Code. Prior to 1974, there were two federal disqualification statutes. One, which is still in effect, 28 U.S.C. §144, provided for peremptory disqualification following the filing of an affidavit of prejudice.[34] The other, an earlier version of 28 U.S.C. §455, provided for disqualification for cause, including "a substantial interest," prior professional involvement in the case, and family relationship with a party or his attorney, but not bias or prejudice.[35] The 1974 amendments to 28 U.S.C. §455, liberalized the statute in two principal ways: (a) they added both bias and the appearance of bias as grounds for disqualification and (b) they greatly increased the scope and breadth of the specific grounds for disqualification based on pecuniary or other interest, family relationship, past or present professional relationship with counsel for a party, and prior professional involvement with a case.

4.2 FINANCIAL INTEREST IN AN ACTION OR PROCEEDING

Canons 3C(1)(c) and 3C(3)(c) provide that a judge should disqualify himself where:

(1)...(c) he knows that he, individually or as a fiduciary, or his spouse or minor child residing in his household, has a financial interest in the subject matter in controversy or in a party to the proceeding, or any other interest that could be substantially affected by the outcome of the proceeding; (d) he or his spouse, or a person within the third degree of relationship to either of them, or the spouse of such a person

...(iii) is known by the judge to have an interest that could be substantially affected by the outcome of the proceeding. (3) For purposes of this section ... (a) "financial interest" means ownership of a legal or equitable interest, *however small,* or a relationship as director, advisor, or other active participant in the affairs of a party [emphasis added].[36]

Identical language is employed in the current federal disqualification-for-cause statute, 28 U.S.C. §455(b)(4), (b)(5)(iii), and (d)(4).

Section 455(b)(4) of the current federal statute and, therefore, Canon 3C(1)(c) of the Code, has been recently construed[37] as requiring disqualification if the judge, his wife, or a minor child residing in his household has any financial interest in the subject matter in controversy or in a party to the proceeding irrespective of whether the outcome of the proceeding could substantially affect that interest.[38] Moreover, the same case held that any interest as a member of a class constitutes a sufficient "interest in a party" to require disqualification, no matter how large the class may be and no matter how small the interest may be.[39] Accordingly, in the states adopting this provision of the Code, the ownership of a judge of even a single share of stock, worth only a few dollars, would disqualify the judge, even if the litigation would have absolutely no effect on the stock's value.[40]

In the case of interests not within the purview of the Code and section 455 definitions of "financial interests" in the subject matters in controversy or in a party, disqualification is required, by the express terms of Canon 3C and section 455, only when the interest "could be substantially affected by the outcome of the proceeding." Accordingly, the courts have declined to require disqualification when the interest will not be affected by the outcome of the proceeding.[41] Thus, in determining whether a particular property interest is ground for disqualification under the Code or section 455, the issue of whether the property interest is an interest in a party or in the subject matter of the litigation is of vital significance. For example, a small stock interest in the corporate parent of a corporate party has been held not to require disqualification because the interest was not an interest in a party or in the subject matter of the litigation and the requisite that the interest "could be substantially affected by the outcome of the litigation" was not met.[42]

In determining whether an alleged interest in the outcome of the proceeding is in fact an interest in the subject matter of the proceeding, the courts have held in the negative when the interest is remote and speculative. For example, in litigation involving a public utility, the fact the judge is a utility customer does not constitute a ground for disqualification either under section 455 or Canon 3C merely because a decision against the utility could result in the state public utility commission granting a refund to the utility's customers.[43] Likewise, the possibility that a corporate nonparty, which is in a position similar to a corporate party, may benefit from the precedent value of a decision in favor of the corporate party does not cause stock owned by the judge in the corporate nonparty to be an interest in the subject matter of the litigation. The stock merely constitutes an interest that might be affected by the outcome of the litigation so that, if the effect of the outcome on its value would not be substantial, disqualification would not be required.[44]

With respect to the per se approach adopted by the ABA Code in specifying a financial interest in a party or the subject matter of the proceeding as a ground for disqualification, a majority of the states adopting the Code have adopted this approach by enacting the exact language of paragraphs (1)(c) and 3(c) of Canon 3C.[45] In fact, at least two states, Indiana and New Jersey, while adopting the per se approach, have modified the Code language to extend the per se approach to other interests. On the other hand, certain states, e.g., Alaska, Arizona, Georgia, Indiana, and Pennsylvania, have quite clearly rejected the per se approach by requiring any financial interest to be substantial before it can serve as a ground for disqualification.

4.3 FAMILY RELATIONSHIP OF A JUDGE TO A PARTY, OR AN OFFICER, DIRECTOR OF A PARTY

Canon 3C(1)(d)(i) of the Code of Judicial Conduct, and its federal counterpart, 28 U.S.C. §455(b)(5)(i), require a judge to disqualify himself whenever:

(d) he or his spouse, or a person within the third degree of relationship to either of them, or the spouse of such a person
   (i) is a party to the proceeding, or an officer, director, or trustee of a party.

In implementing this provision, paragraph 3C(3)(a) and its federal counterpart, 28 U.S.C. §455(d)(2), state that the degree of relationship shall be calculated according to the civil law system.

Under English common law prior to 1789, a judge who was a party was required to disqualify himself, but disqualification was not required when the judge was merely related to a party.[46] A family relationship with a party within the third degree by blood or marriage was, however, recognized as a ground for disqualification by most (but not all) of the more recent decisions in the United States[47] and in most of the state disqualification statutes.[48] Canon 3C(1)(d)(i), therefore, merely codified the prevailing rule on the subject. Insofar as Canon 3C(1)(d)(i) extended the disqualifying effect to the spouse of a person related in at least the third degree to the spouse of a party, the Code expanded the prevailing rule.[49]

4.4 A FAMILY RELATIONSHIP BETWEEN A JUDGE AND COUNSEL IN A PROCEEDING BEFORE HIM OR A PARTNER OR ASSOCIATE OF SUCH COUNSEL

a. Family Relationship to a Lawyer Engaged in the Proceeding

A family relationship between a judge and counsel for a party did not disqualify the judge at common law,[50] and many disqualification statutes do not require disqualification under these circumstances.[51] Also, although a number of statutes do provide for disqualification in the event of a family relationship by blood or affinity between the judge and counsel,[52] none of them expressly applies when the relationship is between the judge's spouse and the attorney's spouse. Canon 3C(1)(d) rectifies all of these omissions by requiring disqualification when a family relationship exists within the third degree, between the judge or his spouse and the lawyer or his spouse.

Canon 3C(1)(d) also eliminates any distinction between an attorney of record pecuniarily interested in the outcome of a litigation by reason of a contingent fee arrangement and an attorney of record without such an interest and has made a family relationship with any attorney acting as such in the litigation a ground for disqualification. Prior to enactment of the Code, some statutes disqualifying judges related to "parties"[53] had been held inapplicable to contingent fee attorneys,[54] while other similar statutes had been held applicable to contingent fee attorneys[55] or attorneys whose fees were to be fixed by the court[56] but not to attorneys without such an interest.[57] Likewise, although several states[58] (but not most states[59]) had a statute disqualifying a judge with a family relationship to an interested person or nonparty, at least two such statutes had been held applicable to contingent fee attorneys of record[60] or attorneys whose fees were to be set by the court[61] but not to attorneys of record without such a pecuniary interest.[62]

b. Family Relationship with a Partner of a Lawyer Engaged in the Proceeding

Generally speaking, even the statutes that disqualify judges related to an attorney in a matter before the judge do not apply to family relationships between judges and partners or associates of trial counsel.[63] The Nebraska and Oregon statutes do, however, apply not only to family relationships between judges and trial counsel, but also to family relationships between judges and partners or associates of trial counsel.[64]

In the remaining states, it is uncertain whether the disqualification statute requires a judge related to a partner of an attorney of record to disqualify himself. As will be demonstrated, both Canon 3C(1) of the ABA Code of Judicial Conduct and its federal equivalent require the judge to disqualify himself in such a case in any state that has adopted Canon 3C(1) without material change.

The two leading federal court decisions applying the federal counterpart of Canon 3C(1), 28 U.S.C. §455, to a family relationship between a judge and a partner of an attorney appearing in a proceeding before the judge are *SCA Services, Inc. v. Morgan*[65] and *Potashnick v. Port City Construction Co.*[66]. In both of these cases, the court held that the partner-relative was "known by the judge to have an interest that could be substantially affected by the proceeding" within the meaning of the provision disqualifying a judge when he or his spouse was related to such a person or his spouse, 28 U.S.C.A. §455(b)(5)(iii), the federal counterpart of Canon 3C(d)(iii), and the court disqualified the judge. Also in *SCA* but not in *Potashnick*[67] the court held, as an additional ground for disqualification, that, under these facts, the judge's "impartiality might reasonably be questioned" within the meaning of the provision disqualifying a judge under such circumstances, 28 U.S.C.A. §455(a), the federal counterpart of Canon 3C(1).

In view of these two decisions, it may be anticipated, in both the federal courts and any Code state, that any judge related in the third degree to a partner of an attorney appearing in a proceeding before the judge may be deemed disqualified on the ground of relationship to a substantially interested person and, probably, also on the ground that his impartiality might reasonably be questioned.[68]

c. Family Relationship to an Associate of a Lawyer Appearing in a Proceeding before the Judge

The Fifth Circuit Court of Appeals, in *United States ex rel. Weinberger v. Equifax, Inc.*,[69] held that a judge is not disqualified from presiding in a proceeding merely because he is the father of an associate of one of the trial attorneys in the proceeding, when the associate neither participates in the proceeding, nor shares in the fees to be derived from it. Under such circumstances: (a) the associate is not "acting as a lawyer in the proceeding" within the meaning of 28 U.S.C. §455(b)(5)(ii); (b) the associate has no "financial interest" in the proceeding under 28 U.S.C. §455(b)(5)(iii); and (c) a ruling by the challenged judge that his own impartiality may not reasonably be questioned under 28 U.S.C. §455 (a) does not constitute an abuse of discretion.

In an identical situation, also involving a father-son relationship between the judge and an associate (the judge's son) of trial counsel, and arising under the Code counterparts of the three provisions construed in *Weinberger*, however, the Georgia Supreme Court, in *Stephens v. Stephens*,[70] disqualified the judge, on the ground that, although the associate was not "acting as a lawyer in the proceeding" and had no "financial interest" which might be "substantially affected by the case," the judge's impartiality might be reasonably questioned.

Applying these two decisions, it seems likely that, in the federal courts and in Code states, judges will not be disqualified, either on the ground of family relationship with an attorney or on the ground of family relationship with an interested person merely because the judge is closely related to an associate of one of the law firms representing a party. Something more, such as participation by the associate in the trial or direct participation by the associate in the fees earned, will have to be shown to disqualify the judge on either of these grounds.

On the other hand, in view of the conflict between these two cases, the odds appear to be more evenly balanced as to whether, in such a case, the courts will disqualify the judge on the ground that his impartiality may be reasonably questioned, even if the associate neither participates in the trial nor directly participates in the fees earned.

4.5 FORMER PROFESSIONAL INVOLVEMENT BY A JUDGE, OR A FORMER PARTNER OR ASSOCIATE OF THE JUDGE, IN A MATTER BEFORE HIM

a. Former Professional Involvement by the Judge Himself in the Proceeding or Matter before Him

At common law, a judge was not required to disqualify himself if he had acted as counsel in the proceeding before the court.[71] A judge was, however, permitted to recuse himself voluntarily in such a case, and judges did so with such frequency as to all but eradicate the common law rule.[72] Most states have now enacted disqualification statutes that have made disqualification mandatory when a judge has previously served as counsel in the proceeding before him.[73] The same was true of the federal disqualification statute enacted prior to the adoption of the code.[74]

Most of the relevant statutes, if read literally, disqualify a judge only if he has been counsel in the "action," "suit," or "proceeding" now before him.[75] A few, however, utilize words such as "cause," "case," and "of counsel," which appear to extend the rule to legal services rendered by the judge-to-be on a matter involved in the suit before suit was actually filed.[76] The rendering of related legal services by a judge before the institution of suit has been held to require disqualification under the broader statutory provisions[77] and, in at least one case, under the narrower type of statute.[78]

When the judge had acted as counsel for a party to the proceeding now before him, in a different, earlier proceeding, and the later proceeding does not involve any of the issues raised in the earlier case, the prior representation has been held insufficient to disqualify the judge.[79] In fact, it has been held that prior representation of a party to the instant action in a different and earlier proceeding does not necessarily disqualify a judge even when the later proceeding involves some of the issues raised in the earlier case.[80] On the other hand, disqualification has been required in the latter situation when the earlier proceeding involved issues of law or fact intimately blended with those in the later proceeding.[81]

Canon 3C(1)(a) of the Code expressly states that a judge should disqualify himself where "he served as lawyer in *the matter in controversy*" (emphasis added). It is, therefore, clear that under the Code the prior representation need not have involved the actual litigation now before the judge. It has, however, been held that, if the prior representation related to a different matter and involved a different cause of action, the judge need not disqualify himself[82] unless it appears that evidence presented in the earlier action also will be presented in the later action[83] or unless a local statute requires a judge to disqualify himself whenever he has represented a party to the proceeding before him with respect to any matter within a specified time period that has not yet elapsed.[84]

b. Professional Involvement by the Judge's Former Law Partner in the Proceeding or Matter before the Judge

If a former law partner of a judge was, while he and the judge were partners, counsel in a proceeding now before the judge, the courts have generally, but not invariably, held that, under principles of partnership or agency law, the acts of the counsel must be attributed to the judge. In such event, the judge has, in various cases, been required to disqualify himself under a typical disqualification statute requiring a judge to disqualify himself when he formerly acted as counsel in the proceeding before him. This has been the result even if the judge did not at any time personally participate in the proceeding[85] and even if the judge's former partner and firm are no longer counsel in the proceeding.[86] Prior to the adoption of the Code, this type of statutory provision was generally the sole possible basis of disqualification.[87] In Louisiana, however, disqualification in this precise situation is mandated by the express terms of the disqualification statutes in both criminal and civil cases.[88]

The adoption of the Code by the supreme courts of most states and by Congress for the federal courts has expressly codified the foregoing holdings. Both Canon 3C(1)(b) of the Code and 28 U.S.C. §455(b)(2) provide that a judge must disqualify himself not only when he personally served as a lawyer in the matter in controversy, but also when "a lawyer with whom he previously practiced law served during such association as a lawyer concerning the matter."

It is clear that Canon 3C(1)(b) requires a judge to disqualify himself when a former partner of his represented a party to the litigation in that very litigation during the period of the partnership. It is, however, equally clear that this Canon does not require a judge to disqualify himself merely because his former law firm represented or counselled a party to the instant litigation in matters unrelated to the instant litigation or any matter involved in it. In *National Auto Brokers v. General Motors Corp,*[89] the Second Circuit Court of Appeals specifically so held.

c. Past Representation of a Party to the Instant Proceeding by a Member of a Firm of Which the Judge Was an Associate

A judge who was formerly an associate in a firm was held not required to disqualify himself from hearing an action handled by the firm during his association, because the judge had no partnership interest in the firm and because the acts of members of the firm were not deemed attributable to the judge. Since the judge had not personally participated in the matter, the Texas disqualification statute was held inapplicable.[90] It appears to be an open question whether, under such circumstances, the judge would be required to disqualify himself under Canon 3C(1)(b), which requires a judge to disqualify himself when a lawyer "with whom he previously practiced law, served during such association as a lawyer concerning the matter." When, however, the judge had personally participated in the matter, he would be disqualified under either a typical disqualification statute[91] or under the Code.

d. Past Status of the Judge as a Supervisor or Department Associate of a Government Attorney Then and Now Handling a Litigation Presently Pending before the Judge

When a judge was formerly employed by the same government agency as another attorney who then was and now is handling a matter now before the judge but the judge did not personally participate in that matter, the judge is not considered to have practiced law with that attorney within the meaning of Canon 3C(1)(b), which disqualifies a judge when a lawyer "with whom he practiced law served during such association as a lawyer concerning the matter" in controversy.[92] The judge is not disqualified even if the judge had been the other attorney's supervisor or department head, unless the circumstances of the prior association are such that his impartiality might reasonably be questioned.[93]

In denying per se disqualification under these circumstances, the Code is in accord with the some prior rule majority rule,[94] although the federal courts and a few state courts required disqualification in such a case.[95]

e. Employment of a Former Law Clerk of the Presiding Judge by a Firm Representing a Party to a Litigation Presently Pending before the Judge

If, when a judge's law clerk accepts an offer of employment from a firm representing a party in an action pending before the judge, the law clerk immediately stops working on the case and does no further work on it during the balance of his clerkship and after joining the law firm, the judge's impartiality may not be reasonably questioned under 28 U.S.C. §455(a) or its counterpart, Canon 3C(1), and the judge is not required to disqualify himself.[96] If, however, the law clerk continues to work on the case as law clerk after he accepts the job offer, an appearance of unfairness is created by the law clerk's presumed intimate knowledge of the case and of the judge's view on the issues. Similarly, an appearance of bias is created by the judge's tolerance of this situation. Consequently, under such circumstances, the judge is required to disqualify himself, even if the law clerk does not work on the case after joining the law firm.[97]

Likewise, if, to the judge's knowledge, the law clerk works on a case after commencing to work for a law firm, the judge is required to disqualify himself on the ground that his impartiality is seriously open to question if he refuses to recuse himself "after being made aware that his former law clerk is working on the case."[98]

4.6 ACTUAL BIAS OR AN APPEARANCE OF BIAS AS GROUNDS FOR DISQUALIFICATION

a. The Development of Actual Bias as a Ground for Disqualification, and the Substitution by the Code of Judicial Conduct of an Objective Test of Bias in Lieu of a Subjective Test

Actual bias gradually became a ground for disqualification in this country toward the end of the nineteenth century, either by revision of the common law or by statute.[99] Today, in statutes listing grounds for disqualification for cause (as distinguished from peremptory disqualification), many states have made actual bias or prejudice a statutory ground for mandatory disqualification.[100] In an even larger number of states, however, neither bias nor an appearance of bias is included in the statutory list of grounds for mandatory disqualification.[101]

With respect to disqualification for bias, the Code's principal contribution is found in Canon 3C(1) of the Code and its federal counterpart, Section 455(a), which require a judge to disqualify himself "in any proceeding in which his impartiality might reasonably be questioned."[102] In applying the latter test, the courts have held that the pertinent inquiry is whether the facts would have caused a reasonable person to question the judge's impartiality.[103]

It has been said, however, that neither actual nor apparent disapproval of a party because of his known conduct requires disqualification unless, as was said by Circuit Judge Kennedy of the Ninth Circuit Court of Appeals in *United States v. Conforte*,[104] it involves "an aversion or hostility of a kind or degree that a fair-minded person could not entirely set aside."

b. The Rule That Bias is Not a Ground for Disqualification Unless of Extrajudicial Origin

Undoubtedly, the most important limitation imposed by the courts upon disqualification for bias prior to adoption of the Code was the requirement that disqualifying bias or prejudice must normally be of extrajudicial origin. Bias generated by occurrences in the proceeding itself was not a ground for disqualification.[105] This rule has been repeatedly reaffirmed under the provisions of both Canon 3C(1) and 28 U.S.C. §455(a) disqualifying judges whose impartiality "might reasonably be questioned,"[106] and those of 28 U.S.C. §144, 28 U.S.C. §455(b)(1), and Canon 3C(1)(b) disqualifying judges who have a personal bias or prejudice against or in favor of a party (§144) or "concerning a party" (§455(b)(1) and Canon 3C(1)(b)).[107]

The broad rule that judicial bias must be extrajudicial in origin has led to a further general rule that judicial rulings, conduct or remarks during a proceeding that manifest bias do not constitute a basis for disqualifying the judge either under section 144[108] or section 455[109] unless the bias is shown to be of extrajudicial origin. An exception to this rule has been recognized, however, in cases "where such pervasive bias is shown by otherwise judicial conduct as would constitute bias against a party,"[110] or would cause failure of the judge to disqualify himself to constitute a denial of due process.[111] A corollary of the general rule that judicial bias must be extrajudicial in origin to be a ground for disqualification is a rule that judicial rulings may not constitute a basis for disqualification.[112] Finally, the courts have been virtually unanimous in holding that insults, threats, or even physical violence by a party toward the judge in the proceeding do not constitute a basis for disqualifying the judge,[113] even if it is found that they necessarily angered the judge,[114] or that they occurred outside the courthouse.[115]

c. Prior Personal Knowledge of Disputed Evidentiary Facts in Case

Canon 3C(1)(a) and 28 U.S.C. §455(b)(1) require disqualification where the judge "has . . . personal knowledge of disputed evidentiary facts concerning the proceeding."[116] When, however, a judge has obtained derogatory information about a party pertinent to the proceeding before him, he is not disqualified if the knowledge was obtained in the same proceeding[117] or acquired in a separate prior proceeding involving the movant or a co-defendant of the movant as a party.[118] The rationale for these results is that the origin of any resulting bias was not extrajudicial.[119]

d. Business Dealings between a Judge and Trial Counsel

Disqualification has been required under 28 U.S.C. §455(a) when the judge has made investments with the lawyer as a co-investor or joint venturer.[120]

e. Remarks Indicative of Prejudgment of the Case

Remarks by the judge during the trial of a criminal case to the effect that he believed the defendant guilty, made outside the presence of the jury, were held not to constitute a ground for disqualification under Canon 3C(1).[121] On the other hand, remarks indicating prejudgement have been held, in certain cases, to require disqualification under Canon 3C(1),[122] especially when the remarks were made before he had heard opposing counsel's argument.[123]

f. Bias against Counsel for Litigant

In the absence of a statute or rule making bias against counsel a per se ground for disqualification, the case law has rejected disqualification based on bias against counsel,[124] particularly when it is based on circumstances that have no connection with that attorney's representation of that party in the instant litigation.[125] Ground for disqualification does, however, exist if the judge's bias against the attorney is sufficient to impair his client's interests.[126] In some states, bias against counsel has been made a per se ground for disqualification by a statute or rule.[127]

Occasionally, an attorney or law firm has sought a blanket disqualification order against a judge, disqualifying him from presiding over any case in which the lawyer or a member of the firm is the attorney of record. Although such a blanket order has been granted in at least one case,[128] it has been denied in at least two other cases.[129]

g. Bias against State as Entitling State to Disqualification of Judge in Criminal Prosecution

Either on the ground of statutory interpretation or constitutional entitlement, the courts have generally held that the state has as great a right as the defendant to have a judge in a criminal trial disqualified for bias.[130] Similarly, statutes providing for peremptory disqualification, when sought by a party averring bias, have been held to inure to the benefit of the state in criminal prosecutions on the theory that the state is a "party."[131]

h. Friendship between the Judge and Any of the Parties or Their Attorneys

Prior to adoption of the Code, friendship between a judge and one of the parties to litigation pending before him was generally held not to be a per se ground for disqualification,[132] but disqualification was required in an instance of close, long-standing friendship where the party had publicly indicated that he had influence with the judge.[133] Friendship between a judge and the attorney for a party has generally not caused judges to recuse themselves voluntarily,[134] although judges have occasionally voluntarily recused themselves for this reason.[135]

i. Alleged Bias of a Judge Who Has Decided a Prior Litigation against the Party to the Instant Litigation Who Seeks to Disqualify the Judge

Deciding a prior litigation against a party is not a ground for disqualification in other matters involving that party.[136] This is so not only when none of the fact issues decided by the judge in the prior litigation is an issue in the later litigation[137] but also when the former litigation involves one or more fact issues present in the later litigation.[138] or related to fact issues in the later litigation.[139] Moreover, this principle has been applied to any combination of civil or criminal actions, including two successive civil actions,[140] two successive criminal actions,[141] a criminal trial followed by a civil trial,[142] and a civil trial followed by a criminal trial.[143]

j. Remarks by Judge in a Prior Proceeding

A judge will not be disqualified from sitting in a criminal proceeding because of remarks or findings pertaining specifically to the facts or law in other cases in which the defendant was also involved, since, as a general rule, disqualification "must instead be predicated on extrajudicial attitudes and conceptions formed outside of the courtroom."[144] Likewise, comments by the judge in a prior trial approving or disapproving a jury verdict generally does not constitute a ground for disqualification of the judge in a later proceeding[145] but have been expressly made a statutory ground for disqualification in one state.[146]

k. Knowledge of Facts Pertinent to Instant Case Acquired from Participation in Prior Litigation

A judge's knowledge of facts pertinent to a pending case, acquired when presiding over prior litigation involving the movant as a party, is not a ground for disqualifying the judge.[147] The courts have so held not only when the conduct involved in the prior litigation is unrelated to that involved in the instant litigation[148] but also when it is either involved in the instant litigation[149] or is related to the conduct involved in that litigation.[150] This principle has been held applicable in the case of successive criminal prosecutions of the movant involving alleged independent crimes, even though the movant had been convicted in the prior prosecution and had been sentenced by the judge in question. Disqualification in such cases has been denied, not only in jury trials[151] but also in bench trials[152] or when there has been a plea of guilty followed by sentencing.[153]

Disqualification based on a judge's knowledge of facts relevant to a litigation pending before him has likewise been denied when the knowledge was acquired while presiding over a prior litigation to which the movant was not a party.[154]

l. Proposed Disqualification of Judge in Criminal Case in Which He Had Previously Rejected a Proposed Plea Bargain or Nolo Contendere Plea

In three federal criminal cases involving jury trials, a federal court of appeals has held that a trial judge was not required to disqualify himself because he had previously rejected a proposed plea bargain.[155] In one of these cases, *United States v. Gallington*,[156] the court reached this result even though the trial judge had questioned the defendant in an effort to satisfy himself that there was a sufficient factual basis for the proposed guilty plea and had secured some admissions from the defendant.[157] Moreover, in both *Gallington* and *United States v. Bunch*,[158] disqualification was held not mandatory even though after the filing of a conditional guilty plea, the judge had examined the pre-sentencing report. The appellate court in each case did, however, indicate that the judge could, in his discretion, have properly recused himself.

The result may be the same in cases where the trial is a bench trial in which the judge is the fact finder and would, therefore, have a greater capacity to injure the defendant had he in fact been biased. Existing precedents seem to indicate that disqualification would ordinarily be denied even if the judge made findings adverse to the movant in the earlier litigation,[159] but that disqualification might be granted if special circumstances of bias were shown[160] or of the judge made adverse findings in the earlier litigation not based on any record evidence.[161]

m. Efforts to Disqualify Judges from Sitting in Retrials of Cases in Which They Had Presided over the Initial Trial

In successive jury trials in the same action, a heavy majority of the courts that have dealt with the question in the absence of a statute expressly requiring disqualification have held that a judge should not be disqualified from presiding over the retrial merely because he presided over the earlier trial.[162]

A contrary rule was, however, prescribed by the Second Circuit Court of Appeals in *United States v. Bryan*[163] for lengthy criminal trials. Since then, the second circuit has made it clear that the *Bryan* rule does not necessarily apply to other situations[164] and has held it inapplicable to the retrial of a short criminal case[165] or to successive trials of different charges against the same defendant[166] or to successive trials of persons charged with participation in the same unlawful conspiracy.[167] Despite these limitations, the rule has, since at least 1977, been applied to all retrials by a local rule in the eastern district of New York[168] and by practice in the district of Connecticut.[169]

In the case of successive bench trials, the situation is less clear. A substantial number of courts have held that the judge should not be disqualified merely because he presided over the first trial and rendered findings adverse to the movant that were reversed on appeal.[170] Disqualification of a judge at the retrial has been required, however, where the reversed findings were unsupported in the record, on the ground that unsupported findings "are evidence that the judge has relied on extrajudicial sources in making such determinations indicating personal bias and prejudice."[171] Even where erroneous findings are based on record evidence, the analysis of relevant factors by the Second Circuit Court of Appeals in *United States v. Robin*[172] suggests that the original judge will be required, or expected, to disqualify himself when he "would reasonably be expected upon remand to have substantial difficulty in putting out of his or her mind previously expressed views determined to be erroneous or based on evidence that must be rejected." This would occur when the erroneous findings were made with particular firmness or were based on strong and weighty evidence that, purely for constitutional or technical reasons, was held inadmissible by the appellate court. *Robin* also indicates that if the second trial is a bench trial, disqualification is more likely. Other pertinent factors would include the nature of the proceeding and the reasons for reversal.[173] For example, disqualification has been required in the second of two successive bench trials where not only did the judge decide key issues against the movant in the first case but also his determinations were reversed because unsupported by record evidence.[174]

In certain states, the majority rule against disqualification in the event of a jury trial in the later proceeding has been abrogated by statutes that require disqualification without distinguishing between bench trials, and jury trials.[175]

In cases involving attempts to disqualify the original judge from presiding over a retrial, the principal dispute has generally been whether the judge's conduct in the first trial demonstrated actual or probable personal bias sufficient to require his disqualification in the retrial.[176] Although the general rule is that a belief or bias as to the merits based on the testimony and evidence at the prior trial is not a ground for disqualification,[177] there is an exception when the belief or bias is so pervasive as to constitute true personal bias against a party.[178]

n. Expression of Opinion on Merits Made in Prior Related Litigation

A party sometimes seeks to disqualify a judge because of adverse remarks pertaining to the merits of a case made in prior related litigation. Ordinarily, disqualification will not be required.[179] Where, however, the judge expressed not only a view on the merits adverse to the party seeking to disqualify him but also the opinion that the party was not a credible witness, disqualification has been required.[180]

o. Prior Expressions of Opinions on Legal Issues in Case at Bar

An extra-judicial public expression of opinion by an appellate or trial judge on a legal issue in a case pending before him, made either before the case was instituted or at least before the judge ascended the bench or knew that the case would be assigned to him, has generally been held not to constitute a ground for disqualifying the judge.[181] The same treatment, of course, has been accorded to rulings on a particular legal issue previously made in other litigation.[182]

p. The Question Whether the Judge before Whom an Alleged Contempt Was Committed, or Who Cited a Party for Indirect Contempt, Must Disqualify Himself from Presiding at the Contempt Proceeding on the Ground of Bias or Likelihood of Bias

The disqualification rules applied in summary contempt proceedings to punish direct contempts differ somewhat from those applicable either in proceedings to punish indirect contempts or in postponed proceedings to punish direct contempts. A direct or constructive contempt is contempt committed in the presence of the court, of which the court necessarily has personal knowledge.[183] Conversely, an indirect contempt is a contempt committed outside the presence of the court, of which the court lacks personal knowledge.[184]

Summary contempt proceedings are employed to punish direct contempts, without any evidentiary hearing. The judge presiding over the trial or hearing during which the alleged contempt was committed determines guilt and pronounces sentence. The United States Supreme Court, in, for example, *Sacher v. United States*,[185] formerly permitted (but did not require) a proceeding to punish a direct contempt committed during the trial to be postponed until the end of the trial and then heard summarily[186] by the trial judge even if the contempt had involved a personal attack on him.[187] In *Offutt v. United States*[188] and *Mayberry v. Pennsylvania*,[189] the court sharply limited the *Sacher* rule. These later cases and other cases require both disqualification and a so-called due process hearing when the judge became personally embroiled with the contemnor[190] or when the nature of the contempt would appear to preclude detached or impartial consideration by the judge despite the lack of any personal embroilment.[191] This is also the rule when the judge has adopted an adversary posture toward the person charged with contempt despite the absence of any personal attack upon the judge.[192]

On the other hand, in the case of indirect contempts, the federal rule has long been that the contemnor is entitled to a due process hearing.[193] In addition, in the case of indirect contempts involving disrespect to a federal judge, the judge has been required to disqualify himself from presiding over the contempt hearing.[194]

4.7 THE QUESTION WHETHER THE JUDGE WHOM A DISQUALIFICATION MOTION SEEKS TO REMOVE IS PERMITTED OR REQUIRED TO RULE ON THE DISQUALIFICATION MOTION

a. Challenges for Cause

Whether or not a peremptory challenge procedure is available, challenges for cause may be made. A challenge for cause necessarily involves a preliminary determination of whether the challenged judge may himself hear and rule on the motion to disqualify. The rules in this regard vary from state to state.[195]

In some states, e.g., Florida, the challenged judge decides not only the sufficiency of the facts alleged in the motion (i.e., whether the facts alleged would require disqualification) but also their truth.[196] In still other states, such as California, both the sufficiency and merits of the motion are decided by a different judge.[197] Finally, in a third group of states, such as Colorado and Georgia, the original judge rules on the sufficiency of the motion, but if he determines that it is sufficient, a different judge holds a hearing and rules on the merits.[198]

b. Peremptory Challenges

The only type of peremptory challenge statute to which the question under consideration truly relates is that typified by the federal and Kansas peremptory disqualification statutes,[199] under which the factual allegations are binding but sufficiency must be determined by the court. Predictably, the rule as to who will determine sufficiency varies from jurisdiction to jurisdiction. In the federal system, the sufficiency question is decided by the challenged judge,[200] while the sufficiency question is decided by a different judge when the identical question arises in Kansas.[201]

4.8 WAIVER OF DISQUALIFIABILITY

At common law, the right of a party to seek and secure an order disqualifying a judge was waivable.[202]

When statutes specify the grounds of disqualification but do not expressly state whether they are waivable, waivability depends, in most jurisdictions, on whether the statute prohibits a judge who is disqualifiable on one of the specified grounds from sitting. In most instances, when the disqualification statute merely specifies particular grounds for disqualification but does not prohibit a judge who is disqualifiable from sitting, the judge's disqualification is deemed nonjurisdictional and, therefore, waivable.[203] Waiver can occur not only by express stipulation or agreement between the parties[204] but also by implication through continued participation in a trial after gaining knowledge of the facts[205] or in pre-trial proceedings resulting in rulings on issues pertinent to the merits[206] or by failure to file promptly both at the first opportunity after learning of the grounds for disqualification and sufficiently in advance of trial to avoid delay.[207] Waiver also can be found when a party fails to follow established requirements as to time or formalities with respect to a motion for disqualification.[208] Conversely, a motion filed after discovery of the ground for disqualification and before the entry of any order going to the merits or substance of the controversy has been held timely even when filed immediately before trial.[209]

In jurisdictions where participation results in a waiver, the cases have varied as to the degree of participation, with knowledge of the ground for disqualification, which has effected a waiver. In some cases, the mere participation in a hearing on any issue pertinent to the merits effected a waiver,[210] while in others a waiver was held to have occurred when the judge had heard the matter and taken it under advisement[211] and, in still others, a waiver was held to have taken place when the judge had issued a ruling.[212]

The failure to move until after the prescribed deadline for so moving has been held not to constitute a waiver when the movant sought disqualification promptly after first discovering the existence of the factual basis for disqualifying the judge.[213] Also, participation in matters resulting in rulings not pertaining to the merits has been held not a waiver.[214] Other courts, however, have held that participation in proceedings resulting in rulings involving the exercise of discretion by the judge constitutes a waiver, even though the rulings do not involve the merits.[215]

When a statute or rule that specifies the grounds for disqualification prohibits judges from sitting in cases in which they can be disqualified, the courts have frequently held that disqualification is nonwaivable, even if the parties have participated in the case on the merits without moving to disqualify the judge.[216] The courts have also refused to permit waiver when the terms of the disqualification statute were so unequivocal as to permit no exception[217] or when the court regarded the policy consideration underlying the statute as so strong as to make waiver undesirable.[218] In fact, disqualification of a judge under a statute prohibiting a judge from sitting under specified circumstances has been held not waivable even by express agreement of the parties.[219]

In a number of states, all or certain specified statutory grounds for disqualification are expressly made waivable by a constitutional or statutory provision or a rule of court.[220] In some states, the waiver must be in writing, or made in open court on the record,[221] and, often, consent of all parties is required.[222]

Finally, Canon 3D of the Code of Judicial Conduct provides that a judge disqualified under Canon 3C(1)(c) or Canon 3C(1)(d) by reason of interest or family relationship to a party, attorneys, or interested person may, instead of withdrawing from the proceeding, disclose on the record the basis of his disqualification; and that if, based on such disclosure, the lawyers, independently of the judge's participation, agree on the record that the judge's relationship is immaterial or that his financial interest is insubstantial, the judge is no longer disqualified and may participate in the proceeding. In at least one jurisdiction, with one judge dissenting, Canons 3C and 3D have been construed as relieving the parties from the necessity of moving to disqualify on any of the foregoing grounds in order to avoid a waiver.[223] On the other hand, the view also has been expressed, with respect to Canons 3C and 3D, that the parties have no obligation to seek to ascertain whether a ground for disqualification exists, but that, if the judge discloses such a ground, a party's failure to then seek to disqualify the judge effects a waiver.[224]

4.9 REMOVAL OF DISQUALIFICATION

The courts are in disagreement on the question of whether removal of a cause of disqualification makes a judge eligible to sit in the case. Both at common law and under a majority of the applicable statutes, removal of the cause of disqualification, as, for example, by the sale by the judge of stock in a corporate party or the dismissal or withdrawal of a party related to the judge, renders the judge eligible.[225] According to a substantial minority of the courts, however, removal does not eliminate the judge's ineligibility.[226]

4.10 EFFECT OF DISQUALIFICATION

At common law, the discretionary rulings and decrees made by a judge subject to disqualification are voidable, rather than void,[227] and, therefore, are not subject to collateral attack.[228] Such rulings are, however, reviewable at common law on the ground of disqualification, on direct appeal,[229] at least if the appellant has not waived the disqualification by failure to file a timely motion to disqualify the judge following discovery of the ground for disqualification.[230] The foregoing rules, that discretionary rulings and decrees by a judge subject to disqualification are voidable rather than void, generally also apply under disqualification statutes or rules that do not expressly forbid disqualifiable judges from sitting.[231]

Under disqualification statutes that declare the grounds for disqualification and expressly forbid the judge to sit, the disqualification is not waivable[232] and orders entered by the judge are void[233] and, therefore, subject to direct appeal on the ground of disqualification[234] even if the order was not preceded by a motion to disqualify the judge[235] and even if the judge did not know of the disqualification when the order was entered.[236] Additionally, in the jurisdictions deeming decrees entered by a judge disqualifed under such a statute to be void, the decree may be collaterally attacked by reason of the judge's disqualification.[237] In jurisdictions in which a disqualification statute prohibiting the judge from sitting authorizes the parties expressly to waive the disqualification, however, the judge's orders and decrees are generally considered voidable rather than void and, therefore, not subject to collateral attack even though the parties did not waive the disqualification.[238]

In some jurisdictions, when the ground for disqualification is based on public policy consideration, the disqualification is nonwaivable and rulings by the judge are void.[239] It follows that, in some jurisdictions applying this principle, some grounds for disqualification render rulings by the judge void, and others do not have that effect.[240]

In Florida, the applicable judicial disqualification statute prescribes the effect of disqualification. The Florida statute provides that: (a) in any case where the grounds for a suggestion of disqualification appear on record but no suggestion of disqualification is filed, the orders, judgments, and decrees entered by the judge shall be valid; (b) when, on a suggestion of disqualification, the judge enters an order declaring himself qualified, the orders, judgments, and decrees entered in the case by the judge shall not be void and shall not be subject to collateral attack; and (c) after an order declaring a judge disqualified has been entered, any party may petition for reconsideration of orders entered by the judge prior to the disqualification order, but, if no such petition is filed, all such prior orders shall be as binding and valid as if they had been entered by a qualified judge.[241]

Now that disqualification is governed by Canon 3C of the Code of Judicial Conduct in virtually all jurisdictions, the courts will have to decide whether the pre-Code rules and statutes relative to express or implied waiver of disqualification have been affected by the express waiver procedure set forth in Canon 3D.

NOTES TO §4.1(a)

1. *See* 6 Bracton, Legibus et Consuetudinibus Anglie 249 (Sr. T. Twiss ed., 1883). *See also* Frank, Disqualification of Judges, 56 Yale L.J. 605, 609–610 (1947); Comment, Disqualification of Judges for Prejudice or Bias—Common Law Evolution, Current Status and the Oregon Experience, 48 Ore. L. Rev. 311, 315–317 (1969) (hereinafter *Disqualification and Oregon*).

2. *See Disqualification and Oregon, supra* note, at 315–319. *Cf.* 1 Blackstone's Commentaries at 361 (3 Lewis ed. p. 1321 1897).

3. E.g., *Dr. Bonham's Case*, 77 Eng. Rep. 648, 8 Co. Rep. 107a, 113b (1609). *See also Derby's (Earl) Case*, 84 Eng. Rep. 1234, 12 Co. Rep. 114 (1619); *Wright v. Crump*, 92 Eng. Rep. 12, 7 Mod. 1 (1702); *Anonymous*, Holt, C. J., 1 Salk. 396 (1698); *City of London v. Wood*, 12 Mod. 669 (1702).

4. E.g., *Matter of Parishes of Great Charte and Kennington*, 93 Eng. Rep. 1107, 2 Str. 1173 (1742).

5. E.g., *Brookes v. Earl of Rivers*, 145 Eng. Rep. 569, Hardres 503 (1660) (defendant married to judge's sister).

6. Even early American cases rejected prior professional involvement as a basis for disqualification. E.g., *Owings v. Gibson*, 9 Ky. 515 (1820); *Den v. Tatem*, 1 Coxe 164 (N.J. 1793); *Bank of North America v. Fitsimons*, 2 Binn. 454 (Pa. 1810).

7. *See* 1 Blackstone, *supra* note 2, at 361 (3 Lewis ed. at 1321).

8. E.g., *Meyer v. San Diego*, 121 Cal. 102, 53 P. 434 (1898); *Bates v. Thompson*, 2 Chip. D. 96 (Vt. 1829); *Sigourney v. Sibley*, 21 Pick. 101 (Mass. 1838); *See also Austin v. Nalle*, 85 Tex. 520, 22 S.W. 668 (1893).

9. E.g., *Gill v. State*, 61 Ala. 169 (1878) (judge held disqualified by relationship to party by consanguinity within fourth degree, despite fact such a ground was not included in the grounds enumerated in the Alabama judicial disqualification statute); *Bayard v. McLane*, 3 Harr. 139 (Del. 1840); *Sanborn v. Fellows*, 22 N.H. 473 (1851); *Bellows v. Pearson*, 19 Johns. 172 (N.Y. 1821).

10. E.g., *Place v. Butternuts*, 28 Barb. 503 (N.Y. 1857). *See also Eggleston v. Smiley*, 17 Johns. 133 (N.Y. 1819); *Pierce v. Sheldon*, 13 Johns. 191 (N.Y. 1816); *Searsburgh Turnpike Co. v. Cutler*, 6 Vt. 315 (1934).

11. E.g., *Tampa St. Ry. & Power Co. v. Tampa Suburban R. Co.*, 30 Fla. 595, 11 So. 562 (1892); *Curtis v. Wilcox*, 74 Mich. 69, 41 N.W. 863 (1882); *Van Rensslaer v. Douglas*, 2 Wend. 290 (N.Y. 1829).

12. See note 6, supra.

13. E.g., *State ex. rel. Barnard v. Board of Education* 19 Wash. 8, 52 P. 317

(1898); *Williams v. Robinson*, 6 Cush. 333 (Mass. 1850). *See Medlin v. Taylor*, 101 Ala. 239, 13 So. 310 (1893) (dictum).

14. E.g., *Walgrove v. Walgrove*, 3 Edw. 241 (N.Y. 1838); *McCauley v. Weller* 12 Cal. 500 (1859); *In re Davis' Estate*, 11 Mont. 1, 27 P. 342 (1944). *See Disqualification and Oregon, supra* note 1, at 327–331 and n. 19.

15. E.g., *In re Davis' Estate, supra* note 14, 11 Mont. at 19, 27 P. at 344; *McCauley, supra* note 14, 12 Cal. at 524.

16. E.g., *Ex parte Cornwell*, 144 Ala. 497, 39 So. 354 (1905). *See Disqualification and Oregon, supra* note 1, at 331.

17. E.g., *Day v. Day*, 12 Idaho 556, 86 Pac. 531 (1906); *Bell v. Bell*, 18 Idaho 636, 111 Pac. 1074, 1076 (1910)(fair trial improbable); *Castleberry v. Jones*, 68 Okla. Crim. 414, 99 P.2d 174 (1940); *Oklahoma ex. rel. Reeves v. Bellah*, 311 P.2d 264 (Okla. Crim. 1957) (doubt or suspicion as to a fair and impartial trial); *State ex. rel. Harden v. Edwards*, 176 Okla. 187, 56 P. 2d 402 (1936) (same; proof of actual prejudice unnecessary); *Leonard v. Wilcox*, 101 Vt. 195, 142 A. 762 (1928).

18. *See Moses v. Julian* 45 N.H. 52(1863)(dictum). *But compare Hutchinson v. Manchester Street Railway*, 73 N.H. 271, 60 A. 1011 (1905) (unconstitutionality of trial by biased judge is an open question).

19. *See King v. Grace*, 293 Mass. 244, 200 N.E. 346, 348 (1936) (dictum); *Thomajamanian v. Odabashium*, 273 Mass. 19, 172 N.E. 232, 233 (1930) (dictum). *Cf. Williams supra* note 13.; *Disqualification and Oregon, supra* note 1.

20. E.g., *In re Murchison*, 349 U.S. 133 (1955); *Board of Medical Examiners v. Steward*, 203 Md 574, 102 A.2d 248 (1954); *Payne v. Lee*, 222 Minn. 269, 24 N.W.2d 259 (1946); *People ex. rel. Przyblinski v. Scott*, 23 Ill. App.2d 167, 161 N.E.2d 705, 706 (1959). *See Disqualification and Oregon, supra* note 1, at 355–356 and n. 269.

NOTES TO §4.1(b)

21. *See Disqualification and Oregon, supra* note 1, at 332, nn. 118–120, and the accompanying text.

22. *See Disqualification and Oregon, supra* note 1, at 333–335, nn. 121–125, and the accompanying text.

23. *Id.*

NOTES TO §4.1(c)

24. 28 U.S.C. §144; Fla. Stat. Ann. §38.10, and Fla R.C.P., R.1.432(d); Kan. Stat. Ann. §20–311d(b). *See Berger v. United States*, 255 U.S. 22 (1921) (judge challenged under 28 U.S.C. §144 must pass on legal sufficiency of affidavit's averments, but neither he nor any other judge may pass on truth of matters alleged); *Davis v. Board of School Commissioners of Mobile County*, 517 F.2d 1044, 1051 (5th Cir. 1975), *cert. denied*, 425 U.S. 944 (1976) (same); *State of Florida v. Cannon*, 163 So.2d 535 (D.C.A. 3d, 1964) (same, as to Florida procedure); *Hulme v. Woleschlagel*, 208 Kan. 385, 493 P.2d 541 (1972) (same, as to Kan. Stat. Ann. §20–311d, except that a judge other than the challenged judge is required to pass on the affidavit's legal sufficiency).

25. E.g., Alaska Stat. Ann. §22.20.022; Cal. Code of Civil Proc. §170(b); Ind.

Code Ann. §33–1–25–1; N.M. Stat. Ann §21–5–9; Ore. Rev. Stat. §§14.260 to .270; S.D. Comp. Laws Ann. §§15–12–20 through 37. *Cf.* Ill. Rev. Stat. Ch. 38, §114.5 (privilege of peremptorily disqualifying judge applied only to defendants in criminal cases). *See Gieffels v. State*, 552 P.2d 661 (Alaska 1976); *Solberg v. Superior Court of City and County of San Francisco*, 137 Cal. Rptr. 460, 561 P.2d 1148, 1158–59 (Cal. In Bank 1977); *U'Ren v. Bagley*, 118 Ore. 77, 245 P. 1074, 46 A.L.R. 1173 (1926)

26. Ariz. R. Civ. P., R. 42(f); Idaho R. Civ. P.R. 40(d)(i); Idaho R. Crim. Proc., R. 25; Ind. Code Ann. §35–36–5–1 (criminal actions); Mo. Supr. Ct. R 51.05; N.D. Cent. Code Ann. §29–15–21; Wis. Stat. Ann. §801.58; Wyo. R. Civ. Proc., R. 40.1(b); Wyo. R. Crim. P., R. 23 (d).

27. *See supra* notes 24–26. In addition to imposing timeliness requirements, some of these states require the affidavit to contain an averment, or be accompanied by a certificate of counsel, that it was filed in good faith and (generally) not for the purpose of delay. E.g., 28 U.S.C. §144 (certificate of counsel); Alaska Stat. Ann. §22.20.022 (affidavit averment); Ore. Rev. Stat. §14.260 (same).

28. E.g., 28 U.S.C. §144; Alaska Stat. Ann. §22.20.022(d); Ind. Code Ann. 35–36–5–1; Wyo. R. Crim. P.R. 23(d).

29. E.g., Cal. Code of Civ. Proc. §170.6(3); Mo. Supr. Ct. R. 51.05 (one per class of parties, classes being defined); Wyo R. Civ. P., R. 40.1(b)(i).

30. E.g., Ariz. R. Civ. Proc., R. 42(f); Idaho R. Civ. Proc., R. 40(d)(1); Wis. Stat. Ann. §801.58(3).

31. E.g., Ore. Rev.Stat. §14.260 (two per party). *But compare U'Ren, supra* note 25 (construing Oregon statute as permitting one per side).

NOTES TO §4.1(d)

32. *See* Martineau, Disciplining Judges for Non-official Conduct: A Survey and Critique of the Law, 10 U. Balt. L. Rev. 225, 228 and n. 19 (1981).

33. Examples of states whose supreme courts have adopted the ABA Code of Judicial Conduct with no substantive change in Canons 3C and 3D include Arkansas, California, Colorado, Connecticut, Florida, Hawaii, Iowa, Kansas, Kentucky, Minnesota, Mississippi, New Hampshire, Nevada, Ohio, Oregon, Tennessee, Washington and Wyoming. Examples of states which have adopted Canons 3C and 3D with only minor substantive changes include Alabama, Alaska, Arizona, Delaware, Georgia, Indiana, Missouri, New Jersey, New Mexico, New York, Oklahoma, Pennsylvania, and West Virginia. These changes have included, for example, amendments requiring a disqualifying financial interest to be substantial (e.g., Alaska, Arizona, Georgia, Indiana, Pennsylvania), disqualifying judges on the ground of family relationships with partners or associates of trial counsel (e.g. Delaware), removing family relationships with trial counsel from the list of disqualifying grounds (e.g. Alabama, Missouri, New York), changing the degree of family relationship to specified persons necessary to disqualification (e.g. Alabama: 4th degree; New York: 6th degree; Oklahoma: 4th degree as to parties and 3rd degree as to lawyers; compare ABA: 3rd degree), disqualifying an appellate judge for sitting as an inferior court judge in the case before him (e.g. New Mexico), expanding Canon 3D's provision for waiver of disqualifying financial interests or family relationships disclosed by the judge (West Virginia), or precluding any such waiver (e.g. New Jersey, Penn-

sylvania). Texas' Canon 3D contains the last-mentioned change and, also, its Canon 3C omits any provision disqualifying judges by reason of family relationship to specified persons. Virginia greatly condenses and modifies Canon 3C. Maine's Canon 3C retains only the general disqualification grounds of bias ("reason to believe that he could not act with complete impartiality") and apparent bias ("his impartiality might reasonably be questioned"); and its Canon 3D omits any provision for waiver of disqualification following disclosure. Finally Louisiana and Michigan merely refer to the existing law of disqualification.

NOTES TO §4.1(e)

34. Under 28 U.S.C. §144, as interpreted by the courts, the facts averred in the affidavit cannot be contested by the judge or opposing party, but they are entitled to contest the legal sufficiency of the facts averred. *Berger, supra* note 24, at 34; *United States v. Ritter*, 540 F.2d 459, 462 (10th Cir. 1976), *cert. denied*, 429 U.S. 951 (1976).

35. Under the express terms of former §455, family relationship required disqualification only when, in the opinion of the challenged judge, it was of such a nature as to render it improper for him to sit in the case.

NOTES TO §4.2

36. From this definition of "financial interest," indirect interests in mutual or common trust fund securities not managed by the judge and securities investments of charitable organizations officered by the judge are excepted; and mutual insurance policy interests and ownership of government securities are excepted unless "the outcome of the proceedings could substantially affect the value of the securities."

37. *In re Cement Antitrust Litigation*, 688 F.2d 1297 (9th Cir. 1982).

38. For criticisms of the per se disqualification rule of 28 U.S.C. §455(b)(4), *see* Note, Judicial Disqualification in the Federal Courts: A Proposal to Conform Statutory Provisions to Underlying Policies, 67 Iowa L. Rev. 525, 530–532 (1982); Note, Judicial Disqualification in the Federal Courts: Maintaining an Appearance of Justice under 28 U.S.C. §455, 1978 U. Ill. L. F. 863, 870–85.

39. *See Cement Antitrust Litigation, supra* note 37 at 1308–1310 (judge required to disqualify by reason of judge's wife's $29.70 stock interest in 7 out of 200,000 class members in antitrust litigation).

40. For pre-code state cases to the same effect, involving statutes disqualifying "interested" judges, *see Tatum v. Southern Pacific Co.* 250 Cal. App.2d 40, 58 Cal. Rptr. 238, 25 A.L.R.3d 1325, 1329 (1967); *City of Vallejo v. Superior Court of Napa Co.*, 199 Cal. 408, 249 P. 1084, 48 A.L.R. 610 (Cal. 1926); *Adams v. Minor*, 121 Cal. 372, 53 P. 815 (1898); and *see also* Ann. 25 A.L.R.3d 1331–1347. The same was true under section 20 of the 1911 judicial code, which was similarly phrased. *In re Honolulu Consolidated Oil Co.*, 243 F. 348 (9th Cir. 1917). Under former 28 U.S.C. §455, which succeeded section 20 of the judicial code, however, disqualification was not required unless the judge had a substantial interest since the statute expressly so provided. E.g., *Minnear Weed Corp. v. Humble Oil & Refining Co.*, 403 F.2d 437 (5th Cir. 1968). *See Lampert v. Hollis Music, Inc..*, 105 F. Supp. 3

(E.D. N.Y. 1952). More often than not, state statutes requiring disqualification on the ground the judge was interested were construed as inapplicable to financial interest of a relative of the judge. E.g., *Goodman v. Wisconsin Electric Power Co.*, 248 Wis. 52, 20 N.W.2d 553, 162 A.L.R. 649, 654 (1945) (wife); *Beasley v. Burt*, 201 Ga. 144, 39 S.E.2d 51 (1946) (wife). *Contra: First National Bank v. Keenan*, 12 S.D. 226, 80 N.W. 1079 (1899) (wife). See Annot. 25 A.L.R.3d 1331, 1342–1344 (1969); Annot. 8 A.L.R. 295–297 (1920).

41. E.g., *In re Virginia Electric & Power Co.*, 539 F.2d 357 (4th Cir. 1976). *Cf. New Mexico Natural Gas Antitrust Litigation*, 620 F.2d 794 (10th Cir. 1980). See Annot. 55 A.L.R. Fed. 650–663; Comment, Meeting the Challenge: Rethinking Judicial Disqualification, 69 Cal. L. Rev. 1445, 1454–1455 and nn. 52 and 53 (1981), and the accompanying text.

42. *United States v. Sellers*, 566 F.2d 884 (4th Cir. 1977).

43. *Virginia Electric & Power, supra* note 41.

44. *Department of Energy v. Brimmer*, 673 F.2d 1287 (Temp. Emerg. Ct. of Apps. 1982).

45. *See supra* note 33 and the accompanying text.

NOTES TO §4.3

46. *See supra* notes 3 and 5, and the accompanying text.

47. *See supra* notes 9 and 10, and the accompanying text.

48. State statutes requiring a judge to disqualify himself when he is related within a degree no closer than the third degree, by consanguinity or affinity to a party, include, *inter alia*, the following: Ala. Code Ann. §12–1–12 (fourth degree); Alaska Stat. Ann. §22.20.020 (third degree); Ark. Stat. Ann. §22.113 (fourth degree); Cal. Code of Civ. Proc. §170(a) (third degree); Colo. Rev. Stat. §16–6–201 (third degree); Conn. Gen. Stat. §51–39 (third degree); Fla. Stat. Ann. §38.02 (third degree); Ga. Code Ann. §15–1–8(a) (sixth degree, computed according to civil law; Hawaii Rev. Stat. §601–7(a) (third degree); Idaho R. Civ. Proc., R. 40(d)(2)(B) (third degree, "computed according to the rules of law"); Ill. Supr. Ct. Rule 67 (third degree, under rules of civil law); Ind. Code Ann. §35–36–5–2 (criminal cases; maximum degree not specified); Ind. Code Ann. §35–1–25–2 (civil cases; sixth degree); Iowa Code Ann. §605.17 (fourth degree); La. Code of Civil Prac. art. 151, (fourth degree); La. Code of Crim. Prac. art. 671 (fourth degree); Miss. Const. art. 6, §165 (degree not stated); Mo. Stat. Ann. §476.180 (same); Mont. Code Ann. §3–1–802 (sixth degree, computed according to the rules of law); Neb. Rev. Stat. §24–315 (degree of parent, child, or sibling); Nev. Rev. Stat. §§1.225, 1.230 (third degree); N.J. S.A. §2:15–49 (third degree, according to common law method); N.Y. Judiciary Law art. 2, §14 (sixth degree, computed by civil law method); Okla. Stat. Ann. tit. 20, §1401 (fourth degree); Ore. Rev. Stat. §14.210(1) (third degree); P.R. Laws tit. 32, App. III, R. 63.1; Tex. Code of Crim. Proc., Tex. Stat. Ann. art. 30.01 (third degree); Tex. Civil Stat. art. 15 (third degree); Wyo. R.Civ. Proc., R. 40.1(b)(2) (degree not stated). Except when stated above, the statute did not state whether the degree of relationship was to be computed according to the civil law or common law. In *In re Dwyer v. Harkins*, 282 Mich. 711, 281 N.W. 766 (1937), *denying reh. of* 282 Mich. 593. 276 N.W. 564 (1937), *cert denied*, 305 U.S. 644 (1938), *reh.*

denied, 305 U.S. 674 (1938), such a statute was construed as referring to degrees of relationship to be determined according to the civil law.

49. None or virtually none of the state disqualification statutes extends disqualification to a family relationship twice removed by marriage from the judge, *see supra* note 48, and the term "related by consanguinity or affinity" in such a statute has been construed as not applicable to such a relationship. *Edison Provision Co. v. Armour & Co.*, 51 Ga. App. 213, 179 S.E. 829 (1935).

NOTES TO §4.4(a)

50. E.g., *McKinney v. Fox*, 309 Ky. 418, 217 S.W.2d 973 (1949); *Johnson v. Moore*, 109 Vt. 282, 196 A. 246 (1938). *See Ex Parte Clanahan*, 261 Ala. 87, 72 So.2d 833, 836, 50 A.L.R.2d 134, 138 (1956); and Annot., 50 A.L.R.2d 143, 144–145 (1956).

51. *See* the statutes for California, Colorado, Florida, Illinois, Louisiana, Nebraska, Nevada, and Oregon, which are cited in note 48.

52. *See* the statutes for Alabama, Alaska, Connecticut, Georgia, Idaho, Indiana, Mississippi, Missouri, North Carolina, Oklahoma, Texas, and Wyoming, which are cited in note 48.

53. E.g., Florida and Texas. *See supra* note 48, *infra* note 54, and the accompanying text.

54. E.g., *Hundley v. State*, 47 Fla. 172, 36 So. 362 (1904); *Norwich Union Fire Ins. Co. v. Standard Drug Co.*, 121 Miss 510, 83 So. 676, 11 A.L.R. 1321 (1920); *Winston v. Masterson* 87 Tex. 200, 27 S.W. 768 (1894); *Missouri K. & T.R. Co. v. Mitcham*, 57 Tex. Civ. App. 134, 121 S.W. 871 (1909). *See* Annot., 50 A.L.R.2d 143, 156–158 (1956). *But compare Postal Mutual Indemnity Co. v. Ellis*, 140 Tex. 570, 169 S.W.2d 482 (1943) (contingent fee interest rendered attorney relative of judge a "party" when amount of fee was subject to determination by the judge).

55. E.g., *Johnson v. State*, 87 Ark. 45, 112 S.W. 143 (1908); *Howell v. Budd*, 91 Cal. 342, 27 P. 747 (1891); *State ex. rel. Mayo v. Pitchford*, 43 Okla. 105, 141 P. 433 (1914); *Ex Parte Bowles*, 164 Md. 318, 165 A. 169 (1933); *Yazoo & M. Valley R. Co. v. Kirk*, 102 Miss. 41, 58 So. 710, 834 (1912). *Compare Gulf States Steel Co. v.Christison*, 228 Ala 622, 154 So. 565 (1934) (family relationship between judge and contingent fee attorney disqualifies judge only if fee is lien upon judgment or decree); *Clanahan*, *supra* note 50, 72 So.2d at 838 (same). *See* Annot., 50 A.L.R.2d 143, 153–155 (1956).

56. E.g., *Brown v. Brown*, 103 Kan. 53, 56, 103 Pac. 1005, 1006 (1918).

57. E.g., *Ex Parte Clanahan*, *supra* note 50; *Strickland Co. v. Union Bkg. Co.*, 42 Ga. App. 645, 157 S.E. 115 (1931). *Cf. Young v. Harris*, 146 Ga. 333, 91 S.E. 37 (1916) (noncontingent fee, to be increased if client successful). *See* Annot., 50 A.L.R. 2d 143, 155–156 (1956).

58. E.g., Fla. Stat. Ann. §38.02 (third degree); Ga. Code Ann. §15–1–8 (6th degree); Ill. Supr. Ct.Rule 67 (third degree). Although the term used by the Georgia statute is "a party interested in the result," it has been construed as including interested nonparties. E.g., *Gray v. Barlow*, 241 Ga. 347, 245 S.E.2d 299 (1978); *Georgia Power Co. v. Watts*, 184 Ga. 135, 190 S.E. 659 (1937).

59. For example, the disqualification statutes in Alabama, Alaska, Arkansas, Colorado, Idaho, Indiana, Louisiana, Montana, Nebraska, New Jersey, New York,

Oklahoma, Oregon, Texas, and Wyoming do not contain any provision making family relationship with an interested person or nonparty a ground for disqualification. *See supra,* note 48.

60. *Chadwick v. State,* 87 Ga. App. 900, 75 S.E.2d 260 (1953); *Vine v. Jones,* 13 S.D. 54, 82 N.W. 82 (1900). On the other hand, efforts to disqualify judges related to attorneys of record on the theory that such relationship made the judges themselves "interested" within the meaning of statutes disqualifying "interested" persons have been unsuccessful. E.g., *Sjobera v. Nordin,* 26 Minn. 501, 5 N.W. 677 (1880); *State v. Ledbetter,* 111 Minn. 110, 126 N.W. 477 (1910). *See* Annot., 50 A.L.R. 2d 143, 152–153 (1956).

61. E.g., *Roberts v. Roberts,* 115 Ga. 259, 41 S.E. 616 (1902).

62. *DeLoach v. State,* 75 Ga. App. 482, 51 S.E.2d 539 (1949) (assistant prosecuting attorney). *Cf. Atlantic Coast Line R. Co. v. McDonald,* 50 Ga. App. 856, 179 S.E. 185 (1935), *cert. denied,* 296 U.S. 621 (1935) (no fee agreement, but compensation hinged on recovery, since client was assetless).

NOTES TO §4.4(b)

63. *See* e.g., the statutes for California, Colorado, Florida, Illinois, Louisiana, and Nevada, which are cited *supra* in note 48.

64. *See* Neb. Rev. Stat. §24–315 (judge related in first degree to partner of attorney for party); Ore. Rev. Stat. §14.210 (judge related in third degree to partner or office associate of attorney for party).

65. 557 F.2d 110 (7th Cir. 1977).

66. 609 F.2d 1101 (5th Cir. 1980).

67. *Potashnick* did, however, rule that, because he had never participated in the proceeding, the lawyer-relative was not "acting as a lawyer in the proceeding" within the meaning of 28 U.S.C.A. §455(b)(5)(ii), and that disqualification was, therefore, not available on that ground.

68. *But compare State v. Edwards,* 420 So.2d 663 (La. 1982) (refusing to disqualify judge who was uncle of law partner of first assistant district attorney, who was prosecutor in case at bar, a criminal proceeding; bias or personal interest on part of judge not alleged).

NOTES TO §4.4(c)

69. 557 F.2d 456 (5th Cir. 1977), *cert. denied,* 434 U.S. 1035 (1978).

70. 249 Ga. 700, 292 S.E.2d 689 (1982).

NOTES TO §4.5(a)

71. E.g., *Townsend v. Hughes,* 2 Mod. 150, 86 Eng. Repr. 994 (K.B. 1676); *Thelusson v. Rendlesham,* 7 H.L. Cases 429, 11 Eng. Repr. 172 (1858); *Lloyd v. Smith,* T.U.P. Charlt. 143 (Ga. 1808); *Hamilton County v. Aurora National Bank,* 89 Neb. 256, 131 N.W. 221 (1911). *See* Annot., 72 A.L.R.2d 443, 456–460 (1960).

72. *See* Annot., 72 A.L.R. 2d 443, 457 (1960).

73. *See* the statutes and rules cited in note 48 with respect to the following

jurisdictions: Alabama, Alaska, Arkansas, California, Colorado, Georgia, Hawaii, Illinois, Indiana, Iowa, Kansas, Louisiana, Missouri, Montana, Nebraska, Nevada, New Jersey, New York, Oklahoma, Oregon, Puerto Rico, Texas, and Wyoming; S.C. Code §14–8–70.

74. 28 U.S.C. §455 (1970).

75. E.g., *See* the disqualification statutes cited in note 48 for the following states: Idaho, Iowa, Montana, Nebraska, and Nevada ("action or proceeding"); Kansas, New Jersey, Puerto Rico, and Wyoming ("action"); Missouri ("suit or proceeding"); and Oregon ("action, suit, or proceeding").

76. E.g., *See* the disqualification statutes cited in note 48 with respect to the following states: Louisiana ("cause"); Colorado, Hawaii, Illinois, and Texas ("case"); Alabama and Georgia ("case or proceeding"); Arkansas and Oklahoma ("cause or proceeding"); New York ("action, claim, matter, motion, or proceeding") and California ("matter" or different "action or proceeding involving any of the same issues"); and S.C. Code §14–8–70 ("case"). *Cf.* N.C. Gen. Stat. §1–83 ("counsel"; change of venue).

77. E.g., *Smith v. Queen Ins. Co.*, 41 Ga. App. 587, 153 S.E. 785 (1930) (construing "cause"); *State ex. rel. Stewart v. Reid*, 114 La. 97, 38 So. 70 (1905) (construing "cause"); *Henry Waterhouse Trust Co. v. Treadway*, 29 Hawaii 256 (1926) (construing "case"); *Slaven v. Wheeler*, 58 Tex. 23 (1882) (construing "case"); *Johnson v. Johnson*, 89 S.W. 1102 (Tex. Civ. App. 1905) (same).

78. E.g., *Leavenworth v. Green River Asphalt Co.*, 101 Kan. 82, 165 P. 824 (1917) (construing "action").

79. E.g., *Carr v. Fife*, 156 U.S. 494 (1895); *Wickhoff v. James*, 159 Cal. App.2d 664, 324 P.2d 661 (1958); *Kerr v. Burns*, 42 Colo. 285, 93 P. 112 (1900); *Harjo v. Chilcoat*, 146 Okla. 62, 294 P. 119 (1930). *See* Annot., 72 A.L.R.2d 443, 467–470 (1960).

80. E.g., *Cleghorn v. Cleghorn*, 66 Cal. 309, 5 Pac. 516 (1885); *Blackburn v. Crawford*, 22 Md. 447 (1864). *See* Annot., 72 A.L.R.2d 443, 469–470 (1960).

81. *Newcome v. Light*, 58 Tex. 141 (1882). *See* Annot., 72 A.L.R.2d 443, 469–470 (1960).

82. *National Auto Brokers v. General Motors Corp.*, 572 F.2d 953, 958 (2d Circ. 1978), *cert. denied*, 439 U.S. 102 (1979).

83. *W.C. Clay Jackson Enterprises, Inc. v. Greyhound Leasing & Financial Corp.*, 467 F. Supp. 801 (D. Puerto Rico 1979).

84. E.g., Cal. Civ. Proc. Code §170(a)(4) (two-year period).

NOTES TO §4.5(b)

85. E.g., *State ex. rel. Ambler v. Hocker*, 34 Fla. 25, 15 So. 581 (1894); *East Rome Town Co. v. Cothram*, 81 Ga. 359, 8 S.E. 737 (1888); *Magoon v. Lord-Young Engineering Co.*, 22 Hawaii 245 (1914); *Merchants National Bank v. Cross*, 283 S.W. 555 (Tex. Civ. App. 1926) (so held irrespective whether judge might have been entitled to share in fee). *See Davis v. Seaward*, 85 Misc. 210, 146 N.Y. Supp. 981 (1914), *aff'd.*, 171 App. Div. 963, 156 N.Y. Supp. 242 (1915) (dictum). *Contra*: *Lowe v. Lowe*, 17 Hawaii 194 (1905); *Fort Worth & D.C. R. Co. v. Mackney*, 83 Tex. 410, 18 S.W. 949 (1892).

86. *M'Laren v. Charrier*, 5 Paige (N.Y.) 530 (1836).

87. *See* the statutes cited, *supra*, in note 73.

88. La. Rev. Stat. Ann. art. 671(3) (criminal cases); La. Rev. Stat. Ann. art. 151(2) (civil cases).

89. *See supra* note 82, 572 F.2d at 958.

NOTES TO §4.5(c)

90. E.g., *Merchants National Bank v. Cross*, 283 S.W. 555 (Tex. Civ. App. 1926). *Cf. supra* note 69, and the accompanying text.

91. *Johnson v. Johnson*, 89 S.W. 1102 (Tex. Civ. App. 1905).

NOTES TO §4.5(d)

92. Justice Rehnquist's memorandum on motion to recuse in *Laird v. Tatum*, 409 U.S. 824 (1974); *United States v. Kelly*, 556 F.2d 257 (5th Cir. 1977); *Muench v. Israel*, 524 F. Supp. 1115 (E.D. Wis. 1981); *People v. Lipa*, 109 Ill. App.3d 610, 440 N.E.2d 1062 (1982); *see* commentary to Canon 3C(1)(b).

93. *See Laird*, *supra* note 92; *Kelly*, *supra* note 92; *Muench*, *supra* note 92; *Lipa*, *supra* note 92; and commentary to Canon 3C(1)(b).

94. E.g., *Payne v. State*, 48 Ala. App. 401, 265 So.2d 185 (Ala. Crim. App. 1972), *cert. denied*, 288 Ala. 748, 265 So.2d 192 (1972), *cert. denied*, 409 U.S. 669 (1972); *Florida ex. rel. Shelton v. Sepe*, 254 So.2d 12 (Fla. App., 3d Dist. 1971); *State of Hawaii v. Midkiff*, 413 P.2d 249 (Hawaii 1966); *People v. Burnett*, 73 Ill. App. 3d 750, 392 N.E.2d 235 (1979); *Kirby v. State*, 78 Miss. 175, 28 So. 846 (1900); *Rodriguez v. State*, 489 S.W.2d 121 (Tex. Crim. Apps. 1972). *See* Annot., 16 A.L.R.4th 556, 560–562 (1982).

95. *United States v. Wilson*, 426 F.2d 268 (6th Cir. 1970); *United States v. Amerine*, 411 F.2d 1130 (6th Cir. 1969); *King v. State*, 246 Ga. 386, 271 S.E.2d 630, 16 A.L.R.4th 545 (1980); *People v. Berry*, 23 App. Div.2d 955, 259 N.Y.S.2d 971 (4th Dept. 1965). *See* Annot., 16 A.L.R.4th 550, 558–560 (1982). *Wilson*, *Amerine*, and *King* are perhaps distinguishable, since the disqualification statute did not merely disqualify any judge who had formerly acted as counsel in the case, but also disqualified any judge who had formerly been "of counsel" in the case. *Kirby* and *Rodriguez*, *supra* note 94, however, construed such a statute as not disqualifying the judge under such circumstances.

NOTES TO §4.5(e)

96. E.g., *Simonson v. General Motors Corp.*, 425 F. Supp. 574 (E.D. Pa. 1976); *Reddy v. Jones*, 419 F. Supp. 1391 (W.D. N.C. 1976). *See Miller Industries v. Caterpillar Tractor Co.*, 516 F. Supp. 84, 88–89 (S.D. Ala. 1980).

97. *Miller Industries*, *supra* note 96, 516 F. Supp, at 88–89.

98. *Fredonia Broadcasting Corp., Inc. v. RCA Corp.*, 569 F.2d 251, 254–257 (5th Cir. 1978). *See Miller Industries*, *supra* note 96, 516 F. Supp. at 88–89.

NOTES TO §§4.6(a)

99. *See supra* §§4.1(a) and 4.1(b).

100. E.g., Alaska Stat. §22.20.020; Cal. Civ. Code §170(a)(5); Colo. Rev. Stat. §16–6–201; Idaho R. Civ. Proc. R. 40(d)(2); Ind. Code Ann. §35–36–5–2; Iowa Code Ann. §605.17; La. Code of Crim. Proc. art. 671(1) (criminal cases); Minn. R. Civ. Proc. 63.02; Nev. Rev. Stat. §1.225(1); Pa. Dist. Justice R. 8A(1); P.R. Laws tit. 32, App. III, R.63.1(e); Wyo. R. Civ. P., R. 40.1(b)(2).

101. Ala. Code Ann. §12–12; Ark. Stat. Ann. §22.113; Conn. Gen. Stat. §51–39; Fla. Stat. Ann. 38.02; Ga. Code Ann. §15–1–8; Ill. Supr. Ct. Rules, R. 66 and 67; La. Code of Civ. Proc. art. 151 (civil cases); Mo. Stat. Ann. §476–180; Miss. Const. art. 6, §165; Mont. Code Ann. §13–1–802; Neb. Rev. Stat. §24–315; N.J.S.A. §2A:15–49; N.Y. Judiciary Law art. 2, §14; Okla. Stat. Ann. tit. 20, §1401; Ore. Rev. Stat. §14.210; S.C. Code Ann. §14–1–130; Tex. Code of Crim. Proc., Tex. Stat. Ann. ch. 30, art. 30.01; Tex. Civ. Stat. tit. 1, art. 15.

102. Whereas canon 3C(1) provides that a judge "should" disqualify himself under such circumstances, 28 U.S. §455(b)(1) provides that he "shall" do so. *See Fredonia, supra* note 98, 569 F.2d at 256–257, which states that section 455 adopted canon 3C's language "with the exception of making the disqualification mandatory by substituting the word 'shall' for the ABA's 'should'."

103. E.g., *see SCA Services, Inc. v. Morgan*, 557 F.2d 110, 116 (5th Cir. 1977); *Parrish v. Board of Commissioners*, 524 F.2d 98, 103 (5th Cir. En Banc 1975), *cert. denied*, 425 U.S. 944 (1976); *Fong v. American Airlines, Inc.*, 431 F. Supp. 1334, 1337 (N.D. Cal. 1977). *See* Annot., 40 A.L.R. Fed. 954–971 (1978).

104. 624 F.2d 869, 881 (9th Cir. 1980) *aff'g in pertinent part* 457 F. Supp. 641 (D. Nev. 1978).

NOTES TO §4.6(b)

105. *See United States v. Grinnell Corp.*, 384 U.S. 563, 583 (1966); *Berger, supra* note 24, 255 U.S. at 31; *Davis, supra* note 24, 517 F.2d at 1051 (applying 28 U.S.C. §144).

106. E.g., *Davis, supra* note 24, 517 F.2d at 1052.

107. E.g., *United States v. Haldeman*, 559 F.2d 31, 131–134, 297 (App. D.C. 1976) (section 144 and present section 455(b)(1), as well as pre–1974 section 455); *Davis, supra* note 24, 517 F.2d at 1051 (section 144, as well as present sections 455(a) and 455(b)(1)). The precedents under section 144 govern the meaning of section 455(b)(1). *See Conforte, supra* note 104, 624 F.2d at 880.

108. E.g., *Smith v. Danyo*, 585 F.2d 83, 87 (3d Cir. 1978); *United States v. Bernstein*, 533 F.2d 775 (2 Cir. 1976), *cert. denied*, 429 U.S. 998 (1976); *Haldeman, supra* note 4–107, 509 F.2d at 131–134; *Inland Freight Lines v. United States*, 212 F.2d 169 (10th Cir. 1953).

109. *See United States v. Holland*, 655 F.2d 44, 46–47 (5th Cir. 1981); *United States v. Boffa*, 513 F. Supp. 505, 510 (D. Del. 1981); *Haldeman, supra* note 107, at 132–133 and n. 297; *City of Cleveland Electric Illuminating Co.*, 503 F. Supp. 368, 372 (N.D. Ohio 1980). *Compare In re International Business Machines Corp.*, 618 F.2d 923, 927–932 (2d Cir. 1980).

110. E.g., see *Holland, supra* note 109, 655 F.2d at 46–47. *See Whitehurst v. Wright*, 592 F.2d 834, 838 (5th Cir. 1979); and *Davis, supra* note 24, 517 F.2d at 1051. *But compare Conforte, supra* note 104, 457 F. Supp. 657, n. 12 (problems of egregious judicial bias of extrajudicial origin should be addressed and resolved under constitutional doctrines of due process and fair play, rather than in context of disqualification statutes).

111. E.g., *Nicodemus v. Chrysler Corp.* 596 F.2d 152 (6th Cir. 1979) (vilification by judge of party in court, clearly showing bias).

112. E.g., *Dee v. Institutional Networks Corp.*, 559 F. Supp. 1281, 1285 (S.D.N.Y. 1983) (under section 455(a)); *Hulme, supra* note 24, 493 P.2d at 550; *Schoonover v. State*, 2 Kan. App.2d 481, 582 P.2d 297 (1978). *See Conforte, supra* note 104, 457 F. Supp. at 652, 657–658, *aff'd on other grounds* (under sections 455(a) and 455(b)(1)). For pre-Code cases to the same effect, *see State ex. rel. Locke v. Sandler*, 156 Fla. 136, 23 So.2d 276 (1945); *Peacock v. State*, 124 Fed. 334, 168 So. 401 (1936). The rule under consideration merely requires that the judge's bias be derived from an extrajudicial source and not that it be expressed in extrajudicial conduct in order to disqualify the judge. *Conforte, supra* note 104, 457 F. Supp. at 657, n. 12.

113. E.g., *United States v. Phillips*, 664 F.2d 971 (5th Cir. 1981) (plot of party to have judge assassinated was learned of by judge during trial); *Wilks v. Israel*, 627 F.2d 32 (7th Cir. 1980) (physical assault by movant on judge); *United States v. Bray*, 546 F.2d 851 (10th Cir. 1976) (movant had accused judge of taking bribe, authored article calling for impeachment of judge, and instigated petition for impeachment); *United States v. Garrison*, 34 Supp. 952, 957 (E.D. La. 1972) (press release by movant castigating judge's decision in prior case); *United States v. Fujimoto*, 101 F Supp. 293, 296 (D. Hawaii 1951), motion for permission to file petition for writ of prohibition or mandamus denied *sub nom Fujimoto v. Wiig*, 344 U.S. 852 (1950) (condemnation of judge by movant's newspaper); *In re Union Leader Corp.*, 292 F.2d 381 (1st Cir. 1961), *cert. denied*, 368 U.S. 927 (1961); *Smith v. District Court for Fourth Judicial District*, 629 P.2d, 1055, 1057 (Colo. En Banc 1981) (threats by defendant in criminal trial to kill judge, which were made to deputy sheriff and repeated by letter to judge); *Yager v. State*, 437 N.E.2d 454 (Ind. 1982) (threats to make citizen's arrest of judge and try him before a "people's court"); *Fitzgerald v. State*, 5 Md. App. 558, 248 A.2d 667 (1968) (movant threw a chart at judge). *But compare Marshall v. Georgia Pacific Corp.*, 484 F. Supp. 629 (E.D. Ark. 1980) (comments by counsel charging judge with racism held justification for recusal by judge in all subsequent cases).

114. *Wilks, supra* note 113.

115. E.g., *Garrison, supra* note 113; *Fujimoto, supra* note 113; *Union Leader, supra* note 113.

NOTES TO §4.6(c)

116. Query whether a case covered by this provision would also be covered by the requirement of canon 3C(1) and 28 U.S.C. §455(a) that a judge disqualify himself "in any proceeding in which his impartiality might reasonably be questioned."

117. E.g., *United States v. Callingham*, 100 F.2d 657 (8th Cir. 1973), *cert. denied*, 416 U.S. 907 (1974) (knowledge acquired by judge by interrogating defendant con-

cerning plea bargain thereafter rejected by judge); *United States v. Foddrell*, 523
F.2d 86 (2d Cir. 1975) (knowledge acquired by reading pre-sentencing report before
sentencing him); *Smith v. United States*, 360 F.2d 590, (5th Cir. 1966).

118. E.g., *United States v. Cowden*, 545 F.2d 257, 265–266 (1st Cir. 1976), *cert.
denied*, 430 U.S. 909 (1977) (knowledge learned in separate trials of co-defendants);
United States v. Boffa, 513 F. Supp. 505, 509–510 (D. Del. 1981) (insufficient basis
for disqualification, whether under 28 U.S.C. §144, 28 U.S.C. §455(a), or 28 U.S.C.
§455(b)(1)); *United States v. Nunn*, 435 F. Supp. 294, 295 (N.D. Ind. 1977) (not
stated whether movant was a party to the prior cases). *See infra* notes 147–154, and
accompanying text.

119. E.g., *see Boffa*, *supra* note 118, 513 F. Supp at 510.

NOTE TO §4.6(d)

120. *Potashnick v. Port City Construction Co.*, 609 F.2d 1101 (5th Cir. 1980).

NOTES TO §4.6(e)

121. E.g., *Moon v. State*, 154 Ga. App. 312, 268 S.E.2d 366 (1981).
122. E.g., *Burrows v. Forrest City*, 543 S.W.2d 488 (Ark. In Banc 1976).
123. *Webbe v. McGhie Land Title Co.*, 549 F.2d 1358 (10th Cir. 1977).

NOTES TO §4.6(f)

124. E.g., *Higgins v. San Diego*, 126 Cal. 303, 58 P. 700, 704, 59 P. 209 (1899);
Head v. State, 160 Ga. App. 4, 285 S.E.2d 735, 739 (1981); *Mann v. State*, 154 Ga.
App. 677, 269 S.E.2d 863, 864 (1980); *Grey v. State*, 450 N.E.2d 125, 128 (Ind.
App. 3d Dist. 1983) (alleged bias arose from intrajudicial source, *viz.* attorney's
behavior); *May v. May*, 150 Ky. 522, 150 S.W. 685 (1912); *Hutchinson v. Manchester
Street R. Co.*, 73 N.H. 271, 60 A. 1011, 1013–1014 (1905); *Clawans v. Waugh*, 10
N.J. Super. 605, 608–609, 77 A.2d 519 (1950); *State v. Case*, 100 N.M. 714, 676
P.2d 241, 243 (1984) (same as in *Grey*, *supra* this note); *Martinez v. Cremona*, 95
N.M. 545, 624 P.2d 54, 59 (Ct. App. 1980), *cert. quashed*, 95 N.M. 593, 624 P.2d
535 (1981). *See Ex Parte N.K. Fairbank Co.*, 194 F. 978, 992 (M.D. Ala. 1912);
Shakin v. Board of Medical Examiners, 254 Cal. App.2d 102, 62 Cal. Rptr. 274,
287, 23 A.L.R.3d 1398, 1414–1415 (1967), *appeal dismissed and cert. denied*, 390
U.S. 410 (1968). *See* Annot., 23 A.L.R.3d 1416, 1420–1422 (1969).

125. E.g., *Mann supra* note 124, 269 S.E.2d at 865.

126. E.g., *Nelson v. Fitzgerald*, 403 P.2d 677 (Alaska 1965); *State ex. rel. Davis
v. Parks*, 141 Fla. 516, 194 So. 613 (1939) (applying peremptory disqualification
statute; affidavit averments of prejudice against attorney and fear client would not
receive fair trial held legally sufficient); *Hayslip v. Douglas*, 400 So.2d 553, 556–557
(Fla. App. 4th Dist. 1981) (same); *Brewton v. Kelly*, 166 So.2d 834, 835 (Fla. App.
1964) (same); *State v. Davis*, 159 Ga. App. 537, 284 S.E.2d 51 (1981); *Hulme*, *supra*
note 24 (same as in *Davis*); *Payne v. Lee*, 222 Minn. 269, 24 N.W.2d 259, 264
(1946). *see Mann*, *supra* note 124, 269 S.E.2d at 865. *Case*, *supra* note 124, 676 P.
2d at 243; *Martinez*, *supra* note 124, 624 P. 2d at 59.

127. E.g., Colo. Rev. Stat. §16–6–201(d); Ore. Rev. Stat. §14–260 (peremptory disqualification by filing of affidavit of prejudice); Wyo. R.C.P., R. 40.1(b)(2). *See People v. the District Court in and for the Third Judicial District*, 560 P.2d 828 (Colo. En Banc 1977); *State v. Superior Court*, 121 Wash. 611, 209 P. 1097 (1920).

128. *Auto Workers Flint Federal Credit Union v. Kogler*, 32 Mich. App. 257, 188 N.W.2d 184 (1971) (disqualifying judge from hearing any case in which law firm is counsel).

129. *Ginsberg v. Holt*, 86 So.2d 650 (Fla. 1956) (motion by attorney); *Clawans*, *supra* note 124 (same).

NOTES TO §4.6(g)

130. *See* Annot., 68 A.L.R.3d 509–523 (1976) and Annot., 115 A.L.R. 866–869 (1938).

131. E.g., *County Attorney of Maricopa County v. Superior Court of Maricopa County*, 11 Ariz. App. 346, 464 P.2d 666 (1970) (disqualification required when application made for change of judge); *State ex. rel. Brown v. Dewell*, 131 Fla. 566, 179 So. 695, 696, 115 A.L.R. 857 (1938) (legally sufficient affidavit averments of prejudice required); *Peters v. Jamieson*, 48 Hawaii 247, 397 P.2d 575, 581–582 (1948) (same); *State v. Kraska*, 294 Minn. 540, 201 N.W.2d 742, 68 A.L.R.3d 505 (1972); *State ex. rel. Tittman v. Hay*, 50 N.M. 370, 60 P.2d 353 (1936); *State v. Franulovitch*, 89 Wash.2d 521, 573 P.2d 1298 (1978) (affidavit averment of prejudice suffices; facts need not be averred); *State ex. rel. Douglas v. Superior Court of Washington*, 121 Wash. 611, 209 P. 1097 (1922). *See* Annot., 68 A.L.R.3d 509–523 (1976).

NOTES TO §4.6(h)

132. E.g., *Bond v. Bond*, 127 Me. 117, 141 A. 833 (1928) (close friendship between family of judge and family of party held insufficient to disqualify judge). *See* Frank, Disqualification of Judges, 56 Yale L.J. 605, 610, n.13 (1947).

133. *Callahan v. Callahan*, 30 Idaho 431, 165 P. 1122 (1917). *Compare* Puerto Rico Laws tit. 32, App. III, R. 63.1(d), (friendship between judge and party or party's attorney requires disqualification when "of such a nature as to thwart the end of justice").

134. *See* Frank, *supra* note 132, at 622.

135. *Id.*

NOTES TO §4.6(i)

136. *Knoll v. Socony Mobil Oil Co.*, 369 F.2d 425, 430 (10th Cir. 1966), *cert. denied*, 386 U.S. 977 (1967); *Barnes v. United States*, 241 F.2d 252, 254 (9th Cir. 1956); *Stein v. Frank*, 575 S.W.3d 399, 402 (Tex. Civ. App. 1978). *See Riojas v. Turner*, 304 F. Supp. 559, 561–562 (D. Utah 1969); Annot. 21 A.L.R.3d 1369, 1371–1373, and §3 (1968).

137. Id., see Annot. supra note 136, *Barnes*, *supra* note 136.

138. E.g., *Lindsay v. Lindsay*, 122 Ala. 578, 158 So. 522, 523 (1934); *McNeil v.*

Continental Casualty Co., 244 So.2d 693, 697–698 (La. App. 1971); and *Musser v. Third Judicial District Court of Salt Lake City*, 148 P.2d 802, 803–804 (Utah 1944).

139. E.g., *Boggs v. Boggs*, 138 Md. 422, 114 A. 474, 481 (1921); *City of Palatka v. Frederick*, 174 So. 82 (Fla. 1937).

140. See *supra* notes 137–139, and the accompanying text.

141. E.g., *United States v. Roberts*, 463 F.2d 372, 374 (4th Cir. 1972); *Wolfson v. Palmieri*, 396 F.2d 121 (2d Cir. 1968); *People v. Vance*, 76 Ill.2d 171, 390 N.E.2d 867, 870 (1979). See *United States v. Scaccia*, 514 F. Supp. 1353, 1355 (N.D. N.Y. 1981). *Cf. United States v. Wolfson*, 558 F.2d 59, 64, n. 17 (2d Cir. 1977).

142. E.g., *Carter v. Director, Patuxent Institution*, 10 Md. App. 247, 269 A.2d 172 (1970). See Annot., 21 A.L.R.3d 1369, at 1374–1375 (1968).

143. E.g., *Barry v. Sigler*, 373 F.2d 835, 836 (8th Cir. 1967); *Wilkes v. United States*, 80 F.2d 285, 289 (9th Cir. 1935); *Boffa, supra* note 118, 513 F. Supp. at 509 (D. Del. 1981); *United States v. Tanner*, 224 La. 505, 69 So.2d 505, 507 (1953); *King v. State*, 391 S.W.2d 637 (Tenn. 1965). See Annot., 21 A.L.R.3d 1369, at 1373–1374 (1968).

NOTES TO §4.6(j)

144. *Boffa, supra* note 118, 513 F. Supp. at 509–510. See *United States v. Partin*, 312 F. Supp. 1355, 1358 (E.D. La. 1970).

145. E.g., *United States v. Valenti*, 120 F. Supp. 80, 86–88 (D. N.J. 1954) (approval of verdict).

146. See *Johnson v. State*, 167 S.E. 900, 900–901 (Ga. App. 1933). *Compare Ingram v. Grimes*, 213 Ga. 652, 100 S.E.2d 914, 915 (1957) (statutory disqualification of judge in event of retrial did not preclude judge from passing sentence following his comments on verdict convicting defendant).

NOTES TO §4.6(k)

147. See *supra* notes 118 and 119 and accompanying text. *A fortiori*, disqualification has been denied when the judge acquired knowledge relevant to the pending litigation in a prior litigation in which the movant was not a party. E.g., *United States v. Partin*, 552 F.2d 621, 639 (5th Cir. 1977), *cert. denied*, 434 U.S. 903 (1977); *United States v. DiLorenzo*, 429 F.2d 216 (2d Cir. 1970).

148. See *infra* notes 151–153, and the accompanying text.

149. See *supra* notes 118 and 138, and the accompanying text.

150. E.g., see *supra* notes 118 and 139, and the accompanying text.

151. E.g., *Wolfson, supra* note 141 (successive securities frauds involving different companies and each involving a jury trial).

152. E.g., *Musser, supra* note 138, 148 P.2d at 803–804.

153. E.g., *United States v. Myers*, 381 F.2d 814 (3d Cir. 1967).

154. *Partin, supra* note 144; *DiLorenzo, supra* note 147. See *Scaccia, supra* note 141.

NOTES TO §4.6(1)

155. E.g., *United States v. Bunch*, 730 F.2d 517 (7th Cir. 1984) (nearest trial judge in another city): *United States v. Bourque*, 541 F.2d 290, 296 (1st Cir. 1976) (two-judge district court); *United States v. Gallington*, 488 F.2d 637, 639–640, 27 A.L.R. Fed. 582 (8th Cir. 1973) *cert. denied*, 416 U.S. 907 (1974).

156. *See supra* note 155.

157. A similar decision was rendered in a federal case in which the trial judge had rejected a *nolo contendere* plea tendered by the defendant. E.g., *see United States v. Cepeda Penes*, 577 F.2d 754, 757 (1st Cir. 1978) (jury trial). In at least one state case, involving a plea bargain breached by the judge, disqualification was required. *Commonwealth v. Felder* 246 Pa. Super. 324, 339, 370 A.2d 1214, (1976) (two dissents on this point; trial had not yet occurred).

158. *See supra* note 155.

159. *See infra* note 170, and the accompanying text.

160. *See infra* notes 173–174, and the accompanying text.

161. *See infra* notes 171 and 174, and the accompanying text.

NOTES TO §4.6(m)

162. E.g., *Hanger v. United States*, 398 F.2d 91, 100–101 (8th Cir. 1968); *Westover v. United States*, 394 F.2d 164, 166–167 (9th Cir. 1968); *Coppedge v. United States*, 311 F.2d 128, 133 (App. D.C. 1962); *Noe v. Commonwealth*, 267 Ky. 607, 103 S.W.2d 104 (1937); *Day v. State*, 2 Md. App. 334, 234 A.2d 894 (1967); *Fry v. Bennett*, 28 N.Y. 324 (1863); *Dowell v. Hall*, 85 Okla. Crim. 92, 185 P.2d 232 (1947).

163. 393 F.2d 90, 91 (2d Cir. 1968) (sometimes cited as *United States v.Simon*, the name of a companion case).

164. *See infra* notes 165–167. *See Partin, supra* note 147, 552 F.2d at 638–639 (describing erosion of *Bryan* pronouncement).

165. E.g., *United States v. Newman*, 481 F.2d 222, 223 (2d Cir. 1973).

166. *Wolfson, supra* note 141, 396 F.2d at 126.

167. *DiLorenzo, supra* note 147, 429 F.2d at 220–221 ("absent special circumstances, judicial economy and calendaring demands often make it desirable that the same judge preside at seriatim trials of co-conspirators").

168. *See* E.D. N.Y. Local Rule 2(d)(2) (1977) and *United States v. Robin*, 553 F.2d 8, 9, n. 1 (2d Cir. 1977).

169. *See Robin, supra* note 168, at 9, n. 1.

170. *Walker v. State*, 84 So. 2d 383 (Ala. App. 1955); *Atlantic & Birmingham Railway Co. v. Mayor and City Council of Cordele*, 128 Ga. 293, 57 S.E. 493 (1907); *State in Interest of Sylvester*, 267 So.2d 585 (La. App. 1972). See *Peacock Records, Inc. v. Checker Records, Inc.*, 430 F.2d 85, 89 (7th Cir. 1970).

171. *Peacock Records, supra* note 170, 430 F.2d at 89; *In re Estate of Hupp*, 178 Kan. 672, 291 P.2d 428 (1955).

172. *See Robin, supra* note 168, 553 F.2d at 10

173. *Id.*

174. *Peacock Records, supra* note 170 ("findings by a trial judge unsupported by

the record are evidence that the judge has relied on extrajudicial sources in making such determinations indicating personal bias and prejudice"); *Estate of Hupp, supra* note 171.

175. E.g., Conn. Gen. Stat. §51–183c. *See State v. Hartley,* 75 Conn. 104, 52 A. 615 (1902). *Cf. Woodsmall v. State,* 181 Ind. 613, 105 N.E. 155 (1914) (statutory right to peremptory change of judge whenever judgment reversed and cause remanded for retrial, provided applicant files affidavit averring judge prejudiced and applicant therefore unable to have a fair trial).

176. E.g., *In re Federal Facilities Realty Trust,* 140 F. Supp. 522 (N.D. Ill. 1956); *Kelly v. New York, N.H. & H.R. Co.,* 139 F. Supp. 319 (D. Mass. 1956); *King v. Superior Court for Maricopa Co.,* 108 Ariz. 492, 502 P.2d 529, 530, 60 A.L.R.3d 172 (1972); *State v. Bohan,* 19 Kan. 28, 52 (1877).

177. *Walker v. State,* 241 Ark. 300, 663, 408 S.W.2d 905 (1966), *cert. denied and app. dism'd,* 386 U.S. 682 (1967); *State ex. rel. Schmidt v. Justice,* 237 So.2d 827 (Fla. App. 1970); *State v. Tawney,* 81 Kan. 162, 105 P. 618 (1909); *State v. Rini,* 153 La. 57, 95 So. 400 (1924), *error dism'd,* 263 U.S. 689 (1924); *Kolowich v. Wayne Circuit Judge,* 264 Mich. 668, 250 N.W. 875 (1933); *Dowell, supra* note 162. *See* Annot., 60 A.L.R.3d 176, 204–208 (1974). *See supra* notes 144, 145, 152, and 170, and the accompanying text.

178. *See Hamm v. Members of Board of Regents of State of Fla.,* 708 F.2d 647, 651 (11th Cir. 1983); *Whitehurst, supra* note 110, 592 F.2d at 838; *Davis, supra* note 24, 517 F.2d at 1051. *Cf. Calhoun v. Superior Court of San Diego Co.,* 51 Cal.2d 257, 331 P.2d 648 (In Bank 1958) (gratuitous expression of opinion required disqualification); *Keating v. Superior Court of City and County of San Francisco,* 45 Cal.2d 440, 289 P.2d 209 (In Bank 1955) (expression of opinion that party willfully testified falsely required disqualification).

NOTES TO §4.6(n)

179. E.g., *Heflin v. State,* 88 Ga. 151, 14 S.E. 112 (1891); *State v. Baldwin,* 178 N.C. 687, 100 S.E. 348, 10 A.L.R. 1112 (1919); *Slayton v. Commonwealth,* 85 Va. 371, 38 S.E.2d 485, 488–489 (1946).

180. E.g., *Kreling v. Superior Court for Los Angeles County,* 63 Cal. App.2d 353, 361–362, 146 P.2d 935, 939 (2d Dist. 1944).

NOTES TO §4.6(o)

181. E.g., *Laird, supra* note 92; *United States v. Bray,* 546 F.2d 851, 857 (10th Cir. 1976); *In re Grblny's Estate,* 147 Neb. 117, 22 N.W.2d 488, 495 (1946); *Judicial Inquiry Commission of West Virginia v. McGraw,* 299 S.E.2d 872 (W. Va. 1983).

182. *Antonello v. Wunsch,* 500 F.2d 1260, 1262 (10th Cir. 1974); *Deal v. Warner,* 369 F. Supp. 174, 177–178 (W.D. Mo. 1973).

NOTES TO §4.6(p)

183. E.g., *Ex Parte Terry,* 128 U.S. 289 (1888); *Fisher v. Pace,* 336 U.S. 155 (1949).

184. E.g., *Nilva v. United States*, 352 U.S. 385 (1957) (refusal to obey subpoenas *duces tecum*); *Cooke v. United States*, 267 U.S. 517, 536 (1925) (letter hand delivered to judge in chambers); *Turkington v. Municipal Court*, 85 Cal. App.2d 631, 193 P.2d 795 (1948) (publication); *La. Grange v. State*, 238 Ind. 689, 153 N.E.2d 593 (1958) (radio broadcast); *State ex. rel. Stanton v. Murray*, 231 Ind. 223, 108 N.E.2d 251 (1952) (newspaper article); *Skolnick v. State*, 397 N.E.2d 986, 995 (Ind. App. 3d Dist. 1979) (leaflets); *In re Merritt*, 391 So.2d 440 (La. 1980) (attorney-contemnor's failure to appear for trial). *But compare Blodgett v. Superior Court*, 210 Cal. 1, 290 Pac. 293, 72 A.L.R. 482 (1930) (filing of contemptuous brief with clerk of court held a direct contempt).

185. 343 U.S. 1, 19 (1952).

186. *Id.*, 343 U.S. at 9–11.

187. *Id.*, 343 U.S. at 11–13.

188. 348 U.S. 11 (1954).

189. 400 U.S. 455 (1971).

190. *Offutt, supra* note 188. *Accord: Taylor v. Hayes*, 418 U.S. 488, 501–503 (1974). *Cf. Johnson v. Mississippi*, 403 U.S. 212 (1971) (in addition to the alleged contempt, contemnor filed suit against judge to enjoin alleged discrimination in jury selection).

191. *Mayberry, supra* note 189 (vilification of judge); *United States v. Seale*, 461 F.2d 345, 351–352 (7th Cir. 1972) (same); *In re Dellinger*, 461 F.2d 389 (7th Cir. 1972) (same).

192. E.g., *Murchison, supra* note 20.

193. E.g., *Cooke, supra* note 184, 267 U.S. at 536–537. *See* F.R. Crim. Proc., R. 42.

194. E.g., *Cooke, supra* note 184, 267 U.S. at 539. *See* F.R. Crim. Proc., R. 42.

NOTES TO 4.7(a)

195. *See Hulme, supra* note 24, 493 P.2d at 545; and see *infra* notes 196 to 198 and the accompanying text. For an exhaustive review of the subject—almost a treatise—*see* the unreported opinion of Judge J. Raymond Kremer in *Rizzo v. Weiner*, C.P. Phila. Co., July Term, 1979, No. 623.

196. E.g., *In re Estate of Carlton*, 378 So.2d 1212, 1216–1221 (Fla. 1980) (stating procedure adopted by the court "is in accord with the great weight of authority").

197. E.g., Cal. Code of Civ. Proc. §170(e) (disqualification motion to be decided by a different judge, agreed on by parties or designated by chairman of judicial council).

198. E.g., Colo. Rev. Stat. §16–6–201(3); *People v. District Court for Third Judicial Distr.*, 560 P.2d 828, 832 (Colo. En Banc 1977); *Stephens v. Stephens*, 249 Ga. 700, 292 S.E.2d 689 (1982).

NOTES TO §4.7(b)

199. 28 U.S.C. §144; Kan. Stat. Ann. §20-311d

200. *Berger v. United States*, 255 U.S. 22, 36 (1921) (affidavit must be by a party and not counsel, but may be on information and belief; and, if legally sufficient and

accompanied by a certificate of good faith by counsel, facts averred may not be disproved, and judge must be replaced); *Wolfson, supra* note 141.

201. *Frey v. Inter-State Savings and Loan Ass'n. of Kansas City*, 226 Kan. 419, 601 P.2d 671 (1979); *Hulme, supra* note 24, 493 P.2d at 545.

NOTES TO §4.8

202. *See* 46 Am. Jur. 2d, Judges, §225 and n. 19, and the accompanying text; 48A C.J.S., Judges, §103a and n. 97, and the accompanying text.

203. *See infra* note 231, and the accompanying text. *See also* Annot., 24 A.L.R.4th 870–949 (1983); Annot., 27 A.L.R.4th 597–666 (1984).

204. *See* 48A C.J.S., Judges §104, nn. 18 and 19, and the accompanying text; and *infra* notes 220 and 221, and the accompanying text.

205. E.g., *Re Marriage of Hopkins*, 74 Cal. App.3d 591, 598–599, 141 Cal. Rptr. 597, 601 (2d Dist. 1977); *Murray v. Commonwealth*, 473 S.W.2d 152 (Ky. 1971); *State v. Benson*, 633 S.W.2d 200, 202 (Mo. App. 1982); *Williams & Mauseth Ins. Brokers, Inc. v. Chapple*, 11 Wash. App. 623, 524 P.2d 431 (1974) (nonjury trial). *See Moore v. State*, 568 S.W.2d 632, 635 (Tenn. Crim. 1978). *See* Annot., 27 A.L.R.4th 597, 616–619 (1984); Annot., 24 A.L.R.4th 870, 887–891, 895 (1983); 48A C.J.S. Judges, §164, nn. 20–29, 35–56.5

206. E.g., Pretrial motions to disqualify were denied in the following cases because preceded by pretrial rulings involving issues pertinent to merits, which rulings are set forth in parentheses: *Reichert v. General Ins. Co.*, 68 Cal.2d 822, 69 Cal. Rptr. 321, 442 P.2d 377, 385–386 (1968) (disqualification motion followed ruling on demurrer to complaint); *People v. Norcutt* 44 Ill.2d 256, 255 N.E.2d 442, 446 (1970); *Oregon State Bar v. Wright*, 280 Or. 693, 573 P.2d 283, 290 (1977) (preliminary injunction; court applied statute precluding disqualification motion after ruling on any motion other than motion for extension). *See* Annot., 27 A.L.R.4th 597, 609–613 (1984).

207. E.g., *Baker v. State*, 52 Ala. App. 699, 296 So.2d 794, 795–796 (1974); *Estate of Wakefield*, 72 Ill. App.2d 128, 221 N.E.2d 788, 789 (1966); *Indianapolis v. L.& G. Realty & Construction Co.*, 132 Ind. App. 17, 70 N.E.2d 908 (960).

208. *Indianapolis, supra* note 207, 170 N.E.2d at 911–912; *State v. Light*, 484 S.W.2d 275 (Mo. 1972); *McNeil v. Continental Casualty Co.*, 244 So.2d 693, 697–698 (La. App. 1971).

209. E.g., *People v. McGlothen*, 26 Ill.2d 392, 196 N.E.2d 319 (1962).

210. E.g., *Pure Milk Products Cooperative v. National Farmers Organization*, 64 Wis.2d 241, 219 N.W.2d 565, 569 (1974). *Cf. Reichert, supra* note 206, 68 Cal.2d at 838, 69 Cal. Rptr. at 330, 442 P.2d at 385–386 (applying California statute precluding disqualification after commencement of hearing on any issue of fact).

211. E.g., *Alameda Conservation Ass'n v. Alameda*, 264 Cal. App.2d 284, 70 Cal. Rptr. 264 (1st Dist. 1968), *cert. denied*, 394 U.S. 906 (1969).

212. *See supra* note 206.

213. E.g., *Wakefield, supra* note 207; *State v. Norman*, 24 Wash. App. 811, 603 P.2d 1280 (1979). *Compare State v. Garcia*, 114 Ariz. 317, 560 P.2d 1224 (rule preserving right to disqualify for cause until ten days after discovery of ground for disqualification even if judge has ruled; peremptory motion must be filed before judge has ruled).

214. E.g., *Sierra Vista v. Cochise Enterprises, Inc.*, 128 Ariz. 467, 626 P.2d 1099 (1979) (peremptory challenge; rule of court governed waiver question); *Marsin v. Udall*, 78 Ariz. 309, 279 P.2d 721 (1955); *Howarth v. Howarth*, 47 Ill. App.2d 177, 197 N.E.2d 736 (1964).

215. E.g., *State v. Cline*, 69 N.M. 305, 366 P.2d 441 (1961); *Re Farrell*, 55 Ore. App. 897, 640 P.2d 652, 654 (1982); *Burns v. Norwesco Marine*, 13 Wash. App. 414, 535 P.2d 860 (1975) (based on statute).

216. E.g., *Vallejo, supra* note 40; *Fry v. Tucker*, 146 Tex. 18, 202 S.W.2d 218 (1947); *Postal Mutual Indemnity, supra* note 54. See 46 Am. Jur. 2d, Judges, §225, n. 20, and the accompanying text; and 48 A. C.J.S., Judges, §103a, nn. 99–100, and the accompanying text. *See also infra* notes 232–238, and the accompanying text.

217. E.g., *Broward County Port Authority v. Ake*, 111 Fla. 132, 150 So. 273 (1933) (disqualification on ground of interest).

218. E.g., *Norton v. Inhabitants of Fayette*, 134 Me. 468, 188 A. 281 (1936) (disqualification by reason of former representation of plaintiff by judge as counsel in same case).

219. E.g., *Hing Yee v. Chung Wa*, 6 Hawaii 304 (1881); *Oakley v. Aspinall*, 3 N.Y. 547 (1850); *Casterella v. Casterella*, 65 A.D.2d 614, 409 N.Y.S.2d 548 (2d Dep't 1978); *Jouett v. Gunn*, 13 Tex. Civ. App. 84, 35 S.W. 194 (1896). *See Seabrook v. First National Bank of Port Lavaca*, 171 S.W. 247, 248 (Tex. Civ. App. 1915).

220. E.g., Ala. Code Ann. §12–1–12 (all statutory grounds); Alaska Stat. §22.20.020(b) (family relationship or prior representation of either party within two years); Ark. Stat. Ann. §22.13 (all statutory grounds); Conn. Gen. Stat. §51–39 same); Fla. Stat. Ann. §38.03 (judge a material witness; or family relationship to party, interested nonparty, or attorney); Ga. Code Ann. §15–1–8(a) (former status as counsel in the proceeding, or as judge, when his ruling or decision is subject of review); Iowa Code Ann. §605.17 (status as party, interest, family relationship, or former representation); Miss. Const. art. 6, §165 (relationship to party by affinity or consanguinity, or interest in any cause); Mo. Stat. Ann. §476.180 (interest in suit, family relationship to either party, or former status as counsel in the proceeding); Neb. Rev. Stat. §24–315 (status as party, interest in cause, family relationship to party, or attorney in cause or co-partner of attorney in cause or former attorney for either party in cause); N.J.R.R. 4 (alleged contempt involving disrespect to or criticism of judge); N.J.R.R. 3:8–2(d) (same); N.Y. Judic. Law art. 2, §14 (ownership of stock or securities of corporate party); Okla. Stat. Ann. tit. 20, §1401 (any statutory ground); Ore. Rev. Stat. §14.210 (family relationship to party or attorney, or former status as attorney for party). *See Georgia Power*, supra note 58.

221. *See supra* note 220 as to Alabama, Connecticut, Florida, New York, and Oklahoma.

222. *See supra* note 220 as to Alabama, Arkansas, Connecticut, Florida, Georgia, Iowa, Mississippi (judges must also consent), Missouri, Nebraska, New York, Oklahoma, and Oregon.

223. *See Adams v. State*, 296 Ark. 548, 601 S.W.2d 001 (1986)

221. *Reilly by Reilly v. Southeastern Penna. Transportation Authority*, 479 A.2d 973, 988–989 (1984).

NOTES TO §4.9

225. E.g., *Kirkland v. Kirkland*, 146 Ga. 347, 91 S.E. 119 (1916); *Bank of Marlinton v. Pocohontas Development Co.*, 88 W. Va. 414, 106 S.E. 881 (1921). *See* 46 Am. Jur. 2d, Judges, § 233.

226. E.g., *Hawley v. Baldwin*, 19 Conn. 585 (1849); *Kells v. Davidson*, 102 Fla. 684, 136 So. 450 (1931). *See* 46 Am. Jur. 2d, Judges, §233.

NOTES TO §4.10

227. *See Carr v. Duhme*, 167 Ind. 76, 78 N.E. 322, 323 (1906) and 46 Am. Jur. 2d, Judges, §231.

228. E.g., *see Sexton v. Barry*, 233 F.2d 220, 224–225 (6th Cir. 1956), *cert. denied*, 352 U.S. 870 (1956) and 46 Am. Jur. 2d, Judges, §231.

229. *See Sexton v. Barry*, *supra* note 228, 233 F.2d at 224–225 and 46 Am Jur. 2d., Judges, §231.

230. *See supra Carr*, note 227, 78 N.E. at 323.

231. *See* 46 Am. Jur. 2d, Judges, §231, n. 6, and the accompanying text; and 48A C.J.S., Judges, §103a, n. 97 and the accompanying text.

232. *Id.*, nn. 8 and 9, and the accompanying text.

233. E.g., *Horton v. Howard*, 70 Mich. 642, 44 N.W. 1112 (1890) (citing cases). *See* 46 Am. Jur. 2d, Judges, §231, n. 8, and the accompanying text; 48A C.J.S., Judges, 158 (citing many cases), n. 42. and the accompanying text.

234. E.g., *In re Hudson*, 301 Mich. 77, 3 N.W.2d 17 (1942); *See Bliss v. Caille Brothers Co. (Bliss v. Taylor)*, 149 Mich 601, 113 N.W. 317, 319 (1907); *Edwards v. Russell*, 21 Wend. 63 (N.Y. 1839); *Fry v. Tucker*, 146 Tex. 18, 202 S.W.2d 218 (1947).

235. *Bliss*, *supra* note 234; *Fry*, *supra* note 234.

236. *Bliss*, *supra* note 234; *Fry*, *supra* note 234.

237. E.g., *Horton*, *supra* note 233; *Gaer v. Bank of Baker*, 111 Mont. 204, 107 P.2d 877, 879 (1940). *See Bliss*, *supra* note 234, 113 N.W. at 319.

238. E.g., *Hines v. Hussey*, 45 Ala. 496 (1871) (statute permitted express waiver); *State v. Hartley*, 75 Conn. 104, 52 A. 615 (1902) (same); *Wood v. Clarke*, 188 Ga. 697, 4 S.E.2d 659, 124 A.L.R. 1077 (1939) (statute permitted waiver).

239. *See* 48A C.J.S. §158, n. 41, and cases cited, and the accompanying text.

240. E.g., *see Wooley v. Superior Court for Stanislaus Co.*, 19 C.A.2d 611, 66 P.2d 680, 687 (1937) (disqualification on ground of interest, family relationship to a party or attorney for a party, or former representation of a party, when established, renders prior rulings void, but bias merely renders future rulings voidable). *See Adams v. State*, 601 S.W.2d at 884; 48A C.J.S. §158, nn. 50–51, and the accompanying text. *Cf.* 46 Am. Jur. 2d, Judges §224, nn. 1–4.

241. Fla. Stat. Ann. §§38.06 to 38.08.

5

Political Activity

5.1 HISTORICAL BACKGROUND IN THE UNITED STATES

Broadly defined, political activity by judges includes both elective activity designed to influence or effect the election or selection of judges, legislators, governmental officers, and executives, and lobbying activity to influence legislative or regulatory action. Until well into this century, there was no established rule against either type of political activity, and even sitting U.S. Supreme Court Justices were wont to engage in both elective[1] and lobbying[2] activities.

Judges have also, until at least the last several decades, engaged in a wide variety of extrajudicial activities of a governmental nature. These have included serving on special committees, commissions, boards, or tribunals appointed by the legislative or executive branches to investigate and make recommendations as to legislative or administrative problems, or to conduct and report on fact-finding investigations.[3] During the early years of the republic, judges even held cabinet offices or served as governors or ambassadors, while continuing to act as judges.[4] Judges from time to time also ran for nonjudicial elective office without first resigning their judicial positions.[5]

Since 1800, the degree of political involvement has been gradually lessening and appears to have reached its nadir in recent years. Prior to the adoption of the American Bar Association Canons of Judicial Ethics in 1924, reduction of judicial involvement in politics and related activities was effected principally through the leadership of certain judges and by a gradual change in judicial behavior, rather than by the adoption of statutes, rules, or codes of ethics. These changes in judicial behavior followed and were perhaps to some extent attributable to the widespread public and congressional criticism of the blatant activities of several U.S. Supreme Court Justices prior to 1820.[6] Although United States Supreme Court Justices continued to accept special committee memberships until well after the middle of this century,[7] they did cease holding cabinet positions and ambassadorships.[8] Similarly, the practice of judges leaving the bench before running for elective nonjudicial office gradually became firmly established after U.S. Supreme Court Justice Hughes resigned from the Court in 1916 to run for president.[9] Interestingly, Hughes did not resign as governor of New York until five months after he was appointed to the U.S. Supreme Court.[10]

The strong opposition of Chief Justices White, Taft, and Stone to even special, temporary memberships on policy-oriented commissions and committees[11] undoubtedly played a major role in the decline of this type of extrajudicial activity.[12]

In 1924 and 1933, the developing sentiment against political and extra-judicial activity by judges was finally codified by the American Bar Association in the form of the ABA Canons of Judicial Ethics. The Canons were first adopted by the American Bar Association in 1924 and were supplemented in 1933 by amendments adding Canons 28 and 30.[13] Thereafter, no less than forty-three states adopted these Canons, at times with modifications.[14]

Succinctly summarized, Canons 28 and 30 generally forbade judges from making political speeches, making or soliciting party contributions, publicly endorsing candidates for political office, participating in party conventions, acting as party leaders or members of party committees, making promises of conduct in office appealing to the appointing or electing power, announcing conclusions of law on disputed issues to secure class support, giving the impression they would administer justice discriminatorily, or becoming a candidate for nonjudicial office without first resigning as judge.[15]

An additional factor that has undoubtedly contributed to the development of stricter standards of judicial conduct has been partisan conflict over judicial nominations by the chief executive, with nominees being attacked by the party out of power on the ground of alleged ethical transgressions. Illustrations include the nomination of Justice Fortas as Chief Justice of the United States, which was challenged on the ground of extrajudicial activities, including advising the president;[16] and the nomination of Circuit Judge Haynsworth to the Supreme Court, which was attacked on the ground he failed to disqualify himself when his stockholdings gave rise to alleged conflicts of interest.[17] Soon after these epic clashes, the ABA drafted and, on August 16, 1972, adopted the Code of Judicial Conduct,[18] which has since also been adopted, with varying revisions, by many state supreme courts.[19]

The Code of Judicial Conduct constitutes a greatly revised and expanded version of the earlier Canons of Judicial Ethics. As will be demonstrated in some detail in §5.3, *infra*, it remedies various deficiencies and ambiguities in the Canons. Perhaps its most notable contribution is the rule established by Canon 7B prohibiting all candidates for judicial office from personally soliciting contributions and public endorsements. Candidates are, however, permitted to establish campaign committees to seek contributions and endorsements.[20] Another of the Code's important contributions is a prohibition of promises of future conduct (other than to faithfully and impartially perform the duties of the office) and statements on pending legal issues. Canon 7B(1)(c) bars these pronouncements even if they do not create an impression of probable future discrimination in favor of the candidate's supporters.[21] A third significant contribution, also contained in Canon 7B(1)(c), is a prohibition of campaign misrepresentations by a candidate as to his own qualifications, record, or conduct.[22] Similarly, misrepresentations as to an opponent's qualifications, record, and conduct are impliedly prohibited by a catchall prohibition in Canon 7B(1)(c) of the Code,[23] relating to misrepresentations as to any "other fact."[24] Finally, Canon 7A(4) of the Code contains a blanket prohibition of all political activity by judges not previously dealt with by Canon 7A, except for political activity on behalf of measures to improve the law, the legal system, or the administration of justice.

5.2 LIMITATIONS IMPOSED BY CONSTITUTIONAL AND STATUTORY PROVISIONS

Many states have constitutional or statutory provisions forbidding judges from also holding any nonjudicial public office.[25] Some of these provisions merely prohibit judges from simultaneously holding judicial and nonjudicial public office, without requiring a judge's resignation before seeking nonjudicial office.[27] Others,[27] and Canon 7A(3) of the ABA Code as adopted in many states,[28] require judges to resign before running for nonjudicial office.

Despite their drastic nature, constitutional provisions requiring judges to resign before running for nonjudicial office have been held not to violate the equal protection clause of the Fourteenth Amendment[29] and, in the case of judges seeking to run for Congress, the federal qualifications clause, Article I, Section 2, Clause 2 of the U.S. Constitution, which prescribes the qualifications for congressional office.[30] These provisions also have been construed as not permitting the judge to take a mere leave of absence while running for another office.[31] The California constitution and the Idaho Code of Judicial Conduct, however, expressly provide that a judge may take a leave of absence without pay while running for nonjudicial office.[32] Similarly, New Mexico permits the judge to take a leave of absence without pay pending the results of the nominating process or until after any primary but requires immediate resignation once a judge has been nominated.[33]

In a number of states, a constitutional or statutory provision prohibits, or formerly prohibited, judges from holding nonjudicial office during the term of their judicial office.[34] When these provisions have been considered relative to a state court judge who sought to run for U.S. Senator or Representative before expiration of his judicial term of office and who had resigned if elected (or whose term would expire before commencement of the congressional term), they have been invalidated as violative of the federal qualifications clause.[35]

In many states, constitutional provisions also prohibit judges from holding office in any political party or organization.[36] Some of these provisions also prohibit judges from taking part in any political campaign,[37] but at least one expressly exempts the judge's own campaign for reelection or retention.[38] Various of these provisions go even further and prohibit judges from contributing to any political party or candidate for political office.[39]

In Florida, where elections for judicial office are nonpartisan,[40] a comprehensive statute regulates political activities by or on behalf of judicial candidates and imposes criminal penalties for violations.[41] Prohibited activities include: (1) participation in any partisan political activities other than personally registering as a member of a party and voting in that party's primary; (2) campaigning as a member of a political party; (3) publicly representing or advertising himself as a member of any political party; (4) endorsing any candidate; (5) making political speeches other than in his own behalf; (6) making contributions to political party funds; (7) accepting contributions from any political party; (8) soliciting contributions for any political party; (9) accepting or retaining a place on any political party committee; (10) making any contribution to any person, group, or organization for its endorsement; (11) agreeing to pay all or any part of any advertisement sponsored by any person, group, or organization endorsing the candidate's candidacy.[42] Candidates for judicial office may, however, accept contributions, but may incur only such expenses as are authorized by law and must accurately record and report their contributions and expenses.[43] Finally, political parties are not permitted to endorse, support, or assist any candidate for judicial office.[44] This prohibition was, however, held to violate the First Amendment insofar as it prohibited political parties from endorsing candidates for election to judicial office, in *Concerned Democrats of Florida v. Reno*.[45]

5.3 LIMITATIONS IMPOSED BY THE CANONS OF JUDICIAL ETHICS AND THEIR SUCCESSOR, THE CODE OF JUDICIAL ETHICS

The ABA Canons of Judicial Ethics made a significant contribution to the regulation of political and other extrajudicial activities. Canon 28 contained a general ban on partisan political activities by judges. In addition, it also prohibited several specific partisan political activities, including the making of political speeches, the making or soliciting of payments of assessments or contributions to party coffers, the public endorsement of candidates for political office and participation in their conventions, serving on any party committee, and acting as party leader. However, when securing office required that a judge be nominated and elected as a candidate of a political party, Canon 28 permitted the candidate to attend and speak at political gatherings and to make campaign contributions to his party. Similarly, Canon 24 prohibited judges from accepting inconsistent duties, and Canon 30 required them to resign before becoming a candidate for any nonjudicial office. Canon 30 also partially regulated campaign activities by prohibiting various types of conduct by judicial candidates, including the following: (a) promises of conduct in office that appealed to the cupidity or prejudices of the electorate; (b) statements in advance on disputed issues to secure voter support; (c) actions creating the impression that, if elected, the candidate would administer his office with bias, partiality, or improper discrimination; (d) conduct that might tend to provide a reasonable suspicion that the judge was using the power or prestige of his office to promote his candidacy or his party; (e) permitting others to do anything on his behalf that would reasonably lead to suspicion of bias, partiality, or improper discrimination.

Canon 7 of the Code of Judicial Conduct, adopted by the ABA in 1972, reiterates, revises, and adds to the political activity provisions of Canons 24, 28, and 30 of the Canons of Judicial Ethics. The revisions and additions include, among others, the following: (a) expanding the prohibition against publicly endorsing candidates for "political office" by prohibiting public endorsement of candidates for "public office";[46] (b) clarifying the prohibition against "political speeches" by prohibiting "speeches for a political organization or candidate";[47] (c) extending the prohibition against accepting or retaining a place on any party committee or acting as party leader by substituting a prohibition forbidding judges to act "as a leader" or hold "any office in a political organization";[48] (d) enlarging the prohibitions against the making or solicitations of contributions to party funds by adding a prohibition of the making or solicitation of any contribution to or for any candidate;[49] (e) broadening the prohibition against "participation in conventions" by prohibiting attendance at political gatherings;[50] (f) adding a prohibition of the purchase of tickets for political party dinners or other functions;[51] (g) clarifying the privileges accorded candidates in partisan judicial elections by expressly entitling them to attend and speak at political gatherings and to make contributions to their party and extending these privileges to candidates in nonpartisan elections and to candidates running in primary elections and making it clear that these privileges are available to both challengers and incumbent judges;[52] (h) inserting a wide ranging prohibition against judges "engaging in any other political activity except on behalf of measures to improve the law, the legal system, or the administration of justice";[53] (i) expanding the prohibitions against promises concerning conduct in office "appealing to the cupidity or prejudices of the appointing or electing power," against prior announcement of "conclusions of law on disputed issues to secure class support," by substituting prohibitions against "pledges or promises of conduct in office other than the faithful and impartial performance of the duties of the office," and against the announcement by the candidate of "his views on disputed legal or political issues;[54] (j) adding a prohibition against any candidate's misrepresenting "his identity, qualifications, present position, *or other fact*" (emphasis added);[55] (k) adding a prohibition forbidding a candidate for elective office to solicit personally either funds or public endorsements for his own campaign, coupled with dispensations permitting him to do so indirectly through campaign committees, and a further dispensation extending the latter privileges to candidates in noncompetitive retention elections when their candidacy has drawn active opposition;[56] (l) clarifying the provision requiring judges who are candidates for nonjudicial office to resign by expressly making it applicable to nonpartisan primaries (not expressly covered by prior Canon 30), as well as party primaries and general elections (expressly covered by Canon 30).[57]

Canons 4 and 5 of the Code of Judicial Conduct deal with quasi-judicial conduct and extrajudicial conduct much more specifically than Canon 24 of the old Canons of Judicial Ethics, which merely prohibited "inconsistent duties." For example, various U.S. Supreme Court Justices were, at one time, disposed to lobby, consult with, or advise members of the executive branches or legislative branches with respect to legislation or administrative or regulatory policies or regulations.[58] This type of activity is proscribed by Canon 4B of the Code of Judicial Conduct, which provides that a judge

may appear at a public hearing before an executive or legislative body or official on matters concerning the law, the legal system, and the administration of justice, and he may otherwise consult with an executive or legislative body or official, but only on matters concerning the administration of justice.

Similarly, Canon 5G specifically precludes service by judges on governmental committees or commissions, which was common up to a few decades ago,[59] by providing that:

A judge should not accept appointment to a governmental committee, commission, or other position that is concerned with issues of fact or policy on matters other than the improvement of the law, the legal system, or the administration of justice.

Finally, Canon 6 of the Code sanctions compensation (plus expense reimbursement) for nonprohibited extrajudicial activities if reasonable in amount and emanating from a source that does not give the appearance of influencing the judge in his judicial duties or otherwise give the appearance of impropriety.

5.4 THE PROVISIONS IN CANON 7 REGULATING SPECIFIC POLITICAL ACTIVITIES, AS ADOPTED IN THE VARIOUS JURISDICTIONS

a. Introduction

The states in which all, or a large number of, judges are selected in partisan elections naturally grant their judges the greatest freedom to engage in political activities. Judges chosen in nonpartisan elections are generally granted less freedom to engage in political activities, and judges who are selected on a nonelective basis, i.e., a commission plan supplemented by noncompetitive retention elections, have the least freedom to engage in political activities.[60]

A comparison of the Canon 7 provisions in each group of states employing a particular principal method of initially selecting major court judges follows. For this purpose, "initial selection" means selection of judges at the beginning of a term of judicial office, as distinguished both from appointments to fill vacancies occurring during a term of office and from noncompetitive retention elections or determinations.[61] The term "principal method" of initial selection means the selection method used in initially selecting judges for a majority of the appellate and general jurisdiction trial courts.

Thus classified, the groups of jurisdictions enacting the Code (District of Columbia and all states other than Illinois, Montana, Rhode Island, Wisconsin, and Maryland[62]) are as follows: partisan election jurisdictions (13): Alabama, Arkansas, Indiana, Kansas, Missouri, Mississippi, New Mexico, New York, North Carolina, Pennsylvania, Tennessee, Texas, and West Virginia; Nonpartisan election jurisdictions (17): Arizona, California, Florida, Georgia, Idaho, Kentucky, Louisiana, Michigan, Minnesota, Nevada, North Dakota, Ohio, Oklahoma, Oregon, South Dakota, Utah, and Washington; commission plan jurisdictions (10): Alaska, Colorado, Delaware, District of Columbia, Hawaii, Iowa, Massachusetts, Nebraska, Vermont, and Wyoming; legislative selection jurisdictions (2): Connecticut and Virginia; executive selection jurisdictions (4): Maine, New Hampshire, New Jersey, and South Carolina.[63]

b. Positions of Leadership in Political Organizations

Canon 7A(1)(a) of the ABA Code prohibits all judges and judicial candidates from acting as a leader of, or holding any office in, any political organization." Canon 7A so provides in forty one of the forty-six Code jurisdictions listed in §5.4(a), including: ten of the thirteen partisan election states; fourteen of the seventeen nonpartisan election states; all of the ten commission plan jurisdictions; both legislative selection states; and all four executive selection states.[65] Three partisan election states[66] and two non-partisan election states have not adopted this provision.[67] The Codes in these states also omit ABA Canon 7A(4)'s prohibition of "any other political activities by judges," which, if adopted, might be construed as prohibiting the holding of leadership positions or offices in political parties. ABA Canon 2A, which has been adopted as part of the Code in each of these five states, does provide that a judge should "conduct himself at all times in a manner that promotes public confidence in the . . . impartiality of the judiciary." This could conceivably be construed as prohibiting judges from holding leadership positions or other offices in a political organization.

In three of the five non-Code states, political leadership activities are expressly forbidden by a court rule embodying the substance of Canon 7A(1)(a)[68] and are necessarily precluded by a provision of the Wisconsin Canons of Judicial Ethics prohibiting judges from being political party members[69] and a provision in Montana criticizing "a judge who becomes the active promoter of the interests of one party as against another."[70]

c. Speeches on Behalf of Political Organizations or Candidates and Public Endorsement of a Candidate for Public Office

Canon 7A(1)(b) of the ABA Code of Judicial Ethics provides that a judge or judicial candidate should not make political speeches or publicly endorse a candidate for office.[71] The states that utilize commission plans, legislative selection, and executive selection all ban speeches and endorsements under their version of Canon 7. The same is true of a majority of the partisan election and nonpartisan election states. In fact, forty-three of the forty-six Code jurisdictions have included these prohibitions in adopting Canon 7.[72]

A few states, although generally prohibiting judges and judicial candidates from speaking on behalf of or publicly endorsing candidates for public office, permit this type of conduct on behalf of other candidates for judicial office, either by expressly authorizing such speeches or endorsements[73] or by confining the prohibitions to speeches or endorsements on behalf of candidates for nonjudicial office.[74]

d. Solicitation of Funds for a Political Organization or Candidate

ABA Canon 7A(1)(c) provides that a judge or judicial candidate should not solicit funds for a political organization or candidate. This prohibition has been adopted without substantial change by ten of thirteen partisan election states,[75] twelve of seventeen nonpartisan election states,[76] all ten commission plan jurisdictions,[77] all four executive selection states,[78] and both legislative selection states.[79]

e. Contributions or Assessments Paid by Judges or Candidates to Political Organizations or Candidates

(i)Introduction

ABA Canon 7A(1)(c) provides that a judge or judicial candidate for judicial office "should not pay an assessment or make a contribution to a political organization or candidate." ABA Canon 7A(2) negates a portion of this prohibition, by providing that "a judge holding an office filled by public election between competing candidates, or a candidate for such office" may, insofar as permitted by law, contribute to a political party or organization.[80] Thus, any version of the Code that contains both of the foregoing provisions permits elective judges and candidates to contribute to political organizations but forbids them to contribute to candidates. Judges holding nonelective positions and judges originally appointed to such positions and retained or seeking retention in noncompetitive retention elections are not permitted to contribute either to political organizations or candidates.

Since contributions to political organizations and contributions to candidates are treated differently by the ABA code, they should be discussed separately.

(ii) Contributions to Political Organizations

The system prohibiting contributions to political organizations by non-elective judges and candidates but expressly permitting such contributions to be made by elective judges, has been adopted in seventeen states: seven of thirteen partisan election states,[81] four of seventeen nonpartisan election states,[82] five of ten commission plan jurisdictions,[83] and one of four executive selection states.[84] Neither of the two legislative selection states has adopted this provision.[85]

In three partisan election states[86] and three nonpartisan election states,[87] contributions to political organizations by judges, whether elective or non-elective, and by elective candidates appear to be permitted. Canon 7 in these states does not prohibit contributions or, more generally, "other political activities," except that in one of these states, Idaho, Canon 7A prohibits "political activities inappropriate to the judicial office." In another of these states, Michigan, all judges and candidates (whether elective or nonelective) are expressly permitted to contribute to political parties.

In Arizona and California, contributions by judges (whether elective or nonelective) and elective candidates to political organizations and candidates are forbidden only if the contributions are in excess of specified individual and aggregate maximums and, therefore, appear to be impliedly permitted when below the maximums.[88] In Ohio, Canon 7A(2) seems, by implication, to permit judges who are not candidates for reelection to contribute to their political party by providing that "a candidate for judicial office may not contribute to his political party in the year in which he is a candidate for reelection.[89]

Finally, in seven nonpartisan election states,[90] five commission plan states,[91] three executive selection states,[92] and two legislative selection states,[93] a general prohibition against contributions by judges (but not candidates) to political organizations is not accompanied by any permissive language authorizing elective judges to make contributions to political organizations or parties. In one of these states, Washington, contributions by elective judges or candidates to political parties or organizations are expressly prohibited.

(iii) Contributions by Judges and Judicial Candidates to Candidates for Public Office

Less consideration need be given to contributions by judges and candidates to candidates for public office, since ABA Canon 7A(1)(c) prohibits all such contributions, and ABA Canon 7A(2) does not authorize them. Consequently, in all the states that have adopted the ABA position on this issue, all such contributions are prohibited.[94]

Twenty-nine of the forty-six Code jurisdictions, consisting of six partisan election states,[95] seven nonpartisan election states,[96] ten commission plan jurisdictions,[97] four executive selection states,[98] and two legislative selection states,[99] expressly forbid contributions by judges or judicial candidates to candidates for public office, irrespective of whether the donee is seeking judicial or nonjudicial office. In one partisan election state[100] and four nonpartisan election states,[101] contributions by judges or judicial candidates to nonjudicial candidates are expressly prohibited, either totally[102] or whenever they exceed specified amounts[103] or under specified circumstances.[104] Contributions to judicial candidates in the latter five states are, however, either expressly permitted[105] or impliedly permitted since the expressed prohibition applies only to nonjudicial candidates.[106] In one partisan election state, contributions by judges or judicial candidates to candidates are expressly permitted, irrespective of whether the candidate is seeking judicial or nonjudicial office.[107] In three partisan election states[108] and four nonpartisan election states,[109] contributions by judges or judicial candidates to candidates for any public office appear to be impliedly permitted, since there is no express prohibition of contributions and no prohibition of "other political activities." In two partisan election states[110] and two nonpartisan election states,[111] which have no prohibition of contributions to candidates for public office, there is a prohibition of "other political activities." Consequently, the legality of contributions in these states appears open.

f. Attendance at Political Gatherings

ABA Canon 7A(1)(c) prohibits judges and judicial candidates from attending political gatherings; but Canon 7A(2) partially countermands this prohibition (and several other Canon 7A(1)(c) prohibitions) and authorizes attendance at political gatherings (and several other types of political activity) by elective judges and judicial candidates. Nonelective judges remain fully subject to all Canon 7A(1)(c) prohibitions and are forbidden to attend political gatherings.

In the forty-six Code jurisdictions, attendance by judges or candidates at political gatherings (i) is specifically prohibited as to all judges and candidates in one nonpartisan election state,[112] four commission plan states,[113] three executive selection states,[114] and two legislative selection states;[115] (ii) is neither specifically prohibited nor specifically authorized, but may nevertheless be prohibited by means of a catchall prohibition of "any other political activity," in two nonpartisan election states[116] and one commission plan state;[117] (iii) is expressly prohibited as to nonelective judges and candidates, but expressly authorized as to elective judges and candidates in six partisan election states,[118] six nonpartisan election states,[119] four commission plan states,[120] and one executive selection state;[121] (iv) is expressly permitted in one partisan election state as to judges and candidates elected by partisan election and is expressly permited in two nonpartisan election states as to elective judges and candidates, but may be impliedly prohibited for other judges and candidates by the provision prohibiting "any other political activity" by judges;[122] (v) is specifically authorized for all judges and judicial candidates without limitation in two partisan election states[123] and two nonpartisan election states;[124] (vi) is specifically authorized as to elective judges and candidates, and is probably permissible as to nonelective judges (because not specifically prohibited and because there is no catchall prohibition of "any other political activity"), in one partisan election state[125] and one nonpartisan election state;[126] (vii) is probably permissible for all judges and candidates in three partisan election states[127] and three nonpartisan election states,[128] in which not only are there no provisions specifically prohibiting or authorizing attendance at political gatherings, but also there is no catchall prohibition against "any other political activity."

Even in states where judges and judicial candidates may attend political gatherings under Canon 7A(2) and, *a fortiori*, in states where Canon 7 is silent on the subject, such conduct would violate prohibitions against judges endorsing candidates for public office if the appearance could be fairly construed as constituting an endorsement of a candidate. This possibility was specifically recognized in the Commentary on California Canon 7A(1), which states:

> Although attendance at political gatherings is not prohibited, any such attendance should be restricted in such a manner as not to constitute a public endorsement of a cause or candidate otherwise prohibited by these Canons.

g. Speeches by a Candidate for Elective Judicial Office on His Own Behalf at Political Gatherings

ABA Canon 7A(2) authorizes a candidate for elective judicial office, including an incumbent judge, to speak on his own behalf at political gatherings when he is a candidate for election or re-election.

In approximately twenty-seven Code states, a candidate for elective judicial office is expressly authorized, generally by a provision substantially identical to Canon 7A(2) to speak at political gatherings. These states include eight partisan election states,[129] thirteen nonpartisan election states,[130] five commission plan jurisdictions,[131] and one executive selection state.[132]

At least three more states should be added to the category just described, since Canon 7 in those states is clearly broad enough to authorize speeches by a candidate in support of his own campaign. In Alabama, Canon 7A(1) states that it is desirable that judicial candidates endeavor not to engage in campaign activities on behalf of candidates for other nonjudicial offices and, thus, clearly sanctions campaign activities such as campaign speeches in support of judicial candidates. Similarly, in Kansas, Canon 7A(2) provides that a candidate for a judicial office selected in a partisan election "may participate on his own behalf in political activity." Finally, in New Mexico, Canon 7A provides that judges "may participate in the political process to the same extent as provided by law for other citizens," provided that he does so in strict conformity with enumerated provisions of the Code.

Another group of fifteen states also appears to permit judicial candidates to speak on their own behalf, not expressly, but by a failure to prohibit such activity. These states include two partisan election states,[133] three nonpartisan election states,[134] five commission plan states,[135] three executive selection states,[136] and two legislative selection states.[137] Although it could be argued that in twelve of these states[138] the prohibition against judges and judicial candidates speaking on behalf of "political organizations or candidates" bars a candidate from speaking on behalf of his own candidacy, it seems unlikely that the framers of this prohibition so intended. Similarly, even though the Code in nine of these fifteen states contains ABA Canon 7A(4)'s "catchall" prohibition of "any other political activity,"[139] it is arguable that a speech by a judge in support of his own candidacy is not "political activity."[140]

Further support for the permissibility of speeches by judges and judicial candidates in support of their own candidacy in states which do not specifically authorize or forbid such speeches is found in ABA Canon 7B, which contemplates campaigns by elective candidates for judicial office. This type of provision is found in Canon 7 in all of the elective states that neither expressly authorize nor forbid speeches by judges or judicial candidates in support of their own campaigns.[141] Although Canon 7, as adopted in all but two of the nonelective states that do not specifically authorize or forbid personal campaign speeches,[142] lacks any provisions pertaining to judicial campaigns,[143] this omission is without significance, since none of these states elects major court judges in competitive elections.[144]

h. Identification by a Judge or Candidate of Himself as a Member of a Political Party

ABA Canon 7 does not contain a specific prohibition barring a judge or judicial candidate from identifying himself as a member of a political party. Similarly, it appears unlikely that a judge's act of identifying himself as a member of a political party would be held to constitute a form of prohibited "political activity" within the meaning of ABA Canon 7A(4)'s general ban on "any other political activity."

In any event, eight partisan election states,[145] five nonpartisan election states,[146] five commission plan states,[147] and one executive selection state[148] specifically permit elective judges and judicial candidates to identify themselves as members of a political party. In Ohio and Tennessee, this authorization specifically extends to judges and judicial candidates generally.[149] In West Virginia, the authorization extends to any judge but, at least literally, does not apply to judicial candidates who are not incumbent judges.[150] New Mexico's version of Canon 7A would undoubtedly be construed as permitting judges and judicial candidates to identify themselves as members of a political party since it provides that judges may participate in the political process to the same extent as other citizens, provided they act impartially and with propriety.[151]

In twenty-three Code states, there is no provision relating to judges or judicial candidates identifying themselves as members of a political party. These states include four partisan election states,[152] nine nonpartisan election states,[153] five commission plan states,[154] three executive selection states,[155] and two legislative selection states.[156] Although a prohibition against "any other political activity"identical or similar to that in ABA Canon 7A(4) is included in the Code in fifteen of these twenty-three states,[157] it appears unlikely that the mere identification by a judge or judicial candidate of his political party would be considered to constitute a "political activity." Accordingly, it is probably permissible in these states for a judge or judicial candidate to identify his political party, provided his act in doing so is not linked with some other activity that is improper, unethical, or violative of some other Code provision.

Finally, in three nonpartisan election states, Kentucky, Washington, and Oregon, elective judges and candidates are prohibited, under specified circumstances, from identifying themselves as members of a political party.[158] In Kentucky, the prohibition only applies when the judge or candidate engages in campaign advertising or speaks on his own behalf; in Oregon, it applies only when the judge publicly identifies himself as a member of a political party beyond registering under the election laws; and, in Washington, the prohibition appears to apply only when a judge attends political gatherings or speaks to such gatherings on his own behalf. Since these three states are all nonpartisan election states, it appears likely that the prohibitions are intended to reinforce the nonpartisan aspects of the elections. In contrast, five nonpartisan election states expressly allow elective judges and judicial candidates to identify their political parties: Louisiana, North Dakota, Ohio, South Dakota, and Utah.[159]

i. Purchasing Tickets to Political Dinners and Functions

Canon 7A(1)(c) prohibits judges and judicial candidates from purchasing tickets for "political party dinners or other functions." Thirty-one of the forty-six Code jurisdictions, six partisan election states,[160] nine nonpartisan election states,[161] ten commission plan jurisdictions,[162] four executive selection states,[163] and two legislative selection jurisdictions[164] have adopted this portion of Canon 7A(1)(c).

In the remaining fifteen Code states, seven partisan election states,[165] and eight non-partisan election states,[166] a candidate's purchase of tickets for political functions is neither prohibited nor authorized. In eight of these fourteen states, four partisan election states,[167] and four nonpartisan election states,[168] Canon 7 of the Code does not contain any prohibition of "other political activities." Therefore, the purchase of tickets to fund-raising events and testimonial dinners is permissible in the latter eight states unless it either amounts to a disguised contribution to a candidate or political organization because it is in excess of reasonable cost or value or is violative of some other portion of Canon 7 in that particular state.[169]

The possibility that the purchase of tickets for testimonial dinners would be held to constitute a political contribution is specifically noted in the commentary to Canon 7A(1)(c) in the California Code, which neither prohibits nor authorizes the purchase of tickets to political functions. Under the commentary, the cost of admission to a political function in excess of the actual cost of the meal is considered a political contribution. The same possibility is emphasized by Canon 7C of the Michigan Code which provides that:

Except as provided in 7B(2)(b) [authorizing the formation by a judicial candidate of committees to secure and manage campaign funds and public statements of support] and (c) [prohibiting such committees from soliciting campaign contributions from lawyers in excess of $100 per lawyer], (1) No judge shall accept a testimonial occasion on his behalf where the tickets are priced to cover more than the reasonable costs thereof, which may include only a nominal gift.

In the remaining six states, two partisan election states,[170] and four non-partisan election states,[171] that neither prohibit nor authorize the purchase of tickets, Canon 7 does contain a prohibition of "other political activities." While the question of whether the purchase of a ticket to a political dinner would constitute a per se violation of that prohibition is open, the answer would seem to depend on the circumstances of the individual case. Apart from that particular question, permissibility of the purchase of tickets to political dinners or functions would probably hinge on the questions of whether the transaction constituted a "contribution," and, if so, whether it was specifically prohibited by the provisions in Canon 7 of the particular state pertaining to contributions.

j. Campaign Rhetoric by Judicial Candidates, including Incumbent Judges

ABA Canon 7B(1)(c) provides that an elective judge or judicial candidate

should not make pledges or promises of conduct in office other than the faithful and impartial performance of the duties of the office; announce his views on disputed legal or political issues; or misrepresent his identity, qualifications, present position, or other fact.

This provision appears in Canon 7 in thirty-five of the forty-six Code states, twelve partisan election states,[172] fifteen nonpartisan election states,[173] seven commission plan states,[174] and one executive selection state.[175] Eleven states lack any such provision: one partisan election state,[176] two nonpartisan election states,[177] three commission plan states,[178] three executive selection states,[179] and two legislative selection states.[180]

In the Code states with such a provision, there are a few variations from the ABA model. Five states, including two partisan election states, Alabama and Texas,[181] and three nonpartisan election states, Michigan, Nevada, and Oregon,[182] omit the prohibition against an announcement by an elective judge or judicial candidate of his views on disputed legal or political issues. In lieu of that provision, Oregon has prohibitions of political activity that "creates a reasonable doubt about a judge's impartiality toward persons, organizations, or factual issues that foreseeably may come before the court on which the judge serves, whether or not actual disqualification becomes necessary" and of political activity that "jeopardizes the confidence of the public or of government officials in the political impartiality of the judicial branch of the government.'"[183] Similarly, Alabama has substituted a provision that requires that an elective judge or candidate "should not announce in advance his conclusions of law on pending litigation";[184] Nevada has an almost identical provision, holding that a judge or candidate should not "indicate his views on pending or impending litigation," but "may campaign on the basis of his ability, experience, and record" and "may answer allegations against his record in office."[185] Kansas has modified the prohibition against statements on disputed legal and political issues by permitting elective judges or candidates to answer allegations directed against their record in office.[186]

Some states have departed from Canon 7B(1)(c)'s description of the judges and candidates subject to its prohibitions with provisions making it applicable only to judicial candidates, including incumbent judges,[187] or to all judges in the state, as well as all judicial candidates,[188] or limiting the application of the prohibitions to judges who are candidates for retention in office.[189]

The principal problem in this area pertains to critical remarks by candidates about their opponents. Pre-Code disciplinary decisions have established two basic principles: (a) factually false statements by one candidate about another are not a ground for discipline if the candidate acted in good faith and reasonably believed the statements to be true[190] but do warrant discipline if the speaker knew or had reason to believe the statements were false;[191] (b) truthful criticisms of an opponent are not grounds for discipline as long as the criticisms are dignified.[192]

The applicability of the rule that factually false derogatory statements are not grounds for discipline if made in good faith and supported by reasonable belief in their truth in disciplinary proceedings under Canon 7B(1)(c) of the Code, is unclear. Canon 7B(1)(c) provides that a candidate should not "misrepresent his identity, qualifications, present position, *or other fact*" (emphasis added). Read literally, a good faith, reasonably supported misrepresentation would violate Canon 7B(1)(c). In view of the pre-Code cases that held or stated that discipline should not be imposed upon judicial candidates for making misrepresentations about an opposing candidate in good faith,[193] however, it seems doubtful that judicial discipline would be imposed under Canon 7B(1)(c) under similar circumstances.

The rule that accurate criticism by a judicial candidate is not a basis for discipline has been held applicable to Canon 7B(1)(c).[194] In fact, the Supreme Court of Kansas has held that factually accurate criticism is not a basis for discipline, even when the criticism is unfair.[195]

k. Solicitation or Acceptance by a Judicial Candidate of Funds or Public Statements of Support for His Own Candidacy in a Competitive Election

Canon 7B(2) of the ABA Code prohibits a judicial candidate, including an incumbent judge, who is seeking election in a "public election between competing candidates," from personally soliciting or accepting campaign funds or public statements of support. Candidates are, however, permitted to establish campaign committees of responsible persons to secure and manage the expenditure of campaign funds and to obtain public statements of support. Canon 7B(2) further provides that such committees are not prohibited from soliciting campaign contributions and support from lawyers.

Either the precise text of ABA Canon 7B(2) or most of its substance has been adopted in twenty-nine of the forty-six Code jurisdictions: ten partisan election states,[196] thirteen nonpartisan election states,[197] five commission plan jurisdictions,[198] and one executive selection state.[199]

Departures from the ABA model are not uncommon. In four of these twenty-nine jurisdictions, Arizona, Michigan, Oregon, and Tennessee, the privilege of having a campaign committee solicit campaign contributions is not in terms limited to elections involving competing candidates; in the remaining twenty-five, the privilege is specifically limited to such elections. In nine of these twenty-nine jurisdictions, two partisan election states,[200] and seven nonpartisan election states,[201] judicial candidates are not forbidden to solicit personally attorneys and others for public statements of support, although they are (as in the case of ABA Canon 7B(2)) forbidden to solicit personally attorneys and others for campaign funds.[202] In Georgia, Canon 7B(2) provides that a judicial candidate may not attend a function at which campaign funds are solicited by a campaign committee acting on the candidate's behalf. In California, Canon 7B(2) prohibits elective candidates from personally soliciting campaign funds but not from accepting them. Judicial candidates in Florida are forbidden by Canon 7B(2) to seek publicly stated support from lawyers. From this it is arguable that soliciting nonattorneys for such endorsements is permitted. In Michigan, Canon 7B(2) forbids the personal solicitation or acceptance of campaign funds or endorsements by candidates only when done "by improper use of his office in violation of B(1)(c)." Finally, also in Michigan, Canon 7B(2)provides that campaign contributions from lawyers may not exceed $100 per lawyer and that any amounts not spent during the campaign must either be returned to the contributors or turned over to the Michigan State Bar's Client Security Fund.

In fourteen of the seventeen remaining Code states, three partisan election states,[203] two nonpartisan election states,[204] four commission plan states,[205] three executive selection states,[206] and two legislative selection states,[207] there are no provisions prohibiting or authorizing solicitation, either by the candidate or a committee, of funds or endorsements for his campaign, except that, in Iowa, Canon 7B(2) authorizes a judge who is an actively opposed candidate in a noncompetitive retention election to establish committees to obtain endorsements and campaign funds. Consequently, it appears that solicitation of funds and endorsements is probably permissible in these states, unless precluded by the prohibition against "other political activities." Such a prohibition is found in ten of the fourteen states, whose Codes are silent on the solicitation issue.[208] It is arguable that direct solicitations by a judicial candidate would violate the prohibition of "any other political activity", but that solicitation through a campaign committee might be sanctioned. In the five jurisdictions that lack a prohibition against "any other political activity,"[209] it can be argued that Canon 7A(1)(c)'s prohibition against soliciting funds for a political organization or candidate is not applicable to solicitations made by either a candidate directly or a committee acting on his behalf. The Code also does not elsewhere appear to create an impediment to solicitations of endorsements, unless solicitations of lawyers who appear before the candidate would be deemed to run afoul of a general canon. General canons that could apply include: (i) Canon 2A's requirement that a lawyer "should at all times conduct himself in a manner that promotes public confidence in the integrity and impartiality of the judiciary"; (ii) the requirement in the commentary on Canon 2 that a judge "must avoid all impropriety and appearance of impropriety"; and (iii) the requirement in ABA Canon 1 that a judge "should himself observe high standards of conduct so that the integrity and independence of the judiciary may be preserved." The surest way to avoid the possibility of charges being brought under these general canons in the five states in question would be for the candidate to operate through a campaign committee.

Colorado's version of Canon 7B(2) is identical to the model Canon, except that it only applies to a judge who is a candidate for "retention in office" and then only when there is active opposition to the judge's retention; it regulates only the solicitation of funds, not endorsements.

Nevada's version of Canon 7B(2) specifically provides that a candidate "may solicit funds for his campaign,"provided he does so within a specified time frame. No mention, however, is made either of campaign committees or of solicitation of endorsements.

Idaho's Canon 7A is virtually identical to Nevada's Canon 7B(2), inasmuch as it expressly excepts the solicitation by a judge of funds for his own judicial campaign from a prohibition forbidding him to directly or indirectly solicit funds for any political organization or candidate.

All of the twenty-nine jurisdictions that have adopted the ABA prohibitions against direct solicitations by a judge or judicial candidate of funds for his own campaign in a competitive election authorize such solicitation by a campaign committee.[210]

Also, with the exception of Arizona and Ohio, all of these jurisdictions authorize multiple solicitation committees, rather than merely one committee.[211] Moreover, with the exception of Arizona and Oklahoma (which merely authorize committee solicitation of campaign contributions), all of them authorize committee solicitations not only of campaign contributions but also public statements of support.[212] Additionally, all but Arizona and Oklahoma specifically authorize the committees to solicit attorneys, and Arizona and Oklahoma do not prohibit solicitation of attorneys by the committees.[213] With respect to Michigan, however, it will be recalled that Canon 7B(2) imposes a $100 ceiling on the amount one attorney may be asked to contribute. Also, Ohio Canon 7B(2) prohibits committees from soliciting or receiving contributions from any employee or appointee of the court, or anyone doing business with the court; the canon adds, however, that the committees may solicit attorneys, presumably intending to except attorneys practicing in the court.

The commentary under ABA Canon 7B(2) caveats that "unless the candidate is required by law to file a list of his campaign contributions, their names should not be revealed to the candidate." Identical commentary appears under that Canon in Arkansas, District of Columbia, Nebraska, New York, North Dakota, South Dakota, Tennessee, Washington, and Wyoming. The evident purpose of this restriction is to relieve judges of the embarrassment and possible appearance of bias that might occur if a judge's known campaign contributors appeared before him in court.

In twenty-two of the twenty-nine states that expressly permit judicial candidates to establish committees to solicit contributions and endorsements in campaigns leading up to competitive elections, the applicable canon requires that the committee act within a specified time frame and stipulates both a beginning date and an ending date.[214] In the other seven states there is no stipulated time frame.[215]

l. Candidates Seeking Retention or Re-election in Noncompetitive Retention Elections

ABA Canon 7B(3) extends the prohibitions and privileges of Canon 7B(2) to incumbent judges running in noncompetitive elections for retention or re-election, if the judge is actively opposed. In such event, Canon 7B(3) provides that the judge "may campaign in response thereto and may obtain public statements of support and campaign funds in the manner provided in subsection B(2)."

Out of the twenty-nine states that have adopted ABA Canon 7B(2), or its substance, twenty-five, including nine partisan election states,[216] ten nonpartisan election states,[217] five commission plan states,[218] and one executive selection state,[219] have adopted either ABA Canon 7B(3) or most of its substantive terms. In addition, two states, Colorado and Iowa, have an equivalent of ABA Canon 7B(3) without having adopted Canon 7B(2).[220] The apparent reason for the omission of Canon 7B(2) is that these states' major court judges are initially selected pursuant to a commission plan and only run in periodic retention elections.[221]

Finally, in five of the states whose Codes contain a version of ABA Canon 7B(?), neither ABA Canon 7B(3) nor its substantive equivalent is included. These five states include two partisan election states, Tennessee, and West

Virginia,[222] and three nonpartisan election states, Georgia, Kentucky, and Ohio.[223]

Presumably, Canon 7B(3) was omitted in Georgia, West Virginia, Kentucky, and Ohio because none of their major court judges run for re-election in noncompetitive retention elections.[224] This does not, however, explain the omission of Canon 7B(3) in Tennessee, since Tennessee's intermediate appellate judges are initially selected under a commission plan system but are re-elected in noncompetitive retention elections.[225] The probable reason for the omission of Canon 7B(3) in Tennessee is that Canon 7B(2) applies to judicial candidates in noncompetitive retention elections as well as in competitive elections.

In Arizona, Florida, Pennsylvania, and Tennessee candidates for retention in noncompetitive retention elections are authorized to obtain endorsements and campaign contributions through campaign committees even if there is no opposition.[226] In Florida, when the retention election candidate certifies that his candidacy has drawn active opposition, he is also entitled to campaign "in any manner authorized by law, subject to the restrictions of subsection B(1)."[227] It is indeed arguable that the language just quoted frees the candidate from the restrictions on direct solicitation by candidates of campaign funds and endorsements imposed by subsection B(2).

On the meaning of the term "active opposition" in ABA Canon 7B(3), the ABA commentary following the canon is helpful. It states that "active opposition" is difficult to define but is intended to include "any form of organized public opposition or an unfavorable bar poll."

5.5 LOBBYING ACTIVITIES BY JUDGES

Lobbying by judges can be either partisan or nonpartisan, depending on whether the judge is acting to advance his political party's program or solely in accordance with his own preferences or goals. Lobbying by a judge can probably be characterized as nonpartisan if the judge acts for reasons of individual conscience. In contrast, if the judge advocates a particular measure because it is part of his party's program, he would appear to be engaged in partisan lobbying activity. In either event, the lobbying would appear to violate Canon 4B if it involved direct lobbying, which is defined as consultation between a judge and a member of the executive or legislative branches. Canon 4B, which has been adopted in many Code states,[228] prohibits any such consultation except at a public legislative or administrative hearing, unless it pertains only to matters concerning the administration of justice. Moreover, even when the judge appears at a public hearing to advocate adoption of a particular measure, Canon 4B states that he may properly do so only if the issue concerns "the law, the legal system, and the administration of justice."

It is arguable, also, that, in states which have adopted the general prohibition by ABA Canon 7A(4) of "any other political activity except on behalf of measures to improve the law, the legal system, or the administration of justice," lobbying by judges not falling within the exceptions specified in Canon 7A(4) violates that canon.

Only Kentucky's version of Canon 7 goes so far as to expressly forbid lobbying. Canon 7A(5) in Kentucky provides that:

No member of the judiciary shall engage in any activity in the nature of lobbying with the executive or legislative branch of the state government on matters affecting the administration of justice without express authority from the Chief Justice.

This provision only pertains to lobbying on matters affecting the administration of justice. Lobbying on other matters is regulated, and apparently prohibited, by Canon 4B, and perhaps Canon 7A(4), of the Kentucky Code, which are identical to ABA Canons 4B and 7A(4).

Direct lobbying was not barred until states began adopting the ABA Code. Previously, the Canons of Judicial Ethics did not contain any provision directly prohibiting direct lobbying on matters not pertaining to the administration of justice.

a. Indirect Lobbying

At one time, politically active judges sought to advance their ideological political goals by having intermediaries lobby important legislators or members of the administration.[229] There is no case law on the question of whether indirect lobbying of this nature would violate Canon 4B.

5.6 INVOLVEMENT OF JUDGES IN CIVIL AND CHARITABLE ACTIVITIES

Under ABA Canon 5B, a judge may participate in civic and charitable activities that do not reflect adversely upon his impartiality or interfere with the performance of his judicial duties.[230]

ABA Canon 5B further provides that, subject to certain limitations, a judge may serve as an officer, director, trustee, or nonlegal adviser of an educational, religious, charitable, fraternal, or civic organization not conducted for the economic or political advantage of its members. The exceptions to this general rule include: (1) Canon 5B(1), which stipulates that a judge should not serve if it is likely that the organization will be engaged in proceedings that would ordinarily come before him or will be regularly engaged in adversary proceedings in any court; (2) Canon 5B(2), which states that a judge should not (i) solicit funds for any educational, religious, charitable, fraternal, or civic organization or (ii) use or permit the use of the prestige of his office for that purpose beyond being listed as an officer, director, or trustee of such an organization or (iii) be a speaker or the guest of honor at an organization's fund-raising events even though he may attend such events; and (3) Canon 5B(3), which provides that a judge should not give investment advice to such an organization, but that he may serve on its board of directors or trustees even though it has the responsibility for approving investment decisions.[231]

5.7 OVERSEEING JUDICIAL POLITICAL ACTIVITY

As is noted in §6(n)(v), *infra*, twenty-four states have expressly included violation of the state's code of judicial conduct or (in the case of Rhode Island) canons of judicial ethics in the enumerated grounds for judicial discipline.[232] A few of these states have prescribed added requirements, e.g., that the code or canon violation be willful (Connecticut, North Dakota, and Oregon); persistent (Delaware); serious (Maine); substantial (Iowa); or likely to result in substantial loss of public respect (Ohio).[233] Furthermore, even in states that have not specifically designated violation of the code or canons as a ground for discipline, the courts have held either that the canons have become binding supplements to the enumerated grounds for judicial discipline or that they should be utilized as nonbinding guides to the meaning of the express grounds.[234]

Finally, the courts have repeatedly disciplined or removed judges for political activities that violated Canon 7 of the Code of Judicial Conduct or one of the Canons of Judicial Ethics pertaining to political activities or some other constitutional or statutory provision or rule of court pertaining to political activity.[235] Political activities that have been held to be grounds for disciplining or removing judges have included: (a) attending political gatherings and acting as ward leader, in violation of Canon 28 of the former New Jersey Canons of Judicial Ethics;[236] (b) campaigning for a candidate for nonjudicial office by giving a speech before a high school group criticizing one of that candidate's opponents and making similar remarks to a reporter with the intent or expectation that they would be published, in violation of Canon 28 of Wisconsin's Code of Judicial Ethics, which is still in effect;[237] (c) making political contributions to the governor in his re-election campaign by helping organize fund-raising events, giving campaign advice, and acting as a local clearinghouse for political patronage, in violation of Canons 1, 2, 7A(2), and 7A(4) of the Missouri Code of Judicial Conduct;[238] (d) direct personal solicitation of contributions for the judge's campaign from an attorney and that attorney's law firm, violative of Canon 7B(2);[239] (e) membership in a partisan political club, attendance at meetings of that club, and payment of dues to that club, in violation of article 5, §29(f) of the Missouri constitution and Missouri Supreme Court Rule 2.28;[240] (f) a surrogate's using his judicial facilities and office for political activities in violation of Canon 2A of the Code as a misuse of public facilities, even though surrogates were exempt by New Jersey Supreme Court Rule 1:17–1 from Canon 7's political activity prohibitions;[241] (g) engaging in partisan political activity in support of a candidate for nonjudicial office by obtaining an affidavit refuting a bribery accusation against that candidate made by his opponents, in violation of Canon 28 of the former New Jersey Canons of Judicial Ethics;[242] (h) partisan political activity unrelated to the judge's own campaign, in violation of Canon 28 of New York's former Canons of Judicial Ethics;[243] (i) false statements of fact made by a judicial candidate about an opponent, with knowledge or reason to know of the falsity.[244]

NOTES TO §5.1

1. E.g., see McKay, The Judiciary and Nonjudicial Activities, 35 Law & Contemp. Prob. 9, Appendix, 27, and 29–31 (1970).

2. See Murphy, The Brandeis/Frankfurter Connection: The Secret Political Activities of Two Supreme Court Justices (1982) (hereinafter cited as Murphy), 3–15, 39–344; McKay, *supra* note 1, at 12–13, 27, 29, 32–34; Murphy, Elements of Extrajudicial Strategy: A Look at the Political Roles of Justices Brandeis and Frankfurter, 69 Geo. L.J. 101, 102–132 (1980) (hereinafter cited as *Elements of Extrajudicial Strategy*); Nathanson, Book Review, The Extra-judicial Activities of Supreme Court Justices: Where Should the Line Be Drawn, 78 Nw. L. Rev. 494–527 (1983); Levy and Murphy, Preserving the Progressive Spirit in a Conservative Time: The Joint Reform Efforts of Justice Brandeis and Professor Frankfurter, 78 Mich. L. Rev. 1252 (1980); Jaffe, Professors and Judges as Advisors to Government: Reflections on the Roosevelt-Frankfurter Relationship, 83 Harv. L. Rev. 366–375 (1969). See *also* Mason, Extra-judicial Work for Judges: The Views of Chief Justice Stone, 67 Harv. L. Rev. 193, 196–199, (1953).

3. E.g., See McKay, *supra* note 1, at 12–13, 25, 27–37; Mason, *supra* note 2, at 194–216.

4. See Mason, *supra* note 2, at 193–194.

5. E.g., See Mason, *supra* note 2, at 194; McKay, *supra* note 1, at 27.

6. See Mason, *supra* note 2, at 193–194.

7. See McKay, *supra* note 1, at 27–37.

8. *Id.*

9. See Murphy, *supra* note 2, at 260–262.

10. See Pusey, Charles Evans Hughes (1951), vol. 1, pp. 272–274. Hughes accepted the appointment to the Court on April 24, 1910, his nomination was confirmed on May 2, 1910, and he qualified as Justice and resigned as governor early in October, 1910. *Id.*

11. E.g., see Mason, *supra* note 2, at 194, n.3; and Mason, Harlan Fiske Stone (1956), at 698–720.

12. See Mason, *supra* note 2, at 194, n.3, and 216.

13. See ABA Canons of Judicial Ethics (hereinafter cited as "ABA-CJE"), and particularly Canons 28 and 30; and *Elements of Extrajudicial Strategy, supra* note 2, at 131.

14. See McKay, *supra* note 1, at 15. Each state-adopted set of Canons shall be

referred to as "CJE," with the abbreviation for the state attached as a prefix (e.g., "N.Y. CJE").

15. *See* ABA-CJE nos. 28 and 30. For an example of a state-adopted version of the ABA-CJE, *see* Alaska CJE Canons 28 and 30.

16. *See* Murphy, *supra* note 2, at 3–4.

17. E.g., *see* Comment, Disqualification of Federal Judges for Bias under 28 U.S.C. Section 144 and Revised Section 455, 45 Fordham L. Rev. 139, 145–146 (1976) (hereinafter cited as *Disqualification of Federal Judges for Bias*) (concluding that Judge Haynesworth's conduct had not violated existing statutory disqualification requirements as currently construed by the courts, but that the U.S. Senate nevertheless believed he should have disqualified himself, and, therefore, that the existing statutory requirements were not strict enough); Comment, Disqualification of Federal Judges—The Need for Better Guidelines, 13 Wake Forest L. Rev. 353, 353–354 (1977) concluding that assaults on propriety of judicial conduct, such as that involving the Haynesworth nomination, resulted in ABA reexamination of the law on disqualification and ABA adoption of greatly revised canons of judicial ethics named the Code of Judicial Conduct, which supplemented the ABA Canons of Judicial Ethics.

18. The Code of Judicial Conduct will be hereinafter cited as "COJC." The ABA version of that Code will be hereinafter cited as ABA-COJC.

19. *See infra* §6.3(n)(v), notes 254–258, and the accompanying text. Each state version of the Code of Judicial Conduct will be cited as "COJC", preceded by the abbreviation for the state (e.g., N.Y. COJC).

20. *See* ABA-COJC Canons 7B(2) and 7B(3).

21. *Compare* ABA-CJE no. 30, which contained similar prohibitions but appeared to condition them upon an impression of probable future discrimination.

22. The ABA-CJE did not contain any prohibition of misrepresentation by a candidate whatsoever, whether as to his own qualifications, record, or conduct or as to any of his competitors' qualifications, record, or conduct.

23. *See supra* note 22.

24. *In re Inquiry Relating to Baker*, 218 Kan. 209, 542 P.2d 701 (1975) (false representations by judicial candidate concerning opponent's pension rights). *Cf.* the following cases imposing bar discipline upon candidates knowingly making false statements concerning competing candidates: *State ex. rel. Nebraska State Bar Ass'n v. Michaelis*, 210 Neb. 545, 316 N.W.2d 46 (1982) (statements by candidate for office of county attorney that respondent "knew or should have known with ordinary care to be false," held violative of Code of Profess. Responsib. DR1–102A(1), (4), (5), and (6); *State Board of Law Examiners v. Spriggs*, 51 70, 155 P.2d 285 (1945); *In re Donahoe*, 90 Wash.2d 173, 580 P.2d 1093 (En Banc 1978) (Code of Profess. Responsib. DR 8–102(A) and (B), held violated); *State v. Russell*, 227 Kan. 897, 610 P.2d 1122 (1980), *cert. denied*, 449 U.S. 983 (1980) (knowingly false accusation that competing candidates for position on Board of Public Utilities had engaged in illegal conduct); *Thatcher v. United States*, 212 F. 801 (6th Cir. 1914), *aff'g.*, 190 F. 969 (Circ. and D. Cts. N.D. Ohio 1911), *reh. denied*, 219 Fed. 173 (6th Cir. 1915), dismissed for want of jurisdiction, 241 U.S. 644 (1916) (knowingly false statements of fact by nonincumbent judicial candidate disparaging incumbents; *In re Thatcher*, 80 Ohio St. 492, 89 N.E. 39 (1909) (same); *Schoolfield v. Bean*, 26 Tenn. App. 30,

167 S.W.2d 359 (1942) (false charges by judicial candidate against opponent's supporters).

NOTES TO §5.2

25. *See infra* notes 26–27 and 32–35. *See also* Bowman, A Judicial Dilemma: Real or Imagined? 83 W. Va. L. Rev. 28, 31–32 (1980). In some states the prohibition extends not only to any other public office but also any other public position of profit. E.g., Alaska Const.art. IV, §14; Pa. Const. art. 5, §16(a); S.C. Const. art. V, §12. In other states the prohibition applies not only to any other public office, but also to any other public employment. E.g., Mo. Ann. Stat. §477.130; Mont. Const. art. VII, §9(3); Nebr. Rev. Stat. §24–202; Wash. Const. art. 4, §15.

26. E.g., Ala. Const. amendm. no. 328, §608(b); Del. Const. art. IV, §4; Me. Const. art. VI, §5.

27. The wording of the provisions varies. Some provide, in substance, that no judge shall become a candidate for nonjudicial office. E.g., Colo. Const. art. VI, §18; N.M. Const. art. VI, §19. Others provide that no judge shall be eligible to become a candidate for nonjudicial office without first resigning. E.g., N.Y. Const. art. 6, §20(b)(2). Still others provide that, if a judge becomes a candidate, he will forfeit his judicial office. E.g., Alaska Const. art. 4, §15; Ariz. Const. art. 6, §28 (Supp.); Minn. Const. art. 6, §6; Mont. Const. art. VII, §10; N.J. Const. art. 6, §7, ¶1; N.Y. Const. art. VI, §20(b)(2); W. Va. Const. art. VIII, §7.

28. *See* COJC Canon 7A(3) in the following states (when renumbered the new number is set forth in parentheses): Alabama (7A(2)); Alaska, Arizona, Arkansas, Colorado (7A(2)); Connecticut (7A(2)); Delaware (7B); District of Columbia, Florida, Iowa (7A(2)); Indiana, Kansas, Kentucky, Louisiana, Massachusetts (7A(2)); Michigan, Minnesota, Missouri, Nebraska, Nevada (7A(2)); New Hampshire (7A(2)); New Jersey (7A(2)); New York, North Carolina, North Dakota, Ohio, Oklahoma, Oregon (7C); Pennsylvania, South Carolina, South Dakota, Tennessee, Utah, Vermont, Virginia (7A(2)); Washington, West Virginia. *Cf.* Hawaii COJC Canon 6B ("a judge who shall become a candidate for elective office shall forfeit his office"). *But compare Nix v. Standing Comm. on Judicial Performance of Okla. Bar Ass'n*, 422 P.2d 203 (Okla. 1966) (canon requiring judges to resign before running for nonjudicial office was merely hortatory, and not binding); and *State v. McCarthy*, 255 Wis. 234, 38 N.W.2d 679 (1949) (similar holding).

29. E.g., *Signorelli v. Evans*, 637 F.2d 853 (2d Cir. 1980); *Roy v. Jones*, 349 F. Supp. 315 (W.D. N.Y. 1972).

30. E.g., *Signorelli, supra* note 29.

31. N.Y. State Commission on Judicial Conduct Report for 1974, p. 337 (construing N.Y. COJC Canon 7A(3), which is identical to ABA COJC Canon 7A(3)).

32. Cal. Const. art. 6, §16; Idaho COJC Canon 7A(3).

33. N.M. COJC Canon 7B.

34. E.g., Idaho Const. art. 5, §9; Iowa Const. art. 5, §5; Mich. Const. art. 6, §20; Nev. Const. art. 6, §11; Wash. Const. art. 4, §15. In some jurisdictions, the prohibition even extends for a short period after expiration of the judge's term. E.g., Mich. Const. art. 6, §20 (one year).

35. E.g., *Stockton v. McFarland*, 56 Ariz. 138, 106 P.2d 328, 329, 332 (1940) (sitting judge); *Riley v. Cordell*, 200 Okla. 390, 194 P.2d 857 (1948) (sitting judge);

Ekwall v. Stadelman, 146 Or. 439, 30P.2d 1037 (1934) (sitting judge); *State ex. rel. Chandler v. Howell*, 104 Wash. 99, 175 P.2d 569 (1918) (judge resigned before running). *See Signorelli, supra* note 29, 637 F.2d at 858.

36. E.g., Alaska Const. art. IV, §14; Ariz. Const. art. 6, §28; Colo. Const. art. VI, §18; Fla. Const. art. 5, §13 (Supp.); Ind. Const. art. 7, §11 (restriction applies to entire term of office); Kan. Const. art. 3, §8; Mo. Const. art. 5, §25(f); Okla Const. art. 7-B, §6; Pa. Const. art. V, §17(a).

37. Ariz. Const. art. 6, §28; Colo. Const. art. VI, §18; Ind. Const. art. 7, §11; Kan. Const. art. 3, §2 (applies only to supreme court justices appointed under the commission plan, or retained in office in a noncompetitive retention election); Mo. Const. art. 5, §25(f).

38. E.g., Arizona Const. art. 6, §28.

39. E.g., see the Colorado, Indiana, and Kansas constitutional provisions cited in note 37, *supra. Compare* Okla. Const. art. 7-B, §6 (applies only to judges appointed under a commission plan or retained in a noncompetitive retention election).

40. *See* Fla. Stat. tit. 9, §§105.011, 105.041(3), 105.071(2), 105.09.

41. Fla. Stat. tit. 9, §§105.071, 105.08, 105.09.

42. *See supra* note 41.

43. Fla. Stat. tit. 9, §105.08.

44. Fla. Stat. tit. 9, §105.09.

45. 493 F. Supp. 60 (S.D. Fla. 1978).

NOTES TO §5.3

46. *Compare* ABA-CJE Canon 28 with ABA-COJC Canon 7A(1)(b).
47. *Compare* ABA-CJE Canon 28 with ABA-COJC Canon 7A(1)(b).
48. *Compare* ABA-CJE Canon 28 with ABA-COJC Canon 7A(1)(a).
49. *Compare* ABA-CJE Canon 28 with ABA-COJC Canon 7A(1)(c).
50. *Compare* ABA-CJE Canon 28 with ABA-COJC Canon 7A(1)(c).
51. *Compare* ABA-CJE Canon 28 with ABA-COJC Canon 7A(1)(c).
52. *Compare* ABA-CJE Canon 28 with ABA-COJC Canon 7A(2).
53. *Compare* ABA-CJE Canon 28 (forbidding judges to engage in partisan activities) with ABA-COJC canon 7A(4) (forbidding judges to engage in "any other political activity," except for those noted in the text accompanying this note and those elsewhere specifically authorized by Canon 7).
54. *Compare* ABA-CJE Canon 30 with ABA-COJC Canon 7B(1)(c).
55. *Compare* ABA-CJE Canon 30 with ABA-COJC Canon 7B(1)(c).
56. *Compare* ABA-CJE Canons 28 and 30 with ABA-COJC Canons 7B(2) (competitive elections) and 7B(3) (noncompetitive retention elections).
57. *Compare* ABA-CJE Canon 30 with ABA-COJC Canon 7A(3).
58. *See supra* notes 2 and 16, and accompanying text.
59. *See supra* note 3, and accompanying text.

NOTES TO §5.4(a)

60. *See* app. §§5.4(b) through §5.4(i), *infra.*

61. The rationale for classifying each jurisdiction according to the method used

in initially selecting a majority of the major trial court judges in that jurisdiction is that it appears likely that the framers and adopters of Canon 7 in any particular jurisdiction would tend to be most influenced by the problems presented by that method of selection. For example, it is believed that, in a jurisdiction where judges were selected at the beginning of each term in partisan elections, the framers and adopters of Canon 7 would have been most influenced by this fact, even if vacancies occurring during terms of office were filled (either finally or temporarily) by a commission plan.

62. In Maryland, Montana, Rhode Island, and Wisconsin, judicial political activities are regulated by the political activity provisions of the outmoded ABA Code of Judicial Ethics. *See* Md. S. Ct. R. 1231, ¶¶XXVII, XXIX; Mont. S. Ct. R. 28, 30; R.I. S. Ct. R. 25, 27; Wisc. S. Ct. R. 60.14, 60.15. In Illinois, such activities are regulated by Ill. S. Ct. R. 70.

63. For a detailed description of the methods of initial selection, final vacancy selection, retention determination, and temporary vacancy selection employed in the fifty states and the District of Columbia, see *supra* §§2.2 to 2.8.

NOTES TO §5.4(b)

64. For convenience of analysis, this prohibition will be referred to in this text, as the "antileadership prohibition."

65. *See* Canon 7A in the District of Columbia and in the forty-five states other than Illinois, Maryland, Montana, Rhode Island, and Wisconsin. In Tennessee, Canon 7A(1) prohibits judges from holding any office in a political organization but does not prohibit them from being active as leader in such an organization.

66. *See* COJC Canon 7A in Alabama, Tennessee, and Texas.

67. *See* Mich. COJC Canon 7A and Ore. COJC Canon 7. Ore. Canon 7B(6) has the effect of an antileadership prohibition, however, since it prohibits a judge from identifying himself or herself as a member of a political party.

68. *See* Ill. S. Ct. R. 70; Md. S. Ct. R. XXVII; R.I. S. Ct. R. 25B.

69. *See* Wis. S. Ct. R. 60.14.

70. *See* Mont. S. Ct. R. 28.

NOTES TO §5.4(c)

71. For convenience, this prohibition will be referred to herein as "the speech and endorsement prohibition."

72. *See* Canon 7A in the Code of Judicial Conduct of each of the forty-six Code jurisdictions listed *supra* in §5.4(a). The only Code jurisdictions that have omitted from Canon 7 the ABA prohibition against speeches or endorsements on behalf of candidates or political organizations are three partisan election states, Alabama, Missouri, and Texas. Further analysis is needed, however, since the code in two of these states contains general language which might to some extent preclude this type of activity. This language includes (a) an apparently nonmandatory Alabama exhortation against judges and candidates becoming engaged in campaign activities for candidates for nonjudicial offices (see Ala. COJC Canon 7A); (b) a Missouri provision prohibiting commission plan judges and judges retained in office by winning

a noncompetitive retention election from taking part in any political campaign (see Mo. COJC Canon 7A(1)); (c) another Missouri provision prohibiting all judges from engaging in "any other political activity except on behalf of measures to improve the law, the legal system or the administration of justice" (see Mo. COJC Canon 7A(4)). On the other hand, the Texas Code seems to clearly permit the activities under consideration, since Canon 7 of that Code omits all of the prohibitory provisions in ABA Canon 7, other than those dealing with certain activities by candidates for judicial office or their adherents in support of their own campaigns.

In Ohio, Canon 7A(1) provides, *inter alia*, that a judge or a candidate for election to judicial office should not make speeches for a political organization or candidate "at a political meeting." The quoted words are not found in ABA 7A(1)(b), and it is arguable that they imply that speeches in favor of a political organization or candidate may be made at a nonpolitical meeting. It is arguable, however, that the making of such a speech would cause an otherwise nonpolitical meeting to become a political meeting.

73. *See* Mich. COJC Canon 7A(1)(b) (speeches); N.C. COJC Canon 7A(1)(b) (endorsements); Pa. COJC Canon 7A(2) (speeches); Tenn. COJC Canon 7A (1)(b) (endorsements). The express authorization in Pennsylvania applies only when the actor holds or seeks a judicial office filled by public election between competing candidates. Also, both in Pennsylvania and in Tennessee, the express authorization of public endorsement or speeches on behalf of a candidate for judicial office is applicable only when the candidate seeks to be elected to the same court as the endorser.

74. *See* Cal. COJC Canon 7A(1)(b) (speeches and endorsements); Mich. COJC Canon 7A(1)(b) (speeches and endorsements); Nev. COJC Canon 7A(1)(b) (endorsements); Ore. COJC Canon 7 (making public statement for, or lending one's name to, with the purpose to elect or defeat candidate for nonjudicial public office, jeopardizing confidence of public or government official in political impartiality of judiciary); and Wash. COJC Canon 7A(1)(b) (endorsements). Although Canon 7 in California and Washington also contains the ABA Canon 7A(4) prohibition of "any other political activity," it appears doubtful that this general language would override the apparent implied authorization described in the text. Also, it is arguable that, when a judge publicly endorses a candidate for judicial office, this constitutes a "measure to improve the administration of justice," such as is expressly excepted from the prohibition of "any other political activity."

NOTES TO §5.4(d)

75. *See* COJC Canon 7A(1)(c) in Arkansas, Indiana, Kansas, Mississippi, New York, North Carolina, Pennsylvania, Tennessee, and West Virginia, and COJC Canon 7A(1) in Alabama. The only partisan election Code states that have omitted or substantially changed this prohibition are Missouri, New Mexico and Texas. Although Missouri's Canon 7 prohibits judges running in partisan elections from soliciting contributions to party funds, it does not prohibit them from soliciting funds for a candidate. Also, Missouri's Canon 7 does not prohibit commission plan judges or judges retained in noncompetitive retention elections from soliciting funds for a political organization or candidate, but prohibits them from taking part in a political campaign (which may amount to the same thing), and sets forth the ABA

Canon 7A(4) prohibition of "any other political activity" verbatim (which also may amount to the same thing). New Mexico omits all ABA prohibitions with respect to political activities other than that pertaining to judges running for nonjudicial office. Finally, Texas omits both the prohibition in question and, also, the other ABA prohibitions dealing with political activities other than activities in connection with the actor's own campaign.

76. *See* COJC Canon 7A(1)(c) in Arizona, Florida, Idaho, Kentucky, Louisiana, Minnesota, Nevada, North Dakota, Oklahoma, South Dakota, Utah, and Washington. The only nonpartisan election code states that have deleted or modified this prohibition are California, Georgia, Michigan, Ohio, and Oregon. *See* Cal. and Ga. COJC Canon 7A(1)(c); Mich. COJC Canon 7A(1); Ohio COJC Canon 7A(1); and Ore. COJC Canon 7A.

California and Washington have both adopted this prohibition insofar as it forbids solicitation of funds for political organizations or candidates for nonjudicial office, but not insofar as it forbids solicitation of funds for candidates for judicial office. Although Canon 7A(3) in both California and Washington forbids "other political activities," it is to be doubted that this general prohibition would preclude an implication of permission to solicit funds for judicial candidates. Georgia's Canon 7A(1)(c) has prohibited solicitations of funds for a political organization, but not solicitation of funds for a candidate; and the permission to solicit funds for a political organization arguably implied from the latter omission is strengthened by the fact that the ABA prohibition of "any other political activity" has been omitted from Georgia's Canon 7. Michigan and Ohio both omit all of the ABA Canon 7A(1)(c) prohibitions, including the prohibition against solicitation of funds for political organizations or candidates. Since Michigan also omits the catchall prohibition of "any other political activities," it is arguable that Michigan impliedly permits such solicitation. Inasmuch as Ohio includes the catchall provision, the contrary conclusion probably applies to Ohio. Finally, in Oregon (which has drastically rewritten ABA Canon 7), since political activity for the purpose of electing or defeating a candidate for a nonjudicial public office, or for a political organization, including solicitation of funds, is prohibited by Canon 7A(4), when, among other things, such activity "jeopardizes the confidence of the public or of government officials in the political impartiality of the judicial branch of the government," there appears to be a good chance, although not a certainty, that solicitation of funds for a nonjudicial candidate or for a political organization is prohibited.

77. *See* COJC Canon 7A(1)(c) in Alaska, Colorado, Delaware, District of Columbia, Iowa, Massachusetts, Nebraska, Vermont, and Wyoming; and Hawaii COJC Canon 6A(1)(c).

78. *See* COJC canon 7A(1)(c) in Maine, New Hampshire, New Jersey, and South Carolina.

79. *See* COJC Canon 7A(1)(c) in Connecticut and Virginia.

NOTES TO §5.4(e)(i)

80. For convenience of discussion, we will refer, in this text, to judges and candidates described by ABA Canon 7A(2) as "a judge holding an office filled by public election between competing candidates, or a candidate for such office," as "elective judges" and "elective candidates"; and we will refer to judges and candidates

selected pursuant to a commission plan, legislative selection plan, or executive selection plan, and not required to thereafter undergo the rigors of a competitive
election, as "nonelective judges" and "nonelective candidates," even if they undergo
noncompetitive retention elections.

NOTES TO §5.4(e)(ii)

81. *See* COJC Canons 7A(1)(c) and 7A(2) in Arkansas, Kansas, Mississippi,
Missouri, New York, Pennsylvania, and West Virginia.

In Kansas and Missouri, the privilege of making contributions is extended only
to judges and candidates holding or seeking offices filled by partisan election. See
Kan. COJC Canon 7A(2) and Mo. COJC Canon 7A(2). This limitation has no
practical effect, since all major court judges in these two states are selected either
on a commission plan basis or on a partisan election basis, and none are selected in
nonpartisan elections. *See supra* notes 75–76 (Chapter 2), and the accompanying
text.

In Tennessee, the foregoing privilege is extended to "a judge or candidate for
judicial office," and, therefore, purports to be available to commission plan judges
as well as partisan election judges. This change in the ABA phraseology does have
a practical effect, since, in Tennessee, even though Supreme Court and major trial
court judges are initially selected by partisan election, intermediate appellate judges
are initially selected on a commission plan basis. *See supra* notes 75–76 (Chapter 2),
and the accompanying text.

In West Virginia, the privilege under consideration is likewise extended to "a
judge," *see* W. Va. COJC Canon 7A(2); but, since all judges in West Virginia (other
than those appointed to fill vacancies temporarily) are chosen by partisan election
(*see supra* notes 66 and 69 (Chapter 2), and the accompanying text), this special
language has no practical significance.

82. *See* COJC Canons 7A(1)(c) and 7A(2) in Louisiana, North Dakota, South
Dakota, and Utah.

Interestingly, S.D. Canon 7A(1)(c) prohibits judges and candidates from paying
an "assessment" to a political organization or candidate, but does not prohibit them
from contributing to a political organization or candidate; and Canon 7A(2) expressly
authorizes a judge or candidate holding an office filled by public election between
competing candidates to contribute to a political party or organization.

83. *See* COJC 7A in Alaska, District of Columbia, Nebraska, Vermont, and
Wyoming.

84. *See* S.C. COJC Canons 7A(1)(c), 7A(2).

85. *See* COJC Canon 7A in Connecticut and Virginia.

86. *See* COJC Canon 7A in Alabama, New Mexico, and Texas.

87. *See* COJC Canon 7A in Idaho, Michigan, and Nevada.

88. *See* COJC Canon 7A(1)(c) in Arizona and California. Although Canon 7,
both in Arizona and in California, has a provision identical to ABA Canon 7A(4)'s
prohibition of "any other political activity," it appears very unlikely that the foregoing interpretation would be affected by that provision.

89. *See* Ohio COJC Canon 7A(2). Although Canon 7 in Ohio has a provision
identical to ABA Canon 7A(4)'s prohibition of "any other political activity," it

seems very unlikely that the foregoing interpretation would be affected by that prohibition.

90. *See* COJC Canons 7A(1)(c) and 7A(2) in Florida, Georgia, Kentucky, Minnesota, Oklahoma, and Washington; and COJC Canon 7A in Oregon. This prohibition in Oregon applies only when one or more of four specified effects occurs.

91. *See* Colo. COJC Canons 7A(1)(c), 7A; Del. COJC Canons 7A(3), 7A(4), 7A; Hawaii COJC Canons 7A(1)(c), 7A; Iowa COJC Canons 7A(1)(c), 7A; Mass. COJC Canons 7A(1)(c), 7A. ABA Canon 7A(2) was totally omitted from each of the foregoing. In one of these commission selection states, Delaware, the Code prohibits not only contributions by judges to political organizations (Canon 7A(3)) but also direct or indirect contributions by judges to political parties (Canon 7A(4)). It is further provided by Canon 7A(4) that any such contribution by a judge's spouse shall be deemed an indirect contribution by the judge in violation of the Code, unless the spouse is individually active in political affairs.

92. *See* Me. COJC Canons 7A (1)(c), 7A; N.H. COJC Canons 7A(1)(c), 7A; N.J. COJC Canons 7A(1)(d), 7A. ABA Canon 7A(2) was totally omitted from each of the foregoing three Codes.

93. *See* COJC Canon 7A(1)(c) and 7A in Connecticut and West Virginia. ABA Canon 7A(2) was totally omitted from the foregoing two Codes.

NOTES TO §5.4(e)(iii)

94. This prohibition represents a change in the law, since the political activity prohibitions of the Canons of Judicial Ethics as still found in four of the five remaining noncode states do not prohibit contributions to candidates for public office. *See* Ill. S. Ct. R. 70; Md. S. Ct. R. XXVII, XXIX; Mont. S. Ct. R. 28, 30; Wisc. S. Ct. R. 60.14, 15. *Contra*: R.I. S. Ct. R. 25 (prohibiting contributions to candidates).

95. *See* COJC Canon 7A(1)(c) in Arkansas, Indiana, Kansas, Mississippi, New York, and Pennsylvania.

96. *See* COJC Canon 7A(1)(c) in Florida, Kentucky, Louisiana, Minnesota, North Dakota, Oklahoma, and Utah.

97. *See* COJC Canon 7A(1)(c) in Alaska, Colorado, Delaware, District of Columbia, Hawaii, Iowa, Massachusetts, Nebraska, Vermont, and Wyoming (prohibition only applies to judges and not candidates in Colorado, Delaware, Hawaii, Iowa, and Massachusetts).

98. *See* COJC Canon 7A(1)(c) in Maine, New Hampshire, and South Carolina; COJC Canon 7A(1)(d) in New Jersey (prohibition only applies to judges and not candidates in Maine, New Hampshire, and New Jersey).

99. *See* COJC Canon 7A(1)(c) in Connecticut and Virginia (prohibition only applies to judges and not candidates in these states).

100. *See* N.C. COJC Canon 7A(1)(d).

101. *See* COJC Canon 7A(1)(c) in Arizona, California, and Washington, and Oregon COJC Canon 7A.

102. *See* N.C. COJC Canon 7A(1)(d); Wash. COJC Canon 7A(1)(c).

103. *See* Ariz. COJC Canon 7A(1)(c), and Cal. COJC Canon 7A(1)(c)

104. *See* Ore. COJC Canon 7A.

105. *See* N.C. COJC Canon 7(1)(b) (contributions to the judicial candidate deemed by the contributor to be the best qualified are expressly permitted).

106. *See* COJC Canon 7A(1)(c) in Arizona, California, and Washington, and Oregon COJC Canon 7A.

107. *See* Tenn. COJC Canon 7A(2) (expressly permits any judge or judicial candidate to contribute "to a political party or candidate").

108. *See* COJC Canon 7A in Alabama, New Mexico, and Texas.

109. *See* COJC Canon 7A in Idaho, Georgia, Michigan, and Nevada.

110. *See* COJC Canon 7A in Missouri (only applies to commission plan judges) and West Virginia (only applies to judges who are not candidates).

111. *See* COJC Canon 7A in Ohio and South Dakota.

NOTES TO §5.4(f)

112. *See* Minn. COJC Canon 7A(1)(c) (permits judge to attend and speak at nonpartisan political gathering during year of elective candidacy).

113. *See* Colo. COJC Canon 7A(1)(c) (attendance at partisan political gathering prohibited); Del. COJC Canon 7A(3); Iowa COJC Canon 7A(1)(c); and Mass. Canon 7A(1)(c).

114. *See* Me. COJC Canon 7A(1)(c); N.H. COJC Canon 7A(1)(c); N.J. Canon 7A(1)(c) (prohibition against judge attending "political functions or functions which are likely to be considered as being political in nature").

115. *See* COJC Canon 7A(1)(c) in Connecticut and Virginia.

116. *See* COJC Canon 7A in Arizona and California (authorizes judicial candidate, whether or not a judge, to speak to political gatherings only on his own behalf).

117. *See* Hawaii COJC Canon 6A.

118. *See* COJC Canons 7A(1)(c) and 7A(2) in Arkansas, Indiana, Kansas, Mississippi, New York, and Pennsylvania. In Kansas, Canon 7A(1)(c) expressly prohibits judges and judicial candidates from attending political gatherings, and Canon 7A(2) authorizes incumbent judges and candidates for judicial offices selected by partisan election to "associate with and contribute to a political party and participate on his own behalf in political activity." It appears uncertain whether Kansas Canon 7A(2)'s requirement that the office sought by a candidate be filled by partisan election would be construed as applicable to incumbent judges also.

119. *See* COJC Canons 7A(1)(c) and 7A(2) in Kentucky, Louisiana, North Dakota, Oklahoma, Utah, and Washington.

120. *See* COJC Canons 7A(1)(c) and 7A(2) in Alaska, District of Columbia, Nebraska, Vermont, and Wyoming.

121. *See* S.C. COJC Canons 7A(1)(c), 7A(2).

122. *See* Mo. COJC Canons 7A(2), 7A(4) (partisan election state) and COJC Canon 7A(2), 7A(4) in Florida and South Dakota (nonpartisan election states).

123. *See* Tenn. COJC Canon 7A (2); W. Va. COJC Canon 7A(2). In West Virginia, the permissive provision in Canon 7A(2) applies only to "judges." *See* W. Va. COJC Canon 7A(2). Possibly, however, the term "judge" would be construed as including candidates for judicial offices. Unlike the other Code provisions cited in this note, the Tennessee language appears to be broad enough to include any candidate for election or re-election even if the election is a noncompetitive retention

election rather than an election between competing candidates. *See* Tenn. COJC Canon 7A(2).

124. *See* Mich. COJC Canon 7A(2); Ohio COJC Canon 7A(2).

125. *See* N.C. COJC Canons 7A(2), 7A.

126. *See* COJC Canons 7A(2) and 7A, in Georgia and South Dakota.

127. *See* COJC Canon 7A in Alabama, New Mexico, and Texas.

128. *See* COJC Canon 7A in Idaho, Nevada, and Oregon.

NOTES TO §5.4(g)

129. *See* COJC Canon 7A(2) in Arkansas, Indiana, Mississippi, Missouri, New York, North Carolina, Pennsylvania, and Tennessee. In Missouri, the privilege under consideration is conferred only on an elective incumbent judge or judicial candidate "where it is necessary that a judge be nominated and elected as a candidate of a political party." This apparent exclusion of candidates in nonpartisan elections from the privilege in question (which ABA Canon 7A(2) extends to all elective candidates) is of no practical significance, since nonpartisan elections are not provided for in Missouri. See Mo. Const. art. 5 §§19, 25(a)–25(d); Mo. Stat. Ann. §478.010 (Supp.).

In Missouri, a judge may speak at political gatherings "on subjects permitted under Canon 4A" which might be construed as permitting campaign speeches on his own behalf, since Canon 4A permits a judge to speak "concerning the administration of justice."

130. *See* COJC Canon 7A(2) in Arizona, California, Florida, Kentucky, Louisiana, Michigan, Minnesota, North Dakota, Ohio, Oklahoma, South Dakota, Utah, and Washington. Canon 7A(2) is more restrictive in Minnesota than in the other states just listed, since it provides that a judicial candidate may speak on his own behalf only "at other than partisan political gatherings during the year in which he is a candidate for election or re-election."

The Michigan language, which provides that "a judge or candidate for judicial office" may speak to political gatherings on his own behalf (or on behalf of other judicial candidates), appear to be literally applicable to nonelective judges and candidates as well as elective judges and candidates. The Arizona, California, and Ohio language likewise appears to be literally applicable to nonelective judges and candidates. It could also be argued that the very term "candidate" implies a forthcoming election, and that the term "speak . . . on his own behalf" (applicable to judges as well as candidates) has a similar connotation.

131. *See* COJC Canon 7A(2) in Alaska, District of Columbia, Nebraska, Vermont, and Wyoming.

132. *See* S.C. COJC Canon 7A(2).

133. *See* COJC Canon 7A in Texas, and West Virginia. West Virginia does, however, authorize judges to speak at political gatherings on subjects permitted under Canon 4A, one of which is the administration of justice.

134. *See* COJC Canon 7A in Idaho, Nevada, and Oregon.

135. *See* COJC Canon 7A in Colorado, Delaware, Hawaii, Iowa, and Massachusetts.

136. *See* COJC Canon 7A in New Hampshire and New Jersey; and Me. COJC Canon 7A(1).

137. *See* COJC Canon 7A in Connecticut and Virginia.

138. *See* COJC Canon 7A(1)(b) in Colorado, Connecticut, Iowa, Maine, Massachusetts, Nevada, New Hampshire, New Jersey, and Virginia; Del. COJC Canon 7A(2); Hawaii COJC Canon 6A(1)(b); and Idaho COJC Canon 7A. Texas totally lacks a prohibition against speeches for political organizations or candidates; West Virginia has such a prohibition, but it applies only when the speaker is not himself a candidate; and Oregon does not have any general prohibition of this nature, but merely prohibits public statements for nonjudicial candidates that have one of various specified effects. *See* Tex. COJC Canon 7A; Ore. COJC Canons 7, 7A; and W. Va. COJC Canon 7A(1)(b).

139. *See* Colo. COJC Canon 7A(1)(d); Conn. COJC Canon 7A(3); Del. COJC Canon 7C; Hawaii COJC Canon 6A(2); Iowa COJC Canon 7A(3); Me. COJC Canon 7A(1)(d); N.H. COJC Canon 7A(3); N.J. COJC Canon 7A(3); W. Va. COJC Canon 7A(4).

140. After defining "political activity" as various activities for "a political purpose or organization," Canon 7 of the Oregon Code defines a political purpose (other than a purpose to promote or influence the passage or defeat of laws or regulations) as "the purpose to elect or defeat one or more candidates for a nonjudicial office." While the various Codes are not in accord as to whether the making of speeches by judges in support of other judicial candidates should be a prohibited political activity, it is arguable the fact that the framers of a number of the Codes concluded in the negative lends weight to the argument that speeches by a judge or judicial candidate in support of his own candidacy is not a "political activity."

141. *See* Idaho COJC Canon 7A; Nev. COJC Canon 7B; Ore. COJC Canon 7B; Tex. COJC Canon 7B; W. Va. COJC Canon 7B.

142. These states are Colorado, Connecticut, Delaware, Hawaii, Iowa, Massachusetts, Maine, New Hampshire, New Jersey, and Virginia. *See supra* notes 135–137, and the accompanying text.

143. Canon 7 in Delaware, Hawaii, Massachusetts, New Hampshire, New Jersey, Maine, Connecticut, and Virginia, all of which are nonelective states, lacks any provisions comparable to those in ABA Canon 7B. The only such nonelective states with any such provision are Colorado and Iowa, and those provisions pertain only to noncompetitive retention elections (*see* Colo. and Iowa COJC Canon 7B), and, in Iowa, to such elections only when the candidate's candidacy has drawn active opposition.

144. *See* Conn. Const. art. V, §2; Del. Const. art. IV, §3; Del. Exec. Order No. 4 (1977); Hawaii Const. art. VI, §3; Me. Const. art. 5, pt. 1, §8; N.H. Const. pt. 2, art. 46; N.J. Const. art. VI, §VI, ¶1; Va. Const. art. 6, §7. *See supra* notes 27, 30, 40, 41, 43–45, 112, 113, 115, 116, 123 (Chapter 2), and the accompanying text.

NOTES TO §5.4(h)3

145. *See* COJC Canon 7A(2) in Arkansas, Indiana, Mississippi, New York, North Carolina, Pennsylvania, Tennessee, and West Virginia.

146. *See* COJC Canon 7A(2) in Louisiana, North Dakota, Ohio, South Dakota, and Utah.

147. *See* COJC Canon 7A(2) in Alaska, District of Columbia, Nebraska, Vermont, and Wyoming.

148. *See* J.C. COJC Canon 7A(2).

149. *See* COJC Canon 7A(2) in Ohio and Tennessee.

150. *See* W. Va. COJC Canon 7A(2). As a practical matter, it seems more likely than not that the term "judge" in West Virginia would be construed as applying to judicial candidates who are not incumbent judges, as well as to incumbent judges.

151. *See* N.M. COJC Canon 7A.

152. *See* COJC Canon 7A in Alabama, Kansas, Missouri, and Texas.

153. *See* COJC Canon 7A in Arizona, California, Florida, Georgia, Idaho, Michigan, Minnesota, Nevada, and Oklahoma.

154. *See* COJC Canon 7A in Colorado, Delaware, Iowa, and Massachusetts and Hawaii COJC Canon 6A.

155. *See* COJC Canon 7A in Maine, New Hampshire, and New Jersey.

156. *See* COJC Canon 7A in Connecticut and West Virginia.

157. *See* Ariz. COJC Canon 7A(4); Cal. COJC Canon 7A(3); Conn. COJC Canon 7A(3); Del. COJC Canon 7C; Fla. COJC Canon 7A(4); Hawaii COJC Canon 6A(2); Iowa COJC Canon 7A(3); Kan. COJC Canon 7A(4); Me. COJC Canon 7A(1)(d); Mo. COJC Canon 7A(4); Minn. COJC Canon 7A(4); N.H. COJC Canon 7A(3); N.J. COJC Canon 7A(3); Okla. COJC Canon 7A(4); Va. COJC Canon 7A(3).

158. Ky. COJC Canon 7A(2); Ore. COJC Canons 7, 7B(6); Wash. COJC Canon 7A(2).

159. *See* note 146, and the accompanying text. In Ohio, the authorization extends to any judge or judicial candidate. *See* Ohio COJC Canon 7A(2).

NOTES TO §5.4(i)

160. *See* COJC Canon 7A(1)(c) in Arkansas, Indiana, Kansas, Mississippi, New York, and Pennsylvania.

161. *See* COJC Canon 7A(1)(c) in Florida, Georgia, Kentucky, Louisiana, Minnesota, North Dakota, Oklahoma, Utah, and Washington.

162. *See* COJC Canon 7A(1)(c) in Alaska, Colorado, District of Columbia, Delaware, Iowa, Massachusetts, Nebraska, Vermont, and Wyoming; and Hawaii COJC Canon 6A(1)(c).

163. *See* COJC Canon 7A(1)(c) in Maine, New Hampshire, New Jersey, and South Carolina.

164. *See* COJC Canon 7A in Connecticut and Virginia.

165. *See* COJC Canon 7A in Alabama, Missouri, New Mexico, North Carolina, Tennessee, Texas, and West Virginia.

166. *See* COJC Canon 7A in Arizona, California, Idaho, Michigan, Nevada, Ohio, Oregon, and South Dakota.

167. *See* COJC Canon 7A in New Mexico, North Carolina, Tennessee, and Texas. *Compare* Tenn. COJC Canon 7A(4) ("a judge should not take a public position on political issues except on behalf of measures to improve the law, the legal system, or the administration of justice").

168. *See* COJC Canon 7A in Idaho, Michigan, Nevada, and Oregon.

169. For a discussion of the provisions in Canon 7 pertaining to political contributions in the various jurisdictions, see §5.4(g), *supra*.

170. *See* Ala. COJC Canon 7A and W. Va. COJC Canon 7A(4). The prohibition

in Alabama is of "political activities inappropriate to the judicial office that he [a judge or candidate] holds or seeks."

171. See COJC Canon 7A(4) in Arizona, Ohio, South Dakota; and Cal. COJC Canon 7A(3).

NOTES TO §5.4(j)

172. See Canon 7B(1)(c) in Alabama, Arkansas, Indiana, Kansas, Mississippi, Missouri, New York, North Carolina, Pennsylvania, Tennessee, Texas, and West Virginia.

173. See Canon 7B(1)(c) in Arizona, Florida, Georgia, Kentucky, Louisiana, Michigan, Minnesota, Nevada, North Dakota, Ohio, Oklahoma, South Dakota, Utah, and Washington; Ore. COJC Canon 7B(3) and (4).

174. See Canon 7B(1)(c) in Alaska, Colorado, District of Columbia, Iowa, Nebraska, Vermont, and Wyoming.

175. See S.C. COJC Canon 7B(1)(c).

176. See N.M. COJC Canon 7.

177. See COJC Canon 7 in California and Idaho.

178. See Del. COJC Canon 7; Hawaii COJC Canon 6; Mass. COJC Canon 7.

179. See COJC Canon 7 in Maine, New Hampshire, and New Jersey.

180. See COJC Canon 7 in Connecticut and Virginia.

181. See COJC Canon 7B(1)(c) in Alabama and Texas.

182. See COJC Canon 7B(1)(c) in Michigan and Nevada; and Oregon. COJC Canon 7B.

183. See Ore. COJC Canons 7A(2), (4).

184. See Ala. COJC Canon 7B(1)(c).

185. See Nev. COJC Canon 7B(1)(c).

186. See Kan. COJC Canon 7B(1)(c).

187. See COJC Canon 7B(1)(c) in Michigan, Nevada, and Ohio.

188. See Ore. COJC Canons 7B(3), (4).

189. See COJC Canon 7B(1)(c) in Colorado and Iowa.

190. In re Freeman, 387 Mich. 617, 198 N.W.2d 289, 290 (1972) (First Amendment precludes bar discipline against judicial candidate for false defamation of opponent, unless made with knowledge that it was false or with reckless disregard of whether it was false or not). See Thatcher v. United States, supra note 24, 212 Fed. at 807; Russell, supra note 24, 610 P.2d at 1127; and Michaelis, supra note 24, 316 N.W.2d at 54.

191. Freeman, supra note 190 (bar discipline against judicial candidate for false defamation of opponent is warranted when the defamatory remark was made with knowledge that it was false or with reckless disregard of whether it was false or not); Re Gorsuch, 76 S.D. 191, 75 N.W.2d 644, 57 A.L.R.2d 1355 (1956) (disbarment proceeding in which judicial candidate was reprimanded for false and derogatory factual statements about his opponent, made without belief in their truth and without reasonable cause for such belief; nondisbarment based upon repentance and provocation); Spriggs, supra note 24 (intemperate and factually false attack by candidate for supreme court on supreme court warranted bar discipline).

192. See Baker, supra note 24 (holding judicial candidate's adverse comments about his opponent's health was legitimate subject of criticism so long as its factual

predicate was not substantially inaccurate, but that false representation that opponent would receive disability pension should be censured since it was a misrepresentation of fact).

193. *See supra* note 190.

194. *Baker, supra* note 24, 542 P.2d at 706.

195. *Id.*, 542 P.2d at 706.

NOTES TO §5.4(k)

196. *See* COJC Canon 7B(2) in Arkansas, Indiana, Kansas, Mississippi, Missouri, New York, North Carolina, Pennsylvania, Tennessee, and West Virginia.

197. *See* COJC Canon 7B(2) in Arizona, California, Florida, Georgia, Kentucky, Michigan, Minnesota, North Dakota, Ohio, Oklahoma, Oregon, South Dakota, and Washington.

198. *See* COJC Canon 7B(2) in Alaska, District of Columbia, Nebraska, Vermont, and Wyoming.

199. *See* S.C. COJC Canon 7B(2).

200. *See* COJC Canon 7B(2) in North Carolina and Tennessee.

201. *See* COJC Canon 7B(2) in Arizona, California, Kentucky, Ohio, Oklahoma, and Washington; and Ore. COJC Canon 7B(7). Ariz. Canon 7B(2) appears to expressly authorize candidates for retention or re-election personally to solicit publicly stated support. Ore. Canon 7B does, however, prohibit a judge from seeking support for himself, or from inviting opposition to another candidate "because of membership by either candidate in a political organization."

202. The presence or absence of the prohibition against "other political activities" might determine whether personal solicitation of publicly stated support is permissible in these nine jurisdictions; that prohibition is present in six of these nine jurisdictions (*see* COJC Canon 7A(4) in Arizona, Kentucky, Ohio, Oklahoma, and Washington and Cal. COJC Canon 7A(3)) and is absent in three of them (*see* COJC Canon 7A in North Carolina, Oregon, and Tennessee).

203. *See* Ala. COJC Canon 7B; N.M. COJC Canon 7; Tex. COJC Canon 7B.

204. *See* COJC Canon 7B in Louisiana and Utah.

205. *See* Del. COJC Canon 7, Mass. COJC Canon 7; Hawaii COJC Canon 6; Iowa COJC Canon 7.

206. *See* COJC Canon 7A in Maine, New Hampshire and New Jersey.

207. *See* COJC Canon 7A in Connecticut and Virginia.

208. *See* La. COJC Canon 7A(4) and Utah COJC Canon 7A(4) (nonpartisan election states); Del. COJC Canon 7C, Hawaii COJC Canon 6A(2); and Iowa COJC Canon 7A(3) (commission plan states); Me. COJC Canon 7A(4); N.H. COJC Canon 7A(3) and N.J. COJC Canon 7A(3) (executive selection states); and Conn. COJC Canon 7A(3) and Va. COJC Canon 7A(3) (legislative selection states).

209. *See* COJC Canon 7A in the following states: Alabama, New Mexico, and Texas (partisan election states); Idaho (a nonpartisan election state); and Massachusetts (a commission plan state).

210. *See supra* notes 196–199.

211. *Id.*

212. *Id.*

213. *Id.*

214. *See* COJC Canon 7B(2) in Alaska, Arkansas, California, District of Columbia, Florida (refers to "the time limitation provided by law"), Indiana, Kansas, Kentucky, Michigan, Mississippi, Nebraska, New York, North Dakota, Ohio, Oklahoma, Pennsylvania, South Carolina, South Dakota, Tennessee, Vermont, Washington, and Wyoming.

215. *See* COJC Canon 7B(2) in Arizona, Minnesota, Missouri, North Carolina, and West Virginia; Ore. COJC Canon 7B(7); Ga. COJC Canon 7C.

NOTES TO §5.4(l)

216. *See* COJC Canon 7B(3) in Arkansas, Indiana, Kansas, Mississippi, Missouri, New York, North Carolina, and Pennsylvania and Tenn. COJC Canon 7B(2). In Tennessee, the substance of both ABA Canon 7B(2) and ABA Canon 7B(3) are combined in a single canon, Canon 7B(2), by the expedient of making Canon 7B(2) applicable to all judicial candidates, without, however, imposing any requisite that candidates in noncompetitive retention elections meet substantial opposition in order to be entitled to the Canon 7B(2) privileges.

217. *See* COJC Canon 7B(3) in Arizona, California, Florida, Minnesota, North Dakota, Oklahoma, South Dakota, and Washington; Mich. COJC Canon 7B(2); Ore. COJC Canon 7B(7). The comments made in note 216 with respect to Tennessee also apply to Michigan and Oregon, except that the applicable canon in Oregon is numbered as Canon 7B(7).

218. *See* COJC Canon 7B(3) in Alaska, District of Columbia, Nebraska, Vermont, and Wyoming.

219. *See* S.C. COJC Canon 7B(3).

220. *See* Colo. COJC Canon 7B(2) and Iowa COJC Canon 7B(2). Although the Colorado Canon merely refers to the subject judges as candidates for "retention in office" without specifically stating that there must be no opponent, such a requirement appears to be probably implicit.

221. *See* §§2.7(b) and 2.7(d), *supra*.

222. *See* COJC Canon 7B in Tennessee, and West Virginia.

223. *See* COJC Canon 7B in Georgia, Kentucky, and Ohio.

224. *See* §§2.5, 2.6, and 2.8.

225. *See* §§2.7(b) and 2.7(d).

226. *See* COJC Canon 7B(3) in Arizona, Florida, and Pennsylvania, and COJC Canon 7B(2) in Tennessee. In Florida, a retention election candidate who has not certified to active opposition is permitted to engage in "limited campaign activities," including not only the conduct authorized by Canon 7B(2), but also interviews with media reporters and editors and appearances and speaking engagements before public gatherings and organizations other than political parties. As is pointed out in the text accompanying note 227, *infra*, however, when a retention candidate certifies that his candidacy has drawn active opposition, he is entitled to thereafter "campaign in any manner authorized by law, subject to the restrictions of subsection B(1)."

227. *See* Fla. COJC Canon 7B(3).

NOTE TO §5.5

228. For illustrative instances where state Codes of Judicial Conduct have adopted ABA Canon 1, verbatim or without any substantive change, see COJC Canon 1 in

Alaska, Arizona, Arkansas, California, Colorado, Connecticut, Delaware (legislative drafting included in activities authorized by Canon 4A), Florida, Georgia, Hawaii, Indiana, Iowa, Kentucky, Louisiana, Maine, Massachusetts, Minnesota, (term "administration of justice" supplemented by term "judicial administration" in Canon 4B), Mississippi, New Hampshire, New Mexico, New York, North Dakota, Ohio, Oklahoma, Oregon, Pennsylvania, South Carolina, South Dakota, Tennessee, Texas, Washington, West Virginia, and Wyoming. For examples of instances where ABA Canon 4 was adopted with one or more minor substantive changes, generally in Canon 4B, see COJC 4 in Alabama, Kansas, Michigan, Missouri, Nevada, New Jersey, North Carolina and Virginia. Examples of the latter include revisions authorizing consultation with executive or legislative bodies or officials on matters concerning the law or legal system, as well as matters concerning the administration of justice (e.g. Alabama, Michigan, Missouri, Nevada), authorizing such consultations without any express limitations on the matters discussed (e.g. North Carolina), deleting any requirement that the authorized activities not cast doubt on the judge's capacity to decide impartially any issue that may come before him (e.g. Kansas, Michigan, Nevada), requiring that the judge not be compensated for any of the activities authorized by Canon 4 (e.g. Virginia), conditioning the teaching activities authorized in ABA Canon 4A upon the judge's securing prior approval of the supreme court (New Jersey), requiring that the matters (pertaining to the administration of justice) with respect to which consultation is authorized by ABA Canon 4B be matters with which the judge has been charged with responsibility by the rules of court (New Jersey), or narrowing the scope of ABA Canon 4C.

NOTE TO §5.5(a)

229. *See* Murphy, *supra* note 2, at 40–44, 158–159, 161–162, 167–168, 281.

NOTES TO §5.6

230. For illustrative instances when state codes have adopted ABA COJC Canon 5B without appreciable substantive change, see COJC Canon 5B in Arkansas, California, Colorado, Connecticut, Delaware, Florida, Georgia, Hawaii, Indiana, Iowa, Kansas, Kentucky, Massachusetts, Minnesota, Mississippi, Missouri, New York, Ohio, Oklahoma, Oregon, Pennsylvania, South Carolina, South Dakota, Tennessee, Texas, Washington, West Virginia, and Wyoming.

231. For instances where, although adopting ABA COJC Canon 5B in the main, state codes have made substantive revisions in it, *see, e.g.*, the following: (a) COJC Canon 5B in Alaska, Arizona, and Maine, in which subsection 1 of ABA Canon 5B has been omitted; (b) COJC Canon 5B in New Mexico, in which subsection 2 of ABA Canon 5B has been omitted; (c) COJC Canon 5B in Louisiana, Michigan and Virginia, in which subsection 3 of ABA Canon 5B has been omitted; (d) COJC Canon 5B in Alabama, in which the ABA stricture in Canon 5B(2) against solicitation of funds for charitable purposes has been made non-mandatory and the ABA prohibition against judges being speakers or guests of honor at fund raising events has been omitted; (e) COJC Canon 5B in Michigan and New Jersey, in which judges are authorized to join and speak in general fund raising appeals; (f) COJC Canon

5B in New Jersey, in which judges are prohibited from being listed as an officer or trustee in any letter or document used in fund solicitation; (g) COJC Canon 5B in North Carolina, which omits the prohibition in ABA Canon 5B(2) against a judge's speaking or being a guest of honor at a fund raising event; and (h) COJC Canon 5B(2) in New Hampshire, which authorizes a judge to solicit funds from specified sources outside the State for purposes connected with judicial education, the judicial system, and the administration of justice.

NOTES TO §5.7

232. *See* §6(n)(v), note 259 (Chapter 6), *infra*, and the accompanying text. The states in question are Alabama, Arkansas, Colorado, Connecticut, Delaware, Hawaii, Iowa, Kansas, Kentucky, Maine, Massachusetts, Minnesota, New Hampshire, North Dakota, Oregon, Pennsylvania, Rhode Island, South Carolina, Tennessee, Texas, Vermont, Washington, West Virginia, and Wisconsin. *Id.*

233. *See* notes 260–264 (Chapter 6), *infra*, and the accompanying text.

234. *See* notes 266–267 (Chapter 6), *infra*, and the accompanying text.

235. E.g., *Baker, supra* note 192; *Matter of Hotchkiss*, 327 N.W.2d 312 (Mich. 1982); *Matter of Bennett*, 403 Mich. 178, 267 N.W.2d 914 (1978); *Matter of Briggs*, 585 S.W.2d 270 (Mo. En Banc 1980); *In re Corning*, 538 S.W.2d 46, 53 (Mo. En Banc 1976); *In the Matter of Conda*, 72 N.J. 229, 370 A.2d 16 (1977); *In re Hayden*, 41 N.J. 443, 197 A.2d 353 (1964); *In re Pagliughi*, 39 N.J. 516, 189 A.2d 219 (1963); *Elias v. Ellenville Chapter of N.A.A.C.P.*, 37 A.D.2d 216, 325 N.Y.S.2d 302 (3d Dept. 1971). *See also* notes 190–195, *supra*, and the accompanying text.

236. *See Pagliughi, supra* note 235 (disbarment proceeding against judge; judge was reprimanded rather than disbarred because "this is the first case involving a violation of Canon 28").

237. *See Bennett, supra* note 235 (judge suspended for one year without pay because of political misconduct and other misconduct).

238. *See Briggs, supra* note 235 (judge removed for political activities and other misconduct).

239. *Hotchkiss, supra* note 235 (public written reprimand).

240. *Corning, supra* note 235. Article 5, §29(f), of the Missouri constitution prohibits commission plan judges from directly or indirectly making any contribution to or holding any office in a political party or organization or taking part in any political campaign; and Missouri Supreme Court Rule 2.28 prohibits judges from either accepting or retaining a place on any party committee or acting as a party leader or engaging generally in partisan activities.

241. *Conda, supra* note 235.

242. *Hayden, supra* note 235 (reprimand, rather than severer discipline, since only a single indiscretion rather than a continued course of partisan political activity).

243. *Elias, supra* note 235 (removal proceeding dismissed without costs because, although respondent judge's partisan political activity violated Canon 28, the judge, a village court justice, acted in the good faith belief that members of the minor judiciary were not subject to Canon 28's restrictions on political activities).

243. *See supra* notes 190–195, and the accompanying text.

6

Judicial Discipline

6.1 SUMMARY OF THE PRINCIPAL METHODS OF DISCIPLINING JUDGES

The principal methods of disciplining judges have been: (i) removal by the executive branch ("executive action"); (ii) legislative removal by impeachment ("impeachment"); (iii) legislative removal by joint resolution of both houses ("joint resolution"); (iv) removal by the governor on address by both houses of the legislature ("address"); (v) removal during a judge's term of office by recall election ("recall"); (vi) removal by defeat in regular elections at the end of a judge's term of office ("non–re-election"); (vii) removal or discipline by a court in proceedings initiated in the courts ("court discipline"); (viii) removal or discipline by disbarring or disciplining judges in their capacities as members of the bar ("bar discipline"); and (ix) removal or discipline in a proceeding initiated before a permanent disciplinary commission or special disciplinary tribunal ("commission discipline").[1]

6.2 SUMMARY OF ALL OF THE METHODS OF JUDICIAL DISCIPLINE

a. Executive Action

Executive action is the oldest method of disciplining judges.[2] In England, judges held their offices "at the king's pleasure"[3] until passage of the Act of Settlement in 1700, which granted judges security of tenure conditioned on good behavior and abolished executive removal except on address of both

Houses of Parliament.[4] Because of the obvious threat to judicial independence, executive action was rejected by the framers of the U.S. Constitution[5] and has virtually disappeared in this country.[6] Apart from removal by the governor on legislative address, the only vestigial remnant of executive action was found in a recently repealed statute in Hawaii that empowered the governor to remove a judge if, and only if, the Commission on Judicial Qualifications recommended removal.[7]

b. Impeachment

Impeachment originated in England in the latter part of the fourteenth century as a method for removal of high-ranking crown officers, including judges. English impeachments were prosecuted by the House of Commons before the House of Lords.[8]

In the United States, impeachment was initially the principal procedure for removing judges.[9] It is still technically available in the federal system[10] and in virtually every state[11] but has been sparsely used.[12]

c. Address

Under removal by "address," which originated with the Act of Settlement, the governor removes a judge after receipt of a concurrent legislative resolution. Its original purpose was to eliminate the king's arbitrary power to remove judges. Address was not provided for in the U.S. Constitution, but four of the original thirteen states, Maryland, Massachusetts, New Hampshire, and South Carolina, did employ address. By 1936, twenty-eight states provided for removal by address, but, by late 1982, this number had been reduced to nineteen.[13] Except in Massachusetts,[14] address has been rarely used in this country.[15]

d. Joint Resolution

A handful of states have adopted "joint resolution" as a method of removal,[16] but it has seldom been used.[17]

e. Recall

Recall, too, has been adopted by only a handful of states[18] but has been employed even less often than impeachment or address.[19]

Although utilized in ancient Babylonia, Greece, and Syracuse, recall was never used in England.[20] It was first adopted in this country in the Articles of Confederation,[21] but was not included in the Constitution. The first state to provide for recall of judges was Oregon in 1908; it was subsequently adopted by California in 1911, Colorado, Arizona, and Nevada in 1912, and Wisconsin in 1926.[22] States in which it is presently employed include Arizona, California, and Wisconsin.[23]

f. Popular Elections Other Than Recall Elections

Although end-of-term partisan elections, nonpartisan elections, and retention elections are regularly held in many states,[24] these devices have rarely resulted in the removal of unfit judges.[25]

g. Disbarment

In some states, efforts have been made to remove judges by having them disbarred in disciplinary proceedings brought against them as lawyers. The theory is that since bar membership is an essential judicial qualification, disbarment has the indirect effect of removing the judge. The courts have been divided as to whether a disbarment or bar discipline proceeding may be validly brought against a sitting judge for official misconduct.[26] Also, the courts that have held that jurisdiction over such proceedings is lacking, have disagreed as to whether this restriction applies to a proceeding to disbar a sitting judge by reason of conduct committed before ascending the bench;[27] and, if the occasion arose, those courts would probably disagree as to whether jurisdiction would exist in proceedings to disbar a sitting judge by reason of conduct that, although committed by him during his term of office, was unrelated to his official duties.[28] On the other hand, practically all of the courts that have denied jurisdiction over a disbarment proceeding against a sitting judge with respect to official misconduct have held that a judge can be disbarred for official misconduct when the action is instituted after he has been removed or otherwise ceased to be a judge.[29] Since a sitting judge may not be disbarred for official misconduct in a number of states, bar discipline has necessarily proved to be an unsatisfactory remedy in those states.

h. Removal of Judges by Proceedings in the Regular Courts without Involvement of Disciplinary Commissions or Special Disciplinary Courts

Apart from recall and defeat in an election, all of the foregoing disciplinary methods involve either action by the executive or action by the legislature. However, judges may also be removed or disciplined in court proceedings. This method has ancient common law roots in the English procedure for removing a judge by a *scire facias* suit in the court of king's bench to annul a judge's letter patent on the ground of misbehavior.[30] Although the courts have recognized that they possess an inherent power to discipline judges by sanctions short of removal,[31] the courts have generally denied any inherent judicial power to remove judges even for misbehavior, usually on the ground that the existence of an express constitutional remedy precludes the implication of an additional remedy.[32]

i. Disciplinary Commissions and Special Disciplinary Courts

A powerful trend has developed during the last twenty-five years toward the use of permanent disciplinary commissions. These bodies, which are normally composed of judges, lawyers, and laymen in varying proportions, conduct investigations and formal hearings on charges of misconduct or unfitness against judges and make and forward to the supreme court findings and recommendations or, in some states, make decisions on the charges, which are binding unless appealed to the supreme court.[33] California, in 1960, was the first state to adopt such a system.[34] Since then, a large number of states have followed suit,[35] so that disciplinary proceedings initiated by or before commissions have now become the predominant form of judicial discipline in this country.

6.3 DISCIPLINARY COMMISSIONS AND SPECIAL DISCIPLINARY COURTS

a. The Number and Types of Disciplinary Systems Involving One or More Disciplinary Commissions or Special Disciplinary Courts

California, in 1960, was the first state to adopt a disciplinary system involving either a disciplinary commission or a special disciplinary court. The California system involved a disciplinary commission that was authorized to: (a) conduct preliminary investigations to determine whether there was sufficient probable cause to warrant formal charges and a formal hearing ("the investigative function"); (b) prefer formal charges and hold formal hearings on those charges ("the hearing function"); and (c) dismiss or sustain the charges and, if sustained, make and submit to the supreme court a recommended decision, including recommended findings of fact and conclusions of law and recommended sanctions ("the recommendatory function"). The state supreme court then rendered a decision containing findings of fact and conclusions of law, dismissing or sustaining charges and imposing sanctions where warranted ("the decisional function"). This system is still in effect.

Since 1960, each of the fifty states, the federal courts, and the District of Columbia have adopted a system for disciplining, removing, or involuntarily retiring judges. These systems employ either one or more disciplinary com missions, a special disciplinary court, or both.[1]

The fifty-two jurisdictions with disciplinary commissions or special disciplinary courts may be divided into jurisdictions with either only one commission or special court, and jurisdictions with two commissions or both a commission and a special court. The systems with only one such commission or special court are frequently referred to as unitary, or "single-tier," systems; and the systems with two such commissions, or a commission and a special court, are frequently referred to as "two-tier" systems.[37] Eight jurisdictions, the United States, Alabama, Delaware, Illinois, Ohio, Oklahoma, West Virginia, and Wisconsin, have two-tier systems;[38] and the remaining forty-four jurisdictions have a unitary or single-tier disciplinary system.[39]

The unitary or single-tier jurisdictions may be further subdivided. In thirty-eight of the forty-four single-tier jurisdictions, the investigative, hearing, and recommendatory functions rest with the disciplinary commission, while the decisional function is lodged with the highest appellate court.[40] In the District of Columbia, Kentucky, Nevada, and New York, however, the decisional function, as well as the investigative and hearing functions, rests with the disciplinary commission; and the only function conferred on the highest appellate court is an appellate function, i.e., the right to review for errors of law.[41]

The systems in Arkansas and Tennessee are unique. The investigative, hearing, and recommending functions rest with the disciplinary commission, but the decisional function is conferred, not upon the highest appellate court, as is usual elsewhere, but upon the state legislature.[42]

In the two-tier jurisdictions, the normal pattern is for the investigative function to be performed by one agency, and for the hearing and decisional functions to rest with another, a permanent special disciplinary court or tribunal. Alabama, Illinois, Ohio, and Oklahoma all fall into this category. The special tribunal's decisions are subject to supreme court review in Alabama and Ohio, while the decisions of the special court in Illinois (termed the Illinois Courts Commission) are not subject to review, and the special court's decisions in Oklahoma (the Court on the Judiciary's Trial Division) are subject to review only by an appellate division of that same special court.[43]

The Delaware disciplinary system also conforms to this pattern, except that it is a three-tier system, with the investigative, hearing, and decisional functions divided among three agencies: the Preliminary Investigatory Committee (investigational function), the Board of Examining Officers (hearing function), and the Court on the Judiciary (decisional function), whose decisions are not subject to review.[44]

Even when a special disciplinary tribunal's decisions are said to be nonreviewable, review by means of writs of mandamus or prohibition will ordinarily be granted, at least when the contention on appeal is that the special tribunal exceeded its jurisdiction.[45]

Atypical two-tier disciplinary systems are found in West Virginia and

Wisconsin, where the investigative function rests in one agency, the hearing function in another, and the decisional function in the state supreme court.[46]

Finally, the new federal court disciplinary system prescribed by the Judicial Councils Reform and Judicial Conduct and Disability Act[47] allocates the investigative and hearing functions to ad hoc investigative panels of district and circuit court judges appointed by the chief judge of the affected circuit (who himself is a member of the panel). The decisional function is allocated to the judicial council for the circuit (or the Judicial Conference of the United States when a matter is referred to it by the judicial council) when discipline short of removal is sought, and to Congress by way of possible impeachment proceedings (on recommendation of the Judicial Conference) when removal is sought.[48]

b. The Constitutionality of the Joinder of Conflicting Functions in the Unitary Disciplinary Commissions

The joinder of the investigative, prosecutorial, and recommendatory functions in a single commission in unitary commission states has been often challenged as violating due process and the principle of separation of powers. To date, these challenges have all been rejected on the ground that, since the decisional function was performed by the supreme court, rather than the commission, the combination of other functions in the commission was not per se prejudicial and had not been shown to be actually prejudicial.[49] It has been held that, in such case, the burden is on the respondent judge to prove bias.[50] In addition, even though the appointment of a master to take testimony has been cited as a factor supporting constitutionality,[51] the combination of the investigative, prosecutorial, hearing, and recommendatory functions in a single commission has been held not to violate due process not only when the testimony was heard by special masters,[52] but also when it was heard by the commission itself.[53]

The emphasis placed by the courts upon the supreme court's decisional function in jurisdictions where the disciplinary commission merely makes a recommendation suggests that the constitutional problem is more acute in jurisdictions like Kentucky, Nevada, and New York, where a unitary commission is also vested with the decisional function, and the supreme court's role is limited to review.[54] In the only decision on the point, involving a disciplinary decision by a special disciplinary court in New York, the former Court on the Judiciary, the combination of functions in that court was, however, held to be constitutional.[55]

c. The Composition and Selectors of the Members of the Various Disciplinary Commissions and Special Disciplinary Courts

In forty of the forty-four single-tier jurisdictions,[56] the disciplinary commission (or special court in Tennessee) is composed of judges, lawyers, and laymen in varying numbers and proportions.[57] The same is true of the nondecisional commissions in four of the eight double-tier or triple-tier jurisdictions.[58] In the decisional special courts or tribunals in the eight double-tier or triple-tier jurisdictions (including the federal courts), judges are the sole members in Delaware, Illinois, Ohio, Wisconsin, and the federal court system; and both judges and lawyers serve in Alabama, Oklahoma, and West Virginia.[59]

In some states, restrictions on membership have been imposed to ensure that the commissions are bipartisan. Typical examples are a requirement that not more than a certain number of the appointive members may belong to the same political party[60] or a requirement that no more than a specified number of members drawn from a particular category may belong to the same political party.[61]

In all but Maryland, Minnesota, and Virginia, the judicial members of the commissions or special courts are chosen by designated courts, judges' associations, chief justices, the state judiciary, or segments of the jurisdiction.[62] In Maryland, the judicial members are chosen by the governor; while in Virginia, they are chosen by the general assembly.[63]

The lawyer members are chosen by a wide variety of selectors, including members of the state bar, the state bar's board of governors, the state bar president, the supreme court, a conference of judges, the chief justice, the chief administrative judge of the trial courts, the governor, the state bar with the advice and consent of the senate, or the governor with the advice and consent of the senate or legislature.[64]

Finally, the lay members of commissions are, in most instances, chosen by the governor. Other selectors occasionally employed include: the governor, with the advice and consent of the general assembly; the court on the judiciary; the supreme court; the supreme court on the governor's recommendation; specified judicial councils or associations; the general assembly; or designated legislative leaders.[65]

In a few instances, the judicial members of disciplinary commissions and special courts may be drawn from all major courts, all major courts other than the highest court, or all major courts other than appellate courts.[66] Generally, however, the statutes require that the members be drawn from specific courts.[67] When considered in the aggregate, i.e. as a single nationwide group, most of the judicial members of the commissions and special courts are required to be trial judges, although a substantial minority are required to be judges of intermediate appellate courts.[68] Only a few are required, or even permitted, to be judges of the state's highest appellate court.[69] Thus, in disciplinary proceedings involving supreme court judges, supreme court judges will not, in most states, play a significant part in proceedings at the administrative level. During the supreme court phase of disciplinary proceedings against supreme court judges, however, this is not the case, since, in all but a handful of states where a panel of judges from courts other than the supreme court is required or authorized,[70] the supreme court usually is required to hear or review the matter.[71] In some instances, a judge who is a commission member is expressly required by a constitutional provision to disqualify himself from sitting in commission proceedings against a member of his own court.[72]

d. The Functions of Investigating the Complaint and Determining whether Probable Cause for Discipline Exists

In each of the unitary commission states, the duties of investigating complaints against judges and determining whether there is probable cause for discipline have been assigned to the commission[73] to be performed, generally, by staff personnel or counsel[74] but occasionally by state or outside investigators[75] or even members of the commission,[76] in conjunction with state counsel[77] or special counsel.[78]

The commissions are generally given the power to subpoena and compel sworn testimony and the production of documents during both the preliminary investigation and formal hearings and to secure court orders compelling compliance with such subpoenas.[79] In at least one state, the commission has been granted the additional power to serve written interrogatories on members of the bar other than the judge involved.[80]

Some states require submission of a verified written complaint,[81] or at least an unverified written complaint,[82] before the commission can launch a preliminary investigation. The proposed ABA Judicial Discipline and Disability Standards, however, recommend that the commission inquire into any charge regardless of the manner in which the charge is made.[83] A few states have expressly adopted this procedure.[84]

Even though an applicable statute or rule requires a verified complaint, or at least a written statement, there is often a provision that permits the commission to dispense with this requirement by authorizing the commission to institute a preliminary investigation on its own motion.[85]

A considerable number of disciplinary systems require that the commission notify the judge during the pendency of the preliminary investigation and afford the judge an opportunity to appear before it and present exculpatory evidence before the commission determines whether there is probable cause or serves formal charges on the judge.[86] Failure to provide the judge with notice and opportunity to present exculpatory matter prior to such determination has been held not to violate due process, even when it violates a commission rule, since the requirements of notice and opportunity to defend apply only to the hearing and not to the investigative stage.[87]

There is disagreement as to whether a judge should be notified during the investigative stage of the identity of the complainant. Some jurisdictions require disclosure,[88] but others do not.[89]

e. Informal Disposition of a Disciplinary Cause before Formal Hearing

After a preliminary investigation, two possible conclusions are: (a) that the conduct, although not warranting a formal hearing, was of such a nature that, if continued, it might ultimately require public censure or removal; or (b) that even though the acts probably constituted misconduct serious enough to warrant formal charges, they were, nevertheless, of a relatively low degree of seriousness. The commissions and legislatures in a number of jurisdictions have developed remedial alternatives to formal hearing procedures to dispose of these types of cases. These include private reprimands,[90] warnings that the judge's conduct would merit discipline if not discontinued, professional counseling, or conditions placed on the judge's future conduct.[91]

f. The Prosecutor of the Charges against the Judge

In most states, prosecuting counsel is selected by the commission from the members of the bar.[92] In other states, the commission is required to ask that the state's highest court appoint prosecuting counsel.[93] In still other states, the attorney general is designated as prosecuting counsel, either absolutely[94] or with the proviso that the commission is authorized to employ other counsel if it believes that the attorney general has a conflict of interest.[95] In yet another group of states, the commission is given an untrammeled choice between the attorney general and counsel selected by it.[96] Finally, one state requires that the commission select a retired judge or a retired state or district attorney as prosecuting counsel.[97]

g. The Appointment of a Panel of Commissioners or of One or More Masters or a Referee to Preside at a Formal Hearing

In practically every state with a unitary disciplinary commission system, the commission is empowered to preside *en banc* over any formal hearing.[98] In several of these states, the commission is also given the option of having the hearing held before a panel of its members.[99] In a majority of the unitary disciplinary systems, the commission may, however, elect to have the formal hearing held before one or more masters, referees, or hearing officers.[100] Generally, the master, or masters, must be selected by the supreme court at the commission's request,[101] although some states require them to be selected by the commission.[102] At times, restrictions on the qualifications or affiliations of the masters are imposed. These include requirements that the master not be a member of the commission[103] or that the master be a judge of a court of record,[104] a judge of one of several specified courts,[105] a judge or lawyer familiar with ruling on motions and admission of evidence,[106] a member of the bar who is neither a judge nor a member of the commission or on its staff,[107] or a "qualified person."[108]

The contention that the use of a master or referee in a disciplinary commission proceeding offends due process because the court or agency rendering the first decision did not hear the evidence or observe the demeanor of the witnesses was rejected by the U.S. Supreme Court in *Mildner v. Gulotta*.[109] None of the statutes or rules provides for a jury trial in disciplinary proceedings;[110] and it has been held that the judge does not have this right.[111]

The other principal constitutional challenge to the use of masters or referees at formal disciplinary hearings arises only when the use of a master or referee is not expressly authorized by the constitutional or statutory provision creating the disciplinary system. Under these circumstances, it has been argued that the use of a master or referee deprives the finder of fact of demeanor evidence and should not be implied. This contention was, however, rejected by the New York Court on the Judiciary in 1975 in *In the Matter of Waltemade*[112].

When masters hear and report on the testimony in a judicial disciplinary proceeding, the commission still has the ultimate responsibility of recommending (or in some states, ordering) discipline or dismissal and, although it may properly give great weight to findings of the masters based on oral testimony, it may (and perhaps should) independently evaluate the evidence. It is free to disregard the master's report and to prepare its own findings of fact and conclusions of law.[113]

h. Confidentiality Restrictions as to Investigations and Hearings by or before Disciplinary Commissions

Commission proceedings, in a majority of the single-tier jurisdictions[114] and a minority of the two-tier jurisdictions[115] are subject to confidentiality restrictions until the commission files a recommendation with the state supreme court or a decision recommending or imposing discipline. Confidentiality ceases in a minority of the single-tier jurisdictions[116] and in a majority of the multi-tier jurisdictions[117] when the commission makes a determination that probable cause exists and/or that a formal hearing is necessary. In several other jurisdictions, the confidentiality restriction is not lifted until the supreme court has issued a final order.[118]

In the jurisdictions terminating confidentiality when a recommendation is filed[119] or discipline imposed,[120] the transcript and other accompanying papers filed with the supreme court also cease to be confidential. When, however, a judge is exonerated after a formal hearing in a jurisdiction in which formal hearings are not open to the public, the records of the proceedings are, in many jurisdictions, permanently protected from public disclosure.[121] Moreover, in a divided decision in *First Amendment Coalition vs. Judicial Inquiry and Review Board*,[122] the Court of Appeals for the Third Circuit held that not only do the press and the public have no First Amendment right to attend a formal judicial disciplinary hearing or to have access to the transcript before the hearing has been completed but also they do not acquire any such right of access to the transcript after completion of the hearing when the commission does not recommend sanctions to the Supreme Court. In so holding, the court reversed the decision below, in which District Judge Pollak had held that the press and public did have a First Amendment right of access to the transcript after (but not before) completion of the formal hearing even when the commission dismissed all charges against the respondent judge. On the other hand, in an analogous decision, in *Landmark Communications, Inc. v. Virginia*,[123] the U.S. Supreme Court held that the First Amendment precludes criminal punishment action against members of the press who secure and publish confidential information about judicial disciplinary proceedings in violation of confidentiality restrictions imposed by state law.

The rules and courts are in conflict as to whether a private complainant's name should be disclosed to the judge.[124] This results from the clash between the policies of protecting complainants from reprisals[125] and of encouraging them to bring instances of judicial misconduct to the commission's attention[126] and the policy of entitling accused judges to confront their accusers and respond to the accusations.[127]

Confidentiality terminates in many jurisdictions when the judge requests that the formal hearing be public[128] or waives confidentiality.[129] In other jurisdictions, the constitutional provision imposing confidentiality may be deemed of such importance that, as a matter of public policy, it cannot be waived.

Specific exceptions to the general confidentiality restrictions also exist. These exceptions entitle the commission to issue explanatory statements when information about the proceeding has become public[130] and to make disclosures to legislative committees for impeachment purposes,[131] to governmental officers or selection commissions for purposes of judicial selection,[132] to courts, commissions, or bar organizations for purposes of bar discipline,[133] or to prosecutors for use in perjury prosecutions.[134]

The commission also may be required or authorized to disclose dismissal of a proceeding or termination of an investigation[135] or the resignation or retirement of a judge following institution of formal proceedings.[136] Finally, a commission may be required to inform the complainant that probable cause has been found lacking or that appropriate corrective action has been taken by the commission (without disclosing the nature of the action).[137]

i. Discovery Proceedings

Disciplinary commission statutes and rules on discovery fall into several categories: (a) those that do not expressly authorize discovery,[138] (b) those that expressly authorize the commission to take depositions or issue sub-poenas, without stating whether the judge also may have discovery;[139] (c) those that expressly authorize the discovery for both the commission and the judge[140] after application to the commission for an order authorizing the discovery;[141] (d) those that expressly authorize discovery for the judge but not the commission;[142] and (e) those that expressly authorize discovery without identifying the parties entitled to obtain such discovery.[143]

Some of the discovery provisions do not expressly state whether they apply to both the investigation and hearing stages,[144] while others expressly apply to both.[145]

In passing on document requests, there appears to have been a tendency to limit discovery to the type generally granted in pre-trial orders, i.e., those designed to obtain trial exhibits and statements from intended trial wit-nesses.[146] Discovery of this nature is expressly required by some commission rules.[147] As might be expected, requests for production of internal com-mission reports, memoranda, and other materials prepared by commission's counsel have been uniformly denied.[148]

Denials of discovery have been sustained on appeal on the grounds of lack of affidavit showing of good cause,[149] lack of prejudice,[150] or sufficient notice of charges and nature of facts sought to be proved.[151] Similarly, the trend in the court decisions has been to deny a judge discovery from com-plainants and witnesses when the commission has not yet determined whether they will be called as witnesses.[152]

j. Evidentiary Rules, Miscellaneous Procedural Rules, and Standards of Proof in Connection with Formal Hearings

(i) Evidentiary Rules

Although the rules of evidence are inapplicable in some jurisdictions, which permit introduction of any relevant and material evidence,[153] most jurisdictions apply the same rules of evidence applicable in a normal trial.[154]

(ii) Statutes of Limitation

Disciplinary proceedings are frequently subject to constitutional or sta-tutory provisions limiting the time period in which a judge's conduct may constitute the basis for discipline. The most typical limitation is one ex-cluding conduct occurring more than a specified number of years before the commencement of the judge's current term of office.[155] Another type limits actionable conduct to events after the judge's current appointment[156] or after he was first elected or appointed to office.[157] Still another type restricts discipline to conduct occurring within a specified time before it was reported to the commission.[158]

(iii) Res Judicata

Because disciplinary orders are often predicated upon the cumulative impact of a continuing course of conduct, the doctrines of *res judicata* and double jeopardy do not preclude commissions and courts in later disciplinary proceedings from reconsidering conduct that was the subject of an earlier disciplinary proceeding against the same judge. This is true even if the earlier proceeding was terminated by dismissal or imposition of milder disciplinary penalty than is being sought in the later proceedings.[159] Conversely, public policy has been held to require that once a commission has completed its formal hearing and voted to dismiss the charges, the proceeding must be deemed terminated.[160]

In a proceeding to discipline a judge after a criminal conviction, the judge is bound by the conviction and is not permitted to re-litigate the underlying facts.[161]

(iv) Resignation as Terminating Commission Jurisdiction over Judge

Resignation does not normally terminate a commission's jurisdiction over a judge, since the question of whether the judge should be disqualified from holding future judicial office is not rendered moot by the resignation.[162]

(v) Self-Incrimination

It is well established that a judge may refuse to testify on the ground of self-incrimination in a judicial disciplinary proceeding,[163] provided he has not waived his privilege by answering questions on the same subject in prior proceedings.[164]

On the other hand, it has been held in New York that such a refusal to testify constitutes either "cause" for removal[165] or establishes unfitness for office.[166]

This is the case not only when the testimony was sought in a grand jury proceeding and pertained to matters other than the judge's judicial conduct,[167] but also when the desired testimony was sought in a judicial disciplinary proceeding.[168] A judge's refusal to waive immunity under a statute granting immunity to witnesses compelled to testify after having first asserted their privilege against self-incrimination also constitutes a basis for removal.[169]

These decisions appear inconsistent with more recent U.S. Supreme Court decisions, holding the privilege against self-incrimination precludes disbarment of a lawyer[170] or discharge of a public official or employee[171] asserting his privilege in a disciplinary proceeding.

No inference of guilt may be drawn in a disciplinary proceeding from the judge's refusal to answer questions on the ground of self-incrimination.[172] Moreover, if a judge was coerced by a disciplinary commission into waiving his privilege against self-incrimination or into waiving immunity under an applicable immunity statute by a threat to remove him for noncooperation, it appears probable that his testimony would be deemed involuntary and thus inadmissible.[173] In the absence of a threat of removal, testimony given by a judge in a disciplinary proceeding because he feared he would not otherwise be able to defend himself would, however, be considered voluntary and admissible.[174]

Finally, if a judge gave immunized testimony in a nondisciplinary setting, such as a grand jury investigation, the testimony's immunized status would not preclude its use in a subsequent proceeding to discipline him, since it would not be considered a criminal proceeding for purposes of the immunity statute.[175]

(vi) Standards Of Proof

It is uniformly recognized that the prosecution bears the burden of establishing that grounds for discipline exist.[176] The only dispute comes on the question of whether the standard is a preponderance of evidence, clear and convincing proof, or proof beyond a reasonable doubt.[177] An overwhelming majority of the disciplinary commission jurisdictions apply the "clear and convincing proof" standard,[178] while a few employ either the "preponderance of the evidence" standard[179] or the "beyond a reasonable doubt" standard.[180]

k. Suspension of Judges Pending Disciplinary or Criminal Proceedings against Them

(i) Express Provision for Suspension Pending Disciplinary Proceedings

Procedures to temporarily suspend judges under disciplinary scrutiny are often provided to maintain confidence in the judiciary.[181] A majority of the jurisdictions employing temporary suspension fix the date on which the disciplinary commission or special court recommends or orders discipline as the date on which suspension commences. This occurs automatically[182] or under a discretionary order entered by the supreme court,[183] the commission,[184] or the supreme court on the recommendation of the commission.[185] When suspended under these circumstances, the judge is entitled to continue to receive compensation in some jurisdictions.[186] In others, the supreme court has discretion to continue or suspend salary,[187] in one or more salary is automatically suspended,[188] and in some there is no provision as to continuance or suspension of salary.[189]

In still other jurisdictions, provision is made for temporary suspension following a commission determination of probable cause and service of formal charges on the judge. This can occur in a variety of ways:

automatically[190] or at the discretion of the commission,[191] the supreme court,[192] or the supreme court on recommendation of the commission.[193] Salary during the temporary suspension is continued as of right in some jurisdictions,[194] but in others continuation or suspension of salary is at the discretion of the supreme court.[195] In some jurisdictions, there is no provision on the subject.[196]

Finally, in a substantial number of jurisdictions, the commission,[197] supreme court,[198] or the supreme court on recommendation of the commission[199] is granted discretion to suspend the judge pending the outcome of the proceeding, without any express requirement that there be a determination of probable cause or its equivalent. Continuation of salary under these circumstances is mandatory in some jurisdictions[200] but, in others, is left to the discretion of the supreme court.[201] In some jurisdictions, there is no provision on the subject.[202]

It has been held that due process does not require that interim suspension with pay be preceded by a hearing.[203]

(ii) Implied Power of Supreme Court to Suspend Pending Disciplinary Proceeding Absent Express Authorization

Under a constitutional provision that granted the supreme court the express power to remove a judge but not the express power to suspend him during the pendency of the removal proceedings, the Texas supreme court, in a 1907 decision, held that the court nevertheless had implied power to suspend the judge.[204]

(iii) Suspension Pending Criminal Proceedings and Following Criminal Convictions

(1) *Suspension Pending Criminal Proceedings.* To avoid any loss of public confidence, many states require or authorize temporary suspension of a judge. In about half of these jurisdictions, the disqualification occurs automatically following indictment;[205] in the remainder, the matter is left to the discretion of the supreme court[206] or the commission.[207] In practically all such jurisdictions, the judge continues to receive his salary.[208]

(2) *Suspension Following Criminal Conviction.* Many jurisdictions make provision for suspension of judges convicted of, or pleading guilty or nolo contendere with respect to, felonies until there has been a final conviction. In some jurisdictions, suspension is automatic or mandatory,[209] while in others suspension is at the discretion of the supreme court,[210] commission,[211] or supreme court on recommendation of the commission.[212] Most of these suspension provisions apply not only to felony convictions but also to convictions for other crimes involving moral turpitude.[213] In practically all instances, the judge's compensation (and their judicial functions) are suspended.[214]

l. The Sanctions That May Be Imposed in a Proceeding Involving a Disciplinary Commission or Special Disciplinary Tribunal

The sanctions that may be imposed in a proceeding involving a disciplinary commission or special disciplinary tribunal vary widely from jurisdiction to jurisdiction. Virtually every state authorizes removal or censure for judicial misconduct.[215] Provision for compulsory retirement in instances of permanent, incapacitating disability is similarly widespread.[216] Other possible sanctions for misconduct include: suspension with or without pay,[217] imposition of a fine,[218] imposition of limitations or conditions on the performance of judicial duties,[219] and disbarment or suspension as a member of the bar.[220] Some disciplinary bodies are also authorized to assess costs against the judge.[221]

While the power of most commissions is limited to recommending drastic sanctions to the supreme court, a number of commissions have the power to impose less drastic disciplinary sanctions, including private admonishment or reprimand.[222]

m. The Role of the Supreme Court in a Jurisdiction in which the Commission Merely Recommends Discipline and the Decisional Function Is Conferred on the Supreme Court Rather Than the Commission

In most jurisdictions where the commission merely recommends discipline, the decisional function is entrusted to the supreme court. The court is required to exercise its independent judgment based on the entire record in determining whether the judge's conduct warrants discipline and, if so, what sanctions should be imposed.[223] In these jurisdictions, the supreme court also has the right to revise, alter, or reject the commission's findings and conclusions[224] and need not accord any weight to them.[225] The supreme courts nevertheless "give substantial consideration and due deference to the Commission's ability to judge the credibility of the witnesses appearing before it."[226]

In jurisdictions where the supreme court applies the foregoing standard of review (herein characterized as the "independent evaluation" standard), the court generally also applies the same standard of proof that the commission is required to apply. If, for example, the standard of proof at the commission level is "clear and convincing evidence," the supreme court generally also applies this standard.[227]

The independent evaluation standard does not require, or authorize, the supreme court of any jurisdiction to hold a *de novo* evidentiary hearing. Rather, the court merely makes a *de novo* determination based on the record compiled below.[228] On the other hand, many jurisdictions authorize the supreme court, in its discretion, to permit the introduction of additional evidence,[229] and at least two jurisdictions expressly authorize the supreme court to remand the matter to the commission to take additional evidence.[230] With one possible exception[231] the additional evidence may be taken before the supreme court or that court's designee.[232]

Since the supreme court's function in the states under consideration is an adjudicative function, rather than a review function, and since the commission's function is merely to make a recommendation, the case must be dismissed if a majority of the court fails, for whatever reason, to adopt the commission's recommendation that the judge be disciplined.[233] In these jurisdictions, moreover, since the governing constitutional or statutory provision predicates supreme court jurisdiction on the filing of a commission recommendation for discipline,[234] a commission decision to dismiss the charges is not reviewable by the supreme court.[235] The same is true of a commission decision to dismiss some, but not all, of the charges.[236]

Even though the supreme court's initial jurisdiction hinges on the filing of a recommendation that action be taken against a judge, the supreme court has the right to enter an order imposing more stringent discipline than that recommended by the commission, even in the absence of a constitutional or statutory provision so providing.[237]

n. The Stated Grounds for Discipline in Judicial Disciplinary Commission Proceedings

(i) Introduction

The four most common grounds for imposing discipline are: (1) willful misconduct in office, (2) willful and persistent failure to perform judicial duties, (3) conduct prejudicial to the administration of justice that brings the judicial office into disrepute, and (4) violation of the applicable code of judicial conduct or canons of judicial ethics, plus variations of each of these four grounds.[238] These grounds, as well as a variety of other grounds utilized in various states, will be discussed in the ensuing subsections.

(ii) Willful Misconduct in Office

In twenty-six jurisdictions, "willful misconduct in office" is a stated ground for discipline.[239] In eleven other states, "misconduct in office" is a stated ground for discipline.[240] Thus, in one form or another, this ground is available in thirty-seven jurisdictions.

The term "willful misconduct in office" has been construed by the California Supreme Court as referring to "unjudicial conduct which a judge acting in his judicial capacity commits in bad faith";[241] and other courts have concurred with this interpretation.[242] "Bad faith," thus used, has been said by the California Supreme Court to encompass at least: (a) the intentional commission of acts that the judge knew, or should have known, were beyond his lawful power, provided actual malice, not mere negligence, motivated the *ultra vires* actions; or (b) acts within a judge's lawful power that were nevertheless committed for a corrupt purpose, i.e., consciously for any purpose other than the faithful discharge of judicial duties.[243] These concepts have been adopted by other courts also.[244]

(iii) Willful and Persistent Failure to Perform Judicial Duties

"Willful and persistent failure to perform judicial duties" is an enumerated ground for discipline in seventeen states[245] and "willful or persistent failure to perform judicial duties" is a ground in ten more states.[246] Also, "persistent failure to perform judicial duties" is a ground in ten additional states;[247] and "willful failure to perform judicial duties" is a ground in four more states.[248] Finally, "failure to perform judicial duties" is a ground in three states.[249] Thus, variations of this particular ground are applicable in forty-four jurisdictions.

(iv) Conduct Prejudicial to the Administration of Justice and/or That Brings the Judicial Office into Disrepute

In twenty-eight jurisdictions, conduct that is either prejudicial to the administration of justice or brings the judicial office into disrepute is a specified ground for discipline. In thirteen of these jurisdictions, the conduct must both be prejudicial to the administration of justice and bring the judicial office into disrepute.[250] In six jurisdictions, either type of conduct suffices to warrant discipline.[251] Finally, seven jurisdictions specify only conduct prejudicial to the administration of justice,[252] and three specify only conduct bringing the judicial office into disrepute.[253]

(v) Violations of the Code of Judicial Conduct or of Canons of Judicial Ethics

Practically every state has adopted a code of judicial conduct.[254] In most states, the code has been derived from the Code of Judicial Conduct, adopted by the American Bar Association in 1972[255] and which succeeded the Canons of Judicial Ethics.[256] In five states, the superseded ABA Canons of Judicial Ethics appear to be still in effect.[257] Generally, the Code of Judicial Conduct has been adopted by a state's supreme court, rather than by the legislature.[258]

In specifying the grounds for judicial discipline, approximately twenty-four states have expressly designated violation of the state's code or canons as a ground for discipline.[259] A few of these states have added requirements that the violation of the code or canons must be willful,[260] persistent,[261] serious,[262] substantial,[263] or of a nature likely to result in substantial loss of public respect.[264] In addition, several states specify violation of the code of professional responsibility, applicable to lawyers, as a ground for discipline.[265]

Even in states that have not specifically included violations of the Code of Judicial Conduct in their constitutional or statutory lists of grounds for discipline, the courts have held either that the canons have become binding supplements to the constitutional or statutory grounds[266] or that the canons should be utilized as guides to the meaning of the constitutional or statutory grounds.[267]

(vi) Incompetence

In seven states, "incompetence" or "incompetence in the performance of judicial duties" is a stated ground for judicial discipline.[268]

(vii) Habitual Intemperance

Habitual intemperance, expressly including in some states, habitual use of drugs, is a stated ground for judicial discipline in many states.[269]

(viii) Conduct Unbecoming a Member of the Judiciary

Conduct unbecoming a member of the judiciary, demonstrating unfitness to hold judicial office[270] or bringing the judicial office into disrepute,[271] is a ground for judicial discipline in certain states.

(ix) Conviction or Commission of Crime or Violation of Law

In a number of jurisdictions, final conviction of a crime of designated seriousness, variously defined as a felony,[272] a crime involving moral turpitude,[273] or either a felony or a crime involving moral turpitude,[274] is a stated ground for judicial discipline. In other states, the commission of a crime of designated seriousness is a ground for discipline.[275] In some states, violation of law is a stated ground for discipline.[276]

(x) Misconduct or Improper Conduct

In some states, misconduct, improper conduct, conduct involving moral turpitude, or the like is a stated ground for judicial discipline.[277]

(xi) Oppression in Office

Oppression in office is a stated ground in certain states.[278]

(xii) Corruption in Office

In certain states, corruption in office is a stated ground for judicial discipline.[279]

(xiii) Gross Partiality in Office

Gross partiality in office is a stated ground for removal in Oklahoma.[280]

(xiv) The Stated Grounds in Tennessee

In addition to the grounds discussed in §§6.3(n)(ii) to 6.3(n)(v), Tennessee has codified the following grounds for judicial discipline:

A persistent pattern of intemperate, irresponsible or injudicious conduct.
A persistent pattern of discourtesy to litigants, witnesses, jurors, court personnel or lawyers.
A persistent pattern of delay in disposing of pending litigation.[281]

(xv) Disbarment

Disbarment is a stated ground for judicial discipline in several states.[282] Even in states where disbarment is not a stated ground for discipline, it would nevertheless be arguable that forefeiture of judicial office would necessarily follow from disbarment, since membership in the state bar is almost always a requisite for eligibility to become a judge of a court of record.[283]

(xvi) Miscellaneous Stated Grounds

Miscellaneous stated grounds include: (a) willful failure to file required financial statements or the filing of fraudulent financial statements,[284] (b) willful refusal to conform to supreme court official policies and directives,[285] or (c) law violations.[286]

o. Specific Types of Courtroom Conduct That Have Been Disciplined—Courtroom Conduct

(i) Abusive, Intemperate, or Sarcastic Treatment of Attorneys, Litigants, or Witnesses

This type of conduct has been disciplined with great frequency.[287]

(ii) Efforts to Coerce Guilty Pleas or Settlements

Efforts by judges to coerce guilty pleas in criminal cases by threatening defendants with severe punishment[288] or to coerce settlements by excessive pressure[289] have been held grounds for discipline. The tactic of terminating a defendant's representation by a voluntary defender when the defendant, but not the voluntary defender, wished to settle, has been held to warrant judicial discipline as an interference with the attorney-client relationship.[290]

(iii) Interrogation of Witnesses in an Adversary Manner

This type of intervention by the judge has been held improper and subject to discipline.[291]

(iv) Comments on the Merits

Comments by the judge on the merits of a case pending before him have been held to justify discipline.[292]

(v) Judge's Failure to Disqualify Himself When He Has a
Material Conflict of Interest or Bias or an Appearance of a
Material Conflict of Interest or Bias

This type of conduct has subjected judges to discipline, both before and after the adoption of Canon 3C of the Code of Judicial Conduct, which defines situations in which the judge should disqualify himself.[293]

(vi) Abuse of the Contempt Power

Abuse of the contempt power has from time to time resulted in discipline.[294]

(vii) Consideration of Ex Parte Communications

Except as authorized by law, a judge is forbidden by Canon 3A(4) of the ABA Code of Judicial Conduct to initiate or consider ex parte communications concerning a pending or impending proceeding. Conduct of the type prohibited by this canon has frequently been held a basis for judicial discipline.[295]

(viii) Ex Parte Judgments or Orders

The entry of ex parte judgments and orders is apt to violate the requirement in ABA Canon 3A(4) that every interested party be accorded a full hearing and has often given rise to judicial discipline.[296]

(ix) Deliberate and Knowing Disregard of the Law

Although good faith errors of law are not a basis for discipline,[297] deliberate disregard of the law is a ground for discipline.[298]

(x) Delay in Deciding Cases

Although delay in deciding a particular case has not been a ground for discipline unless accompanied by corruption,[299] discipline has been imposed when there was a pattern of delay.[300]

(xi) Partiality

Undue partiality by the judge during the trial of a case has been held a ground for discipline.[301] Partiality in rendering a decision, motivated by hostility to the attorney against whom the decision was rendered, also has been disciplined.[302]

(xii) Altering or Directing the Alteration of Court Records

The alteration of, or giving of directions to alter, court records has given rise to severe sanctions, particularly when intended to conceal other improper judicial conduct, such as "fixing" of traffic cases.[303]

(xiii) Incompetence

At least in states in which incompetence is a stated ground for judicial discipline, incompetence has resulted in discipline.[304]

(xiv) Intoxication While Sitting in Court

Intoxication while on the bench has been censured or reprimanded.[305]

p. Out-of-Court Conduct Related to the Judge's Judicial Duties that Has Resulted in Discipline

(i) Nepotism and Favoritism in Making Appointments

ABA Canon 3(b)(4) requires that a judge appoint officials and employees "only on the basis of merit, avoiding nepotism and favoritism." Violations of this canon have resulted in discipline.[306] Moreover, when there is an appearance of favoritism, discipline will be imposed even if the persons appointed were competent.[307]

(ii) Receipt of Bribe in Return for Promised Judicial Action

Needless to say, this type of conduct has resulted in removal from office.[308]

(iii) Embezzlement of Court Funds

Such conduct necessarily results in removal.[309]

(iv) Publicizing Criticisms of Other Judges, or of Efforts to Secure Rule Changes

The publicizing of criticisms of other judges[310] or of efforts to secure rule changes[311] has been held subject to censure.

(v) Participation in Arrests

Participation by a judge in arrests has been held violative of Canon 2A of the Code of Judicial Conduct as giving the appearance of partiality and has, therefore, been disciplined.[312]

q. Out-of-Court Conduct Not Related to Judicial Duties that Has Been the Basis of Discipline

(i) Business Affiliations and Fiduciary Relationships

Canon 5C(1) of the ABA Code of Judicial Conduct prohibits financial and business dealings by a judge "that tend to reflect adversely on his impartiality, interfere with the proper performance of his judicial duties exploit his judicial position, or involve him in frequent transactions with

lawyers or persons likely to come before the court on which he serves."[313]
In addition, Canon 5C(2), which has been adopted in a number of states,[314]
provides that:

Subject to the requirements of subsection (1), a judge may hold and manage investments, including real estate, and engage in other remunerative activity, but should
not serve as an officer, director, manager, advisor, or employee of any business.

In jurisdictions that do not provide adequate judicial salaries, one alternative
version of Canon 5C(2), which has been adopted in some states,[315] omits
the prohibition against business affiliations and permits judges to engage in
the operation of a business. A second alternative to Canon 5C(2), which
also has been adopted in a limited number of states,[316] permits judges to
engage generally in the operation of a business but prohibits them from
operating certain specified types of business deemed affected with a public
interest, including banks, public utilities, or insurance companies.

Violations of the foregoing canons, and of similar canons of the former
Canons of Judicial Ethics, have resulted in discipline being imposed.[317] For
example, business dealings by a judge with a lawyer likely to appear before
him have been proscribed because they created an appearance of partiality
on the part of the judge.[318]

Likewise, service by a judge on the board of directors of a business concern
has been disciplined, when prohibited per se by an applicable canon[319] or,
even if not prohibited per se, when the judge permitted the concern to
publicize and thereby exploit his judicial position.[320] Moreover, exploitation
by a judge of his judicial office by dealing on behalf of a business enterprise
with persons likely to be influenced thereby has resulted in discipline.[321]

Canon 5D also precludes a judge from acting as a fiduciary, except for
the estate, trust, or person of a member of his family and then only if such
service will not interfere with the proper performance of his judicial duties.
Even family fiduciary relationships are prohibited when it is likely that the
judge will be engaged in proceedings that would ordinarily come before him
or if the estate, trust, or ward becomes involved in adversary proceedings
in the court on which he serves or one under its appellate jurisdiction.

(ii) Investments

The prohibition in Canon 5C(1) against financial business dealings by a
judge that "tend to reflect adversely upon his impartiality, interfere with
the proper performance of his judicial duties, exploit his judicial position,
or involve him in frequent transactions with lawyers or persons likely to
come before the court on which he serves" necessarily applies to investments
by judges. The most obvious illustration of an investment that would tend
to reflect adversely on a judge's partiality would, of course, be an investment
in a concern that was from time to time a party to proceedings in the judge's

court.[322] Canon 5C(3) also seeks to discourage further the acquisition or retention by judges of investments of this sort by providing that a judge should manage his investments to minimize the number of cases in which he is disqualified and that, as soon as he can do so without serious financial detriment, he should divest himself of investments and other financial interests that might require frequent disqualification.[323]

An investment interfering with the proper performance of the judge's duties would, of course, include one that caused the judge to absent himself from court to an undue extent.[324] An investment that would tend to exploit a judge's judicial position would exist if the enterprise sought or accepted the business of lawyers who practiced in the judge's court. Finally, an investment of the type just described would tend to involve the judge in frequent transactions with lawyers likely to come before the judge's court if the judge played an active role in the management of the enterprise.[325]

Canon 5C(7) also affects a judge's investments and business affiliations by providing that information acquired by a judge in his judicial capacity should not be used or disclosed by him in financial dealings or for any other purposes not related to his judicial duties.

(iii) Other Employment

(1) *Business Employment*. The permissibility of business employment would depend on whether Canon 5C(2) or alternatives 1 and 2 to Canon 5C(2) were in effect in the judge's state. Even if generally permissible, a judge's employment would still have to avoid the prohibitions contained in Canon 5C(1).

(2) *Quasi-Judicial Employment*. Canon 4 outlines permissible quasi-judicial activities for judges.[326] Canon 4A permits judges to be involved in legal education, but since Canon 3A(5) requires a judge to "dispose promptly of the business of the court," any such role should not unduly impinge on the judge's time. Reasonable compensation for permitted activities is allowed by canon 6(A).

(iv) Acceptance of Gifts, Bequests, Favors or Loans

Subsections (a) and (b) of Canon 5C(4) of the ABA Code of Judicial Conduct permit a judge and members of his family residing in his household to accept various types of gifts, bequests, favors and loans specified in those subsections. Subsection (c) of Canon 5C(4) prohibits a judge or a member of his family residing in his household from accepting any gift, bequest, favor or loan if the donor is a party or other person whose interests have come, or are likely to come, before the judge; any gift, bequest, favor or loan whose value exceeds $100 must be reported. Gifts accepted in violation of this Canon subject the judge to discipline, even if there is no showing that the gift came with "strings attached".[327] The same is true of a failure to report gifts over $100.[328] Canon 5C(4) has been widely adopted.[329]

(v) Law Violation

Judges convicted of, or committing, felonies or other crimes involving moral turpitude might be disciplined under stated grounds pertaining to the conviction or commission of a specified type of crime[330] or conduct prejudicial to the administration of justice and/or that brings the judicial office into disrepute;[331] or, in three states, conduct unbecoming a member of the judiciary;[332] or, in Arkansas, law violation.[333] Also, in any state that specifies canon violations as a ground for judicial discipline, the judge might be disciplined under Canon 1 requiring high standards of conduct; Canon 2, requiring the avoidance of impropriety and the appearance of impropriety in all the judge's activities; or Canon 2A, requiring conduct promoting public confidence.[334]

(vi) Disgraceful or Immoral Personal Conduct

Disgraceful or immoral personal conduct has been disciplined in a number of cases.[335] As to sexual immorality, several cases have held it may subject a judge to discipline,[336] but one case has held otherwise.[337] Public brawling and rude, obnoxious, and insulting behavior in public has been disciplined.[338]

(vii) Political Activity

Chapter 5 deals with Canon 7 of the ABA Code of Judicial Conduct, regulating political activities by judges.

(viii) Civic and Charitable Activity

Canon 5B of the ABA Code of Judicial Conduct regulates a judge's civic and charitable activities. A judge is permitted to engage in civil and charitable activities that do not reflect adversely upon his impartiality or interfere with the performance of his judicial duties (Canon 5B). Board memberships or other positions with nonpolitical, nonprofit, civic, charitable, educational, religious, or fraternal organizations are permitted, provided the organization is not likely to appear in court before him or to be regularly engaged in adversary proceedings in any court (Canons 5B and 5B(1)). A judge is prohibited from soliciting funds for such organizations or from using or permitting the prestige of his judicial office to be used for that purpose. Similarly, a judge is prohibited from being a speaker or the guest of honor at such an organization's fund raising events, but he may attend such events (Canon 5B(2)). Finally, judges are not permitted to give investment advice to such organizations but may serve on their boards of directors or trustees, even though those bodies have the responsibility for approving investment decisions (Canon 5B(3)).

(ix) Public Disagreement with the Law as Presently Prescribed by the Constitution or Legislature

Published articles by a judge disagreeing with the present state of the law are not improper as long as the judge does not advocate disobedience and does not give the impression that he himself will not apply the law as presently written.[339]

r. Conduct during a Previous Term of Office or before Ascending the Bench or before the Enactment Authorizing the Instant Type of Disciplinary Proceeding

The majority view is that, unless barred by a constitutional or statutory time limitation,[340] conduct of a judge during a previous term of office, before ascending to the bench, or before creation of the commission, may constitute the basis for removal or other discipline.[341] Several courts, however, have barred consideration of conduct in a previous term when the judge has been elected by the voters with knowledge of the misconduct on the theory that, by re-electing the judge, the electorate has forgiven the judge.[342] The forgiveness concept has, however, been held inapplicable when it has not been shown that the electorate knew of the misconduct when they re-elected the judge.[343] Also, it has been held inapplicable when the remedy selected is censure, rather than removal.[344]

On the theory that the forgiveness doctrine is predicated on the hypothesis that the judge's re-election shows that he would have been re-elected even if he had been removed from office because of his misconduct, the forgiveness doctrine has been held inapplicable when, in the particular state, judges removed on the ground of misconduct are disqualified from holding future office.[345]

s. Compulsory Retirement or Suspension on the Ground of Disability

In virtually every state plus the District of Columbia, the provisions on judicial discipline are accompanied by provisions for involuntary retirement of disabled judges.[346] These same provisions also frequently provide for temporary suspension (in lieu of retirement) of temporarily disabled judges;[347] many disability statutes provide for automatic or discretionary disqualification or suspension of a judge pending court action on a recommendation by the commission that the judge be involuntarily retired on the ground of disability.[348]

Since these provisions pertain primarily to the removal of disabled judges, this subject is discussed in greater detail in Chapter 7.

NOTE TO §6.1

1. *See* Schoenbaum, A Historical Look at Judicial Discipline, 54 Chi-Kent L. Rev. 1, 1–22, 24–25 (1977), Cameron, The Inherent Power of a State's Highest Court in Disciplining the Judiciary, 54 Chi-Kent L. Rev. 1b, 1b–16 (1977), Gasperini, An

derson, and McGinley, Judicial Removal in New York: A New Look, 40 Fordh. L. Rev. 1, 3–4, 15–16, 27–34, 37–39 (1971)

NOTES TO §6.2(a)

2. *See* Schoenbaum, *supra* note 1, at 2; and Shartel, Retirement and Removal of Judges, 20 J. Am. Jud. Soc'y. 133, 142 (1936).

3. *See* Schoenbaum, *supra* note 1, at 2–3.

4. 12 and 13 Will. 3, c.2, §3(1700).

5. *See* U.S. Const. arts. II and III; and Schoenbaum, *supra* note 1, at 3–4.

6. *See* Schoenbaum, *supra* note 1, at 3–4.

7. Hawaii Rev. Stat. §610–13 (Supp. 1969), repealed and replaced by Hawaii Const. art. VI, §5 (conferring on supreme court power to discipline judges on recommendation of a disciplinary commission). *See* Schoenbaum, *supra* note 1, at 3–4.

NOTES TO §6.2(b)

8. *See* Clarke, The Origins of Impeachment, in Oxford Essays in Medieval History (1934); and Schoenbaum, *supra* note 1, at 5, nn. 24 and 25, and the accompanying text.

9. *See* Schoenbaum, *supra* note 1, at 5, n. 25, and the accompanying text; and *see* Berger, Impeachment of Judges and "Good Behavior" Tenure, 79 Yale L.J. 1475 (1966); and Note, Remedies for Judicial Misconduct and Disability: Removal and Discipline of Judges, 41 N.Y. L. Rev. 149, 163 (1966) (hereinafter cited as *Remedies*).

10. U.S. Const. art. I, §§2(5), 3(6); U.S. Const. art. II, §4; U.S. Const. art. III, §2(3).

11. *See* Schoenbaum, *supra* note 1, at 24–27 (Table I); *see* Moser, Populism, a Wisconsin Heritage: Its Effect on Judicial Accountability in the State, 66 Marqu. L. Rev. 1, 4 (1982).

12. *See* Moser, *supra* note 11, at 7–8.

NOTES TO §6.2(c)

13. *See* Moser, *supra* note 11, at 14; Schoenbaum, *supra* note 1 at 4.

14. *See* Moser, *supra* note 11, at 14–15.

15. *See* Moser, *supra* note 11, at 14; Schoenbaum, *supra* note 1, at 4; *Remedies*, *supra* note 9, at 164.

NOTES TO §6.2(d)

16. E.g., Kan. Const. art. 3, §16; N.Y. Const. art. 6, §23(a) (as to judges of Court of Appeals and justices of Supreme Court); N.C. Const. art. IV, §17(1) (as to mental or physical incapacity only); Wash. Const. art. 4, §8

17. *Cf.* Moser, *supra* note 11, at 13–15.

NOTES TO §6.2(e)

18. *See* Cameron, The Inherent Power of a State's Highest Court to Discipline the Judiciary, 59 Chi-Kent L. Rev. 45, 45, n. 4 (1977).

19. *See* Schoenbaum, *supra* note 1, nn. 35–43, and the accompanying text.

20. *See* Moser, *supra* note 11, at 33–35.

21. Articles of Confederation art V (1778), executed by its signators on various dates through March 1, 1781. *See* Moser, *supra* note 11, n. 238, and the accompanying text.

22. *See* Schoenbaum, *supra* note 1, at 8.

23. Ariz. Const. art. VIII, §1; Cal. Const. art. 23, §1; Wisc. Const. art. 13, §12. *See* Comment, Judicial Discipline—Does It Exist in Pennsylvania? 84 Dick. L. Rev. 447, 449, n. 17 (1980).

NOTES TO §6.2(f)

24. *See* supra §§2.5, 2.6, 2.7(d) and 2.8; and *see* Schoenbaum, *supra* note 1 at 9–10.

25. *See* Schoenbaum, *supra* note 1, at 9–10.

NOTES TO §6.2(g)

26. Illustrative decisions sustaining jurisdiction include *Gordon v. Clinkscales*, 215 Ga. 843, 114, S.E. 2d 15 (1960) (petition to disbar stated good cause of action); *State ex. rel. Nebraska Bar Ass'n v. Conover*, 166 Neb. 132, 88 N.W.2d 135 (1958) (judgment of disbarment); *In re Mattera*, 34 N.J. 259, 168 A.2d 38 (1961) (sustaining jurisdiction to disbar); *Mahoning County Bar Ass'n v. Franko*, 168 Ohio St. 17, 151 N.E.2d 17 (1958), *cert. denied*, 358 U.S. 932 (1959) (indefinite suspension of license to practice law ordered). For other cases so holding, *see infra* notes 77 and 79 (Chapter 7), and the accompanying text. Illustrative cases denying jurisdiction include: *Alabama State Bar ex. rel. Steiner v. Moore* 213 So.2d 404 (Ala. 1968); *State Bar of Cal. v. Superior Court for Los Angeles Co.*, 207 Cal. 323, 278 Pac. 432 (1929); *Petition of Colorado Bar Ass'n*, 137 Colo. 357, 325 P.2d 932, 937 (1958); *Chambers v. Central Committee of Oklahoma Bar Ass'n*, 203 Okla. 583, 224 P.2d 583 (1950). For other cases so holding, *see infra* notes 77 and 80 (Chapter 7), and the accompanying text. *See also* Annot., 57 A.L.R.3d 1150, 1158–1160 (1974); and Annot., 53 A.L.R.3d 305, 306–307 (1957)

27. *Compare Matter of Riley*, 142 Ariz. 604, 691 P.2d 695, 698 (In Banc 1984) (sustaining jurisdiction) and *In re Mills*, 539 S.W.2d 447 (Mo. En Banc 1976) (same) with *In re Proposed Disciplinary Action by the Florida Bar*, 103 So.2d 632 (Fla. 1958) (denying jurisdiction).

28. *Compare Riley*, *supra*, note 27, 691 P.2d at 698 ("jurisdiction in disciplinary proceedings [against incumbent judges] should depend on the position the individual held at the time of the alleged misconduct"), *In re Wehrman*, 327 S.W.2d 743, 744 (Kan. 1959) ("no act of misconduct shall be the subject of disciplinary action [against a sitting judge] unless the act is at the time capable of commission by any member of the bar without being specifically set apart from other lawyers") and *In re Watson*,

71 Nev. 227, 286 P.2d 254, 255, 53 A.L.R.2d 301 (1955) ("as to those in judicial office, however, our judicial authority [to impose bar discipline] must be held limited to the field of action outside of official duties").

29. Jurisdiction was sustained in *Florida Bar v. McCain*, 330 So.2d 712 (Fla. 1976) (former supreme court judge); *State ex. rel. Oklahoma Bar Ass'n v. James*, 463 P.2d 772 (Okla. 1969); *Louisiana State Bar Ass'n v. Funderburk*, 284 So.2d 564 (La. 1973) (based on constitutional provision authorizing disbarment proceedings against judges); *In re Hasler*, 447 S.W.2d 65 (Mo. En Banc 1969) and *Schoolfield v. Tennessee Bar Ass'n*, 209 Tenn. 304, 353 S.W.2d 401 (1961) (findings in impeachment trial held conclusive by waiver of collateral estoppel in disbarment proceeding). Jurisdiction was denied in *In re Meraux*, 202 La. 736, 12 So.2d 798 (1943) (decided before enactment of constitutional provision relied upon in *Funderburk*); and *Re Jones*, 202 La. 2d, 729, 12 So. 2d 795 (1943) (same). *See infra* notes 82 to 86 (Chapter 7), and the accompanying text.

NOTES TO §6.2(h)

30. *See also* Schoenbaum, *supra* note 1 at 14; Cameron, *supra* note 1, at 47; and Shartel, Federal Judges—Appointment, Supervision, and Removal: Some Possibilities under the Constitution (pts. 1–3) 28 Mich. L. Rev. 485, 723, 870, 882 (1930).

31. E.g., *In re Municipal Court of Cedar Rapids*, 188 N.W.2nd 354 (Iowa 1971) (censure); *In re DeSaulnier*, 279 N.E.2d 296, 308 (Mass. 1971) (order enjoining judge from exercising judicial powers and duties); *Ransford v. Graham*, 374 Mich. 194, 131 N.W.2d 201 (1964) (same; salary not suspended); *In re Graham*, 366 Mich. 268, 114 N.W.2d 333, 337 (1962); *In re Mussman*, 112 N.H. 99, 289 A.2d 403 (1979) (power to suspend recognized); *In re Kading*, 70 Wis.2d 508, 522–523, 235 N.W.2d 409, 415–416 (1975). *See In re DeSaulnier*, 274 N.E.2d 454, 456 (Mass. 1971).

32. E.g., *Municipal Court supra* note 31, 188 N.W.2d at 358; *Graham*, *supra* note 31, 114 N.W.2d at 337; *DeSaulnier*, *supra* note 31, 279 N.E.2d at 308; *Mussman*, *supra* note 31, 289 A.2d at 404. *See Ransford*, *supra* note 31, 131 N.W.2d at 203. *But compare* Shartel, *supra* note 6–30, at 891–88; and Comment, Limitations of Article on the Proposed Judicial Removal Machinery: S. 1506, 118 Pa. L. Rev. 1064, 1067–69 (1970). However, a few decades ago, constitutional provisions were enacted in a few states conferring express constitutional power upon the state's highest appellate court to remove judges on specified grounds without the assistance of any disciplinary commission. *See* Cameron, *supra* note 1 at 51; Schoenbaum, *supra* note 1, at 16–18. These provisions have, as a general proposition, been superseded by substitution of disciplinary commission systems. *Id.*, at 21–22.

NOTES TO §6.2(i)

33. *See infra* §6.3(a); and Schoenbaum, *supra* note 1, at 19–22.

34. *See* Schoenbaum, *supra* note 1, at 20.

35. *Id.*, at 21–22, and Table I on pp. 24–27. *See also* Tesitor and Sinks, Judicial Conduct Organizations (Am. Jud. Soc., 2d ed. 1980), at 3–10, 12–49 (Tables 1–7) and 83–84; and Gasperini, *supra* note 1, at 37–39 (App. B).

NOTES TO §6.3(a)

36. *See infra* notes 41–46 and 48–50; and Tesitor and Sinks, *supra* note 35, at 19–27.

37. *See* Greenberg, The Illinois "Two-Tier" Judicial Disciplinary System: Five Years and Counting, 54 Chi-Kent L. Rev. 69–112 (1977); Gillis and Fieldman, Michigan's Unitary System of Judicial Discipline: A Comparison with Illinois' Two-Tier Approach, 54 Chi-Kent L. Rev. 117–136 (1977); Cohn, Comparing One and Two-Tier Systems, 63 Judicature 244–248 (1978).

38. *See infra* notes 42 to 44 and 46 to 48; and Tesitor and Sinks, *supra* note 35, at 12–13, 16–18, 19–21, 24–25, 27, 83–85.

39. *See infra* notes 40–42; and Tesitor and Sinks, *supra* note 35 at 12–27.

40. The thirty-eight jurisdictions consist of all of the remaining jurisdictions other than Arkansas, Kentucky, Nevada, New York, Tennessee, and the District of Columbia. E.g., Alaska Const. art. IV, §10; Alaska Stat. §§22.30.011, .70; Ariz. Const. art. 6.1, §§3, 4; Cal. Const. art. 6, §18 (Supp.); Colo. Const. art. 6, §23(3) (Supp.); Conn. Gen. Stat. §§51–51h to 51r (commission may itself impose lesser degrees of discipline); Fla. Const. art. 5, §12; Ga. Const. art. 6, §7, ¶¶VI-VIII; Hawaii Const. art. VI, §5; Hawaii S. Ct. R. 26; Idaho Code Ann. 1–2101 to 2103; Ind. Const. art. 7, §11; Ind. Code §§33–2.1–5–19 to 22, 33–2.1–6–22 and 25; Iowa Const. art. 5, §19; Iowa Code Ann. §§605.26 to .30; Kan. S. Ct. R. 620 to 624; La. Const. art. 5, §25; La. S. Ct. R. 23; Me. Rev. Stat. tit. 4, §9B; Me. S. Ct. Order of July 5, 1978 (establishing Committee on Judicial Responsibility and Disability, hereinafter cited as "Me. S. Ct. Order") §§6–10; Me. Comm. Judic. Responsib. and Disab. Rules, pp. 1–3; Md. Const. art. IV, §§4A, 4B; Mass. Gen. Laws ch. 211C, §§1, 2; Mass. Rules of Comm. on Judic. Conduct R. 23; Mich. Const. art. 6, §30; Minn. Stat. Ann. §490.15; Miss. Const. art. 6, §177A; Mo. Const. art. 5, §24; Mont. Const. art. VII, §11; Nebr. Const. art. V, §30; Nebr. Rev. Stat. §§721–728; N.J. S. Ct. R. 39; N.J. Const. art. 6, §6, ¶1; N.J. Stat. Ann. §§1B–1 to 11; N.J. Appell. Pract. Rules, R. 2:15–12 to 14; N.H.S. Ct. R. 39 (9), (10), (11); N.M. Const. art. VI, §32; N.C. Gen. Stat. §7A–375 to 376, 378; N.D. Cent. Code §§27–23–01 to 03; Ore. Const. art. VII, §8; Ore. Rev. Stat. §§1.410–1.430; Pa. Const. art. 5, §18; R.I. Gen. Laws §§8–16–1 to 8–16–9; S.C. Const. art. V, §13; S.C. S. Ct. R. 34; S.D. Const. art. V, §9; S.D. Comp. Laws Ann. §16–1A–1 to 13; Tex. Const. art. 5, §1-a (Supp.); Utah Const. art. VIII, §28; Utah Code Ann. §§78–7–28 to 30; Va. Code §2.1–37.16 (Supp.) to 4; Vt. Const. art II, §30; Vt. S. Ct. Rules for Discip. Control of Judges, R. 11; Va. Const. art. VI, §10; Wash. Const. art. IV, §31; Wyo. Const. art. 5, §6.

Any cross-reference hereinafter in any footnote to a previously cited set of rules will generally merely refer to them as "Rules" and will identify the state involved immediately before the latter term (e.g., "Minn. Rules").

41. D.C. Code §11–1152, 1526 to 1529; Ky. Const. §121; Ky. Rev. Stat. 934.340; Ky. Judic. Retirem. and Removal Comm. Rules, RR. 4.020 to .025, .170-.180, .220, .250-.290; Nev. Const. art. 6, §21; N.Y. Const. art. 6, §22; N.Y. Judic. Law §§44, 47; N.Y. State Comm. on Judic. Conduct Rules, R. 7000.11 to .7, .9.

42. Ark. Stat. Ann. §§22–1001 to 1005; Tenn. Code Ann. §§17–5–201 to 313
In Tennessee, the commission is named the Court of the Judiciary. Id.

43. E.g., Ala. Const. amend. no. 328, §§6.17–6.18; Ill. Const. art. 6, §15; Ohio Rev. Code Ann. §§2701.11–.12; Okla. Const. art. 7-A, §§1–7; Okla. Stat. Ann. §§1651–1658.

44. *See* Del. Const. art. IV, ¶37.

45. *People ex. rel. Harrod v. The Illinois Courts Commission*, 69 Ill.2d 445, 372 N.E.2d 52 (1977).

46. W. Va. Const. art. VIII, §8 (supreme court may discipline judge in all ways short of removal; removal may only be by impeachment); W. Va. Rules of Proc. for Handling of Complaints against Justices, Judges and Magistrates, R. I to III; Wis. Const. art. VII, §11; Wis. Stat. Ann. §§757.81–.91.

47. 28 U.S.C. 372. *See* Neisser, The New Federal Judicial Discipline Act: Some Questions Congress Didn't Answer, 65 Judicature 143–160 (1981); Burbank, Procedural Rulemaking under the Judicial Councils Reform and Judicial Conduct and Disability Act of 1980, 131 U. Pa. L. Rev. 283–348 (1982); Burbank, The Federal Judicial Discipline Act: Is Decentralized Self-Regulation Working? 67 Judicature 183–199 (1983).

48. *See* 28 U.S.C. 372.

NOTES TO §6.3(b)

49. E.g., *In re Hanson*, 532 P.2d 303, 305–307 (Alaska 1975); *McCartney v. Commission on Judicial Qualifications*, 12 Cal.3d 512, 116 Cal. Rptr., 260, 267, 526 P.2d 268, 275, n.7 (En Banc 1974); *In re Kelly*, 238 So.2d 565, 570–571 (Fla. 1970); *In re Haggerty*, 257 La.1, 241 So.2d 469, 472 (1970); *In re Diener*, 268 Md. 659, 304 A.2d 587 (1973); *In the Matter of Del Rio*, 400 Mich. 665, 256 N.W.2d 727, 736–737 (1977); *In the Matter of Mikesell*, 396 Mich. 517, 243 N.W.2d 86, 91–92 (1976); *In the Matter of Duncan*, 541 S.W.2d 564 (Mo. En Banc 1976); *In re Mills*, 539 S.W.2d 447 (Mo. En Banc 1976); *In re Nowell*, 293 N.C. 235, 237 S.E.2d 246, 252–253 (1977). *See* Peskoe, Procedures for Judicial Discipline: Type of Commission, Due Process and Right to Counsel, 54 Chi-Kent L. Rev. 147, 151–153 (1977).

50. *See Del Rio, supra* note 49, 256 N.W.2d at 737.

51. Id.

52. E.g., *Del Rio, McCartney,* and *Mikesell, supra* note 49. *McCartney* rejected the contention that due process was violated by the fact that, during the investigative phase of the proceeding, the commission had read and considered investigative field reports of the prosecuting attorney's field agents. *See McCartney*, 526 P.2d at 275, n.7. *Del Rio* stressed the fact that it reviewed *de novo* the commission's findings and recommendations.

53. E.g., *Hanson, Kelly, Haggerty* and *Nowell, supra* note 49. *Hanson*, 532 P.2d at 307, specifically rejected the contention that, when the commission had the option to hear the matter itself or appoint a special master to do so, it was constitutionally required to appoint a special master.

54. *See* Ky. Const. §121; Nev. Const. art. 6, §21; N.Y. Const. art. 6, §22; N.Y. Judic. Law §44(7). *See also* Tesitor and Sinks, *supra* note 35, at 14–15, 22–24.

55. *Friedman v. State of New York*, 24 N.Y.2d 528, 301 N.Y.S.2d 484, 249 N.E.2d 369, 375, 377–379 (1969), appeal dismissed, 397 U.S. 317 (1970). *But compare Duncan, supra* note 49, 541 S.W.2d at 566 ("a fair trial and a fair tribunal are essential

to due process and the combination of prosecutor and judge in one body creates a high probability of unfairness").

NOTES TO §6.3(c)

56. It will be recalled that the double-tier or triple-tier jurisdictions are the United States, Alabama, Delaware, Illinois, Ohio, Oklahoma, West Virginia, and Wisconsin, and the single-tier jurisdictions are the remaining forty-three states and the District of Columbia. *See supra* notes 38 and 39, and the accompanying text.

57. The forty single-tier jurisdictions referred to are all of the forty-four single tier jurisdictions referred to in note 56 other than Arkansas, Hawaii, South Carolina, and Utah. *See supra* notes 40–42 as to Michigan, Mississippi, Missouri, Montana, Nevada, New Hampshire, New Mexico, Pennsylvania, and Wyoming, *and see* Alaska Const. art. IV, §10; Alaska Stat. §22.30.010; Ariz. Const. art. VI.I, §1; Cal. Const. art. VI, 6 §8 (Supp.); Colo. Const. art. VI, §23(3)(a); Conn. Gen. Stat. §51–51k; D.C. Code §11–1522; Fla. Const. art. 5, §12(a)1; Ind. Const. art. 7, §9; Ind. Code §33–2.1–6.2; Ga. Const. art. 6, 27, §6; Idaho Code §1–2101; Iowa Code Ann. §605.26; Kan. S. Ct. R. 602; Ky. Const. §121; La. Const. art. V, §25; Me. S.Ct. Order §1; Md. Const. art. IV, §4A; Mass. Gen. Laws Ann. ch. 211C, §1; Minn. Bd. on Judic. Stds. R. 1(a); Nebr. Rev. Stat. §24–715; N.J. Appell. Pract. Rules R. 2:15–2; N.Y. Const. art. 6, §22; N.C. Gen. Stat. §7A–375; N.D. Cent. Code §27–23–02; Ore. Rev. Stat. §1.410; R.I. Gen. Laws §§8–16–1 and 6–9; S.D. Comp. Laws Ann. §16–1A–2; Tenn. Code Ann. §17–5–201; Tex. Const. art. 5, §1-A (2); Va. Code Ann. §2.1–37.3, Vt. S. Ct. Rules for Discipl. Control of Judges R. 4; Wash. Const. art. 4, §31 (amend. 71); Wash. Rev. Code Ann. §2.64.020. *See also* Tesitor and Sinks, *supra* note 35, at 28 to 39. Id. at 18–27. In the other four single-tier jurisdictions, the required members are: resident electors in Arkansas; lawyers and laymen in Hawaii; judges and lawyers in South Carolina; and legislators and bar commissioners in Utah. Ark. Stat. §22–1002; Hawaii S. Ct. R. 8.1(a); S.C. Supr. Ct. R. 34; Utah Code Ann. §78–7–27. *See* also Tesitor and Sinks, supra note 35, at 28, 30, 36–37.

58. The four jurisdictions referred to in the text are Alabama, Illinois, West Virginia, and Wisconsin. The members of the nondecisional commissions in the remaining double-tier or triple-tier jurisdictions are lawyers and laymen in the case of the investigative commission and judges in the case of the hearing commission in Delaware, lawyers in Ohio; lawyers and laymen in Oklahoma; and federal district or circuit judges in the case of investigative panels in federal disciplinary proceedings. *See* 28 U.S.C. 372; Ala. Const. amend. no. 328(a), §6.17; Del. Ct. on Judiciary R. 3, 5; Ill. Const. art. VI, §§15(b), (e); Ohio S. Ct. Rules for Govt. of Judic. of Ohio R. II(1); Okla. Stat. Ann. Tit. 20, §1653; W. Va. S.Ct. Rules of Proc. for Handling Complaints against Justices, Judges and Magistrates R. I(A)(1); Wis. Stat. Ann. §757.83 (Supp.).

59. 28 U.S. §372; Ala. Const. amend. no. 328, §6.18(a); Del. Const. art. IV, §37; Ill. Const. art. VI, §15(e); Ohio Rev. Code Ann. §270.11; Okla. Const. art. 7A, §§2(a)–2(c); W. Va. Rules, *supra* note 58, R. II(A)(1); Wis. Stat. Ann. §757.87(3). There are, however, eight judges and only one lawyer on each of the divisions (trial and appellate) of the Oklahoma Court of the Judiciary. Okla. Const. art. 7-A,

60. E.g., Ky. Rev. Stat. §34.310; Nev. Const. art. 6, §21(4).

61. Iowa Code Ann. §605.26; S.D. Comp. Laws Ann. §16–1A–2.

62. E.g., designated court or courts (Alaska, Arizona, California, Colorado, Connecticut, Florida, Hawaii, Kentucky, Louisiana, Massachusetts, Michigan, Missouri, Nevada, New Mexico, Oregon, Pennsylvania, South Carolina, Texas, Utah); chief justice of supreme court (United States, District of Columbia, Illinois, Iowa, Nebraska, New York, North Carolina, Ohio, West Virginia); judiciary of state (Mississippi) or state trial courts (North Dakota, Wyoming); judicial conference (South Dakota); governor (Maryland); governor with senate confirmation (Minnesota); each house of legislature (Virginia). See supra notes 57–59. For purposes of this treatise, the District of Columbia court of appeal is deemed to be that District's highest or "supreme court").

63. See supra note 57.

64. E.g., state bar members (Michigan); state bar's board of governors (Alabama, Arizona, California, Florida, Idaho, Kentucky, Missouri, Nebraska, Nevada, New Mexico, North Carolina, North Dakota, Oregon, Texas, Utah, Wyoming); state bar president (South Dakota); supreme court (Hawaii, Vermont); conference of judges (Louisiana); chief administrative judge of trial courts (Massachusetts); governor with confirmation by senate (Colorado, Minnesota, Rhode Island) or legislature in joint session (Alaska) or each house of legislature (Virginia); governing body of state bar, with confirmation by senate (Idaho). See supra notes 57–59.

65. E.g., governor (Alabama, District of Columbia, Florida, Illinois, Kentucky, Maryland, Massachusetts, Nebraska, Nevada, New Mexico, New York, North Carolina, North Dakota, Pennsylvania, South Dakota, Utah) or chief executive (District of Columbia); governor with senate confirmation (Arizona, California, Colorado, Idaho, Iowa, Minnesota, Oregon, Rhode Island, Texas, Wisconsin, Wyoming) or confirmation by legislature (Connecticut); supreme court (Hawaii, Vermont); legislature (District of Columbia) or each house of legislature (Virginia). See supra notes 57–58.

66. All major courts (Maryland, Nevada, Oregon); all major courts other than supreme court (Massachusetts); all major courts other than appellate courts (New York, 2 judges; another from App. Div.). See supra notes 57–59.

67. Jurisdictions in which judges are drawn in varying numbers from one, some or all of their supreme court ("S"), intermediate appellate court ("IA"), major trial courts ("MT"), trial courts of specialized jurisdiction ("ST"), or inferior trial courts ("IT") are the following: Alabama (S, MT), Alaska (S, IA, MT), Arizona (IA, MT, IT), California (IA, MT, IT), Colorado (MT, IT), Connecticut (MT), Delaware (Ct. on Judic.: S, MT, ST), District of Columbia (MT), Florida (IA, MT, IT), Idaho (chief justice ex officio), Illinois (Judic. Inquiry Bd.: MT; Cts. Comm.: S, IA, MT), Iowa (MT), Louisiana (IA, MT), Michigan (IA, MT, IT), Minnesota (MT, two ITs), Mississippi (MT, ST, two ITs), Missouri (IA, MT), Montana (MT), Nebraska (S, MT, two ITs), New York (IA and any non-appellate court), North Carolina (IA, MT, IT), North Dakota (MT, IT), Oklahoma (Ct. on Judic. Trial Div.:MT; Ct. on Judic. App. Div.: S, IA, MT), Pennsylvania (IA, MT), Rhode Island (IA, MT), South Carolina (MT, IT), South Dakota (MT) Texas (IA, MT), Tennessee (IA, MT), Virginia (MT, IT), West Virginia (Judic. Invest. Bd.: MT, IT; Judic. Hrg. Bd.: MT, IT), and Wyoming (MT). See supra notes 57 to 59.

68. See supra notes 67 and notes 57 to 59.

69. *See supra* note 67 and notes 57 to 59. Jurisdictions requiring one or more of the commission members to be drawn from the supreme court include: Alaska, Delaware, Idaho, Nebraska and Oklahoma; and jurisdictions permitting, but not requiring, one or more of the commission members to be drawn from the supreme court include Maryland, Nevada, and Oregon. *See supra* notes 57–59.

70. E.g., Cal. Const. art. VI, §18 (Supp.) (authorizes substitute panel); Fla. Const. art. 5, §12(h) (requires substitute panel); Miss. Const. art. 6, §177A (same). *Accord*: ABA Approved Draft of Stds. Rel. to Judic. Discipl. and Disab. Retirem. §7.14 (hereinafter cited as "ABA Stds."). *Compare* Minn. Rules, *supra* note 57, R. 12(h) (members of supreme court "shall disqualify themselves under Minn. St. 2.74, subd. 2, as they deem necessary").

71. *See supra* notes 40–48 and the accompanying text.

72. E.g., Nev. Const. art. 6, §21(8); Okla. Const. art. 7-A, §6(a) (district judge disqualified from becoming a member either of trial division or of appellate division of Court on Judiciary if respondent judge is a judge of a court within former's judicial district).

NOTES TO §6.3(d)

73. *Id. See* Alaska Stat. §22.30.011; Ariz. Comm. on Judic. Qualifics. Rules of Proc., R. 2; Ark. Stat. Ann. §22–1003; Cal. Rules of Ct. R. 904; Colo. Rules of Proc. of Comm. on Jud. Qualifics. R. 5; Conn. Gen. Stat. §51–51l; D.C. Code §11–1527; Fla. Const. art. 5, §12; Fla. Jud. Qualifics. Comm. Rules R. 6; Ga. Jud. Qualifics. Comm. Rules R. 3; Hawaii Comm. on Judic. Discipl. Rules, S. Ct. R. 26.2 to .6; Ind. Code §§33–2.1–5–6, 33–2.1–6–9; Iowa Code Ann. §605.29(1); Ky. S. Ct. Rules R. 4.170; Me. S. Ct. Order, *supra* note 40, §6; Md. Const. art. IV, §4B; Mass. Gen. Laws Ann. Tit. 311C, §2; Mass. Rules, *supra* note 40, R. 11–12; Minn. Rules, *supra* note 57, R. 6(a) and (c); Mo. Const. art. 5, §24(1); Mo. Bar and Judic. Rules, R. 12.06(a), 1208(a); Mont. Const. art. VII, §11(2); Nebr. Rev. Stat. §24–721; Nev. Const. art. 6, §21(7); N.M. Const. art. VI, §32; N.M. Stat. Ann. §§34–10–2.1, 3 and 4; N.Y. Const. art. 6, §22(a); N.Y. Judic. Law §§44(1) to 4; N.Y. Comm. on Judic. Conduct Rules R. 7000.1 to 3; N.D. Cent. Code §27–23.02; Ore. Rev. Stat. 1.420(1); Pa. Const. art. 5, §18(e); R.I. Gen. Laws §§8–16–4(b), (c); S.C. Supr. Ct. R. 34(10); S.D. Const. art. V, §9; S.D.S. Ct Rules of Proc. Implementing Powers and Duties of Judic. Qualifics. Comm. R. 5; Tex. Const. art. 5, §1–9(7); Tex. Rev. Civ. Stat. art. 5966a, §§2, 5A; Utah Code Ann. §78–7–30(1); Vt. Rules, *supra* note 57, R. 6(6); Va. Code §2.1–37.4; Wyo. S. Ct. Rules titled Wyo. Judic. Supervis. Comm. Rules R. 9.

74. E.g., Ark. Stat. Ann. §§22–1004(a), (b); Iowa Code Ann. §605.29 (investigative employees); S.D. Comp. Laws Ann. §16–1A–7. *See* ABA Stds. §2.8(d); Tesitor & Sinks, *supra* note 35, at 60, 62, 63, 68, 69, 73, 75, 77, 78 (instances where commission staff included counsel)

75. E.g., Ariz. Rules, *supra* note 6–73, R. 2C (special investigator or investigative agency); Ind. Code §§33.21–5–6(b), 33–1.1–6–9(c) (special investigators); Okla. Comp. Laws Ann. tit. 20, §1658 (state investigators or state bar association).

76. E.g., Ind. Code §§33–2.1–5–6(b), 33–2.1–6–9(c).

77. E.g., Nebr. Rev. Stat. §24–724 (counsel provided by his attorney general); Penn. State Stat. 11.160(d) (attorney general).

78. E.g., Ariz. Rules, *supra* note 73, R. 2C; Mass. Rules, *supra* note 73, R. 2(1) and 11; Nebr. Rev. Stat. §24–724. *See Matter of McKenney*, 424 N.E.2d 194, 196 (Mass. 1981).

79. E.g., Ala. Judic. Inquiry Comm. Rules of Proc. R. 10; Alaska Stat. §22.30.066; Ark. Stat. Ann. §22–1003(4); Cal. Govt. Code §§68750–68753; Conn. Gen. Stat. §510; D.C. Code 11–1527(c), (d); La. Rev. Stat. Ann. §13–36; La. S. Ct. Rules R. XXIII, §5; Minn. Rules, *supra* note 57, R. 2(e); N.M. Stat. §34, §§27–30; Va. Code §§2.1–37.9 to .12.

80. E.g., Del. Ct. on Judic. Rules of Proc. R. 3(e).

81. E.g., Ark. Stat. Ann. §22–1004(a); R.I. Comm. on Judic. Tenure and Discipl. Rules R. 3(b).

82. E.g., Conn. Gen. Stat. §51–51l; Del. Ct. on Judic. R. 3; D.C. Code §1527(a)(i); Mass. Gen. Laws art. 211c, §2.

83. *See* ABA Stds., *supra* note 70, §4.1, and the accompanying commentary.

84. E.g., Colo. Rules, *supra* note 73, R. 5(c); Minn. Rules, *supra* note 57, R. 6(a), (c); Mo. Const. art. 5, §24(2); Pa. Const. art. 5, §18(c); Tex. Rev. Civ. Stat. Ann. §1-a(7). Query whether provisions authorizing investigation of a "complaint" would be so construed. Examples of such provisions include: Miss. Code Ann. §9–19–21; Mont. Const. art. VII, §11(2); N.Y. Const. art. 6, §22; La. S. Ct. R. XXIII, §3(a).

85. E.g., Ala. Judic. Inqu. Comm. R. 6; Alaska Stat. Ann. §22.30.011(a); Ariz. Rules, *supra* note 73, R. 2(A); Cal. Rules, *supra* note 73, R. 904; Ind. Code Ann. §§2.1–5–5 and 6, 33–2.1–6–8; Ky. Rules, *supra* note 73, R. 4.170; S.C. S. Ct. R. 34 (10).

86. E.g., Cal. Rules, *supra* note 73, R. 904(b); Del. Rules, *supra* note 80, R. 3(d); Fla. Rules, *supra* note 73, R. 6(b); Ill. Judicial Inquiry Bd. R. 4(e); Ind. Code §33–2.1–5–6(b); Ky. Supr. Ct, R. 4.170(4); La. Rules, *supra* note 79, R. XXIII, §3(b); Mich. Gen. Ct. Rules, R. 932.7(b); S.D. Rules, *supra* note 73, R. 5(b); Wyo. Rules, *supra* note 73, R. 9(d); *cf.* Hawaii Supr. Ct. R. 26.6(c) ("notice that a complaint has been made may be given to the judge named in that complaint").

87. E.g., *McCartney, supra* note 49. *Cf. In re Inquiry concerning Judge, No.64, Bill J. Martin*, 275 S.E.2d 412 (N.C. 1981); *In re Carrillo*, 542 S.W.2d 105 (Tex. 1976).

88. E.g., Cal. Rules, *supra* note 73 R. 904(b); Me. S. Ct. Order, *supra* note 40; S.D. Rules, *supra* note 72, R. 5(b); Wyo. Rules, *supra* note 72, R. 9(d). *See infra* notes 124 to 127, and the accompanying text.

89. E.g., Ill. Judic. Inqu. Bd. R. 4(e) (judge not to be informed of grievant's name unless circumstances require otherwise); *Mikesell, supra* note 49. (commission had discretion to withhold citizen complainant's identity notwithstanding filing by judge of written consent to disclosure); Gillis and Fieldman, *supra* note 37, at 120 (favoring nondisclosure). *See infra* notes 124–127, and accompanying text.

NOTES TO §6.3(e)

90. E.g., Cal. Rules, *supra* note 73, R. 904(d); Conn. Gen. Stat. §51–51(n); Minn. Rules, *supra* note 73, R. 6(g); Miss. Code Ann. §9–19–11.

91. E.g., Ariz. Rules, *supra* note 73, R. 2E; Colo. Const. art. VI, §23(3)(e); Ga. Rules, *supra* note 74, R. 3; Minn. Rules, *supra* note 57, R. 6(g) (verbatim copy

of ABA Stds. R. 6(g)); Mo. Rules, *supra* note 73, R. 12.075; N.Y. Judic. Law art. 2-A, §44(10); N.Y. Rules, *supra* note 73, R. 7000.3(c); R.I. Gen. Laws Ann. §8–16–4(c); Wyo. Rules, *supra* note 73, R. 9(e)(2). *cf.* Tenn. Code Ann. §17–5–306 (cease and desist order re minor infractions). *See* ABA Stds. R.6(g); Todd and Proctor, Burden of Proof, Sanctions, and Confidentiality, 54 Chi-Kent L. Rev. 177, 184–185 (1977); and Gillis and Fieldman, *supra* note 37, at 132–134.

NOTES TO §6.3(f)

92. E.g., Ariz. Rules, *supra* note 73, R. 6A; Del. Rules, *supra* note 80, R. 9(c)(3); Fla. Rules, *supra* note 73, R. 7(a); La. Rules, *supra* note 79, R. XXIII, §§2(d), 15; Me. Supr. Ct. Order, *supra* note 40, §3; Tex. Rev. Stat. Ann. art. 5966a, §2.

93. E.g., Hawaii Rules, *supra* note 73, R. 26.7, 26.9; Mass. Rules, *supra* note 73, R. 2(1) and 11(a).

94. E.g., Iowa Code Ann. §§605.29(2), 30(2).

95. Ala. Rules, *supra* note 79, R. 15.

96. E.g., Ky. Rules, *supra* note 73, §4.110; Mo. Rules, *supra* note 73, R. 12.05; Tex. Rev. Civ. Stat. Ann. §5966a, §2.

97. Tenn. Code Ann. §17–5–312.

NOTES TO §6.3(g)

98. E.g., Alaska Comm. on Judic. Qualifics. Rules R. 9; Ariz. Rules, *supra* note 73, R. 6A; Cal. Rules, *supra* note 73, R. 907; Colo. Const. art. VI, §23(e); Ga. S. Ct. R. 5; Idaho Code Ann. §1–2103; Ind. Code §§33–2.1–5–9, 33–2.1–6–12; Mass. Rules, *supra* note 40, R. 16(b); Minn. Rules, *supra* note 73, R. 9(a), 16B; Mont. Rev. Code Ann. §3–1–1106(2); Nebr. Const. art. V, §30(1); N.M. Const. art. VI, §32; N.Y. Const. art. 22(a); N.Y. Jud. Law §§43(1), 44(2); Ore. Rev. Stat. §1.420; R.I. Rules, *supra* note 81, R. 10; (commission required to sit en banc); Tex. Const. art. 5, §1-a(8); Utah Code Ann. §78–7–30(1); Wyo. Rules, *supra* note 73, R. 12(f) (commission required to set en banc).

99. E.g., Mass. Rules, *supra* note 40, R. 16(b); Minn. Rules, *supra* note 73, R. 9(a); N.Y. Jud. Law. art. 2-A, §43(1). *See* ABA Stds., *supra* note 70, §§5, 9, at 38 (recommending use of panel of commissioners where commission workload too great for en banc hearings; no commissioner involved in investigation should serve on panel).

100. E.g., *See supra* note 98, as to Arizona, California, Colorado, Georgia, Idaho, Indiana, Massachusetts, Minnesota, New York, Oregon, Texas, and Utah. *Cf.* S.C. S.Ct. Rules, *supra* note 73, R. 34(2)(e), (8), (13), and (14) (hearing must be before three masters but commissions may take additional evidence after receiving masters' report).

101. E.g., *See supra* note 98 at to California, Colorado, Georgia, Idaho, Indiana, Massachusetts, Oregon, and Texas.

102. E.g., *see supra* note 98 as to Arizona, New Mexico, and New York. *Compare* S.C. S. Ct. Rules, *supra* note 73, R. 34(8).

103. E.g., *see supra* note 98 as to Arizona, Massachusetts, and New York.

104. E.g., *see supra* note 98 as to Montana, Nebraska, and New Mexico.

105. E.g., Tex. Const. art. 5, §1-a(8).

106. E.g., Minn. Rules, *supra* note 73, R. 9(a).

107. E.g., N.Y. Jud. Law §2-A, §43(2).

108. Ore. Stat. Ann. §1.420(b).

109. 425 U.S. 901 (1976), *aff'g.* 405 F.Supp. 182, 195 (E.D. N.Y. 1975).

110. *See supra* note 73, and also notes 98 to 100.

111. E.g., *Sharpe v. State ex. rel. Oklahoma Bar Ass'n.* 448 P.2d 301, 306–307 (Okla. 1968), *cert. denied*, 384 U.S. 904 (1968). *Compare In re Daly*, 284 Minn. 567, 171 N.W.2d 818 (1969) (attorney has no right to jury trial in disciplinary proceedings against him); *In re Northwestern Bonding Co.*, 16 N.C. App.2d 272, 192 S.E.2d 33 (1972), appeal dismissed, 282 N.C. 426, 192 S.E.2d 837 (1972).

112. 37 N.Y.2d nn, oo-pp. (Ct. on Judic. 1975) (five-to-one decision). *Cf.* Williams, The Historical and Constitutional Bases for the Senate's Power to Use Masters or Committees to Receive Evidence in Impeachment Trials, 50 N.Y.U. L. Rev. 512, *et. seq.* (1975) (use by U.S. Senate of master or referee in impeachment trials is impliedly authorized by U.S. Constitution) *But see* Gasperini, *supra* note 1, at 24–25.

113. *See Geiler v. Comm. on Judic. Qualifics.*, 110 Cal. Rptr. 201, 515 P.2d 1, 4 (1973), *cert. denied*, 417 U.S. 932 (1974).

NOTES TO §6.3(h)

114. Single-tier jurisdictions with rules to this effect, where the commission merely recommends and does not itself impose discipline, include, among others, the following: Ariz. Rules, *supra* note 73, R. 10; Cal. Rules, *supra* note 73, R. 902; Colo. Const. art. V, §23(g); Colo. Rules, *supra* note 73, R. 3(a); Conn. Gen. Stat. §51–51l; Ga. Rules, *supra* note 73, R. 18; Hawaii Supr. Ct. R. 26.4; Hawaii Rev. Stat. §§610–3(a), (b), 610–12(b) (repealed); Idaho Code §1–2103; La. Rules, *supra* note 79, R. XXIII, §23(a); Me. S. Ct. Order, *supra* note 40, §8; Md. Const. art. IV, §4B(a); Mass. Rules, *supra* note 40, R. 3; Mo. Supr. Ct. R. 12, 23; Mont. Const. art. VII, §11(4); Mont. Rev. Codes Ann. 11–1105, 1107(2), 1121 to 1126; Nebr. Rev. Stat. §24–726; Nev. Const. art. 6, §21(5)(a); Nev. Comm. on Judic. Discipl. Rules R. 4(a); N.H. Supr. Ct. R. 40(3); N.M. Const. art. VI, §32; N.C. Gen. Stat. §7A–377; Pa. Const. art. 5, §18(h); R.I. Gen. Laws 18–16–4(c); S.D. Rules, *supra* note 73, R. 4; Tex. Const. art. 5, §1-a(10); Va. Code Ann. §2.1–37.13; Vt. Stat. Ann. §8–16–4(c); Wyo. Rules, *supra* note 73, R. 7. *Cf.* Alaska Stat. §22.30.011(b) (hearing is private unless public hearing is requested by judge); Miss. Const. art. 6, §177a (all proceedings before commission shall be confidential unless commission unanimously votes to contrary). Single-tier jurisdictions with such a confidentiality rule, in which the commission issues a final disciplinary order, include the following: D.C. Code §11–1528(a); Ky. Rules, *supra* note 73, R. 4.130; N.Y. Judic. Law art. 2-A, §45.

115. 28 U.S.C. §372(c)(14); Del. Const. art. IV, §37; Del. Rules, *supra* note 80, R. 10(d); Ohio S. Ct. Rules for Govt. of Judic. R. II(21), III(2) and (5).

116. Ark. Stat. §22–1004(b); Fla. Const. art. 5, §12(d); Fla. Rules, *supra* note 73, R. 10(a); Ind. Code Ann. §§33–2.1–5–3, 33-2.1–6–6; Minn. Rules, *supra* note 57, R. 5; Ore. Rev. Stat. §§1.420(2), 1440; Vt. Rules, *supra* note 57, R. 6(7) to (9).

Even in these jurisdictions, however, in which the formal hearing is public, the commission's deliberations are nevertheless confidential. *In re Inquiry concerning a Judge, Gridley*, 417 So.2d 950 (Fla. 1982).

117. Ala. Const. amend. no. 328, §6.17(b); Ill. Const. art. 6, §15(c); W. Va. Rules, *supra* note 58, R. I(B)(5), II(B)(10), and III(C)(9); Wis. Stat. Ann. §757.93.

118. E.g., S.C. S. Ct. R. 34, §33; Utah Code Ann. §78–7-30(3).

119. *See supra* note 114 as to Arizona, California, Colorado, Georgia, Idaho, Louisiana, Maryland, Pennsylvania, Texas, Virginia, and Wyoming.

120. E.g., D.C. Code Ann. §11–1528(a); N.Y. Judic. Law art. 2-A, §44(7).

121. *See supra* notes 114, 115, 118 and 120 as to Delaware, District of Columbia, Hawaii, Kentucky (record remains confidential unless supreme court orders otherwise), Louisiana, Maine, Massachusetts, Nevada, New Hampshire and South Carolina.

122. 3d Cir., Feb. 14, 1986, Nos. 84–1153 & 83–1164, rev'g 579 F. Supp. 192 (E.D. Pa. 1984). *But compare First Amendment Coalition v. Judicial Inquiry and Review Bd.*, 501 Pa. 129, 460 A.2d 722 (Pa. 1983) (denying petition to mandamus commission to disclose hearing transcript on ground disclosure prohibited by Pa. Const. art. 5, §18).

123. 435 U.S. 829 (1978).

124. *See supra* notes 88 and 89.

125. *See Forbes v. Earle*, 298 So.2d 1, 4 (Fla. 1974); *Landmark Communications, Inc. v. Virginia*, 217 Va. 699, 233 S.E.2d 120, 129–130 (1977), *rev'd on other grounds by Landmark, supra* note 122. *Compare Landmark, supra* note 122, 435 U.S. at 833.

126. *See Forbes, supra* note 125, 298 So.2d at 4; *Mikesell, supra* note 49, 243 N.W.2d at 94; *Landmark, supra* note 125, 233 S.E.2d at 129–130.

127. The rules requiring disclosure are necessarily based on this policy.

128. *See supra* notes 114 and 115 as to Alaska, Arizona, Georgia, Kentucky, Maine, New York, Ohio, and Rhode Island. *See also* R.I. Rules, *supra* note 81, R. 10.

129. E.g., Mass. Rules, *supra* note 40, R. 3(c); Minn. Rules, *supra* note 57, R. 5(a)(3) (waiver during preliminary investigation, prior to filing of formal charges); Ohio Rules, *supra* note 115, R. II(21)(b). *See* ABA Proposed Stds., *supra* note 70, §4.8. Such a waiver by a judge has however, been held not to terminate confidentiality protection afforded to witnesses and citizen complainants, e.g., *Mikesell*, supra note 49, 243 N.W.2d at 93–94.

130. E.g., Ga. Rules, *supra* note 73, R. 18(c); Ind. Code Ann. §33–2.1–5–6(c) (authorizing public response by commission to public statement by complainant concerning commission finding of lack of probable cause); Minn. Rules, *supra* note 57, R. 5(b); Tex. Const. art. 5, §1-a(10), Vt. Rules, *supra* note 57, R. 6(12), (14). *Cf.* Ky. S. Ct. R. 4.130(1). *See* ABA Proposed Stds., *supra* note 70, §4.9.

131. E.g., Miss. Code Ann. §9–19–21(4); Vt. Rules, *supra* note 57, R. 6(9).

132. E.g., Me. Supr. Ct. Order, *supra* note 40, §8(1); Minn. Rules, *supra* note 57, R. 5(c); Vt. Rules, *supra* note 57, R. 6(9).

133. E.g., Ky. S. Ct. R. 4.130; Ohio Rules, *supra* note 115, R. II(21)(c).

134. E.g., D.C. Code §11–1528; Ga. Rules, *supra* note 73, R.18(b); Va. Code Ann. §2.1–37.13.

135. E.g., Cal. Rules, *supra* note 73, R. 902(b)(2); Mass. Rules, *supra* note 40, R. 3(f).

136. E.g., Cal. Rules, *supra* note 73, R. 902(b)(4).

137. *Id.*, R. 902(b)(5); Vt. Supr. Ct. Rules, *supra* note 57, R. 6(13).

NOTES TO §6.3(i)

138. E.g., Alabama, Arizona, Delaware, Florida, Georgia, Hawaii, and South Dakota Rules, *supra* notes 73, 79, and 80; Ohio Rules, *supra* note 115; Me. S. Ct. Order, *supra* note 40.

139. E.g., D.C. Code §11–1527(c); Nebr. Rev. Stat. §24–721.

140. E.g., La. Rules, *supra* note 79, R. 23, §5; Mass. Rules, *supra* note 40, R. 15 (documents, statements, and depositions); Minn. Rules, *supra* note 57, R. 2(e) (depositions and documents); Mo. Rules, *supra* note 73, R. 12.12 (same); N.Y. Rules, *supra* note 73, R. 7000.3, 7000.6(h); Tex. Const. art. 5, §1–a(7), (8) and (11)Va. Code Ann. §2.1–37.12 (depositions); Vt. Rules, *supra* note 57, R. 8(4).

141. *See supra* note 140.

142. E.g., *see* Ky. Rules, *supra* note 73, R. 4. 170 (4).

143. E.g., Cal. Govt. Code §§68750–68754; W. Va. Rules, *supra* note 58, R. III(8) (subpoenas for witnesses or documents on request).

144. E.g., Nebr. Rev. Stat. §24–721.

145. E.g., D.C. Code §11–1527.

146. E.g., *Del Rio, supra* note 49, 256 N.W.2d at 735–736; *In the Matter of Byrne*, 47 N.Y.2d(b), (d), 420 N.Y.S.2d 70, 72 (N.Y. Ct. on Judiciary 1978); *In the Matter of McMahon*, 47 N.Y.2d(m), (o) (N.Y. Ct. on Judiciary 1978). *See* Peskoe, *supra* note 49, at 168.

147. E.g., R.I. Rules, *supra* note 81, R. 9; N.Y. Rules, *supra* note 73, R. 7000.6(h).

148. *Byrne, supra* note 146, 47 N.Y.2d at (d). 420 N.Y.S.2d at 72. *Cf. Crooks v. State Bar*, 3 Cal. 3d 346, 355, 475 P.2d 872, 878, 90 Cal. Rptr. 600, 606 (In Bank 1970) (disciplinary proceeding against attorney); Peskoe, *supra* note 49, at 168.

149. E.g., *McCartney, supra* note 49, 526 P.2d at 273–274 (denial of application for leave to take depositions; due process clause held not violated).

150. *In re DuPont*, 322 So.2d 180, 183 (La. 1975).

151. E.g., *Haggerty, supra* note 49, 241 So.2d at 475–476 (denial of application for additional particulars not in violation of due process as long as charges give notice of alleged misconduct).

152. E.g., *Mikesell, supra* note 49, 396 Mich. at 517, 243 N.W.2d at 92–94.

NOTES TO §6.3(j)(i)

153. E.g., La. Judic. Comm. Rules,R. VIII. *See Haggerty, supra* note 49, 241 So.2d at 476–477.

154. E.g., Fla. Rules, *supra* note 73, R. 15; Ky. S. Ct. R. 4.240; Mo. S. Ct. R. 12.20; Ohio Rules, *supra* note 115, R. III (10); R.I. Rules, *supra* note 81, R. 12 (excludes evidence inadmissible in civil case tried to a court without a jury); S.C. S. Ct. R. 34(14)(a); S.D. Rules, *supra* note 73, R. 9; Wyo. Rules, *supra* note 73, R. 12(g).

NOTES TO §6.3(j)(ii)

155. E.g., Alaska Stat. Ann. §22.30.011; Cal. Const. art. VI, §18(c) (Supp.); Wyo. Const. art. 5, §6(e) (six years). *But compare* Minn. Stat. Ann. §490.16 (expressly provides there is no limitation).

156. E.g., Del. Const. art. IV., §37.

157. E.g., Ohio Rev. Code Ann. §2701.12.

158. E.g., Mass. Gen. Stat. Ann., ch. 211C, §2 (one year); N.D. Cent. Code (§27–23–03(3) (six years).

NOTES TO §6.3(j)(iii)

159. E.g., *Kelly, supra* note 49, 238 So.2d at 570.

160. *In re Dekle*, 308 So. 2d 4, 5 (Fla. 1975).

161. *In the Matter of Coruzzi*, 95 N.J. 557, 472 A.2d 546 (1984).

NOTE TO §6.3(j)(iv)

162. *In re Peoples*, 296 N.C. 109, 250 S.E.2d 890, 909–914 (1978); N.Y. Judic. Law art. 2-A, §47 (resignation of judge after commission recommendation of removal, but before removal decree, does not terminate jurisdiction, but subsequent removal decree renders judge ineligible for future judicial office).

NOTES TO §6.3(j)(v)

163. *See In re Sarisohn*, 27 A.D.2d 466, 469, 280 N.Y.S.2d 237, 243 (2d Dep't 1967) (recognizing judge's constitutional right to refuse to testify, but removing him from office on ground refusal to testify showed unfitness for judicial office); ABA Stds. *supra* note 69, §5.13, commentary.

164. *See Haggerty, supra* note 49, at 473 (voluntary statement filed by judge with commission waived his privilege).

165. *See In the Matter of Osterman*, 13 N.Y.2d (a), (o)-(q) (1963).

166. *See Sarisohn, supra* note 163, 27 A.D.2d at 469, 280 N.Y.S.2d at 243.

167. *Osterman, supra* note 165.

168. *Sarisohn, supra* note 163.

169. *Osterman, supra* note 165.

170. *Spevack v. Klein*, 385 U.S. 511, 87 S. Ct. 625 (1967) (attorney had refused to testify, since not entitled to immunity), overruling a contrary decision in *Cohen v. Hurley*, 366 U.S. 117 (1961) (similar facts).

171. *Lefkowitz v. Cunningham*, 431 U.S. 801 (1977) (refusal to waive immunity held not a valid basis for discharge); *Gardner v. Broderick*, 392 U.S. 273 (1968) (same); *Sanitation Men Ass'n v. Commissioner of Sanitation*, 392 U.S. 280 (1968) (same). *Cf. Lefkowitz v. Turley*, 414 U.S. 70 (1973) (same; public contractor). *But compare DeWalt v. Barger*, 490 F.Supp. 1262, 1271–1272 (M.D. Pa. 1980) (refusal to give immunized testimony held a valid basis for discharge).

172. E.g., *see* Cal. Rules, *supra* note 73, R. 908(b).

173. *See Garrity v. New Jersey*, 385 U.S. 493 (1967) (public employees may not

be prosecuted on basis of incriminating testimony given by them under threat of discharge if they exercised privilege against self-incrimination).

174. E.g., *Pinkney v. District of Columbia*, 439 F.Supp. 519, 534 (D.D.C. 1977).

175. *Napolitano v. Ward*, 457 F.2d 279 (7th Cir. 1972).

NOTES TO §6.3(j)(vi)

176. E.g., *Hanson, supra* note 49, 532 P.2d at 307–308; *Geiler, supra* note 113, 515 P.2d at 4.

177. *See infra* notes 178–180, and the accompanying text.

178. E.g., Hawaii Ct. R. 26.09(f); Mich. Gen. Ct. R. 932.4 (conduct "clearly prejudicial to the administration of justice" constitutes disciplinary "misconduct in office"); Miss. Comm. on Judic. Perf. Rules, R. 8D; Ohio Rules, *supra* note 115, R. III(6); Wis. Stat. Ann. §757.89; *Hanson, supra* note 49, 532 P.2d at 307–308; *Geiler, supra* note 113, 515 P.2d at 4; *In re LaMotte*, 341 So.2d 513, 516 (Fla. 1977); *In re Rome*, 218 Kan. 198, 206, 542 P.2d 676, 684 (1975); *Haggerty, supra* note 49, 241 So.2d at 479; *Diener, supra* note 49, 304 A.2d at 594; *Nowell, supra* note 49, 293 N.C. at 247, 237 S.E.2d at 254; *In the Matter of Cieminski*, 270 N.W.2d 321, 326 (N.D. 1978); *In the Matter of Field*, 281 Ore. 623, 576 P.2d 348, 351 (In Banc 1978); *In the Matter of Heuermann*, 240 N.W.2d 603, 605–606 (S.D. 1976) (rejecting "beyond reasonable doubt" standard because proceeding not a criminal proceeding). *See* Overton, Grounds for Judicial Discipline in the Context of Judicial Disciplinary Commissions, 54 Chi-Kent L. Rev. 59, 63, n. 38 (1977).

179. E.g., N.Y. Rules, *supra* note 73, R. 7000.6(i); *In re Terry*, 262 Ind. 667, 323 N.E.2d 192, 194, n.2 (1975), *cert. denied*, 423 U.S. 867 (1975); *Duncan, supra* note 49, 541 S.W.2d at 569; *In re Brown*, 512 S.W.2d 317, 319–320 (Tex. 1974). *See* Overton, *supra* note 178 and n. 39.

180. E.g., N.J. Stat. Ann. §2A:1B–9 (removal proceeding before supreme court); *Coruzzi, supra* note 161, 472 A.2d at 552.

NOTES TO §6.3(k)(i)

181. *See* Gillis and Fieldman, *supra* note 37, at 134–135.

182. E.g., Alaska Stat. Ann. §22.30.070(a); Ariz. Const. art. 6.1, §2; Conn. Gen. Stat. §51–51j; D.C. Code §11–1526(c)(1); Ind. Const. art. 7, §11; Minn. Stat. Ann. §490.16(1); Mo. Const. art. 5, §24(4); N.D. Cent. Code §27–23–03(1); S.D. Comp. Laws Ann. §16–1A–10; Wyo. Const. art. 5, §6(c). *But compare* S.D. Rules, *supra* note 73, R. 17(b) and 20 (supreme court has discretion to suspend judge when commission has recommended suspension).

183. E.g., N.Y. Const. art. 12, §22(e); Vt. Rules, *supra* note 57, R. 5(1).

184. E.g., 28 U.S.C. §372(6)(B)(iv).

185. E.g., La. Const. art. 5, §25(C); S.D. Rules, *supra* note 73, R. 17(b), 20. *But compare* S.D. Comp. Laws Ann. §16–1A–10 (suspension automatic).

186. E.g., *see supra* note 182 as to Alaska, Arizona, Indiana, Minnesota, Missouri, North Dakota, South Dakota, and Wyoming.

187. E.g., N.Y. Const. art. 6, §22(g) (salary continues unless supreme court directs otherwise).

188. E.g., D.C. Code §1526(c)(1).
189. E.g., 28 U.S.C. §372(6)(B)(iv); Conn. Gen. Stat. §51–51s.
190. E.g., Ala. Const. amend. no. 328, 619; Mont. Rev. Code Ann. §3–1–1109.
191. E.g., D.C. Code §1526(c)(3); Iowa Code Ann. §605.29(2); Ky. Rules, *supra* note 73, R. 4.020(a); Nev. Const. art. 6, §21(7).
192. E.g., Wis. Stat. Ann. §757.95.
193. E.g., Fla. Const. art. 5, §12(f); Miss. Const. art. 6, §177a; S.C. Supr. Ct. R. 34(23); Tex. Const. art. 5, §1-a(6); Wis. Stat. Ann. §757.95.
194. E.g., Ala. Const. amend. no. 328, §6.19; Ky. Rules, *supra* note 73, R. 4.020(a); Mont. Rev. Code Ann. §3–1–1109.
195. E.g., Fla. Const. art. 5, §12.
196. E.g., *see supra* notes 191 and 193 as to Florida, Iowa, Mississippi, Nevada, South Carolina, and Wisconsin.
197. E.g., Okla. Const. art. 7-A, §4(d) (discretion of Okla. Ct. on Judic., Trial Divis.).
198. E.g., Hawaii Rules, *supra* note 73, R. 26.12(d)(1); Minn. Rules, *supra* note 57, R. 7(d)(1); Miss. Code Ann. §9–19–13; N.J.S.A. §2A:1B–5; Ore. Rev. Stat. §1.420(5); W. Va. Rules, *supra* note 58, R. II(J)(2).
199. E.g., Colo. Rules, *supra* note 73, R. 5(k); Mich. Gen. Ct. R. 9.220; Miss. Code Ann. §9–19–13; R.I. Gen. Laws §§8–166 to 8–167; Tex. Const. art. 5, §1-a(6); Wis. Stat. Ann. §757.95.
200. E.g., Colo. Rules, *supra* note 73, R. 5(k); Hawaii Rules, *supra* note 73, R. 26. 12(d)(1); Minn. Rules, *supra* note 57, R. 7(d)(1); Miss. Code Ann. §9–19–13.
201. E.g., N.J.S.A. §2A:1B–5; Miss. Const. art. 6, §177a; Okla. Const. art. 7-A, §4(d); Tex. Const. art. 5, §1-a(6); W. Va. Rules, *supra* note 58, R. II(J)(2).
202. E.g., Okla. Const. art. 7-A, §4(d); Ore. Rev. Stat. §1.420.(5); Wis. Stat. Ann. §757.95.
203. *Del Rio, supra* note 49, 256 N.W.2d at 734.

NOTE TO §6.3(k)(ii)

204. *Griner v. Thomas*, 101 Tex. 36, 104 S.W. 1058 (1907) (statute authorizing suspension held impliedly authorized by constitutional removal provision).

NOTES TO §6.3(k)(iii)(1)

205. E.g., Hawaii Rules, *supra* note 73, R. 26.12(a); and Ohio Rules, *supra* note 115, R. III(1)(b). *See supra* note 182 as to Alaska, Arizona, Indiana, Minnesota, Missouri, North Dakota, South Dakota, and Wyoming; and note 190 as to Alabama. *Cf.* ABA Stds, *supra* note 70, and ensuing commentary.
206. E.g., Nebr. Const. art. 5, §30(3); N.Y. Const. art. 6, §22(e); Vt. Rules, *supra* note 57, R. 5(1).
207. E.g., Tex. Const. art. 5, §1-a(6)(A).
208. *See supra* note 182 as to Alaska, Arizona, Hawaii, Indiana, Minnesota, Missouri, North Dakota, South Dakota, and Wyoming; note 183, as to Vermont; note 190 as to Alabama; and Hawaii Rules *supra* note 73, R. 26.12 (a) and (b). *Cf.* N.Y. Const. art. 6, 22(g) (salary continues unless N.Y. Court of Appeals directs

otherwise); Tex. Const. art. 5, §1-a(6) (suspension is with or without pay, as determined by commission).

NOTES TO §6.3(k)(iii)(2)

209. E.g., Colo. Const. art. VI, §23(2); D.C. Code §11-1526(c)(1); Ohio Rules, *supra* note 115, R. II(8)(a); Okla. Const. art. VIII, §1; R.I. Gen. Laws §8-16-8(a); Vt. Rules, *supra* note 57, R. 5(2).

210. E.g., Ariz. Const. art. 6.1, §3 (supreme court can act on recommendation of commission or on its own motion); Ind. Const. art. 7, §11 (same); Mich. Const. art. 6, §30(2); Minn. Stat. Ann. §490.16(2) (same); Nebr. Const. art. V, §30(4); N.D. Cent. Code §27-13-03(2) (same); S.D. Comp. Laws §16-1A-12 (same); Utah Code Ann. 78-7-28(3) (either commission or supreme court can suspend); Wyoming Const. art. 5, §6(d).

211. E.g., D.C. Code §11-1526(c)(1). *Cf.* Mo. Const. art. 5, §24 (on recommendation of commission, supreme court shall suspend judge). *See supra* note 210 as to Utah.

212. Alaska Stat. Ann. §23.30.070(b); La. Const. art. 5, §25(c); Miss. Const. art. 6, §177A; Mont. Rev. Code Ann. §3-1-1110.

213. E. g., *see* notes 209–212 as to Alaska, Arizona, Colorado, Minnesota, Missouri, North Dakota, Nebraska, Rhode Island, South Dakota, and Wyoming. *Cf.* note 209 as to Vermont (felonies and misdemeanors adversely affecting judge's ability to perform his duties).

214. *See* notes 209–212, as to Alaska, Arizona, Colorado, District of Columbia, Indiana, Minnesota, Montana, Nebraska, North Dakota, Oklahoma, South Dakota, Utah, and Vermont; and *see* R.I. Gen. Laws §8-16-8(a). *Compare* La. Const. art. 5, §25(c) (salary suspension is up to discretion of supreme court on recommendation of commission).

NOTES TO §6.3(1)

215. *See supra* notes 40 to 44, and accompanying text, as to Alabama, Alaska, Arizona, California, Colorado, Connecticut, Delaware, Florida, District of Columbia, Hawaii, Idaho, Illinois, Kentucky, Maine, Maryland, Massachusetts, Michigan, Minnesota, Mississippi, Missouri, Montana, Nebraska, Nevada, New York, North Carolina, North Dakota, Ohio, Oklahoma, Oregon, Pennsylvania, Rhode Island, South Dakota, Texas, Utah, Virginia, and Washington. *Cf.* 28 U.S.C.A. §§372(c)(6)-(8) (censure, reprimand, or recommendation of impeachment to house of representatives); Tenn. Code Ann. §§17-5-309 to 311 (removal recommendation transmitted to General Assembly); W. Va. Const. art. VIII, §8 (removal only by impeachment). *See also* Tesitor and Sinks, *supra* note 35, at 44-46.

216. *See supra* notes 40-47; Tesitor and Sinks, *supra* note 35, at 44-46; and ABA Proposed Stds., *supra* note 70, §§8.1-8.8.

217. *See supra* notes 40-43 and 46 as to Alabama, Alaska, Colorado, Connecticut, Georgia, Hawaii, Illinois, Kentucky, Louisiana, Michigan, Mississippi, Montana, Nebraska, Ohio, Oregon, Pennsylvania, Rhode Island, South Carolina, Tennessee, Utah, Vermont, Washington, and West Virginia. *See also* Iowa Code Ann. §605.27

(suspension without salary for not more than twelve months); and *Del Rio, supra* note 49, 256 N.W.2d at 729, 753, and n.4 (suspension beyond remainder of term of office).

218. E.g., Minn. Rules, *supra* note 57, R. 10(d)(6).

219. E.g., *Id.*, R. 10 (d)(4).

220. E.g., *see* Mass. Rules, *supra* note 40, R. 23(a) (disbarment); Minn. Rules, *supra* note 57, R. 10(d)(3) (bar discipline); Miss. Code Ann. §9–19–17 (suspension); Tesitor and Sinks, *supra* note 35 at 44–46; Todd and Proctor, *supra* note 91, at 188–189; ABA Stds., *supra* note 70, §§1.1, 6.6, 6.7(c), 7.11.

221. E.g., La. Supr. Ct. R. 23, §22 (commission may assess costs subject to review by supreme court); Minn. Rules, *supra* note 57, R. 10(d)(7).

222. E.g., Cal. Const. art. 6, §18(c) (Supp.); Colo. Const. art. VI, §23(e) (Supp.) (informal remedial action); Md. Const. art. IV, §4B (reprimand); Nebr. Const. art. V, §30 (private reprimand); R.I. Gen. Laws §8–16–4(c) (same); Tex. Const. art. 5, §1-a(8) (Supp.) (private or public reprimand).

NOTES TO §6.3(m)

223. E.g., *Hanson, supra* note 49, 532 P.2d at 308–309 (overruling *In re Robson,* 500 P.2d 657 [Alaska 1982]); *Geiler, supra* note 113, 515 P.2d at 4; *Kelly, supra* note 49, 238 So. 2d at 571; *Diener, supra* note 49, 304 A.2d at 594; *In the Matter of Buford,* 577 S.W.2d 809, 813–821 (Mo. En Banc, 1979) (rejecting "substantial evidence test"); *Nowell, supra* note 49, 237 S.E.2d at 252–253; *In re Martin,* 245 S.E.2d 766, 772 (N.C. 1978); *Cieminski, supra* note 178, 270 N.E.2d at 326; *In the Matter of Field,* 281 Ore. 623, 576 P.2d 348, 351 (1978); *Heuermann, supra* note 178, 240 N.W.2d at 606; *In re Brown,* 512 S.W.2d 317, 320 (Tex. 1974).

224. E.g., *see Spruance v. Commission on Judicial Qualifications,* 119 Cal. Rptr. 841, 532 P.2d 1209, 1212–1213, and n. 5 (Cal. In Bank 1975); *Buford, supra* note 223, 577 S.W.2d at 813–814.

225. E.g., *see Brown, supra* note 223, 512 S.W.2d at 320.

226. E.g., *see In re Anderson,* 412 So.2d 743, 746 (Miss. 1982).

227. E.g., *Spruance, supra* note 224, 532 P.2d at 1212–1213; *Diener, supra* note 49, 304A.2d at 594.

228. *See supra* note 223, and the accompanying text.

229. E.g., Colo. Const. art. VI, §23(3)(c); Idaho Code §1–2103; La. Supr. Ct. R. 23, §13; Nebr. Rev. Stat. §24–723; Pa. Const. art. 5, §18(h); S.C. Supr. Ct. R. 34(21)(d). According to *Brown, supra* note 223, 512 S.W.2d at 320, however, additional evidence may be introduced before the supreme court only by moving for leave to adduce the additional evidence, showing good cause, and securing an order granting such leave.

230. E.g., La. Supr. Ct. R. 23, §13; Minn. Rules, *supra* note 57 R. 12(d)(1). The latter rule authorizes this procedure if "the court desires an expansion of the record or additional finding with respect either to the recommendation for discipline or to the sanction to be imposed." *Id.*

231. S.C. Rules, *supra* note 73, §34(21)(d) (supreme court may direct that additional evidence be taken before its designee and filed as part of the record before the court).

232. *See supra* notes 223–230.

233. *In re Syzmanski*, 400 Mich. 469, 255 N.W.2d 601 (1977).

234. E.g., *Geiler, supra* note 113, 515 P.2d at 4; *Spruance, supra* note 224, 532 P.2d at 1212, n.5.

235. E.g., *Spruance, supra* note 224, 532 P.2d at 1212, n.5; *Mikesell, supra* note 49, 243 N.W.2d at 89–90.

236. E.g., *Spruance, supra* note 224, 532 P.2d at 1217, n.5.

237. E.g., *Diener, supra* note 49, 304 A.2d at 600; *In re Scott*, 377 Mass. 364, 370, 386 N.E.2d 218, 221 (1979); *In re Hardy*, 294 N.C. 90, 240 S.E.2d 367, 372–373 (1978) (three dissents on this point). *Compare* N.Y. Const. art. 6, §22(d) (giving decisional function to commission, but empowering Court of Appeals to "impose a less or more severe sanction prescribed by this section than the one determined by the commission, or impose no sanctions").

NOTE TO §6.3(n)(i)

238. *See infra* §§6.3(n)(ii) to 6.3(n)v.

NOTES TO §6.3(n)(ii)

239. Alaska Stat. Ann §22.30.011; Ariz. Const. art. 6.1, §4; Cal. Const. art. VI, §18(c); Cal. Rules, *supra* note 73, R. 904(a); Colo. Const. art. VI, §23(d); Del. Const. art. IV, §37; D.C. Code §11–1526(a)(2); Ga. Const. art. 6, §7, ¶7; Hawaii Rules, *supra* note 73, R. 26.5; Idaho Code Ann. §1–2103; Ill. Const. art. 6, §15; Ind. Const. art. 7, §11; Iowa Code Ann. §605.27; La. Const. art. 5, §25; Mass. Gen. Laws Ann. ch. 211C, §2; Minn. Rules, *supra* note 57, R. 4(a); Miss. Const. art. 6, §175 (willful misdemeanor in office); Mont. Const. art. VII, §11(3)(b); Nebr. Rev. Stat. Ann. §24–722; Nev. Const. art. 6, §21; N.M. Const. art. 6, §32; N.C. Gen. Stat. §7A–376; N.D. Cent. Code §27–23–03; Ore. Const. art. VII, §8(1) ("willful misconduct in a judicial office where such misconduct bears a demonstrable relationship to the effective performance of judicial duties"); S.D. Const. art. V, §9; Tenn. Code Ann. §17–5–302; Utah Code Ann. §78–7–28.

240. Ala. Const. amend. no. 328, §6.18(a); Ky. S. Ct. R. 4.020; Md. Const. art. IV, §4B(b); Mich. Const. art. 6, §30(2); Mo. Const. art. 5, §24(3) ("misconduct"); N.J.S.A. §2A:1B–2; N.Y. Const. art. 6, §22(a); Pa. Const. art. 5, §18(d); Vt. Rules, *supra* note 57, R. 2 (misfeasance or malfeasance in office); Va. Const. art. VI, §10 ("misconduct while in office"); Wyo. Const. art. 5, §6(e).

241. *See Spruance, supra* note 224, 532 P.2d at 1221; *Geiler, supra* note 113, 515 P.2d at 11.

242. *Anderson, supra* note 226, 412 So.2d at 745; *Nowell, supra* note 49, 237 S.E.2d at 255; *In the Matter of Martinez*, 99 N.M. 198, 656 P.2d 861, 865–866 (1982).

243. *See Spruance, supra* note 224, 532 P.2d at 221; *Geiler, supra* note 113, 515 P.2d at 9.

244. *Martinez, supra* note 242, 656 P.2d at 865; *Nowell, supra* note 49, 237 N.E.2d at 255.

NOTES TO §6.3(n)(iii)

245. *See supra* notes 239 and 240 as to Alaska, Arizona, California, Delaware, District of Columbia, Georgia, Idaho, Indiana, Louisiana, Mississippi, Montana, New Mexico, North Carolina, South Dakota, Vermont, Wyoming; and *see* Conn. Gen. Stat. §51–51i.

246. *See supra* note 239 as to Colorado, Massachusetts, Nevada, Oregon, and Tennessee; and *see* Fla. Const. art. 5, §12(f); Tex. Const. art. 5, §1-a(6)(A); Tex. Rev. Civ. Stat. Ann. art. 5966a, §6B; Wis. Stat. Ann. §757.81.

247. *See supra* notes 239 and 240 as to Illinois, Iowa, Kentucky, Maryland, Michigan, New York, Utah, and Virginia; and *see* Minn. Stat. Ann. §490.16(3); R.I. Gen. Laws §8–16–4(b); S.C. S. Ct. R. 34(1)(b).

248. *See supra* notes 239–240 as to Missouri, Nebraska, New Jersey and North Dakota.

249. *See supra* note 240 as to Alabama and Pennsylvania; and *see* Okla. Const. art. VII-A, §1 (gross neglect of duty).

NOTES TO §6.3(n)(iv)

250. *See supra* notes 239, 240, and 245 as to Arizona, California, Connecticut, Georgia, Idaho, Illinois, Indiana, Louisiana (conduct must be persistent and public), Mississippi, North Carolina, South Dakota, Utah, and Vermont; *see infra* note 251 as to Minnesota.

251. *See supra* notes 239 and 240 as to Alaska, District of Columbia, Hawaii, Minnesota, Pennsylvania, and Tennessee. *See also* Minn. Rules, *supra* note 73, R. 4(a). *But compare* Minn. Const. art. 6, §9; and Minn. Stat. Ann. §490.16(3).

252. *See supra* notes 239 and 240 as to Maryland, Massachusetts, Michigan (conduct "clearly" prejudicial), New York (conduct "on or off the bench"), Virginia, and Wyoming. *See supra* note 251 as to Minnesota.

253. *See supra* notes 239 and 246 as to Iowa and Rhode Island (conduct that brings the judicial office into *serious* disrepute"); and *see* Ohio Rev. Code Ann. §2701.12 ("a violation of such of the canons of judicial ethics as would result in a substantial loss of public respect for the office" (emphasis added)); and Tex. Const. art. 5, §1-(a)(b) (willful or persistent conduct).

NOTES TO §6.3(n)(v)

254. *See* Martineau, Disciplining Judges for Nonofficial Conduct: A Survey and Critique of the Law, 10 U. Balt. L. Rev. 225, 228 (1981); and *supra* notes 62 and 63 (Chapter 5).

255. *See* Martineau, *supra* note 254, at 228. The Code of Judicial Conduct, both as prepared and recommended by the ABA and as adopted by many states (sometimes with revisions and sometimes without revisions), will be hereinafter cited as "COJC."

256. *See* Martineau, *supra* note 254, at 228.

257. *See supra* notes 62 and 63, and the accompanying text.

258. E.g., *see* Codes of Judicial Conduct in Arizona, Arkansas, Florida, Iowa,

Kentucky, Louisiana, Minnesota, Missouri, New Mexico, and Ohio. *But compare* those in California (adopted by Conference of California Judges) and New York (adopted by New York State Bar Association).

259. *See supra* notes 239, 240, 245, 246, 247, and 253 as to Alabama, Colorado, Connecticut, Delaware, Hawaii, Iowa, Kentucky, Massachusetts, North Dakota, Ohio, Oregon, Pennsylvania, South Carolina, Tennessee, Texas, Vermont, and Wisconsin. *See also* Ark. Stat. Ann. §22–1004; Me. Supr. Ct. Order, *supra* note 40, par. 9; Md. R. Proc. 1231(15) (violation of any canon is prejudicial to proper administration of justice); N.H. Rev. Stat. Ann. §490.4; Pa. Const. art. 5, §17(b), 18(d); Wash. Const. art. IV, §31; W. Va. Const. art. 8, §8; W. Va. Rules, *supra* note 58, R. III(C)(13).

260. *See supra* notes 239, 245, and 246 as to Connecticut, North Dakota, Oregon, Texas, and Wisconsin.

261. Del. Const. art. IV, §37.

262. Me. Supr. Ct. Order, *supra* note 40, par. 9.

263. Iowa Code Ann. §605.27.

264. Ohio Rev. Code Ann. §2701.12.

265. *See supra* notes 239, 240, 247, and 259 as to Minnesota, Pennsylvania, South Carolina, Tennessee, and Vermont.

266. E.g., *Halleck v. Berliner*, 427 F.Supp. 1225, 1240 (D.D.C. 1977); *In the Matter of Babineaux*, 346 So.2d 676, 678–679 (La. 1977) (deliberate violation of Code of Judicial Conduct constitutes "persistent and public conduct prejudicial to the administration of justice that brings the judicial office into disrepute"). *See In re Foster*, 318 A.2d 523, 533 (Md. 1974) ("the commission noted that Rule [of Judicial Ethics] 13 (now Rule 14) makes any violation of the Rules of Judicial Ethics conduct prejudicial to the administration of justice").

267. *See Cannon v. Commission on Judicial Qualifications*, 122 Cal. Rptr. 898, 537 P.2d 898, 918, n.22 (In Bank 1975); *Spruance, supra* note 224, 532 P.2d at 1221; *Haggerty, supra* note 49, 241 So.2d at 474; *Foster, supra* note 267, 318 A.2d 523, 534–535 (Md. 1974); *In re Nowell*, 293 N.C. 235, 237 S.E.2d 235, 252 (1977). *Cf. People ex. rel. Harrod v. Illinois Courts Comm.*, 69 Ill.2d 445, 372 N.E.2d 52, 63–64 (1978) (code supplies guides to interpretation of vague constitutional standards, and only conduct in violation of code may be subject to complaint before commission).

NOTE TO §6.3(n)(vi)

268. *See supra* notes 240, 245, 246, 247, 250, 253, and 259 as to Connecticut, Kentucky, Missouri, Oregon, South Carolina, and Texas; and note 251 as to Minnesota.

NOTE TO §6.3(n)(vii)

269. *See supra* notes 239, 240, 245, 246, 247, and 249 as to Alaska, Arizona, California, Colorado, Connecticut, Georgia, Idaho, Iowa, Massachusetts, Michigan, Mississippi, Missouri, Montana, Nebraska, Nevada, New Mexico, New York, North Carolina, North Dakota, Oklahoma, Oregon, Rhode Island, South Carolina, South Dakota, Utah, Vermont, Wisconsin, Wyoming.

NOTES TO §6.3(n)(viii)

270. E.g., Fla. Const. art. 5, §12(f). *Cf.* N.J.S.A. §2A:1B–2 ("other conduct evidencing unfitness").
271. E.g., Minn. Rules, *supra* note 57, R. 4(a).

NOTES TO §6.3(n)(ix)

272. *See supra* notes 239, 240, and 247 as to Hawaii, Kentucky, Louisiana, Michigan, Minnesota, Mississippi, Utah, Vermont, and Wisconsin.
273. *See supra* notes 239, 247, and 253 as to Georgia, Missouri, Nebraska, North Carolina, Ohio, and South Carolina; and *see* Ohio Rev. Code Ann. §2701.12, and Ohio Rules, *supra* note 115, R. II(5)(a). See also Del. Const. art. IV, §37 (the commission, after appointment, of an offense involving moral turpitude)
274. *See supra* notes 239 and 245 as to Alaska, Connecticut, and Oregon.
275. E.g., Me. Supr. Ct. Order, *supra* note 40, par. 9 ("a crime the nature of which casts into doubt his continued willingness to conform his conduct to the Code of Judicial Conduct"); Mo. Const. art. 5, §24 ("commission of a crime" or "any offense involving moral turpitude"); N.J. Const. art. 6, §§7, 1 ("misdemeanor committed during their respective continuance in office"); Okla. Const. art. VII-A, §1; Tex. Rev. Civ. Stat. art. 5966, §6B (willfully violates a provision of the Texas penal statutes).
276. E.g., Ark. Stat. Ann. §22–1004.

NOTE TO §6.3(n)(x)

277. E.g., Cal. Rules, *supra* note 73, R. 904 ("engaged in an improper action or dereliction of duty"); Mo. Const. art. 5, §24 ("misconduct"); Ohio Rev. Code Ann. §2701.12 ("any misconduct involving moral turpitude").

NOTE TO §6.3(n)(xi)

278. E.g., Mo. Const. art. 5, §24(3); Okla. Const. art. VII-A, §1.

NOTE TO §6.3(n)(xii)

279. E.g., Mo. Const. art. 5, §24(3); Okla. Const. art. VII-A, §1.

NOTE TO §6.3(n)(xiii)

280. E.g., Okla. Const. art. VII-A, §1.

NOTE TO §6.3(n)(xiv)

281. Tenn. Code Ann. §17–5–302.

NOTES TO §6.3(n)(xv)

282. E.g., *see* Conn. Gen. Stat. §51–51i(7), Nebr. Rev. Stat. Ann. §24–722; Ohio Rev. Code, §2701.12A(3).

283. E.g., Alaska Const. art. IV, §4; Alaska Stat. Ann. §§22.05.070, 22.10.090; Colo. Const. art. VI, §8; D.C. Code §11–1501(b); Fla. Const. art. 5, §8; Ill. Const. art. 6, §11; Ind. Const. art. 7, §10; Kan. Const. art. 3, §2(n); La. Const. art. V, §24; Mont. Const. art. VII, §9; N.J. Const. art. 6, §§6, 2; Pa. Stat. Ann. §2873(b)(1). *See supra* §6.2(g).

NOTES TO §6.3(n)(xvi)

284. E.g., Conn. Gen. Stat. Ann. §51–51i.
285. E.g., Ky. Supr. Ct. R. 4.020.
286. E.g., Ark. Stat. Ann. §22–1004.

NOTE TO §6.3(o)(i)

287. *McCartney, supra* note 49, 526 P.2d at 283–284 (constituted willful or prejudicial misconduct; censured); *In re Glickfeld*, 92 Cal. Rptr. 278, 479 P.2d 638 (Cal. In Bank 1971) (constituted "prejudicial conduct"; censured); *In re Inquiry concerning a Judge, Re Lantz*, 402 So.2d 1144 (Fla. 1981) (violated Canons 1 and 3(A)(3) of Code of Judicial Conduct; reprimanded); *Del Rio, supra* note 49, 256 N.W.2d at 749–753; *In re McDonough*, 296 N.W.2d 648, 686 (Minn. 1979) (violated Canon 3(A)(3); censured); *In re Fullwood*, 518 S.W.2d 22 (Mo. En Banc 1975) (violated various canons; suspended); *Mikesell, supra* note 49 (suspended); *In the Matter of Albano*, 75 N.J. 509, 384 A.2d 144 (1978) (violated Canon 3(a)(3); reprimanded); *In the Matter of Yengo*, 72 N.J. 425, 371 A.2d 41 (1977) (violated Canon 3(a)(3)); *In the Matter of Mertens*, 56 A.D.2d 456, 392 N.Y.S.2d 860, 863–865, 869–870 (1st Dep't 1977).

NOTES TO §6.3(o)(ii)

288. E.g., *Del Rio, supra* note 49, 256 N.W.2d at 741–742, 752–753 (suspended for five years).

289. E.g., *Mertens, supra* note 287, 392 N.Y.S.2d at 869–870 (threats to report nonsettling insurance company defendants to the Superintendent of Insurance as companies that did not bargain in good faith).

290. E.g., *Geiler, supra* note 113, 515 P.2d at 10–11 (removed).

NOTE TO §6.3(o)(iii)

291. E.g., *Mikesell, supra* note 49, 243 N.W. 2d at 96–100, *McCartney, supra* note 49, 526 P.2d at 280, 282–283. *See* Gillis and Fieldman, *supra* note 37 at 133.

NOTE TO §6.3(o)(iv)

292. E.g., *Matter of Seraphim*, 97 Wis.2d 485, 294 N.W.2d 483, 499 (1980) (violated rule 15 of Wisconsin Code of Judicial Ethics, which proscribed such comments).

NOTE TO §6.3(o)(v)

293. E.g., *Cincinnati Bar Ass'n v. Heitzler*, 32 Ohio St.2d 214, 291 N.E.2d 477, 486 (1972) (disbarment proceeding); *In the Matter of Lombardi*, 49 N.Y.2d (v)-(w) (1980); *In re Martin*, 275 S.E.2d 412, 418, 423–424 (N.C.1981) (held "willful misconduct in office"). *See infra* §7.11(b)(vi).

NOTE TO §6.3(o)(vi)

294. E.g., *In re Crowell*, 379 So.2d 107 (Fla. 1979) (demonstrated unfitness for judicial office; removed); *Del Rio, supra* note 49, 256 N.W.2d at 746, 751–753 (five-year suspension); *Yengo, supra* note 287, 371 A.2d at 53 (held misconduct in office and conduct evidencing unfitness for office and judicial incompetence; removed).

NOTE TO §6.3(o)(vii)

295. E.g., *In re Dekle*, 308 So.2d 5 (Fla. 1975) (violation of Canon 3A(4) of Fla. COJC); *In re Lowry*, Unreported Order, Dkt. No. 284–79 (Vt. 1979) (same). *Compare* Buckley, The Commission on Judicial Qualification: An Attempt to Deal with Judicial Misconduct, 3 U.S.F.L. Rev. 244, 246–248 (1969) (consideration by judge of off-the-record information).

NOTE TO §6.3(o)(viii)

296. E.g., *Buford, supra* note 223, 577 S.W.2d at 823–824 (violated Mo. COCJ Canon 3(A)(4)s requirement of opportunity for hearing; thirty-day suspension for this and other conduct); *In re Hardy*, 294 N.C. 90, 240 S.E.2d 367 (1978) (entry of dismissal of judgment or acquittal in criminal prosecution without notice to prosecutor; censured); *Nowell, supra* note 49 (same; only censured, since motives not corrupt); *In the Matter of Edens*, 290 N.C. 299, 226 S.E.2d 5 (1976) (same; censured).

NOTES TO §6.3(o)(ix)

297. *Matter of Troy*, 364 Mass. 15, 306 N.E.2d 203, 217–218 (1973); *Murtagh v. Maglio*, 9 A.D.2d 515, 195 N.Y.S.2d 900, 905 (2d Dept. 1960). *Accord*: Hawaii Supr. Ct. R. 26.5(b); Mass. Rules, *supra* note 40, R. 8.

298. Scott, *supra* note 237, 386 N.E.2d 218, 220–221 (public reprimand or censure, plus restrictions on assignments). *See Harrod, supra* note 43, 372 N.E.2d at 63.

NOTES TO §6.3(o)(x)

299. *In re Charge of Judicial Misconduct*, 593 F.2d 879 (9th Cir. 1979).

300. E.g., *Municipal Court of the City of Cedar Rapids*, 188 N.W.2d 354 (Iowa 1971).

NOTES TO §6.3(o)(xi)

301. E.g, *Del Rio, supra* note 49, 256 N.W.2d at 745 (repeated instances of partiality; five-year suspension for this and other reasons). *See* Buckley, *supra* note 295, at 248–250.

302. *State ex. rel. Commission on Judicial Qualifications v. Rome*, 623 P.2d 1307 (Kan. 1981) (removed from office).

NOTE TO §6.3(o)(xii)

303. *In the Matter of Jones*, 47 N.Y.2d (mmm) (Ct. on Judiciary 1979).

NOTE TO §6.3(o)(xiii)

304. E.g., *Field, supra* note 223 (removed from office).

NOTE TO §6.3(o)(xiv)

305. E.g. *Stark County Bar Ass'n v. Weber*, 190 N.E.2d 918, 918 (Ohio 1978).

NOTE TO §6.3(p)(i)

306. E.g., *In the Matter of Bonin*, 378 N.E.2d 669 (Mass. 1978) (held violative of Canons 3B(4) and 2A of Mass. COJC; censured and suspended).

307. *Id.*

NOTE TO §6.3(p)(ii)

308. E.g., *In the Matter of Bates*, 555 S.W.2d 420 (Tex. 1977).

NOTE TO §6.3(p)(iii)

309. E.g., *In re Anderson*, 412 So.2d 743 (Miss. 1982) (violated Canons 1, 2A, and 3B of Miss. COJC, and constituted "willful misconduct").

NOTES TO §6.3(p)(iv)

310. E.g., *McDonough, supra* note 287, 296 N.W.2d at 671–672, 687, 695–696 (censure and fine).

311. E.g., *Kelly, supra* note 49 (four-to-three decision) (violated canons of Fla. COJC requiring cooperation between judges and prohibiting arbitrary or extreme judicial conduct; reprimand).

NOTE TO §6.3(p)(v)

312. E.g., *West Virginia Judicial Inquiry Comm. v. Dostert*, 271 S.E.2d 427 (W.Va. 1980) (six-month suspension without pay).

NOTES TO §6.3(q)(i)

313. E.g., COJC Canon 5C(1) in Arkansas, Alaska, Arizona, California, Colorado, Connecticut, Delaware, Florida, Hawaii, Indiana, Iowa, Kansas, Kentucky, Louisiana, Maine, Michigan, Minnesota, Mississippi, Missouri, New Jersey, New Hampshire, New Mexico, New York, North Carolina, North Dakota, Ohio, Oklahoma, Oregon, Pennsylvania, South Carolina, South Dakota, Tennessee, Texas, Virginia, Washington, West Virginia, Wyoming. Alabama, Georgia, Massachusetts, and Washington have adopted ABA Canon 5C(1), except that Alabama, Georgia and Washington have omitted the prohibition of dealings that tend to involve the judge "in frequent transactions with lawyers or persons likely to come before the court on which he serves"; and, perhaps due to a typographical error, Massachusetts has omitted language prohibiting dealings tending to exploitation of the judge's judicial position.

314. E.g., COJC Canon 5C(2) in Arkansas, Alaska, Colorado, Florida, Hawaii, Iowa, Maine, Michigan, Minnesota, New Hampshire, New York, North Carolina, Ohio, South Carolina, Tennessee, Washington, Wyoming. Cf. Ill. S. Ct. R. 63. For variations of this ABA canon, which are substantially identical to it except as indicated in the parentheses following the names of the states, *see, e.g.,* COJC Canon 5C(2) in Arizona (judge may act as an officer, director, advisor, or employee of "a closely held business"), Delaware, Masschusetts (authorization of "other remunerative activity" restricted to activity "permitted by Canon 4"), New Jersey (omits authorization to "engage in other remunerative activity"), Texas (judge may not be officer, director, or manager of a "publicly owned business," viz., a business having more than ten stockholders), Virginia (judge may act as an officer, director, or non-legal advisor of a "family business"). In Mississippi and Missouri, ABA Canon 5C(2) is omitted from COJC Canon 5C.

315. *E.g.,* COJC Canon 5C(2) in Alabama, Connecticut, Georgia, Indiana, Kentucky, North Dakota, Pennsylvania, and South Dakota. *Cf.* COJC Canon 5C(2) in New Mexico (authorizes other remunerative activity, and omits ABA proviso prohibiting judge from acting as an officer, director, manager, advisor, or employee of any business), and West Virginia (same, except prohibits judge from allowing his name "to so appear in connection with such business, except as may be required by law").

316. *E.g.,* COJC Canon 5C(2) in California Kansas, Oklahoma and Oregon; and Nev. COCJ Canon 5C(3). *Cf.* COJC Canon 5C(2) in Louisiana (authorizes "other remunerative activity," and prohibits judge from serving with specified public interest institutions). In California, Nevada, and Oklahoma, Canon 5C(2) prohibits advertising appearing on the power or prestige of the judge's office.

317. *See infra* notes 318–321.

318. E.g., *In re Welch*, 388 A.2d 535 (Md. 1978) (violated former Md. Canons of Judic. Ethics 4 and 25 and Md. rule 9; censured).

319. E.g., *Babineaux, supra* note 266 (violation of canon 5C(2) held "persistent and public conduct prejudicial to administration of justice that brings the judicial office into disrepute"; suspension without pay until resignation as corporate director).

320. E.g., *Heitzler, supra* note 293 (violated former Ohio Canon of Judic. Ethics 25; indefinitely suspended from practice of law).

321. E.g., *Foster, supra* note 266 (violated Md. Canon of Judic. Ethics 24 and Md. Rule of Judic. Ethics 9; censured).

NOTES TO §6.3(q)(ii)

322. E.g., *Heitzler, supra* note 293, 291 N.E.2d at 487 (indefinite suspension from practice of law).

323. *Id.* Code provisions identical or substantially identical to ABA Canon 5C(3) include, *e.g.*, COJC Canon 5C(3) in Arizona, Arkansas, California, Colorado, Connecticut, Delaware, Florida, Georgia, Hawaii, Indiana, Iowa, Kansas, Kentucky, Louisiana, Maine, Massachusetts, Michigan, Minnesota, New Hampshire, New Jersey, New Mexico, New York, North Carolina, North Dakota, Ohio, Oklahoma, Oregon, Pennsylvania, South Dakota, Tennessee, Texas, West Virginia, Washington and Wyoming; COJC Canon 5C(2) in Mississippi, Missouri; and COJC Canon 5C(4) in Nevada. Alabama omits ABA Canon 5C(3)'s divestiture requirements. Also, Virginia's Canon 5C omits ABA Canon 5C(3).

324. E.g., *Troy, supra* note 297, 306 N.E.2d at 232–234.

325. *Welch, supra* note 318, and accompanying text (censured).

NOTE TO §6.3(q)(iii)(2)

326. *See Napolitano v. Ward*, 457 F.2d 271, 284 (7th Cir. 1972) (violations of Canon 4 are disciplinable).

NOTES TO §6.3(q)(iv)

327. E.g., *Seraphim, supra* note 292, 294 N.W.2d at 498–499 (three-year suspension without compensation).

328. *Id.*, at 488–489, 491, 498, 500, and n.1.

329. States which have adopted ABA Canon 5C(4) and (5) without appreciable substantive change include, *e.g.*, Arkansas, California, Florida, Georgia, Indiana, Iowa, Kansas, Kentucky, Maine, Massachusetts, Michigan (value of gift to judge incident to public testimonial may not exceed $100), Minnesota, Mississippi, Missouri, Nevada, New Hampshire, New Jersey (gift incident to public testimonial must be "of nominal value"), New Mexico, New York, North Carolina, North Dakota, Ohio, (same as Michigan), Oklahoma, Oregon, South Carolina, South Dakota, Tennessee, Texas, Washington, West Virginia, and Wyoming. States which, although they have adopted ABA Canons 5C(4) and (5) in the main, have made one

or more appreciable substantive changes therein, include, e.g. Arizona and Michigan. States which have adopted ABA Canon 5C(4) in a greatly condensed form include, e.g., Alabama, Louisiana and Virginia. Pennsylvania has altogether omitted ABA Canons 5C(4) and (5).

NOTES TO §6.3(q)(v)

330. *See supra* §6.3(n)(ix).

331. E.g., *In re Judge No. 491*, 249 Ga. 30, 287 S.E.2d 2 (1982) (judge pleaded nolo contendere to charge of crime involving moral turpitude; removed). *See supra* §6.3(n)(iv).

332. *See supra* §6.3(n)(viii). *See also* notes 270–271.

333. *See supra* note 276, and the accompanying text.

334. E.g., *In re Conduct of Roth*, 293 Ore. 179. 645 P.2d 1064 (In Banc 1982) (censured); *Duncan, supra* note 49, 541 S.W.2d at 571 (removed).

NOTES TO §6.3(q)(vi)

335. E.g., *Haggerty, supra* note 49 (removed). *See supra* §§6.3(n)(iv), 6(3)(n)(viii), 6.3(n)(x).

336. E.g., *Heitzler, supra* note 293, 291 N.E.2d at 482; *In re Inquiry concerning a Judge, No. 76–13*, 336 So.2d 1175 (Fla. 1976) (reprimand and restriction on sitting in criminal cases); *Seraphim, supra* note 292; *cf. Haggerty, supra* note 49.

337. *In the Matter of Dalessandro*, 483 Pa. 431, 397 A.2d 773 (Pa. 1976).

338. *Matter of Johnson*, 568 P.2d 855 (Wyo. 1977) (conduct described in text held prejudicial conduct bringing judicial office into disrepute; censure and reprimand).

NOTE TO §6.3(q)(ix)

339. *In re Inquiry concerning a Judge, Gridley*, 417 So.2d 950, 954–955 (Fla. 1982).

NOTES TO §6.3(r)

340. *See supra* §6.3(j)(ii).

341. E.g., *In the Matter of Bennett*, 403 Mich. 178, 267 N.W.2d 914, 920 (district judge disciplined for conduct committed while a probate judge, and while a candidate for district judge, but not in connection with that candidacy); *Sharpe, supra* note 111 (conduct during previous or preceding term made grounds for removal by statute); *Heuermann, supra* note 178, 240 N.W.2d at 607–608 (conduct occurring before creation of commission); *Seraphim, supra* note 292, 294 N.W.2d at 490–491 (conduct occurring before effective date of constitutional amendment authorizing discipline or removal by court following recommendation by commission but after adoption of current Code of Judicial Conduct). *See also* Cal. Const. art. VI, §18(c) (authorizing discipline with respect to conduct occurring within six years before commencement of current term of office); and Utah Code Ann. §78-7-28 (judge may be disciplined for "willful misconduct in office in any term of office subsequent

to the enactment of this section"). *See* Buckley, *supra* note 295 at 252, n. 11 (California's six-year limitation period commencing six years prior to commencement of current term was added to obviate argument pre-term misconduct not disciplinable).

342. E.g., *State ex. rel. Turner v. Earle*, 295 So.2d 609 (Fla. 1974); *In re Laughlin*, 153 Tex. 183, 265 S.W.2d 805, 808 (1954). *But compare In re Boyd*, 308 So.2d 13, 22 (Fla. 1975).

343. E.g., *In re Martin*, 275 S.E.2d 412, 423 (1981); *In the Matter of Carrillo*, 542 S.W.2d 105, 110–111 (Tex. 1976); *see In re Brown*, *supra* note 223, 512 S.W.2d at 320–321.

344. *Id.*, 512 S.W.2d at 321.

345. E.g., *Martin*, *supra* note 342, 275 S.E.2d at 422–423.

NOTES TO §6.3(s)

346. *See* Tesitor and Sinks, *supra* note 35, Table 5, at 44–46. *See infra* §7.13.

347. *See infra* §7.13.

348. *See*, e.g., *supra* note 182 as to Alaska, Arizona, Minnesota, Missouri, North Dakota, South Dakota, Wyoming (automatic suspension); and notes 177–179 as to New York, South Dakota, and Vermont (discretionary suspension).

7

Removal of Judges

7.1 INTRODUCTION

The only truly viable method of removal currently used in this country is removal through proceedings before a disciplinary commission. The ancient but inefficient and largely obsolete remedies of impeachment, address, joint resolution, and recall are still theoretically available in many states, however and will, therefore, be discussed in this chapter, albeit not as extensively as disciplinary commission proceedings.

7.2 REMOVAL BY EXECUTIVE ACTION

Removal of judges by executive action has become totally obsolete even in England, where it was used centuries ago. This method has not been utilized in this country since the American Revolution.[1]

7.3 IMPEACHMENT

Impeachment is still an available removal procedure in practically every jurisdiction in this country.[2] With a few exceptions,[3] the great majority of the constitutional and statutory impeachment provisions specify the grounds for impeachment.[4] The grounds for impeachment appear to fall into three broad categories: (a) grounds that, although they have frequently been given a broader interpretation,[5] arguably connote criminality or illegality; (b) grounds encompassing conduct that, although not necessarily criminal or illegal, is wrongful, unethical, improper, or abusive; and (c) grounds reaching conduct that, although neither illegal nor improper, shows incompetency in judicial office. More specific grounds may be grouped within these three broad categories as shown in the following sections.

a. Illegality Grounds

"High crimes,"[6] "misdemeanors involving moral turpitude,"[7] "crimes,"[8] "misdemeanors,"[9] "misdemeanors in office,"[10] "corrupt conduct in office" or "corruption in office,"[11] "corrupt conduct" or "corruption,"[12] "treason,"[13] and "bribery."[14]

b. Impropriety Grounds

"Malfeasance in office,"[15] "gross or serious misconduct in office,"[16] "misbehavior in office" or "misconduct in office,"[17] "willful neglect of duty,"[18] "misconduct" (in only one jurisdiction),[19] "habitual drunkenness" or "drunkenness,"[20] plus, in one jurisdiction, "gross immorality."[21]

c. Incompetency Grounds

"Maladministration" or "malpractice in office,"[22] "neglect of duty,"[23] and "incompetency."[24]

A sizeable number of jurisdictions specify grounds falling solely in the illegality group.[25] An even larger group, however, lists grounds that fall not only into the illegality but also into the impropriety group[26] or in all three groups[27] or into the illegality group and the incompetency group.[28] Finally, a small handful of jurisdictions list no grounds falling into the illegality group but only grounds falling into the impropriety group[29] or the incompetency group[30] or both.[31] Probably, however, the impropriety or incompetency grounds in the last-mentioned small handful of jurisdictions which pertain to misconduct in office, malfeasance or misfeasance in office, or maladministration, would be construed as applying to criminal as well as noncriminal official misbehavior or maladministration.

The existing impeachment remedies have been criticized as not reaching conduct that, although not involving criminality and moral turpitude, is nevertheless indicative of unfitness to hold judicial office.[32] This criticism is applicable to those jurisdictions with impeachment provisions that fall only into the illegality group unless terms such as "misdemeanors" are construed to reach conduct that, although neither criminal nor corrupt, is improper. This interpretation of misdemeanors was often advanced during the Watergate impeachment proceedings.

In addition to the limited grounds for impeachment in a number of jurisdictions, the other principal flaws in impeachment are that: (a) impeachment does not provide any remedy short of removal;[33] (b) legislatures are ill equipped as fact finders;[34] (c) impeachment is unduly expensive and takes the entire legislature away from its legislative duties;[35] and (d) impeachment proceedings are apt to be actuated by undue partisanship.[36] For all of the above reasons, impeachment is largely ineffective as a disciplinary remedy.

Despite its inherent defects, impeachment remains viable since many of the more modern removal systems, providing for court-imposed discipline of judges with the assistance of disciplinary commissions or discipline imposed by such commissions or by special courts, have explicitly preserved impeachment.[37]

Although federal impeachment proceedings always have been tried by the full Senate,[38] the suggestion has been made that the problem of conflicting legislative obligations could be alleviated by delegating the duty to hold a hearing to a committee or one or more special masters,[39] pursuant to an unused Senate rule authorizing these alternatives.[40]

The courts have frequently held that, because a removal proceeding commenced by a disciplinary commission is not a criminal proceeding, the prosecutors' burden of proof is to establish the charges by "clear and convincing evidence," rather than by proof "beyond a reasonable doubt."[41] It has also been held, however, that an impeachment proceeding is sufficiently like a criminal proceeding to commend the "reasonable doubt" standard.[42]

The impeachment provisions in the federal Constitution provide that a party convicted in an impeachment proceeding shall be subject in that proceeding only to removal from office but "shall nevertheless be liable and subject to indictment, trial, judgment, and punishment according to law."[43] A judge or other impeachable civil officer of the United States may, however, be indicted, tried, convicted, and punished in a criminal proceeding before, as well as after, the institution of an impeachment proceeding.[44]

The typical state impeachment provision, like its federal counterpart, provides that the lower house shall have the sole power of impeachment and that the upper house shall have the sole power to try all impeachments.[45] The requisite majorities required for impeachment and conviction vary from jurisdiction to jurisdiction, both as to the percentage required to impeach or convict and also as to whether the required majority applies to all elected members of the branch of the legislature or merely to those members present and voting.[46]

In Missouri, appellate and circuit court judges impeached by the house of representatives are tried before the supreme court or, in the case of supreme court judges, a special commission of seven eminent jurists elected by the senate.[47] In Nebraska, judges impeached by a majority of the elected members of the unicameral legislature are tried by the supreme court or, in the case of supreme court judges, by the judges of the district court.[48]

7.4 ADDRESS AND JOINT OR CONCURRENT RESOLUTIONS

Address and joint resolution differ in that, with address, the governor removes the judge on the address of both houses of the legislature,[49] whereas, with a joint or concurrent resolution, removal is effected by the legislature itself without participation by the governor.[50] In all but a few instances, the required majority is of all of the members of each house, rather than merely a majority of those present and voting, and usually must be a two-thirds majority.[51] In most instances, the required ground or charge is merely "cause," "good cause," "reasonable cause," "reasonable cause that is not sufficient ground for impeachment," "charges," or "complaint."[52]

Some address procedures provide that the governor "may" remove the judge on the address of both houses,[53] but others provide that the governor "shall" remove the judge.[54] The use of the word "may" in these statutes appears to indicate that the governor has discretion when confronted with a joint resolution requesting him to remove a judge.

All but a few of the address and joint resolution provisions entitle the accused judge to notice of the charges and a hearing.[55] The federal due process clause would probably mandate these procedures in those states whose statutes do not expressly so provide.[56] It is an open question, however, whether the required "hearing" would have to be a full-fledged trial.[57]

7.5 RECALL

The removal device known as recall is presently available to remove judges of courts of record in only a handful of states, including Arizona, California, Oregon, and Wisconsin.[58] Under the typical recall procedure, the presentation of a petition signed by a specified percentage of the voters in a designated geographical area (usually the area within the judge's jurisdiction) results in a special election being held in which the eligible voters determine whether to retain the judge in office.[59]

The requirements as to the class and percentage of voters who are required to sign the recall petition varies from state to state. In Arizona, for example, the petition must be signed by the "number of qualified electors equalling 25 percent of the number of votes cast at the last preceding general election for all the candidates for the office held by the officer."[60] In Wisconsin, on the other hand, the petition must be signed by the number of electors equal to at least 25 percent of the vote cast for the office of governor at the last preceding election, in the state, county, or district from which such officer is to be recalled."[61]

In addition to the onerous signature requirement, another common limitation specifies the frequency with which a particular judge may be subjected to a recall election. In Arizona, for example, only one recall petition and special election with respect to a particular judge is permissible during the same term of office, unless the petitioners pay the expenses of any additional election.[62] In Wisconsin, only one recall petition and special election against the same judge is permitted during the term for which he was elected.[63]

In Arizona, advisory recall elections may be held in order to advise U. S.

Senate and the President of the United States that the Arizona voters wish a federal judge to be removed.[64] The petition must be signed by 15 percent of the electors casting votes for the governor in the pertinent judicial district in the preceding election. The recommendation is not transmitted to Washington unless it is approved by a majority of the voters at the next general election. As of 1983, no advisory recall petition had ever been filed against a federal judge in Arizona.[65]

Recall has been criticized because, although it ascertains and carries out the wishes of the electorate, it does not provide a procedure for hearing and adjudicating charges of misconduct or unfitness due to disability against a judge.[66]

7.6 REMOVAL IN REGULARLY SCHEDULED ELECTIONS

Obviously, any election involving an incumbent judge has the potential of removing the judge. The voters, however, are generally insufficiently acquainted with the qualities and merits of any of the candidates, including the incumbent, to be able to exercise an informed judgment on the question of removal or retention.[67] Consequently, it appears likely that removal in regularly scheduled competitive elections or noncompetitive retention elections will usually occur only when the judge has been guilty of extreme misbehavior that has been highly publicized.[68]

7.7 REMOVAL OF JUDGES IN COURT PROCEEDINGS NOT PRECEDED BY ANY INVESTIGATION BY OR HEARING BEFORE A DISCIPLINARY COMMISSION

The courts have generally held that the existence of express constitutional removal remedies negates any implied judicial power to remove judges.[69] Constitutional provisions were enacted a few decades ago in a small number of states, including Alabama, Indiana, Louisiana, New Jersey, and Texas, empowering the state supreme court to remove judges without the assistance of a disciplinary commission.[70] However, amendatory constitutional provisions in Alabama, Indiana, Louisiana, and Texas and rules of court in New Jersey have been adopted providing for disciplinary commissions to conduct investigations and hearings and make recommendations to the state supreme court concerning complaints against judges.[71] Accordingly, as a practical matter, judicial disciplinary action unaided by disciplinary commissions is now a thing of the past in this country. Even in states such as Texas, where the prior constitutional provision for judicial removal proceedings was not repealed by the commission plan amendments,[72] it appears highly unlikely that such proceedings will ever again be instituted now that the commission plan procedures are available.

7.8 DISBARMENT OF JUDGES

a. The Distinction between Disbarment as an Ancillary Sanction in a Judicial Disciplinary Proceeding and Disbarment in a Bar Disciplinary Proceeding

A decree imposing sanctions in a judicial disciplinary proceeding may, in some jurisdictions, include not only sanctions against the judge as a judge, but also sanctions against him as a member of the bar.[73] Whether this will be deemed necessary or appropriate will generally depend on whether the conduct involves moral turpitude. Judges may be removed from the bench on the ground of unfitness evidenced by misconduct not involving moral turpiture; the prevailing view, however, is that a judge removed from the bench on such a ground generally should not be disbarred.[74]

Prior to the adoption of disciplinary commission systems, the unsatisfactory nature of direct removal methods, such as impeachment, led bar associations to seek to remove judges of courts of record indirectly by disbarring them.[75] The theory was that since bar membership is invariably a requisite for judicial eligibility for judgeships on courts of record,[76] disbarment would effect the removal of such a judge. However, the courts were in disagreement not only as to whether disbarment has the effect of removing such a judge from the bench,[77] but also whether they had jurisdiction over proceedings to disbar judges.[78]

b. Bar Discipline Proceedings to Disbar or Discipline Sitting Judges for Judicial Misconduct

In cases involving bar discipline proceedings against sitting judges seeking to disbar or suspend them as attorneys based on judicial misconduct, jurisdiction has been sustained in a considerable number of cases[79] and has been denied in a smaller number of cases.[80] In cases sustaining jurisdiction, the courts normally reasoned that judges should not be immune from bar discipline for violating ethical rules governing the bar merely because they were judges and the challenged conduct was committed in the performance of their judicial duties.[81] The cases denying jurisdiction have turned on a variety of theories. Some courts have held that the availability of other judicial removal remedies had the effect of excluding indirect removal by disbarment.[82] Other courts have held that subjecting sitting judges to efforts to disbar them would infringe upon their judicial independence[83] or that judges should not be disciplined as attorneys for conduct occurring while they were prohibited, as judges, from practicing law[84] or that conduct by a judge in his judicial capacities (rather than his capacity as an attorney) is not subject to bar discipline.[85]

c. Bar Discipline of Sitting Judges for off-the-Bench Conduct Unrelated to Their Judicial Functions

The courts appear to disagree as to whether jurisdiction exists.[86]

d. Bar Discipline of Sitting Judges for Conduct Occurring before They Ascended the Bench

Here again, jurisdiction has been sustained by some courts and denied by others.[87]

e. Bar Discipline of Former Sitting Judges for Judicial Misconduct

Except for the Louisiana supreme court,[88] even the courts that have rejected jurisdiction in proceedings to impose bar discipline on sitting judges have unanimously sustained jurisdiction when the proceeding was instituted after the judge had been removed, resigned, or for any other reason ceased to be a judge.[89] *A fortiori*, decisions to the same effect have been rendered both by courts that have never had occasion to determine whether jurisdiction exists to impose bar discipline on sitting judges[90] and by courts that have sustained such jurisdiction as against sitting judges.[91]

Even courts that have recognized that a former judge may be subjected to bar discipline for conduct in office have declined to impose sanctions when the judicial conduct, while oppressive or improper, did not involve moral turpitude.[92]

7.9 REMOVAL IN PROCEEDINGS INITIALLY HANDLED BY DISCIPLINARY COMMISSION

a. Introduction

Judicial discipline through permanent disciplinary commissions has come into existence during the last quarter of a century. During that short period, this type of system has been adopted in all fifty states plus the District of Columbia.[93]

b. The Number and Types of Disciplinary Systems Involving One or More Disciplinary Commissions or Special Disciplinary Courts and the Allocation of Functions between Them and the State Supreme Court

In most states, there is a single commission that screens, investigates, hears, and makes recommendations to the supreme court concerning complaints against judges.[94] In a handful of the states with a single commission or a special court, the commission or special court issues the disciplinary orders itself, and the supreme court merely performs a review function.[95] In another small but slightly larger group of states, the screening, investigative, hearing, recommendatory, decisional, and reviewing functions are divided in varying ways between a permanent investigative commission, a permanent decisional commission or special court, and the state supreme court (which performs either a reviewing function, a decisional function, or no function).[96]

7.10 THE PRINCIPLES APPLIED BY THE COURTS IN DECIDING WHETHER TO REMOVE A JUDGE OR IMPOSE A LESS STRINGENT FORM OF DISCIPLINE

a. The Significance of the Presence or Absence of Moral Turpitude or Bad Faith

Although the presence or absence of moral turpitude and bad faith both have a significant bearing on the type of discipline imposed, these states of mind are quite different and have a different bearing on the removal question. Whereas moral turpitude virtually guarantees removal, [97] bad faith merely creates a strong likelihood, but not a certainty, of removal.[98]

Moral turpitude has generally been equated to dishonesty or corruption.[99] On the other hand, "bad faith" has been defined as encompassing both the intentional commission of acts that a judge knew, or should have known, were beyond his power, provided his intention involved actual malice, or the commission of acts within a judge's lawful power "for a corrupt purpose," i. e., for any purpose other than the faithful discharge of judicial duties,[100] and has been equated to willful misconduct.[101]

Conduct involving moral turpitude that has resulted in removal has included: acceptance of a bribe,[102] fraud,[103] extortion,[104] embezzlement,[105] and commission of a felony or crime involving moral turpitude.[106] Criminal conduct may be established either by direct proof of the conduct (if not yet adjudicated in criminal proceedings)[107] or by proof of a criminal conviction (if a final conviction has been rendered).[108] When a criminal action involving the subject matter of the disciplinary proceeding is pending, a commission or supreme court may, in its discretion, either refuse to stay the commission proceeding[109] or grant a stay pending the outcome of the criminal proceeding.[110] When a final criminal conviction has been rendered, it is binding on the judge in the disciplinary proceeding.[111] Until a conviction has become final, it may not be used as evidence of guilt in the commission proceeding.[112]

b. The Rule Exempting Errors in Decisions or Errors of Judgment from Removal or Other Discipline When Bad Faith Is Not Shown

It is well established that decisional or judgmental errors, mistakes in statutory interpretation, and errors as to the scope of his powers or of limitations on them do not subject a judge to removal or any other form of discipline.[113] Erroneous rulings are, however, subject to discipline, including removal, when made in bad faith.[114]

c. The Concept to The Effect That the Determination of Whether to Remove Will Depend on Whether the Pattern or Cumulative Effect of All of the Judge's Allegedly Wrongful Acts Shows Unfitness for Judicial Office

Although conduct requiring removal may be shown by proof of specific major incidents that demonstrate unfitness for judicial office, removal also must be ordered if the pattern or cumulative effect of the judge's allegedly wrongful acts, considered in their totality, shows that the judge is morally or temperamentally unfit for judicial office, even though no vindictive or corrupt motive has been shown and even if the acts forming the pattern are ostensibly innocuous if considered separately.[115]

It has, moreover, been specifically held that when a pattern of misconduct has been established by proof of numerous instances of misconduct, the instances of misconduct found in the record are sufficient to justify removal, even if the court assumes the proposition that the judge's conduct was free from fault in all other cases.[116]

d. The Significance of Both the Magnitude of the Violation and the Probability of the Violation's Recurrence

Factors that have a significant bearing on the decision of whether to remove the judge or discipline him in a less stringent manner include the magnitude of the violation and the probability of recurrence.[117] For example, proof that the judge has already altered his mode of conduct since the incident complained of would tend to establish probability of nonrecurrence.[118] Expressions of contriteness and assurances of nonrepetition may be deemed by the court or commission to have the same effect.[119] On the other hand, unsuccessful efforts to discontinue the unsuitable behavior would have a contrary tendency.[120]

e. The Effect of Proof of Mitigating Circumstances

Patterns of misconduct in court, such as abusiveness, intemperateness, excessive and partisan interrogation of witnesses, and various combinations of the same have often been sufficiently overcome by proof of mitigating circumstances to persuade a supreme court to reject removal in favor of public censure. Such mitigating circumstances have included: proof that the misconduct was caused by inexperience on the bench;[121] ignorance of the law;[122] illness;[123] proof of redeeming judicial qualities, such as conscientiousness and efforts to be just and fair in formulating decisions;[124] and cessation of the wrongful conduct.[125]

Likewise, nonofficial conduct that might otherwise result in removal from office has been held sufficiently mitigated by proof of extenuating circumstances or behavior to be dealt with by public censure, rather than removal. Such circumstances have included, for example, discontinuance of the offending conduct, coupled with absence of corruption and moral turpitude,[126] and efficiency and conscientiousness in the courtroom.[127]

7.11 THE TYPES OF CONDUCT THAT HAVE BEEN DISCIPLINED BY REMOVAL FROM OFFICE

a. Introduction

Many, and perhaps most, of the cases heard by judicial disciplinary commissions involve charges of not only multiple incidents, but also several different types of alleged misconduct. In such a case, it is therefore often difficult to determine the precise significance of any particular type of conduct with respect to a commission or supreme court recommendation or decision to remove the judge.

b. Official Misconduct

(i) Corrupt Conduct in Office

Corrupt official conduct,[128] such as the acceptance of bribes in return for judicial favors,[129] extortion based on threats of unfavorable court rulings,[130] and embezzlement of court funds,[131] always results in removal.

(ii) Denial of Constitutional Rights

Next to corruption in office, a pattern of denying parties' their constitutional rights is the type of official conduct involving the greatest likelihood of removal. Patterns of conduct of this nature that have resulted in removal ention of parties' right to due process[132] and the denial or interference with parties' right to counsel.[133]

(iii) Partiality in Courtroom Behavior

Although generally combined with other types of conduct in cases in which judges have been removed, untoward partiality in the courtroom is considered to be a serious breach of judicial ethics and a significant basis for possible removal. Examples of conduct evidencing undue partiality that, in combination with other misconduct, has resulted in removal, include extensive questioning by the judge of witnesses in a partisan manner,[134] the making of comments (whether or not in the presence of the jury) indicating a belief in the merits of the case,[135] and partiality in decision, when deliberate.[136]

(iv) Abuse of Contempt Power

Abuse of the contempt power is taken very seriously in proceedings to discipline a judge and has several times played a substantial role in the removal of a judge.[137] Such abuses have included repeated instances of summarily holding lawyers in contempt without any substantial basis[138] or of arbitrarily holding not only lawyers, but also parties, relatives of parties, or others, in contempt without any substantial basis.[139]

(v) The Coercing or Attempted Coercing of Parties to Plead Guilty or Settle by Threatening Adverse Judicial Action if They Do Not Accede

Coercion of parties to plead guilty, settle, or take other action by threatening adverse judicial action if they do not accede is also considered to be serious misconduct and has resulted in removal orders.[140] In one disciplinary proceeding in which the court censured, rather than removed, the judge, despite his having coerced a party into settling in a single instance, the court nevertheless stated that this type of intimidation is one of the gravest types of judicial misconduct, since it deprives the intimidated party of his right to a hearing.[141]

(vi) Improper Failure of Judge to Disqualify Himself When He Has a Material Conflict of Interest or Bias or an Appearance of a Material Conflict of Interest or Bias

Canon 3C(1) of the Code of Judicial Conduct requires a judge to disqualify himself in a proceeding "in which his impartiality might reasonably be questioned," and then sets forth an illustrative, but not exhaustive, list of situations in which application of this test requires disqualification.[142]

Knowing violations of this Canon or similar statutory prohibitions have often been the subject of discipline.[143] Some of those decisions have resulted in removal or sanctions tantamount to removal,[111] and some have resulted in censure,[145] depending on the seriousness of the conflict, interest, or bias; the existence or nonexistence of corrupt motive or knowledge of the conflict; and the nature and extent of other misconduct.[146]

(vii) Intemperate, Abusive, or Discourteous Treatment of Litigants, Attorneys, or Witnesses

Intemperate, abusive, or discourteous treatment of litigants, attorneys, or witnesses violative of Canon 3A(3) of the Code of Judicial Ethics has frequently subjected judges to judicial discipline[147] and has played an important role in state supreme court determinations to remove judges from office or impose sanctions on them equivalent to removal.[148]

(viii) Incompetence

In most states, incompetence is not a stated ground for judicial discipline.[149] In at least one state, where incompetence is a ground, a judge has been removed for "generally incompetent performance of judicial duties."[150] Repeated disregard of parties' constitutional rights to counsel and a hearing, abusive issuance of bench warrants, and arrogance toward counsel formed part of the picture and were treated as evidence of the judge's general incompetence.[151]

(ix) Initiation or Receipt and Consideration of Ex Parte Communications

The initiation of and consideration by a judge of an *ex parte* communication relative to a pending or impending proceeding in any court violates Canon 3A(4) of the Code of Judicial Conduct and has, from time to time, been the subject of judicial discipline.[152] In a celebrated Florida case, *In re Dekle*,[153] a Supreme Court justice was reprimanded for receiving from an attorney a draft opinion and using it copiously in drafting an opinion dispositive of major litigation. Although the justice testified that he had not known that the attorney's draft had not been given to opposing counsel, the Supreme Court held that he had nevertheless violated Canon 3(A) (4) because he had negligently failed to determine that it was not an *ex parte* memorandum. The Florida Supreme Court specifically stated that, had the judge known that the memorandum was sent to him *ex parte*, it would have removed him from office.[154]

c. Nonofficial Conduct

(i) Business Affiliations, Fiduciaryships, and Investments

From time to time, the courts have removed, suspended, or otherwise disciplined judges for violating Canon 5C.[155] The violations have included: holding corporate directorships or ownerships in violation of the juridic tion's version of Canon 5C(2);[156] an affiliation with a business that greatly interfered with the judge's performance of his judicial duties and in which the judge caused county personnel and equipment to be used;[157] exploitation by the judge of his judicial office by permitting a business corporation, of which he was a director, to circulate a brochure with the names and pictures of all officers and directors including himself;[158] and improper failure of a judge to disqualify himself in a case in which a corporation, of which he was a director, was a party.[159]

(ii) Acceptance of Gifts, Bequests, Loans, or Favors[160]

In *In the Matter of Seraphim*,[161] a judge was removed from office because, among other types of misconduct, he had heard and rendered sentences in criminal proceedings against an automobile dealer while he was leasing an automobile from the dealer at approximately one-third the normal rate.

(iii) Law Violations

The conviction of a felony or misdemeanor involving moral turpitude is, of course, a per se ground for removal in virtually every state.[162] Also, the commission of criminal or illegal conduct has caused or played a part in the removal of judges even though they were not criminally prosecuted for, or convicted of, the conduct.[163]

Disgraceful or immoral private misconduct that seriously reflects upon a judge's reputation for good character may lead to his removal, particularly when combined with other types of misconduct.[164]

(iv) Political Activity[165]

In re Briggs is the leading case in which a judge has been removed from office for political activity forbidden under Canon 7.[166] In that case, the judge had violated various Canons of the Missouri Code of Judicial Conduct by arranging political party fund-raising meetings, acting as a patronage clearinghouse for his political party and political counsel for the governor, and making both direct and indirect campaign contributions to the governor, the latter having been made through his wife from commingled marital funds.

Other such cases are discussed in Chapter 5.[167]

7.12 EFFECT OF INVOLUNTARY REMOVAL OF JUDGE FOR DISCIPLINARY REASONS ON COMPENSATION AND BENEFITS

As a general rule, a final order by a state court of last resort removing a judge from office for disciplinary reasons has the effect of terminating not only the judge's right to further compensation[168] but also his right to a pension or retirement allowance.[169] Despite loss of his pension or retirement allowance rights, the judge is generally expressly entitled to the return of his contributions to the retirement fund.[170]

7.13 COMPULSORY RETIREMENT OR SUSPENSION ON THE GROUND OF DISABILITY

In practically every state,[171] the provisions governing judicial discipline provide for involuntary retirement of judges on the ground of disability.[172]

In some jurisdictions, disabilities that result in involuntary retirement are variously described as "disability"[173] or as "mental or physical disability"[174] that prevents or seriously interferes with the judge's performance of his judicial duties and is permanent or likely to be permanent.[175] In a number of other jurisdictions, the description is substantially the same, except that the disability is merely described as "permanent," rather than as permanent or likely to be permanent;[176] and in several such jurisdictions, the description of the disability does not include any express requisite that the disability be permanent or likely to be permanent.[177] In others, there is no express requirement that the disability interfere with performance of the judge's judicial duties; in some of these there is an express requirement of permanency[178] and, in others, there is no such requirement.[179] Finally, in at least one jurisdiction, the judge must be eligible for retirement.[180]

The investigatory, hearing, recommendatory, and decisional functions with respect to involuntary retirement on the ground of disability are almost invariably allocated between commission and court in the same manner as in the case of proceedings to impose discipline for misconduct.[181]

Typically, in cases of temporary disability, temporary suspension, pending termination of the disability, is authorized,[182] often (but not invariably) with mandatory pay. Also, automatic disqualification or suspension pending supreme court action on a commission recommendation of involuntary retirement is frequently provided for.[183]

Habitual intemperance is generally a ground for discipline rather than involuntary retirement,[184] but it is a ground for involuntary disability retirement in the District of Columbia.[185] Similarly, whereas incompetence is generally a basis for discipline,[186] it is a ground for involuntary retirement in Oklahoma.[187]

The typical provision for involuntary retirement by reason of disability provides that the retirement shall be deemed to have been voluntary.[188] Presumably, the purpose of this provision is to make it clear that an involuntarily retired judge is entitled to the same disability benefits or retirement benefits that he would have received had he retired voluntarily on the ground of disability. Some involuntary disability provisions expressly provide that the retiree shall be entitled to retirement benefits.[189] Although a retiree generally ceases to receive compensation when involuntarily retired, at least one state provides that an involuntary retiree's retirement shall be "with or without compensation."[190]

In one case when the supreme court found that the respondent's conduct was attributable to senility, it disapproved commission findings of "prejudicial conduct" and, instead, ordered that the respondent be involuntarily retired on the ground of disability.[191] Conversely, in another jurisdiction, the court held that it could not involuntarily retire the judge when the commission had recommended removal and not retirement. Moreover, since the judge had not requested disability retirement when the case was before the commission, the court would not remand the case to the commission for a determination as to whether the judge should be involuntarily retired.[192]

Because the only procedure for removing federal district, appellate, or Supreme Court judges or justices is impeachment,[193] federal judges are not removable for disability.[194] Instead, where, after investigation, a special committee appointed by the chief judge of the circuit reports that a judge is disabled, the judicial council attempts to deal with the problem either:(a) by requesting that the judge voluntarily retire on the basis that the service requirements otherwise applicable to his pension rights would not apply[195] or (b) by ordering that, on a temporary basis for a certain time, no further cases be assigned to that judge.[196]

NOTE TO §7.2

1. See supra§6.2(a).

NOTES TO §7.3

2. E.g., U. S. Const. art. I, §§3(6), (7) and art. II, §4; Ala. Const. art. VII, §§173–174; Ala. Code Ann. §§38–311 to 322; Alaska Const. art. II, §20 and art. IV, §12; Alaska Stat. §§22.05.120, 170; Ariz. Const. art. 8, pt. 2, §2; Ariz. Rev. Stat. Ann. §§38–311 to 322; Ark. Const. art. 15, §1; Ark. Stat. Ann. §§12–2201 to 12–2223; Cal. Const. art. 4, §18; Colo. Const. art. XIII, §§1–2; Conn. Const. art. 5, §2 and art. 9, §§1–3; Del. Const. art. IV, §§1, 2; Fla. Const. art. 3, §17; Ga. Const. art. 3, §7, ¶¶1–3; Hawaii Const. art. III, §20; Idaho Const. art. 5, §§3–4; Idaho Code §§19–4001 to 4016; Ill. Const. art. 4, §14; Ind. Const. art. 6, §7; Ind. Code §§5–8–1–1 to 5–8–1–18; Iowa Const. art. 3, §20; Iowa Code Ann. §§68.1 to 14; Kan. Stat. Ann. §§37–101 to 117; Ky. Const. §§66–68; Ky. Rev. Stat. §§63.020 to .055; La. Const. art. 10, §24; Md. Const. art. III, §26 and art. IV, §4; Me. Const. art. IV, pt. 1, §8 and pt. 2, §7, and art. IX, §5; Mass. Const. pt. 2, c. 1, art. VI and VII; Mich. Const. art. 11, §7; Minn. Const. art. 8, §§1–4; Miss. Const. art. 4, §§49–52; Mo. Const. art. VII, §§1–3; Mo. Ann. Stat. §§106.020 to .210; Mont. Const. art. V, §13; Mont. Rev. Code Ann. §§5–5–401 to 433; Nev. Const. art. 7, §§1, 2; N. H. Const. pt. 2, art. 36, 38–40; N. J. Const. art. 7, §1, ¶¶1–3; N. J. Const. art. 7, §2, ¶1; N. M. Const. art. IV, §§35, 36; N. Y. Const. art. 6, §24; N. Y. Public Law art. 15-A, §§415–428; N. C. Const. art. IV, §§1, 4; N. C. Gen.

Stat. §123–5; N. D. Const. art. XI, §§8–10; Ohio Const. art. II, §§23–24; Okla. Const. art. VIII, §§1–6; Pa. Const. art. 6, §§4–6; P. R. Const. art. III, §21; R. I. Const. art. 10, §4, and art. 11, §§1–3; S. C. Const. art. XV, §§1–2; S. D. Const. art. XVI, §§1–8; Tenn. Const. art. V, §§1–4; Tenn. Code Ann. §§8–46–101 to 108; Tex. Const. art. XV, §§1–5; Utah Const. art. VI, §§16–20; Vt. Const. ch. II, §§57–59; Va. Const. art. IV, §17; Wash. Const. art V, §§1–2; W. Va. Const. art. 4, §9; W. Va. Code §6–6–3; Wis. Const. art. 7, §1; Wyo. Const. art. 3, §§17–18. *But compare* Nebr. Const. art. III, §17 (supreme court tries impeachments of all judges, except panel of district court judges tries impeachments of supreme court judges). *See supra* notes 10 to 12 (chapter 6), and the accompanying text. Oregon does not have the impeachment remedy. See Ore. Const. art. VII. See *infra* note 37.

3. *See supra* note 2, as to Connecticut, Georgia, Hawaii, Illinois, Maryland, Nebraska, New York, and Texas.

4. U. S. Const. art. 2, §3(4); Ala. Const. art. VII, §173; Alaska Stat. §§22.05.120 and 170; Ariz. Const. art. 8, pt. 2, §1; Ariz. Rev. Stat. §38–311; Ark. Const. art. 15, §1, Ark. Stat. Ann. §12–2201; Cal. Const. art. 4, §18; Colo. Const. art. XIII, §2; Del. Const. art. VII, §2; Fla. Const. art. 3, §17(a); Idaho Code §19–4001; Ind. Const. art. 6, §7; Ind. Code §5–8–1–1; Iowa Const. art. 3, §20; Kan. Stat. Ann. §37–101; Ky. Const. §68; La. Const. art. 10, §24(A); Me. Const. art. IX, §5; Mass. Const. pt. 2, c.1, §2, art. 8; Mich. Const. art. 11, §8; Minn. Const. art. 8, §2; Miss. Const. art. 4, §50; Mo. Const. art. VII, §1; Mont. Rev. Code Ann. §5–5–401; Nev. Const. art. 7, §2; Nev. Rev. Stat. §§283.140; N. H. Const. pt. 2, art. 38; N. J. Const. art. 7, §2, ¶1; N. M. Const. art. IV, §36; N. C. Gen. Stat. §123–5; N. D. Const. Code art. XI, §10; Ohio Const. art. II, §24; Okla. Const. art. VIII, §1; Pa. Const. art. 6, §6; P. R. Const. art. III, ¶21; R. I. Const. art. 10 §4; S. C. Const. art. XV, §1; S. D. Const. art XVI, §3; Tenn. Const. art. 5, §4; Utah Const. art VI, §19; Vt. Const. ch. II, §58; Va. Const. art. IV, §17; Wash. Const. art. 5, §2; W. Va. Const. art. 4, §9; W. Va. Code §6–6–3; Wis. Const. art. 7, §1; Wyo. Const. art. 3, §18. Compare Ga. Code Ann. §15–6–13 (fails to specify grounds for impeachment except states failure of disqualified superior court judge to substitute another superior court judge is ground for impeachment).

5. *See* Fenton, The Scope of the Impeachment Power, 65 Nw. U. L. Rev. 719, 731–745 (specific bases of federal impeachment convictions of judges for high crimes and misdemeanors have included serious official misconduct as well as criminal conduct, but have not included nonofficial misconduct of a noncriminal nature).

NOTES TO §7.3(a)

6. E. g., *see supra* note 4 as to United States, Arizona, Arkansas, Colorado, Delaware, Mississippi, South Carolina ("serious crime"), Utah, Washington, West Virginia and Wyoming.

7. E. g., *see supra* note 4 as to Alabama and Puerto Rico

8. E. g., *see supra* note 4 as to Maryland, Michigan, Minnesota, New Mexico, North Dakota, South Dakota, Tennessee, Virginia, and Wisconsin.

9. E. g., *see supra* note 4 as to United States, Colorado, Iowa, Michigan, Minnesota, Nevada, New Jersey, New Mexico, Virginia, Washington, West Vir-

10. E. g., *see supra* note 4 as to Delaware, Florida, Indiana, Kansas, Kentucky, Maine, Mississippi, Rhode Island and South Dakota.

11. E. g., *see supra* note 4 as to Michigan, Minnesota, Missouri, New Hampshire, Oklahoma, and Wisconsin.

12. E. g., *see supra* note 4 as to North Dakota, South Dakota, Virginia, and West Virginia.

13. E. g., *see supra* note 4 as to United States, Delaware, Mississippi, and Puerto Rico.

14. E. g., *see supra* note 4 as to United States, Delaware, Mississippi, New Hampshire, and Puerto Rico.

NOTES TO §7.3(b)

15. E. g., *see supra* note 4 as to Alabama, Alaska, Arizona, Colorado, Iowa, Louisiana, Nevada, New Mexico, North Carolina, North Dakota, South Dakota, Utah, Virginia, Washington, and Wyoming.

16. E. g., *see supra* note 4 as to Arkansas, Louisiana, and South Carolina ("serious misconduct in office").

17. E. g., *see supra* note 4 as to California, Maryland, Pennsylvania ("misbehavior in office"), and Massachusetts ("misconduct in office").

18. E. g., *see supra* note 4 as to Maryland, Missouri, and Oklahoma.

19. E. g., *see supra* note 4 as to Missouri.

20. E. g., *see supra* note 4 as to Missouri, North Dakota, Oklahoma ("habitual drunkenness"), and South Dakota ("drunkenness").

21. E. g., *see supra* note 4 as to West Virginia.

22. E. g., *see supra* note 4 as to Massachusetts, New Hampshire, Vermont ("maladministration in office"), and New Hampshire ("malpractice in office").

23. E. g., *see supra* note 4 as to West Virginia.

24. E. g., *see supra* note 4 as to Maryland, Missouri, Oklahoma, South Dakota ("gross incompetency"), and West Virginia.

25. E. g., *see supra* note 4 as to United States, Delaware, Florida, Idaho, Indiana, Kansas, Kentucky, Maine, Michigan, Minnesota, Mississippi, New Jersey, Ohio, Puerto Rico, Tennessee, and Wisconsin.

26. E. g., *see supra* note 4 as to Alabama, Arizona, Arkansas, Colorado, Iowa, Louisiana, Montana, Nevada, North Carolina, New Mexico, North Dakota, South Carolina, Utah, Virginia, Washington, and Wyoming.

27. E. g., *see supra* note 4 as to Missouri, New Hampshire, Oklahoma, and West Virginia.

28. E. g., *see supra* note 4 as to New Hampshire.

29. E. g., *see supra* note 4 as to Alaska, California, and Pennsylvania.

30. E. g., *see supra* note 4 as to Vermont.

31. E. g., *see supra* note 4 as to Massachusetts.

32. *See* Schoenbaum, *supra* note 1 (Chapter 6), at 7; 32 N. Y. St. B. A. Rep. 40 (1878).

33. *See* Schoenbaum, *.supra* note 1 (Chapter 6), at 7.

34. *See Remedies, supra* note 9 (Chapter 6), at 164.

35. *See* Buckley, *supra* note 295 (Chapter 6), at 250; Moser, *supra* note 11

(Chapter 6), at 7–8, 12; *Remedies, supra* note 9, at 164; Williams, *supra* note 112 (Chapter 6), at 516. *See also Forbes v. Earle*, 298 So. 2d 1, 3 (Fla. 1974).

36. *See Schoenbaum, supra* note 1, (Chapter 6), at 5–6.

37. E. g., Conn. Gen. Stat. ch. 872a, §§51–51i; Fla. Const. art. 5, §12(g); Idaho Code Ann. §1–2103; Nev. Const. art. 6, §21; N. M. Const. art. VI, §32; N. D. Const. art. VI, §12; Pa. Const. art. 5, §18(n); Tenn. Code Ann. §17–5–313; Tex. Const. art 1-a, §13; Vt. Rules, *supra* note 73, R. 3(2). For a case so holding or stating, *see*, e. g., *Thaler v. State of New York*, 79 Misc.2d 621, 360 N. Y. S.2d 986, 990 (Ct. Cl. 1974).

38. *See* Williams, *supra* note 112 (chapter 6), at 516–518.

39. *Id.* The contention that the impeachment provisions in the federal constitution do not authorize this type of delegation has been met by the counter arguments that the English House of Lords used committees to hear evidence several times in the early seventeenth century (*see* Williams, *supra* note 112 (Chapter 6), at 528–531), that such a rule is authorized by the provisions in the U. S. Constitution that each House may "determine the rules of its proceedings," U. S. Const. art. I, §5(2) (*see* Williams, *supra* note 112 (Chapter 6), at 558–560), and by the provision that Congress may make all laws necessary to execute congressional powers, U. S. Const. art. I, §8(18) (*see* Williams, *supra* note 112 (Chapter 6), at 560–563, reviewing analogous precedents). It has been further contended that a senate-appointed committee or set of masters in an impeachment trial could prepare and submit to the Senate proposed findings, conclusions, and recommendations, provided the Senate is not bound to follow them (*see* Williams, *supra* note 112 (Chapter 6), at 586–589). Finally, it has been argued that this suggested procedure is not in violation either of the due process clause in the Fifth Amendment or of the confrontation clause in the Sixth Amendment or of the impeachment clauses of the U. S. Constitution (*see* Williams, *supra* note 112 (Chapter 6), at 590–618).

40. Rules of Procedure and Practice in the Senate When Sitting on Impeachment Trials XI, Senate Manual, S. Doc. No. 92–1, 92d Cong., 1st Sess. 137–138 (1971).

41. *See supra* notes 178–180 (Chapter 6), and the accompanying text.

42. *Alonzo v. State ex. rel. Booth*, 283 Ala. 607, 219 So.2d 858 (1969). *Accord*: *Coruzzi, supra* note 161 (Chapter 6), 472 A.2d at 552. See *supra* note 180 (Chapter 6) and the accompanying text.

43. U. S. Const. art. I, §3(7).

44. *United States v. Hastings*, 681 F.2d 706 (11th Cir. 1982); *United States v. Isaacs*, 493 F.2d 1124 (7th Cir. 1974), *cert. denied*, 417 U. S. 976 (1974) (federal judge).

45. *Compare* U. S. Const. art. I, §§2(5), 3(6) with state impeachment provisions cited, *supra* note 2.

46. E. g., *compare* U. S. Const. art. I, §§2(5), 3(6) (simple majority of elected house members required to impeach, and two-thirds of senators present and voting required to convict) with Del. Const. art. VI, §1 (two-thirds of all house members required to impeach, and two-thirds of all senate members present and voting required to convict); Nev. Const. art. 7, §1 (simple majority of all elected house members requisite to impeach, and two-thirds of all elected senator members required to convict); and Wisc. Const. art. 7, §1 (simple majority of all elected house members needed to impeach, and two thirds of senate members present requisite to convict).

47. Mo. Const. art. VII, §§2, 3.

48. Nebr. Const. art. III, §17.

NOTES TO §7.4

49. E. g., Ark. Const. art. 15, §2; Del. Const. art. III, §13; Me. Const. art. IX, §5; Mich. Const. art. 6, §25; Miss. Const. art. 4, §53; Tex. Const. art. XI, §8; Tex. Rev. Civ. Stat. Ann. art. 5964; Wis. Const. art. 7, §11 (term "address" used, but governor not mentioned). *Compare* Pa. Const. art. 6, §7 (only elected judges of courts not of record). *Compare* N. Y. Const. art. 6, §§23(b), (c) (judges of certain courts may be removed by senate on recommendation of governor).

50. E. g., Kan. Const. art. 3, §16; N. Y. Const. art. 6, §§23(a), (c) (judges of Court of Appeals and Supreme Court); N. C. Const. art. IV, §17(1) (removal by joint resolution limited to mental and physical disability); Ohio Const. art. IV, §17; Tenn. Const. art. 6, §6; Wash. Const. art. 4, §8.

51. *See supra* notes 49 and 50. A two-thirds majority of all of the members in each house (whether or not voting or present) is required in Arkansas, Delaware, Kansas, Michigan, Mississippi, New York, North Carolina, Ohio, Tennessee, Texas, and Wisconsin. *Id.* A three-quarters majority of all of the members (whether or not voting or present) is required in Washington. Maine merely requires a removal resolution by both houses and Pennsylvania merely requires a removal resolution by the senate, which sounds like a simple majority (Maine) or two-thirds majority (Pennsylvania) of those present and voting. *Id.*

52. *See supra* notes 49 and 50 as to Arkansas, Delaware, Kansas, Maine, Michigan, Mississippi, Ohio ("complaint"), Pennsylvania, and Tennessee ("charges"). *But compare* Texas Rev. Civ. Stat. Ann. art. 5964 (Supp.) ("willful neglect of duty, incompetency, habitual drunkenness, oppression in office, breach of trust, or other reasonable cause"); Washington Const. art. 4, §8 ("incompetency, corruption, malfeasance, or delinquency in office or other sufficient cause").

53. *See supra* note 49 as to Arkansas, Delaware, and Maine.

54. *See supra* note 49 as to Michigan, Mississippi, Pennsylvania, and Texas.

55. *See supra* notes 49 and 50 as to Kansas, Maine, Mississippi, New York, Ohio, Texas, Washington, and Wisconsin.

56. *Compare Haggerty, supra* note 49 (Chapter 6), 241 So.2d at 479 (judge entitled to due process, privilege against self-incrimination, right to counsel, and production and examination of witnesses in disciplinary commission proceeding).

57. Schoenbaum, *supra* note 1 (Chapter 6), at 4, opines that, although the judge is entitled to notice and opportunity to be heard, there is no trial, nor does he have the right to present a defense, as he does in an impeachment trial. The due process rights enunciated in *Haggerty, supra* note 49 (Chapter 6), 241 So.2d at 479, and described *supra* in note 56, seem, however, to include a right to present witnesses and to cross examine prosecution witnesses.

NOTES TO §7.5

58. E. g, Ariz. Const. art. VIII, pt. 1, §§1 6 (applies to any public officer); Ariz. Rev. Stat. §§19 201 to 234 (partly Supp.) (same); Cal. Const. art. 23, §1

(applies to every elective public officer); Ore. Const. art. II, §18 (same); Wis. Const. art. XIII, §12 (Supp.) (applies to "any elective officer"); Wis. Stat. §9.10 (same). *See* Buckley, *supra* 295 (chapter 6), at 250; Cameron, supra note 1 (Chapter 6), at 45, n. 4; Moser, *supra* note 11 (Chapter 6), at 33–44; Schoenbaum, *supra* note 1 (Chapter 6), at 8–9; Comment, Judicial Discipline—Does It Exist in Pennsylvania? 84 Dick. L. Rev. 447, 449, n. 18 (1977); Note, Discipline and Removal of the Judiciary in Arizona, 13 Law and Social Order 85, 87–90 (1973); *Remedies, supra* note 9 (Chapter 6), at 164–165.

59. *See supra* note 58 as to Arizona, California, Oregon, and Wisconsin, *See also* Schoenbaum, *supra* note 1, at 8.

60. Ariz. Rev. Stat. Ann. §19–201.

61. Wis. Const. art. XIII, §12.

62. Ariz. Rev. Stat. Ann. §19–202B.

63. Wis. Const. art. XIII, §12.

64. Ariz. Rev. Stat. Ann. §§19–231 to 233 (partly Supp.). *See* Frankel, Judicial Conduct and Removal for Cause in California, 36 S. Cal. L. Rev. 72, 75–76 (1936).

65. *See* Note, *supra* note 58, at 88.

66. *See* Frankel, Judicial Conduct and Removal for Cause in California, 36 S. Cal. L. Rev. at 75–76.

NOTES TO §7.6

67. *See* Schoenbaum, *supra* note 1 (Chapter 6), at 9–10; and Note, Selection and Discipline of State Judges in Texas, 14 Houston L.Rev. 672, 681–682, 686–687 (1977).

68. *See* Schoenbaum, *supra* note 1 (Chapter 6), at 10.

NOTES TO §7.7

69. *See supra* note 32 (Chapter 6), and the accompanying text.

70. E. g., Ala. Const. of 1901, §174; Ala. Code tit. 41, §§178, 180–182, 201; La. Const. of 1921, art. IX, §§1, 5; N. J. Const. of 1947, art. VI, §6, ¶4, and art. VII, §3 (West. Cum. Supp. 1977–1978); Tex. Const. art. V, §6 (1891); Tex. Const. art. XV, §6. *See* Schoenbaum *supra* note 1 (Chapter 6), at 13–18. Cf. Ore. Const. art. VII, §6; But see *Mattera, supra* note 26 (chapter 6, 168A 2d at 43 (Supreme Court not authorized to remove judges, since legislature had not implemented constitutional provision).

71. *See supra* notes 40 and 43 (Chapter 6), and the accompanying text. *See also Pittam v. Maynard*, 103 Idaho 177, 646 P.2d 419 (1982) (statute providing for judicial removal had been impliedly repealed by constitutional provision and statute creating judicial disciplinary commission system). In Alabama, investigations are conducted by an investigation agency named the judicial inquiry commission and hearings and decisions are held and rendered by a special court called the court on the judiciary. Ala. Const. Amendment no. 328, §§6.17, 6.18.

NOTES TO §7.8(a)

73. *See supra* note 220 (Chapter 6), and the accompanying text.

74. E. g., *Cannon, supra* note 267 (Chapter 6), 537 P.2d at 918.

75. *See infra* notes 79–87 and *supra* notes 26–29 (Chapter 6), and the accompanying text. *See* Schoenbaum, *supra* note 1, (Chapter 6), at 10–13.

76. E. g., Alaska Const. art. IV, §4; Cal. Const. art. 6, §23; Colo. Const. art. VI, §8; D. C. Code §11–1501(b); Fla. Const. art. 5, §8; Ga. Code §15–18–3; Ill. Const. art. 6, §2; Ind. Const. art. 7, §10; Kan. Const. art. 3, §2(c); La. Const. art. IV, §24; Mont. Const. art. VII, §9; N. J. Const. art. 6, §6, ¶2.

77. *Compare State ex. rel. Saxbe v. Franko*, 168 Ohio St. 338, 154 N. E.2d 751 (1958) (disbarment automatically effects removal) and *Heitzler, supra* note 293 (Chapter 6), 291 N. E.2d at 483 (bar disciplinary proceedings may result in disqualification of a judge because he is required to be a lawyer) with *Re Silkman*, 88 App. Div. 102, 84 N. Y. Supp. 1025, 1028 (disbarment would not effect removal) (1903) and *Re Strahl*, 201 App. Div. 729, 195 N. Y. Supp. 385 (1922) (same).

78. *See supra* notes 26–28 (Chapter 6), and the accompanying text; and *see infra* notes 79–87, and the accompanying text.

NOTES TO §7.8(b)

79. E. g., *Gordon, supra* note 26 (Chapter 6) (good cause of action for disbarment of superior court judge alleged); *In re DeSaulnier*, 274 N. E.2d 454 (Mass. 1971); *In re Littell*, 294 N. E.2d 126 (Ind. 1973) (two-year suspension from practice of law); *Mattera, supra* note 26 (Chapter 6); *Heitzler, supra* note 293 (Chapter 6) (indefinite suspension from practice of law); *Mahoning supra* note 26 (Chapter 6) (same); *Jenkins v. Oregon State Bar*, 405 P.2d 525 (Ore. En Banc 1965); *In re Burton*, 67 Utah 118, 246 Pac. 188 (1926) (censured); *In re Stolen*, 193 Wis. 602, 214 N. W. 379, 55 A. L. R. 1355 (1927). *Cf. In re McGarry*, 380 Ill. 359, 44 N. E.2d (1942) (judicial acts not subject to bar discipline unless immoral, dishonest, criminal, or fraudulent); *Petition of Board of Commissioners of State Bar*, 65 N. M. 332, 337 P.2d 400 (1959) (same holding as in *McGarry*). *Compare Re Gibbs*, 51 S. D. 464, 214 N. W. 850 (1927) (jurisdiction to impose bar discipline for judicial acts exists, but should not be assumed absent an extraordinary situation). *See supra* note 26 (Chapter 6), and the accompanying text. *See also* Annot. 53 A. L. R.2d 305–312 (1957); Annot. 57 A. L. R.3d 1150–1182 (1974).

80. E. g., Alabama State Bar *supra* note 26 (Chapter 6); *Colorado Bar Ass'n, supra* note 26 (Chapter 6) (1958); *Investigation of Circuit Judge*, 93 So.2d 601 (Fla. En Banc 1957); *Proposed Disciplinary Action, supra* note 27 (Chapter 6); *Wehrman, supra* note 28 (Chapter 6); *Strahl, supra* note 77; *Silkman, supra* note 77 (violation by surrogate of restriction on practice of law); *Re Watson*, 71 Nev. 227, 286 P. 2d 254, 53 A. L. R.2d 301 (1955); *Chambers, supra* note 26 (Chapter 6).

81. *See supra* note 79 and the accompanying text.

82. E. g., *see Alabama State Bar, supra* note 26 (Chapter 6); *State Bar of California, supra* note 26 (Chapter 6); *Investigation of Circuit Judge, supra* note 80; *Chambers, supra* note 26 (Chapter 6).

83. E. g., *Chambers, supra* note 26 (Chapter 6).

84. E. g., *State Bar of California, supra* note 26 (Chapter 6); *Investigation of Circuit Judge, supra* note 80; *Chambers, supra* note 26 (Chapter 6); *Strahl, supra* note 77; *Silkman, supra* note 77.

85. E. g., *Alabama State Bar, supra* note 26 (Chapter 6).

NOTE TO §7.8(c)

86. *See supra* note 28 (Chapter 6) and the accompanying text. *See also supra* note 29 (Chapter 6) and the accompanying text.

NOTE TO §7.8(d)

87. *See supra* note 27 (Chapter 6) and the accompanying text. *See also supra* note 28 (Chapter 6) and the accompanying text.

NOTES TO §7.8(e)

88. *Meraux, supra* note 29 (Chapter 6). *Re Jones, supra* note 29 (Chapter 6).

89. E. g., *see McCain, supra* note 29 (Chapter 6) (four-one-two decision); *Hasler, supra* note 29 (Chapter 6); and *James, supra* note 29 (Chapter 6). *See also* Annot. 57 A. L. R.3d 1150–1182 (1973).

90. E. g., Schoolfield, *supra* note 29 (Chapter 6). *Accord:* ABA Stds., *supra* note 70 (Chapter 6), §3.2, and commentary thereunder.

91. E. g., *Matter of Vasser,* 75 N. J. 357, 382 A.2d 1114 (1978); *Re Orsini,* 37 N. J. 500, 181 A.2d 771 (1962).

92. E. g., *State ex. rel. Oklahoma Bar Ass'n v. Sullivan,* 596 P.2d 864 (Okla. 1979).

NOTE TO §7.9(a)

93. *See supra*§§6.2(i) and 6.3(a).

NOTES TO §7.9(b)

94. *See supra* note 40 (Chapter 6), and the accompanying text. *Cf. supra* note 42 (Chapter 6) and accompanying text.

95. *See supra* note 41 (Chapter 6), and the accompanying text.

96. *See supra* notes 43–48 (Chapter 6), and the accompanying text. In Delaware, the investigative, hearing and decisional functions are divided between two agencies and a special court. See *supra* note 44 (Chapter 6) and the accompanying text.

NOTES TO §7.10(a)

97. E. g., *see Coruzzi, supra* note 161 (Chapter 6), at 550 (judge who accepts a bribe must be removed); *In re Peoples,* 296 N. C. 109,250 S. E.2d 890, 918 (1978), *cert. denied,* 442 U.S. 929 (1979).

98. *Coruzzi, Supra* note 161 (Chapter 6), 705 P. 2d at 1774–1775 and

n.21 (judge removed); and *Geiler, supra* note 113 (Chapter 6), 515 P.2d at 9–12 and n.11 (same) with *McCartney, supra* note 49 (Chapter 6), 526 P. 2d at 281–282, 287–288 (removal denied).

99. E. g., *see Geiler, supra* note 113 (Chapter 6), 515 P.2d at 12; *In re Martin*, 295 N. C. 291, 245 S. E.2d 766 (1978) (same).

100. E. g., *see Spruance, supra* note 224 (Chapter 6), 532 P.2d at 1221; and *Geiler, supra* note 113 (Chapter 6), 515 P.2d at 11.

101. E. g., *see Geiler, supra* note 113 (Chapter 6), 515 P.2d at 9.

102. E. g., *Coruzzi, supra* note 161 (Chapter 6); *Bates, supra* note 308 (Chapter 6).

103. E. g., *In re LaMotte*, 341 So.2d 513 (Fla. 1977); *Matter of Carrillo, supra* note 72.

104. *In the Matter of Alonzo*, 223 So.2d 585 (Ala. 1968).

105. *Anderson, supra* note 309 (Chapter 6).

106. *Bates supra* note 308 (Chapter 6) (bribe).

107. *Id.*

108. *Cornett v. Judicial Retirement and Removal Comm.*, 625 S. W.2d 564 (Ky. 1981).

109. *See Bates, supra* note 308 (Chapter 6) (sustaining failure of master and commission to grant a stay).

110. *See Cornett, supra* note 108 (remanded to commission for discretionary determination by commission whether to grant stay).

111. *See Coruzzi, supra* note 161 (Chapter 6), 472 A.2d at 551–554.

112. *See Cornett, supra* note 108, 625 S. W.2d at 568–569.

NOTES TO §7.10(b)

113. E. g., *Murtagh, supra* note 297 (Chapter 6), 195 N. Y. S.2d at 905. *See Overton, supra* note 178 (Chapter 6), at 65–67.

114. E. g., *Cannon, supra* note 267 (Chapter 6), 537 P.2d at 918 (judge removed).

NOTES TO §7.10(c)

115. E. g., *see Crowell, supra* note 294 (Chapter 6), 379 So.2d at 110 (long-continued abuse of the contempt power; judge removed). *See also Kelly, supra* note 49 (Chapter 6),238 So.2d at 566 (pattern of hostility toward many attorneys, court officials, and fellow judges; judge reprimanded but warned continuation of pattern might result in removal).

116. *Yengo, supra* note 287 (Chapter 6), 371 A.2d at 57.

NOTES TO §7.10(d)

117. *See Field, supra* note 223 (Chapter 6), 576 P.2d at 354.

118. E. g., *Scott, supra* note 237 (Chapter 6), 386 N. E.2d at 221.

119. *Id.*

120. *Field, supra* note 223 (Chapter 6), 576 P.2d, at 355.

NOTES TO §7.10(e)

121. E. g., *McCartney, supra* note 49 (Chapter 6), 526 P.2d at 287.
122. E. g., *In the Matter of Kuehnel,* 413 N. Y. S.2d 809 (Ct. on Judic. 1978).
123. E. g., *McDonough, supra* note 287 (Chapter 6), 296 N. W.2d at 697.
124. E. g., *McCartney, supra* note 49 (Chapter 6), 526 P.2d at 288.
125. E.g., *Scott, supra* note 237 (Chapter 6), 386 N. E.2d at 221.
126. E.g., *Scott, supra* note 237 (Chapter 6),386 N. E.2d at 221.
127. E. g., *Johnson, supra* note 338 (Chapter 6), 568 P.2d at 867.

NOTES TO §7.11(b)(i)

128. E. g., *see Martin, supra* note 99, 245 S. E.2d at 775.
129. *See supra* note 102, and the accompanying text.
130. E. g., *See Alonzo, supra* note 104; *Littell, supra* note 79.
131. E. g., *see Anderson, supra* note 309 (Chapter 6).

NOTES TO §7.11(b)(ii)

132. E. g., *Crowell, supra* note 294 (Chapter 6); *Yengo, supra* note 287 (Chapter 6).
133. E. g., *Geiler, supra* note 113 (Chapter 6); *Cannon, supra* note 267 (Chapter 6).

NOTES TO §7.11(b)(iii)

134. *In the Matter of Waltemade,* 37 N. Y.2d (nn) (1975).
135. E. g., *Seraphim, supra* note 292 (Chapter 6), 294 N. W.2d at 499–500 (Wisc. Code of Judic. Ethics, R. 15, proscribed any judicial comment on pending proceedings, whether or not shown to have affected outcome).
136. *State ex. rel. Commission on Judicial Qualifications v. Rome, supra* note 302 (Chapter 6), 623 P.2d at 1317. *See supra* notes 301-302 (Chapter 6), and accompanying text.

NOTES TO §7.11(b)(iv)

137. E. g., *Cannon supra* note 267 (Chapter 6), 537 P.2d at 907–912; *Crowell, supra* note 294 (Chapter 6); *Yengo, supra* note 287 (Chapter 6), 371 A.2d at 53 to 57. *Cf. Del Rio, supra* note 49 (Chapter 6), 256 N. W.2d at 751 (1977) (five-year suspension without pay instead of removal).
138. E. g., *Cannon, supra* note 267 (Chapter 6), 537 P.2d at 907–912; *Yengo, supra* note 287 (Chapter 6), 371A.2d at 53–57; *Del Rio supra* note 49 (Chapter 6), 256 N. W.2d at 751.
139. E. g., *Crowell, supra* note 294 (Chapter 6), 573 So. 2d at 108–110.

NOTES TO §7.11(b)(v)

140. E. g., *Del Rio, supra* note 49 (Chapter 6), 256 N. W.2d at 741–742. *Cf. Mertens, supra* note 287 (Chapter 6), 392 N. Y. S.2d at 869–870 (judge censured). *See supra* notes 288–290 (Chapter 6), and the accompanying text.

141. *See McDonough, supra* note 287 (Chapter 6), 296 N. W.2d at 675–676, 696.

NOTES TO §7.11(b)(vi)

142. *See supra* Chapter 4.

143. *See supra* note 293 (Chapter 6), and the accompanying text.

144. E. g., *see Heitzler, supra* note 293 (Chapter 6), 291 N. E.2d at 485–488.

145. E. g., *see Lombardi* and *Martin, supra* note 293 (Chapter 6).

146. *See Heitzler, Lombardi,* and *Martin, supra* note 293 (Chapter 6).

NOTES TO §7.11(b)(vii)

147. *See supra* note 287 (Chapter 6), and the accompanying text.

148. *See Del Rio supra* note 49 (Chapter 6), 256 N. W.2d at 749–753; *Yengo, supra* note 287 (Chapter 6), 371 A.2d at 56–57.

NOTES TO §7.11(b)(viii)

149. *See* note 268 (Chapter 6), and the accompanying text; and Tesitor and Sinks, *supra* note 35 (Chapter 6), at 40–43 *See also supra* notes 239–240, 245–247, 249, 251, 253, 259, 273, 283 (Chapter 6) as to the states not listed in note 268 (Chapter 6).

150. *Field, supra* note 223 (Chapter 6), 576 P.2d at 354. *See* Ore. Const. art. VII, §8(1).

151. *Field, supra* note 223 (Chapter 6).

NOTES TO §7.11(b)(ix)

152. *See supra* note 295 (Chapter 6), and the accompanying text.

153. *Dekle, supra* note 295 (Chapter 6).

154. *Id.* at 11.

NOTES TO §7.11(c)(i)

155. As to Canon 5C generally, *see supra* §§6.3(q)(i) to 6.3(q)(iv).

156. *Babineaux, supra* note 266 (Chapter 6) (officerships and directorships in financial institutions and other institutions affected with a public interest in violation of Louisiana's version of ABA Canon 5C(2); state supreme court removed judges, with proviso removal would not take effect if judges resigned their officerships and directorships within a specified grace period).

157. *Troy, supra* note 297 (Chapter 6).

158. *Heitzler, supra* note 293 (Chapter 6).

159. *Id.*

230   The Judiciary

NOTES TO §7.11(c)(ii)

160. See *Supra* §6.3(q)(iv).
161. *Seraphim, supra* note 292 (Chapter 6).

NOTES TO §7.11(c)(iii)

162. *See supra* notes 272–275 (Chapter 6), 102–106, 108–112, and the accompanying text.
163. *See supra* notes 275–277 (Chapter 6) and 107, and the accompanying text. *See also Haggerty, supra* note 49 (Chapter 6) (judge removed because of disgraceful conduct in his personal life, including illegal gambling); *Duncan, supra* note 49 (Chapter 6) (judge removed because of illegal trespass by breaking into neighbor's home to search for weapons because of threats by neighbor against judge's children; conduct violated ABA Canon 2A, which requires judges to respect and comply with the law).
164. *Haggerty, supra* note 49 (Chapter 6) (judge removed because he had participated in and brought pornographic films and two prostitutes to a stag party, and had engaged in frequent illegal gambling through a bookie). *Cf. Heitzler, supra* note 293 (Chapter 6) (judge indefinitely suspended for various items of misconduct, one of which consisted of trips with a woman to whom he was not married while he was still married but separated from his wife).

NOTES TO §7.11(c)(iv)

165. *See supra* Chapter 5 for comprehensive discussion of the restrictions imposed on political activities by judges.
166. *See Briggs, supra* note 235 (Chapter 5) and the accompanying text.
167. For discussion of other decisions disciplining judges by reason of prohibited political activities, *see supra* §5.7.

NOTES TO §7.12

168. E. g., Ala. Const. amend. no. 317(3); Colo. Const. art VI, §23; Del. Const. art IV, §37; D. C. Code§11–1526(c); Ga. Const. art. 6, §13, ¶ 3 (b); Mont. Rev. Code Ann. §3–1–1111(2); Pa. Const. art. 5, §18(h). *But compare* Md. Const. art. IV, §4(B)(b) (a judge removed for disciplinary reasons "shall have the rights and privileges accruing from his judicial service only to the extent prescribed by the order of removal").
169. E. g., Cal. Govt. Code §75033; Mo. Ann. Stat. §476.480; N. C. Gen. Stat. Ann. §7A–36; S. D. Comp. Laws Ann. §16–1A–13; Va. Const. art. VI, §10; Wyo. Const. art. 5, §6(f). *But compare* Mont. Code Ann. §19–5–503 (annuity of actuarial value equivalent to accumulated deductions and present value of state annuity then standing in credit).
170. E. g., Cal. Govt. Code §75033.1; S. D. Comp. Laws Ann. §16–1A–13; Va. Const. art. VI, §10. *See In re Peoples*, 296 N. C. 109, 250 S. E.2d 890, 914 (1978), cert. denied, 442 U. S. 929 (1979).

NOTES TO §7.13

171. *See* Tesitor and Sinks, *supra* note 35 (Chapter 6), at 40–43; and Wash. Const. art. IV, §31 (amend. 71). The District of Columbia and all states in the country, except New Hampshire and Oregon, provide for involuntary retirement, by reason of disability, in commission-initiated proceedings; New Hampshire and Oregon have separate statutory procedures for involuntarily retiring disabled judges. *See* Tesitor and Sinks, *supra* note 5 (Chapter 6) at 40–43, as supplemented by Wash. Const. art. IV, §31 (amend. 71).

172. E. g., *see* U. S. C. §372; Ala. Const. amend. no. 328, §6.18(a); Alaska Stat. §22.30.011; Ariz. Const. art. 6.1, §4; Ark. Stat. Ann. §§22–1003 to 1004; Conn. Gen. Stat. §§51–49; Cal. Const. art. 6, §18; Colo. Const. art. VI, §23; Del. Const. art. IV, §37; D. C. Code §11–1526; Fla. Const. art. 5, §12; Ga. Const. art. 6, §7, ¶¶7–8; Hawaii Const. art. VI, §5; Hawaii S. Ct. R. 26; Idaho Code Ann. §1–2103; Ill. Const. art. 6, §15; Ind. Const. art. 7, §11; Iowa Code Ann. §605.27(1); Ky. Const. §121; Kan. Const. art. III, §15; Ky. Rules, *supra* note 73 (Chapter 6), R. 4.020(a); La. Const. art. 5, §25(C); Me. Supr. Ct. Order, *supra* note 40, §10; Md. Const. art. IV, §4B(b); Mass. Rules, *supra* note 40, R. 20, 23; Mich. Const. art. 6, §30(2); Minn. Const. art. 6, §9; Minn. Stat. Ann. §490.16; Miss. Const. art. 6, §177A; Mo. Const. art. 5, §24; Mont. Const. art. VII, §11(3)(a); Nebr. Const. art. V, §30; Nebr. Rev. Stat. §24–722; Nev. Const. art. 6, §§21(1), 21(6)(b); N. M. Const. art. VI, §32; N. Y. Const. art. 6, §22(a); N. C. Gen. Stat. §7A–376; N. D. Cent. Code §27–23–03; Ohio Rev. Code Ann. §§2701.11, 12(B); Okla. Const. art. VII-A, §1; Pa. Const. art. 5, §18; R. I. Gen. Laws §8–16–9; S. C. Const. art. V, §13; S. C. S. Ct. R. 34; S. D. Const. art. V, §9; Tenn. Code Ann. §17–5–303; Tex. Const. art. 5, §1-a(6)(B); Utah Code Ann. §§78–7–28 to 30; Vt. Rules, *supra* note 73 (Chapter 6), R. 2, 6, 11; Va. Const. art. VI, §10; Wash. Const. art. IV, §31, W. Va. Const. art. 8, §8; Wis. Const. art. 7, §11; Wis. Stat. Ann. §§757.81-.91; Wyo. Const. art. 5, §6(e).

173. *See supra* note 172 as to Alaska, Arizona, Colorado, Idaho, Indiana, Louisiana, Maryland, Minnesota, New Mexico, North Dakota, Rhode Island, South Carolina, Texas, and Wyoming. *Cf.* note 72 as to Utah (disability that seriously interferes with the performance of judicial duties).

174. *See supra* note 172 as to Mississippi, Nebraska, North Carolina, Tennessee, Vermont, and Wisconsin.

175. *See supra* notes 173 and 174, and the accompanying text.

176. *See supra* note 172 as to Iowa, Michigan, Missouri, New York, Ohio, Oklahoma, and Wisconsin (described as physical and mental disability in these states), and Florida ("disability").

177. E. g., *see supra* note 172 as to Alabama, Hawaii, Kentucky, Maine, Rhode Island, and South Dakota.

178. E. g., *see supra* note 172 as to Rhode Island ("physical and mental disability").

179. E. g, *see supra* note 172 as to Hawaii (merely "disability") and Kentucky (same).

180. E. g., *see supra* note 172 as to Rhode Island.

181. *See supra* notes 172, 40–48 (Chapter 6), and the accompanying text.

182. E. g., Ala. Const. amend. no. 328, §6.18(a) (suspension with or without pay); Ill. Const. art. 6, §15(e) (suspension with or without pay); Iowa Code Ann. §605.29(2); La. Const. art. 5, 25 (C); Minn. Rules, *supra* note 57 (Chapter 6), R. 9(e) (suspension with pay); Okla. Ct. on Judic. Rules, Trial Div., R. 10 (suspension with or without pay); R. I. Gen. Laws §§8–16–4(d), 8–16–7(a) (temporary suspension by supreme court on recommendation by commission following completion of hearings before commission); Utah Code Ann. §§78–7–28(3), 78–7–30(1), (2) (no salary for the period of suspension); Wisc. Stat. Ann. §757.95.

183. E. g., *see supra* note 182 (Chapter 6) as to Alaska, Arizona, Minnesota, Missouri, North Dakota, South Dakota, and Wyoming.

184. *See* §6.3 (n)(vii).

185. D. C. Code §11–1526(b).

186. *See* §6.3 (n)(vi).

187. Okla. Const. art. VII-A, §1(c).

188. E. g., Cal. Const. art. VI, §18(d); Ind. Const. art. 7, §11; N. D. Cent. Code §27–23–03(4); Va. Const. art. VI, §10; Wyo. Const. art. 5, §6(f).

189. E. g., Okla. Const. art. 7-A, §4(d); Wyo. Const. art. 5, §6(f).

190. Okla. Const. art. VII-A, §1(c).

191. *McComb v. Commission on Judicial Performance*, 138 Cal. Rptr. 459, 564 P.2d, 1, 4, 8 (1977).

192. *In re Corning*, 538 S. W.2d 46 (Mo. En Banc 1976).

193. U.S. Const art. I, §2(5); art. I, §§3(6), 3(7); art. II, §4; art. III, §2.

194. 28 U. S. C. A. §372.

195. 28 U. S. C. A. §372(c)(6)(B)(iii).

196. 28 U. S. C. A. §372(c)(6)(B)(iv).

8

Civil and Criminal Liability

8.1 JUDICIAL IMMUNITY FROM CIVIL LIABILITY

a. Historical Development of Judicial Immunity from Civil Liability

Historically, there has been a correlation between judicial immunity and the right of parties to appeal from adverse decisions. In England, in the tenth and eleventh centuries, there was no right of appeal, but disappointed litigants were entitled to charge judges handing down unfavorable judgements with "falsehood," later termed "false judgment." The litigant could then seek nullification of the judgment and a fine against the judge, called an "amercement," payable to the court in which the challenge against the judgment was instituted.[1] Initially, the complaining party could either limit the challenge to alleged errors of law or contest the record through trial by combat.[2]

Gradually, these means of imposing liability on judges were supplanted by appeals to higher courts. In appeals from courts of record, the doctrines of sanctity or nonimpeachability of the record and conclusiveness of the trial court's findings of fact developed to limit the appeals to alleged errors of law.[3] With the development of appellate remedies, the need for suits to impose liability on judges became redundant, and a doctrine of judicial immunity from civil and (at least to some extent) criminal liability for judicial acts developed.[4]

Although preceded by a number of cases recognizing criminal[5] and civil immunity,[6] the leading case holding a judge immune from civil liability for damages is *Floyd v. Barker*, decided by Lord Coke in 1607.[7] The policy reasons underlying the doctrine of judicial immunity cited by Lord Coke were: (a) the need for finality of decisions; (b) the protection of judicial independence; (c) the avoidance of "continual calumniations" and perjuries against even the most sincere judges; and (d) protection of the system of justice from falling into disrepute. Since *Floyd v. Barker*, judicial immunity from civil liability in damages for official acts has been adopted by the great weight of authority, both in England[8] and in the United States.[9]

Damage actions in which American courts have applied this doctrine have included not only actions based on common law causes of actions, but also actions under the federal Civil Rights Acts.[10] The common law causes of action to which doctrine of judicial immunity has been applied have been diverse and have included false arrest, false imprisonment, malicious prosecution, wrongful disbarment, assault, assault and battery, wrongful search and seizure, wrongful garnishment, negligence, libel, and slander.[11]

b. Overview of Judicial Immunity from Civil Liability

The principal feature of the generally accepted doctrine of judicial immunity from civil liability is that, if the questioned acts satisfy certain criteria, judges are absolutely immune from civil liability, regardless of whether they acted in good faith or maliciously. The principal limitations on the doctrine of judicial immunity from civil liability are that the challenged acts must have been "judicial acts" and that they must not have been clearly outside the scope of the court's general jurisdiction.

c. The Requisite That the Challenged Act or Omission Must Not Have Been Clearly Outside the Court's General Jurisdiction

For considerably more than a century, the general rule in the United States has been that, even if a judge has exceeded his jurisdiction, he is immune from civil liability, even for malicious conduct, provided there is not a clear lack of general jurisdiction over the subject matter.[12] When, however, there is a clear lack of general jurisdiction, the American rule is that the judge is subject to civil liability.[13] In such event, it has been held that even the judge's good faith belief that he had jurisdiction will not immunize him from liability for damages, but will merely mitigate the damages.[14]

When a court has jurisdiction over a general class of cases, but not over a particular case following within that general class the judge's act in deciding (albeit erroneously) that the court has jurisdiction over a particular case is a judicial act, which should be protected against liability. When, however, a court lacks jurisdiction not only over a particular case but also over the general class of cases into which it falls, the judge's assumption of jurisdiction is not a judicial act, but rather a wrong that is practically willful and that should not be immune from liability.[15]

In addition to the many cases that have considered the effect of deficiencies in subject matter jurisdiction, a few cases have considered the effect of lack of personal jurisdiction. The few decisions are divided as to whether civil immunity should be granted, with some cases denying immunity[16] and others granting immunity.[17] Perhaps the reason for the lesser incidence of this type of case is that judges are less apt to act when they lack jurisdiction over the person than when they lack jurisdiction over the subject matter.

d. The Requisite That the Challenged Act Must Have Been a Judicial Act

Judicial civil immunity also requires that the challenged act must have been a "judicial act."[18] This requirement dates at least to Lord Coke's 1607 opinion in *Floyd v. Barker*.[19] In the federal courts, the principles governing the determination of whether an act is a "judicial act" were laid down by the U. S. Supreme Court in 1978 in *Stump v. Sparkman*, which involved an *ex parte* order signed by a circuit court judge directing the sterilization of a fifteen-year-old girl.[20] According to Justice White's majority opinion[21]:

The relevant cases demonstrate that the factors determining whether an act by a judge is a "judicial" one relate to the nature of the act itself, *i. e. whether it is a function performed by a judge*, and to the expectations of the parties, *i. e., whether they dealt with the judge in his judicial capacity* [emphasis added].

Applying these tests, the majority in *Stump* held that, even though the judge had acted without filing, docketing, notice, hearing, or appointment of a guardian *ad litem* or attorney for the girl, his act in signing the sterilization order was a "judicial" act. The majority's grounds were that the signing of an order is "the type of an act normally performed only by judges," and that "he did so in his capacity as a circuit court Judge."[22]

In addition to the tests specified by the majority in *Stump v. Sparkman*, the courts have repeatedly held that a key question in determining whether an act was a judicial act is whether it was ministerial. If it was, the doctrine of absolute immunity is inapplicable.[23] The leading case on the distinction between ministerial and judicial acts is *Ex Parte Virginia*.[24] There the selection of a jury by a judge was held to be ministerial rather than judicial, and therefore indictable, since similar acts could be and often were performed by persons other than judges.[25] It must be noted that there is a contrary, and apparently growing, view recognized in recent federal decisions[26] and the Restatement of Torts,[27] holding that administrative acts by judges are entitled to the same absolute immunity accorded to discretionary acts customarily performed by judges.

The issuance of arrest warrants has frequently resulted in efforts to impose civil liability on judges. Mere error in determining whether there was probable cause for the issuance of the warrant has been held not a basis for imposing liability, since the determination of probable cause is itself a judicial function.[28] Conversely, when a magistrate directed a police officer to arrest someone not named in a warrant, for an offense not committed in the magistrate's presence, the magistrate's act was not a judicial act, and he was not immune from civil liability.[29]

Some types of courtroom behavior are so unlike normal judicial conduct that the judge has been held subject to civil liability. A judge who physically evicted an individual from his courtroom was held to be acting extrajudicially and, therefore, not protected against civil liability unless the judge acted in good faith.[30] The court emphasized that the judge was performing an act normally performed by a sheriff or bailiff, for which a sheriff and bailiff would have had only qualified immunity.[31]

In a suit by the parents of a little girl murdered by a paroled convict, the judge's failure to call the defendant's recidivism to the prosecuting attorney's attention, to sentence him as a recidivist, or to order him treated as a mentally disordered sex offender, each in violation of a state statute, were held judicial, rather than ministerial, acts and, therefore, protected by absolute judicial immunity.[32]

The promulgation by judges of rules governing the bar has been held a legislative, rather than a judicial function, and, therefore, subject to the immunity rule applicable to the legislative function, rather than that applicable to the judicial function.[33] This distinction is, however, academic, since the legislative function is also protected by an absolute immunity.[34]

e. The Absolute Nature of Judicial Immunity from Civil Liability for Judicial Acts Not Clearly Outside the Court's General Jurisdiction Over the Subject Matter

According to the weight of authority in the United States, immunity for acts not clearly outside the court's general jurisdiction is absolute rather than qualified. Thus, a judge is immune from civil liability regardless of whether he acted in good or bad faith, innocently or knowingly and willfully, honestly or corruptly, or with good intentions or maliciously.[35] The rule is the same in England.[36]

In many jurisdictions the courts have explained that the reason for granting immunity even if the judge acted maliciously or corruptly is not to protect malicious or dishonest judges, but rather to protect honest and sincere judges from unfounded efforts by disgruntled parties to charge them with liability. The aim is to safeguard and foster judicial independence[37] and avoid the chilling effect civil liability would have on qualified candidates for judicial office.[38] Louisiana is the only state to have adopted the contrary view that a judge of a court of general jurisdiction who acts maliciously, corruptly, or in bad faith is not immune from civil liability even when he is not acting in excess of his jurisdiction.[39]

There is, however, a split in authority as to whether judges of inferior or limited jurisdiction are immune from civil liability when they act corruptly, maliciously, or in bad faith. Although a majority of the courts in the United States appear to apply the doctrine of absolute judicial immunity to inferior court judges under these circumstances,[40] a few courts have held to the contrary.[41]

f. Civil Suits against Judges Seeking Equitable Relief Not Based on Any of the Federal Civil Rights Acts

At common law, there are two conflicting lines of authority on the question whether judges are immune from actions seeking equitable or declaratory relief with respect to their judicial acts. The majority rule appears to be that judges are not immune from equitable or declaratory relief,[42] but there is a substantial minority position.[43]

The majority rule declining to grant immunity in equitable actions has been said to be based on the proposition that judicial immunity should not be extended any further than is needed to ensure judicial independence, and that judicial immunity from equitable relief is not needed.[44]

The converse view has been explained on the grounds that innocent judges would be just as inconvenienced in equitable actions and that judicial immunity from equitable relief is, therefore, as necessary to judicial independence as judicial immunity from liability for damages.[45]

g. Judicial Immunity from Civil Liability in Damage Actions Based on the Federal Civil Rights Acts

During the last several decades, many damage actions have been brought against state court judges alleging violations of the due process, equal protection and other guarantees of the U. S. Constitution. These actions, predicated on §1 of the federal Civil Rights Act of 1871,[46] have been brought in the federal courts.[47] The latter statutory provision, which has sometimes been called the "Ku Klux Klan Act" and is herein referred to as "§1983" (since codified as 42 U. S. Code §1983), provides that every person who, "under color of any statute, ordinance, regulation, custom, or usage of any state," subjects or causes to be subjected any person to the deprivation of any rights, privileges, or immunities secured by the federal Constitution or federal law shall be liable to that person for damages or equitable relief.

Since §1983 does not expressly exclude judges, there was, prior to 1951, considerable uncertainty and confusion both as to whether judges had immunity from liability for judicial acts in damage actions under §1983 and as to whether any immunity would be absolute or qualified (i. e., contingent on good faith).[48] In 1951, the U. S. Supreme Court, in *Tenney v. Brandhove*,[49] held that state legislators were absolutely immune from liability for legislative acts in damage actions under §1983. Thereafter, the federal courts, other than the Third Circuit Court of Appeals, unanimously applied the absolute judicial immunity concept to damage actions under §1983,[50] and the Third Circuit Court of Appeals followed suit in 1966.[51] Finally, in 1967, in *Pierson v. Ray*,[52] the United States Supreme Court endorsed the rule applied in these cases and specifically held that judges are absolutely immune from liability for damages in actions under §1983 for judicial acts constituting civil rights violations.

Since then, *Pierson* has been reaffirmed and extended by the United States Supreme Court in its 1978 decision in *Stump*. There, the Court held that the common law doctrine that judicial acts in excess of jurisdiction, but not clearly outside all jurisdiction, are absolutely immune from damage liability is equally applicable to damage actions under §1983.[53] The absolute immunity doctrine of *Pierson* and *Stump* has, since 1978, been applied by the United States District Court for the Eastern District of Pennsylvania to a judicial act alleged to be induced by bribery or collusion;[54] the Court granted a motion to dismiss a complaint which contained that allegation.

h. Judicial Nonimmunity From Liability in Actions Seeking Equitable Relief under the Federal Civil Rights Acts

In §1983 actions seeking equitable or declaratory relief against judicial acts by state court judges, the federal courts have overwhelmingly held that judges have no immunity.[55] The United States Supreme Court discussed this question in 1980 in *Supreme Court of Virginia v. Consumers Union of the United States, Inc.*[56] Although the Court found it unnecessary to decide the question, it pointed out that six federal circuit courts of appeal had held that judges lack immunity in §1983 actions seeking equitable or declaratory relief, and that the Court had "never held that judicial immunity absolutely insulates judges from declaratory or injunctive relief with respect to their judicial acts."[57]

i. Derivative Immunity of Nonjudges for Judicial Acts Committed by Judges Pursuant to Conspiracy with the Nonjudges

Section 1983 imposes damage liability upon every person who "under color of" state law subjects or causes any person to be subjected to deprivation of any civil right. In 1945, in *Screws v. United States*,[58] the United States Supreme Court held that acts of a state official that cause a deprivation of civil rights are to be deemed "under color of" state law, even when those acts are violative of state law. It is also accepted that private persons conspiring with state officials to deprive others of their civil rights are also acting "under color of" state law within the meaning of §1983.[59]

In 1965, in *Haldane v. Chagnon*,[60] the Ninth Circuit Court of Appeals considered the question of whether co-conspirators who were not state officials shared the officials' absolute immunity. The court held that private persons cannot be held liable under §1983 unless they conspire with a state official against whom the plaintiffs have a valid claim. The *Haldane* rule has, at times, been referred to as the doctrine of derivative immunity.[61] Following *Haldane*, some federal courts adopted the doctrine of derivative immunity,[62] while others rejected it.[63] Finally, in 1980, in *Dennis v. Sparks*,[64] the U. S. Supreme Court settled the matter by emphatically rejecting the doctrine of derivative immunity.

8.2 JUDICIAL IMMUNITY FROM CRIMINAL LIABILITY

a. Judicial Immunity from Criminal Liability for Misfeasance, Malfeasance, or Nonfeasance in Office.

In some states, e. g., Kentucky, malfeasance (called "misfeasance" in that state) in office is not a common law crime[65] and, to constitute a crime, must be specifically made a crime by statute. In other states, however, e. g., Pennsylvania, malfeasance in office is a common law crime.[66]

Where malfeasance in office is a common law crime and the alleged malfeasance involves the performance of a discretionary act, it has been held that a judge cannot be found guilty unless he is shown to have acted in bad faith or corruptly.[67] The judge thus has a qualified immunity. The only situation in which the judge lacks even a qualified immunity is when he has breached a positive, statutory duty.[68] Similarly, bad faith must generally be shown to establish the statutory crime of malfeasance or nonfeasance in office, even if the statute does not expressly make bad faith an element of the crime.[69] *A fortiori*, when the statute requires that the malfeasance or neglect of duty be "willful," the courts have generally applied the statute as written and required that the judge's act or omission be willful and have sometimes additionally required that it be with a corrupt motive.[70] Likewise, when applied to judicial acts by a judge, the statutory offense of "willful and malicious oppression in office" has been construed as requiring that the act must have been knowingly and corruptly done.[71]

Analogously, moreover, when a judge is cited for criminal contempt by reason of a violation of the applicable rules of court, he cannot be found to have been guilty of contempt unless he acted in bad faith or corruptly.[72]

b. Judicial Immunity from Criminal Liability for Statutory Offenses Peculiarly Applicable to Judges, Other Than Misfeasance or Nonfeasance in Office

Whether immunity applies under statutes prohibiting and imposing criminal penalties upon judicial acts other than malfeasance or nonfeasance in office turns on the statute itself. While some such criminal statutes have been applied to judges without mention of the judge's state of mind,[73] conviction under others has been held to require a showing of bad faith.[74] Bad faith was not mentioned as a relevant consideration in various cases where the allegedly unlawful judicial act did not involve the exercise of judicial discretion, e. g., acts that were ministerial[75] or were unconditionally prohibited.[76]

There are certain judicial crimes in which corruptness is an inherent part of the crime. Such crimes include the solicitation, acceptance, or receipt of bribes or promises of bribes in return for promised judicial favors, or conspiracies or agreements to solicit or accept such bribes.[77] Since this type of crime necessarily involves bad faith, failure of the prosecution to prove bad faith would constitute a failure to establish the crime. Conversely, inasmuch as absolute immunity is not even available as a defense against a charge of malfeasance in office,[78] it follows, *a fortiori*, that absolute immunity is no defense against charges of corrupt judicial conduct of the types described above.[79]

c. Judicial Immunity from Criminal Liability for Discretionary Judicial Acts under Criminal Prohibitions Not Particularly Applicable to Judges

Under these circumstances, it has been held that a judge has a qualified immunity with respect to discretionary acts that are allegedly violative of a statutory or common law criminal prohibition that is applicable to the community in general and not particularly aimed at judges.[80]

d. Judicial Immunity from Criminal Liability under the Federal Civil Rights Acts

In 1879, in *Ex Parte Virginia*,[81] the United States Supreme Court first dealt with the question of whether judges are immune from criminal liability under the federal Civil Rights Acts for violating federal constitutional rights. The Court determined that the challenged judicial act, *viz.*, the exclusion of negroes from juries in violation of the federal Civil Rights Act of March 1, 1875,[82] was a ministerial act, rather than a discretionary judicial act and that the judicial immunity doctrine was inapplicable. The Court expressed no opinion as to whether discretionary judicial acts are immune from criminal prosecution under the federal Civil Rights Acts.

The latter question was, however, presented in 1944 in *United States v. Chaplin*,[83] where a discretionary judicial act by a state court judge within his jurisdiction was prosecuted under the criminal provisions of the federal Civil Rights Acts. The Court ruled that the act was immune.

A subsequent pronouncement (albeit *obiter dicta*) by the United States Supreme Court in 1974 in *O'Shea v. Littleton* (an action seeking equitable relief under the federal Civil Rights Acts),[84] however, has indicated that judicial acts in violation of federal constitutional rights are not necessarily immune from criminal liability under the federal Civil Rights Acts. According to the Court:[85]

we have never held that the performance of the duties of judicial, legislative, or executive officers, requires or contemplates the immunization of otherwise criminal deprivations of constitutional rights. *Cf. Ex Parte Virginia*, 100 U. S. 339 (1880). On the contrary, the judicially fashioned doctrine of official immunity does not reach "so far as to immunize criminal conduct proscribed by an Act of Congress" *Gravel v. United States*, 408 U. S. 606, 627 (1972).

The exact boundaries of judicial immunity from criminal liability under the federal Civil Rights Acts must be settled in future cases, but it seems at least likely that judges' criminal liability for judicial acts violative of federal constitutional rights will depend on the existence or nonexistence of bad faith. The availability of good faith as a defense received indirect support in the Eleventh Circuit Court of Appeals in *United States v. Hastings*.[86] There, in considering federal criminal prosecutions of judges generally, the court said that, although there is no absolute immunity for acts committed by judges in their official capacities,[87] there may be a qualified common law immunity immunizing such acts from criminal prosecution when committed in good faith.[88]

In recent years, the federal courts have authoritatively established that a federal criminal prosecution of a federal judge may be brought prior to removal of the judge from office and notwithstanding a pending impeachment proceeding against the judge.[89]

8.3 JUDICIAL IMMUNITY FROM CIVIL AND CRIMINAL LIABILITY FOR DEFAMATION

a. Judicial Immunity from Civil Liability for Defamation

(i) Introduction

A judge performing a judicial act or function is absolutely immune from liability for damages for any oral or written defamation, provided only that the communication is relevant to the matters before the judge.[90] This rule of judicial immunity is part of the broader rule that oral or written communications by participants in judicial proceedings, uttered or written during the course of the proceedings and relevant to the subject matter of the proceedings, are absolutely privileged.[91] It is, of course, also an application of the rule that judicial acts are immune from civil liability.[92]

The rule of absolute judicial immunity, or privilege, for defamatory communications is subject to three significant limitations: (i) the communication must have been uttered or written by the judge in the performance of a judicial function; (ii) the communication must have been relevant to the matters before the judge; and (iii) the function being performed must not have been clearly beyond all possible jurisdiction, i. e., the judge must at least have had "colorable jurisdiction."

(ii) Defamatory Statements by a Judge Are Not Absolutely Privileged Unless Made in the Course of the Performance by Him of a Judicial Function

To be absolutely privileged, a defamatory communication must have been uttered or written by the judge while performing a judicial function.[93] For example, it has been held that defamatory remarks by a judge concerning a party or witness are not absolutely privileged when made "after the case is determined and the judicial duty is performed."[94] Conversely, a letter by a judge to a prison warden, detailing information useful for future parole purposes concerning a convict previously sentenced by the judge, was held to be an absolutely privileged judicial act.[95]

Close questions arise as to just when a matter has terminated so as to defeat application of the privilege to subsequent defamatory remarks. Defamatory comments concerning counsel while the judge was walking through the courtroom, after having adjourned a trial for the day, were held to present a triable issue of fact as to whether the trial had been terminated and the judge divested of his absolute privilege.[96]

Still another borderline situation involves the publication, in unofficial reports, of opinions by judges containing allegedly libelous matter. In *Murray v. Brancato*,[97] in which the judge had personally forwarded his opinion to the publisher of the unofficial reports, a divided New York Court of Appeals held that the judge was not legally required to forward his opinion to the unofficial reporter. Therefore, his act was not a "judicial act" and was not absolutely privileged. A contrary decision was rendered by the Second Circuit Court of Appeals a few years later, however, in *Garfield v. Palmieri*.[98] Moreover, even in New York, it has been held that, when the judge is required by law to transmit his opinion to the reporter, his act is absolutely privileged.[99] Also, a judge is not liable for defamatory matter in his opinion when he does not participate in its transmission to the reporter.[100]

Statements by a judge outside the courtroom are privileged if made in the course of his performance of a judicial function.[101] Conversely, it has been held that remarks made by a judge inside the courtroom are not privileged unless the judge is "acting at the time as a judge in the course of his official duties".[102]

(iii) To Be Absolutely Privileged, a Statement or Communication by a Judge Performing a Judicial Function Need Merely Have Some Reference to the Matter before the Judge and Need Not Be Relevant to an Issue Before the Court

In the case of defamatory statements by parties, attorneys, and witnesses, the overwhelming majority view is that such a statement is absolutely privileged if made in the course of a judicial proceeding, and relevant to the proceeding, irrespective of whether the statement is relevant to any issue before the judge.[103] The courts are in disagreement as to whether the requisite of relevancy to the proceeding applies to judges. According to one line of authority, this relevancy requirement applies to defamation by judges.[104] Other courts, in Massachusetts, New York, Washington, and England, for example, however, have held that this relevancy requirement applies only to parties, attorneys, and witnesses and not to judges.[105]

(iv) In Order That a Statement Made by a Judge While Performing a Judicial Function Be Absolutely Privileged, the Function Being Performed Must Not Have Been Clearly Beyond All Possible Jurisdiction

The broad rule of judicial immunity for judicial acts, as prescribed by *Bradley* and its progeny, extends to acts in excess of jurisdiction as long as they are not clearly beyond all jurisdiction.[106] This principle has been applied by various courts in defamation suits, in which the courts have ruled that defamatory statements made by participants in the course of a judicial proceeding are absolutely privileged. This is the rule even if jurisdiction over the subject matter is lacking, provided there is "colorable jurisdiction". over the subject matter.[107] Presumably, this principle would be held equally applicable to defamation suits against judges.

Another line of cases has prescribed an apparently contrary principle: The absence of jurisdiction over the subject matter defeats absolute privilege.[108] In fact, it has been held that lack of jurisdiction over the subject matter precludes absolute privilege, even if the alleged defamer believed in good faith that the court had jurisdiction over the subject matter.[109] This rule has been explained on the ground that the lack of jurisdiction has the effect of depriving the defamed person of the opportunity to prove that the defamation is false.[110]

*(v) Statutes Making Communications in Judicial Proceedings
Absolutely Immune from Liability in Damages*

A handful of states, including California, Idaho, Montana, North Dakota, Oklahoma, Puerto Rico, South Dakota, and Utah, have statutes pertaining to civil liability, which provide that a publication made in any judicial proceeding is privileged.[111] These statutes have been construed as providing for an absolute privilege, rather than a qualified privilege.[112]

Some of these statutes also confer an absolute privilege on communications made in the proper discharge of an official duty.[113] Although not as broad as the privilege with respect to judicial proceedings, this privilege for official communications would seem to apply to most judicial acts.

In *Bradford v. Pette*,[114] the question arose as to whether the New York Civil Practice Act granting immunity for publication of "a fair and true report of a judicial . . . proceeding" protected a judge who causes an opinion he had authored to be published in an unofficial reporter. The court answered this question in the affirmative, but held that this privilege was qualified, available only if the defendant acted in good faith and from proper motives.

b. Judicial Immunity from Criminal Liability for Defamation

In a number of states, libel is still a common law rather than a statutory crime[115] and, thus, subject to the applicable common law privileges.[116] One of the oldest common law privileges is a judge's immunity from criminal prosecution for libels published by him in judicial proceedings or in the performance of his other judicial duties.[117] In a number of states, however, the crime of libel is currently defined by statute. In those states, there is a question of whether a judge's common law privileges are still in full force and in effect in prosecutions for criminal libel or criminal defamation. In a number of these states, this question is answered in the affirmative by the statute itself, since the applicable statutory provision either expressly provides for a privilege for judges[118] or provides for a privilege for participants in judicial proceedings[119] or contains a general exemption for privileged communications.[120]

On the other hand, some of the statutory provisions concerning criminal defamation provide no defenses or privileges other than the defense of truth and therefore do not expressly exempt communications for judges or communications in judicial proceedings;[121] and even the defense of truth is sometimes, but not always, conditioned upon the communication having being made with good motives and for justifiable ends.[122] Still other criminal defamation statutes, although providing general defenses or privileges other than that of truth, likewise do not expressly provide for any privilege relating specifically to communications by judges or communications pertaining to judicial proceedings.[123] Although there appears to be no direct authority, what little analogous authority exists involving statutory libel actions in which common law defenses were held available, suggests that common law privileges pertaining to communications by judges or communications in judicial proceedings remain available even in the states that do not expressly codify those privileges, including not only those that do not expressly codify any other privileges, but also those that provide for a statutory defense of truth or codify one or more of the other common law privileges.[124]

NOTES TO §8.1(a)

1. *See* Block, *Stump v. Sparkman* and the History of Judicial Immunity, Duke L. J. 879, 881–883 (1980).

2. *Id.*, at 881–882.

3. *Id.*, at 882–883.

4. *Id.*, at 884–885.

5. *Id.*, at 884; 6 W. Holdsworth, A History of English Law 235–236 (2d ed. 1937).

6. *See* Block, *supra* note 1, at 884, n. 24, and the accompanying text; *Floyd v. Barker*, 12 Coke Rep. 23, 77 Engl. Repr. 1305, 1306–1307 (Star Chamber 1607) (discussing and citing cases); *Yates v. Lansing*, 9 Johns, 395, 408–409 (N. Y. 1811) (discussing and citing pre–1607 cases).

7. *Floyd*, *supra* note 6.

8. E. g., *see Miller v. Hope*, 2 Shaw, Sc. App. Cas. 125 (H. of L. 1824); *Fray v. Blackburn*, 3 B. and S. 576, 122 Eng. Repr. 217 (1863); *Haggard v. Pelicier Freres* (1892) A. C. 61; *Anderson v. Gorrie*, L. R. (1895) 1 Q. B. 668; *Bottomley v. Brougham* (1908) 1 K. B. 584.

9. E. g., *Dennis v. Sparks*, 449 U. S. 24 (1980); *Stump v. Sparkman*, 435 U. S. 349 (six-three decision) (1978); *Pierson v. Ray*, 386 U. S. 547 (1967); *Bradley v. Fisher*, 80 U. S. (13 Wall.) 335 (1872); *Randall v. Brigham*, 74 U. S. (7 Wall.) 523 (1869); *O'Bryan v. Chandler*, 352 F.2d 987 (10th Cir. 1965), *cert. denied*, 384 U. S. 926 (1966); *Heasley v. Davies*, 342 F.2d 786 (8th Cir. 1965); *Busteed v. Parsons*, 54 Ala. 393 (1876); *Evans v. Copins*, 26 Ariz. App. 96, 546 P.2d 365 (1976); *Pickett v. Wallace*, 57 Cal. 555, 557 (1881); *Turpen v. Booth*, 56 Cal. 65, 69 (1880) (grand jurors); *Reverend Mother Pauline v. Bray*, 168 Cal. App.2d 384, 335 P.2d 1018, (1959); *Perry v. Meikle*, 102 Cal. App.2d 602, 228 P.2d 17, 19–20 (1951); *Singer v. Bogen*, 305 P.2d 893 (Cal. App. 1957); *Platz v. Marion*, 35 Cal. App. 241, 169 P. 697, 700 (1918); *Phelps v. Sill*, 1 Day's Reps. 315, 329 (Conn. 1804); *McDaniel v. Harrell*, 81 Fla. 66, 87 So. 631, 632 (1921); *Rivello v. Cooper*, 322 So. 602 (Fla. App., 4th Dist. 1975); *Smith v. Hancock*, 156 Ga. App. 80, 256 S. E.2d 627, 628 (1979); *State v. Taylor*, 425 P.2d 1014, 1019 (Hawaii 1967); *Holland v. Lutz*, 194 Kans. 712, 401 P.2d 1015, 1019–1020 (1965); *Berry v. Bass*, 157 La. 81, 102 So. 76 (1924); *Cleveland v. State*, 380 So.2d 105 (La. App. 1979); *Conques v. Hardy*, 337 So.2d 627 (La. App. 1976); *Rush v. Buckley*, 100 Me. 322 (1905); *Allard v. Estes*, 292 Mass. 187, 195–196, 191 N. E. 884 (1935); *Olepa v. Mapleton*, 2 Mich. App 734, 141 N. W. 2d 350, 351–352 (1966); *Grove v. Van Duyn*, 44 N. J. L. 654 (1882); *Taylor v. Doremus*, 1 Harr. (N. J.) 473, 475 (1838); *Galindo v. Western States*

Collection Co., 82 N. M. 149, 477 P.2d 325 (1970); *Lange v. Benedict*, 73 N. Y. 12, 27 (1878); *Austin v. Vrooman*, 128 N. Y. 229, 28 N. E. 477 (1891); *Doran v. Savoca*, 39 Misc.2d 430, 240 N. Y. S.2d 835 (Sup. Ct., Albany Co. 1963); *Gans v. Callaghan*, 238 N. Y. Supp. 599 (Sup. Ct., King Co. 1930); *Voll v. Steel*, 141 Ohio, St. 293, 47 N. E.2d 991 (1943); *Allen v. Holbrook*, 103 Utah 319, 135 P.2d 242, 103 Utah 319 (1943); *Burgess v. Towne*, 13 Wash. App. 954, 538 P.2d 559 (1975); *Linde v. Bentley*, 482 P.2d 121, 123 (Wyo. 1971). *But cf. Pratt v. Gardner*, 56 Mass. (2 Gray.) 63 (1848)(judge immune when court had jurisdiction over subject matter and person). *See* 46 Am. Jur. 2d, Judges, §§72–83; *Id.*, §§72–83 (Supp.).

10. *See infra* §§8.1(g)–8.1(i).

11. E. g., *see supra*, note 9:*Doran, Burgess, Holland,* and *Voll* (false arrest); *Rush, Platz, Rivello, Holland, Grove,* and *Heasley* (false imprisonment); *Rivello* (malicious prosecution); *Randall* and *Bradley* (assault); *Grove* (assault); *Allen* (wrongful search and seizure); *Galindo* (wrongful garnishment); *Rivello* (negligence). *See* also *Comm. v. Cauffel*, 79 Pa. Super. 597, 600–603 (assault and battery) (1922). As to libel and slander, *see infra* §8.3.

NOTES TO §8.1(c)

12. E. g., *see Stump, Bradley, O'Bryan, Turpen, Reverend Mother Pauline, Perry, Singer, Holland, Berry, Conques, Allard, Rush, Lange, Austin,* and *Burgess, supra*, note 9. *See* 48A C. J. S., Judges §§86, 87, nn. 1–3, 22–27, and the accompanying text.

13. E. g., *see Spires v. Bottorf*, 317 F.2d 273 (7th Cir. 1963), *Cert. denied*, 379 U. S. 938 (1964); *Manning v. Ketcham*, 58 F.2d 948 (6th Cir. 1932); *Vickrey v. Donivan*, 59 N. M. 90, 279 P.2d 853 (1955); *Utley v. City of Independence*, 402 P.2d 91 (Ore. En Banc 1965). *See Stump, supra* note 9, 435 U. S. at 356–357; and *Bradley, supra* note 9, 13 Wall. at 351–352. *See* 48A C. J. S., Judges, §§86, 87, nn. 7–8, and the accompanying text.

14. E. g., *Manning, supra* note 13.

15. *See Grove, supra* note 9, 44 N. J. L. at 660–661.

16. E. g., *Taylor, supra* note 9, 1 Harr. (N. J.) at 476, 482; *Beaurain v. Sir William Scott*, 3 Campb. 388, 170 Eng. Rep. 1420(1813). *Cf. Lange, supra*, note 9, 73 N. Y. at 20.

17. E. g., *Galindo, supra*, note 9. *Cf. Conques supra* note 9 (granting immunity for arresting nine-year-old child since judge acted in good faith, even though juvenile jurisdiction was lacking).

NOTES TO §8.1(d)

18. *See infra* notes 19–32. *See* also 46 Am. Jur. 2d, Judges §§72, 82, 83; 48A C.J. S., Judges §§86, 89–90; Restateme. , Torts, 2d §895(d) and comment (c).

19. *See Floyd, supra* note 6, 73 Eng. Repr. at 1306.

20. *See Stump, supra* note 9.

21. *Id*, 435 U. S. at 362.

22. *Id.*, at 362–363.

23. E. g., *Ex Parte Virginia*, 100 U. S. 339, 348–349 (1879) (not immune from

criminal liability); *Doe v. County of Lake Indiana*, 399 F.Supp. 553, 556–558 (N. D. Ind. 1975); *Shore v. Howard*, 414 F.Supp. 379, 385–386 (N. D. Tex. 1976) (not immune from civil liability). *See* 46 Am. Jur. 2d, Judges §§82, 83; Wilson, Judicial Immunity—To Be or Not to Be, 25 How. L. J. 809, 814–815 (1982). *But compare Hodge v. Sharpe*, 287 S. W. 2d 596 (Ky. 1956).

24. *Ex Parte Virginia, supra* note 23.

25. *Id.*, 100 U. S. at 348.

26. E. g., *Garfield v. Palmieri*, 193 F.Supp. 137, 143–144 (S. D. 1961), *Aff'd on same ground*, 297 F.2d 526, 527 (2d Cir. 1962), *cert. denied*, 369 U. S. 871 (1962); *Martin v. Wyzanski*, 191 F.Supp. 931 (D. Mass. 1961).

27. Restatement of Torts, 2d, §585, comment (c).

28. E. g., *Allen, supra* note 9, 135 P.2d at 248. *Cf. Frazier v. Moffat*, 239 P.2d 123 (Cal. App., 2d Dist. 1950) (exercise by magistrate of statutory power to orally order arrest of person committing public offenses in magistrate's presence).

29. *Yates v. Village of Hoffman Estates*, 209 F.Supp. 757 (N. D. Ill. 1962).

30. *Gregory v. Thompson*, 500 F.2d 60 (9th Cir. 1974).

31. *Id.*

32. *Berry v. State*, 400 So.2d 80, 82–84 (Fla. App. 1981).

33. *Supreme Court of Virginia v. Consumers Union of the United States*, 446 U. S. 719 (1980).

34. *Id.* (legislative immunity rule held a bar to recovery of attorney's fees, but not a bar to declaratory and injunctive relief.

NOTES TO §8.1(e)

35. *Stump, supra* note 9, 435 U. S. at 356 (action under 42 U. S. C. §1983); *Pierson, supra* note 9, at 554 (action under 42 U. S. C. §1983); *Smith v. Bacon*, 699 F.2d 434, 436 (8th Cir. 1983) (action under 42 U. S. C. §1983); *Slotnick v. Staviskey*, 560 F.2d 31, 32 (1st Cir. 1977) (action under 42 U. S. C. §1983); *Evans, supra* note 9, 546 P.2d 366; *Turpen, supra* note 9, 56 Cal. at 69; *Reverend Mother Pauline, supra* note 9, 355 P.2d at 1019–1020; *Perry, supra* note 9, 228 P.2d at 19; *McDaniel, supra* note 9, 87 So. at 632; *Smith, supra* note 9, 256 S. E.2d at 628; *Berry, supra* note 32, 400 So.2d at 80; *Mundy v. McDonald*, 216 Mich. 444, 453, 85 N. W. 877, 880–881, 20 A. L. R. 398 (1921); *Lange, supra* note 9, 73 N. Y. at 27. *See also* 48A C. J. S., Judges §87 at 697; 46 Am. Jur. 2d, Judges, §79.

36. E. g., *Anderson, supra* note 8; *Fray, supra* note 8, 132 Eng. Rep. at 217.

37. E. g., *see Pierson, supra* note 9, 386 U. S. at 554.

38. *United States v. Chaplin*, 54 F.Supp. 926, 934 (S. D. Cal. 1944) (granting immunity from criminal liability; remarks applied to immunity from civil liability as well as immunity from criminal liability). *Cf. Conques, supra* note 9, 337 So.2d at 631 (stating reason for granting judge qualified immunity). In Louisiana, the state in which *Conques* was decided, even judicial immunity from civil liability is a qualified immunity. *See infra* note 39, and the accompanying text.

39. *See Berry, supra* note 9, 102 So. at 79; *Cleveland, supra* note 9, 380 So.2d at 105.

40. E. g., *Yasell v. Goff*, 12 F.2d 396, 56 A. L. R. 1239 (2d Cir. 1926), *aff'd*, 275 U. S. 503 (1927); *McGlasker v. Calton*, 397 F. Supp. 525 (M. D. Ala. 1975) *aff'd without opinion*, 524 F.2d 1230 (5th Cir. 1975); *Wilson v. Hirst*, 67 Ariz. 197, 193

P.2d 461 (1948); *Davis v. Burris*, 51 Ariz. 220, 75 P.2d 689 (1938); *Taliaferro v. Contra Costa County*, 182 Cal. App.2d 587, 592, 6 Cal. Rptr. 231, 234 (1960); *Perry, supra* note 9; *Gordon v. District Court of Fifth Judicial District*, 36 Nev. 1, 131 Pac. 134 (1913); *Virtu Boutique, Inc. v. Job's Lane Candle Shop, Inc.*, 51 A. D.2d 813, 380 N. Y. S.2d 263 (2d Dept. 1976); *Whitehead v. De Andrea*, 60 N.Y.S. 2d44 (Sup. Ct., N. Y. Co. 1945); *Landseidel v. Coleman*, 47 N. D. 275, 181 N. W. 593, 13 A. L. R. 1339 (1921); *Waugh v. Dibbens*, 61 Okla. 221, 160 Pac. 589 (1916); *Berry v. Smith*, 148 Va. 424, 139 S. E. 252, 55 A. L. R. 279 (1927); *Burgess v. Towne*, 13 Wash. App. 954, 538 P.2d 559 (1975); *Baylis v. Strickland* (1940) 1 Man. & G. 591, 133 Eng. Rep. 469 (per *Tindal*, C. J.). *See* 46 Am. Jur. 2d, Judges, 979.

41. E. g., *Williamson v. Lacy*, 86 Me. 80, 29 Atl. 943, 945 (1893). *See Webb v. Fisher*, 109 Tenn. 701, 72 S. W. 110, 110–111 (1903); *In re McNair*, 324 Pa. 48, 187 A. 498, 502, 106 A. L. R. 1373 (1936) (magistrates immune from liability for erroneous judicial acts, so long as they act in good faith); and 46 Am. Jur. 2d, Judges §79. *Cf. Broom v. Douglas*, 175 Ala. 268, 57 So. 860, 862 (1912) (inferior court judge acting in excess of jurisdiction but not in absence of general jurisdiction of subject matter is immune only if he acted in good faith; if he had jurisdiction over subject matter, he is immune even if good faith lacking).

NOTES TO §8.1(f)

42. E. g., *Shore, supra* note 23, 414 F.Supp. at 385–386. *See* 48A C. J. S. Judges, §86, nn. 14–17, and the accompanying text.

43. E. g., *Town of Hopkins, South Carolina v. Cobb*, 466 F.Supp. 1215, 1218–1219 (D. S. C. 1979). *See* 48A C. J. S. Judges, §86, pp. 693–694, nn. 18–21, and the accompanying text.

44. E. g., *see Shore supra* note 23, 414 F.Supp. at 385.

45. *See Town of Hopkins, supra* note 43, 466 F.Supp. at 1218–1219.

NOTES TO §8.1(g)

46. Act of April 20, 1871, ch. 22, §1, 17 Stat. 13, 42 U. S. C. §1983.

47. Examples of such Civil Rights Act suits against judges (with the section of 42 U. S. C. sued on set forth in the parentheses following each citation) include, *inter alia*, the following: *Dennis, supra* note 9 (§1983); *Supreme Court of Virginia, supra* note 33 (§1983); *Stump, supra* note 9 (§1983); *Pierson, supra* note 9, (§1983); *Ex parte Virginia, supra* note 23 (Act of March 1, 1875, 18 Stat. pt. 3, 336, prohibiting discrimination in selection of any jury); *Smith, supra* note 35 (§1983); *Harper v. Merckle*, 648 F.2d 848 (5th Cir. 1981) (§1983); *Lopez v. Vanderwater*, 620 F.2d 1229 (7th Cir. 1980) (§1983); *Slavin v. Curry*, 574 F.2d 1256 (5th Cir. 1978) (§§1983, 1985); *Perez v. Borchers*, 567 F.2d 285 (5th Cir. 1978) (§§1983, 1985, 1986, 1988); *Slotnick, supra* note 35 (§1983); *Kurz v. State of Michigan*, 548 F.2d 172 (6th Cir. 1977) (§§1981, 1983, 1985); *Kermit Construction Corp. v. Banco Credito v. Ahorro Ponceno*, 547 F.2d 1 (1st Cir. 1976) (§§1983, 1985, 1986); *Guedry v. Ford*, 431 F.2d 660 (5th Cir. 1970) (§1983); *Haldane v. Chagnon*, 345 F.2d 60 (9th Cir. 1965) (§§1981–1988); *Shore, supra* note 23 (§§1982, 1983, 1985, 1986), *Wade v. Bethesda Hospital*, 337 F.Supp. 671 (U. D. Ohio 1971) (§§1983, 1985(3)). The counts in these

actions based on federal Civil Rights Acts have at times been supplemented by pendent counts alleging common law causes of action. E. g., *Stump, supra* note 9.

48. E. g., *compare McShane v. Moldoran,* 172 F.2d 1016 (6th Cir. 1949) (no immunity as to judges conspiring with others to deprive plaintiff of federal civil rights); *Burt v. City of New York,* 156 F.2d 791 (2d Cir. 1946) (same); *Picking v. Pennsylvania RR,* 151 F.2d 250–251 (3d Cir. 1945) (same); with *Bottone v. Lindsley,* 170 F.2d 705, 707 (10th Cir. 1948) (judge immune unless state court proceeding a complete nullity and judge actuated by specific purpose to effect civil right violation), and *Chaplin, supra* note 38, 54 F.Supp. at 928–932 (absolute immunity from criminal as well as civil liability). *See Block, supra* note 1, at 505.

49. 341 U. S. 367 (1951).

50. E. g., *Stift v. Lynch,* 267 F.2d 237 (7th Cir. 1959); *Cuiksa v. City of Mansfield,* 250 F.2d 700 (6th Cir. 1957); *Kenney v. Fox,* 232 F.2d 288 (6th Cir. 1956); *Tate v. Arnold,* 223 F.2d 782, 785 (8th Cir. 1955); *Cawley v. Warren,* 216 F.2d 74 (7th Cir. 1954); *Peters v. Carson,* 126 F.Supp. 137, 142 (W. D. Pa. 1954); *Ginsburg v. Stern,* 125 F.Supp. 596, 602 (W. D. Pa. 1954), *aff'd per curiam on different ground,* 225 F.2d 245 (3d Cir. 1955); *Morgan v. Sylvester,* 125 F.Supp. 380 (S. D. N. Y. 1954), *aff'd per curiam,* 220 F.2d 758 (2d Cir. 1955); *Souther v. Reid,* 101F.Supp. 806 (E. D. Va. 1951).

51. *Bauers v. Heisel,* 361 F.2d 581 (3d Cir. 1966), *cert. denied,* 386 U. S. 1021 (1967).

52. *Pierson, supra* note 9.

53. *Stump, supra* note 9.

54. *Strawbridge v. Bednarik,* 460 F.Supp. 1171, 1172 (E. D. Pa. 1978).

NOTES TO §8.1(h)

55. E. g., *Harris v. Harvey,* 605 F.2d 330, 335, n.7 (7th Cir. 1979); *Heimbach v. Village of Lyons,* 597 F.2d 344, 347 (2d Cir. 1979); *Slavin, supra* note 47, 574 F.2d at 1264; *Shipp v. Todd,* 568 F.2d 133, 134 (9th Cir. 1978); *Timmerman v. Brown,* 528 F.2d 811, 814 (4th Cir. 1975); *Fowler v. Alexander,* 478 F.2d 694, 696 (4th Cir. 1973); *Shore, supra* note 23 414 F.Supp. at 3385–386. *See Briggs v. Goodwin,* 569 F.2d 10, 15, n.4 (App. D. C. 1977); *Jacobson v. Schaefer,* 441 F.2d 127, 130 (7th Cir. 1971). *Cf. Doe supra* note 23, 399 F.Supp. at 557–559 (sustaining suit for equitable and declaratory relief against ministerial or administrative acts by judicial defendants).

56. *Supreme Court of Virginia, supra* note 33, 446 U. S. at 734–736.

57. *Id.* at 735 and n.13.

NOTES TO §8.1(i)

58. 325 U. S. 91, 107–113(1945).

59. *See Adickes v. S. H. Kress & Co.,* 398 U. S. 144, 152 (1970). *Cf. United States v. Price,* 383 U. S. 787, 794 (1965) (18 U. S. C. §242, the criminal counterpart of §1983, held applicable to private person conspiring with state official).

60. 345 F.2d 601 (9th Cir. 1965).

61. *See* Comment, The Abolition of the Doctrine of Derivative Immunity in the

Fifth Circuit; *Sparks v. Duval County Ranch Co.*, 32 Ala. L. Rev. 251–256 (1980); Comment, Derivative Immunity for Private Attempts to Corrupt the Judiciary in Violation of 42 U. S. C §1983: *Sparks v. Duval County Ranch Co.*, 14 Ga. L. Rev. 344–367 (1980).

62. E. g., *Perez*, *supra* note 47, 567 F.2d at 287; *Kurz*, *supra* note 47, 548 F.2d at 175; *Hansen v. Ahlgrimm*, 520 F.2d 768, 770–771 (7th Cir. 1974); *Guedry*, *supra* note 47, 431 F.2d at 664. *Cf. Hazo v. Geltz*, 537 F.2d 747, 749 (3d Cir. 1976).

63. *White v. Bloom*, 621 F.2d 276, 281 (8th Cir. 1980); *Kermit*, *supra* note 47, 547 F.2d at 3.

64. *Dennis*, *supra* note 9.

NOTES TO §8.2(a)

65. E. g., *Commonwealth v. Tartar*, 239 S. W.2d 265 (Ky. 1951).

66. E. g., *McNair*, *supra* note 41, 187 Atl. at 501.

67. *Id*, 187 Atl. at 501. Contra: *The King v. Saintsbury*, 4 D. & E. 451, 457, 2 Rev. Rep. 433, 438(1791). *Compare*, however, the minority view expressed in a dictum in *Hamilton v. Williams*, 26 Ala. 527, 533 (1855), to the effect that judges are absolutely immune from criminal liability for judicial acts.

68. *See McNair*, *supra* note 41, 187 Atl. at 501.

69. E. g., *Commonwealth v. Robbins*, 232 Ky. 115, 22 S. W.2d 440 (1929) (statutory crime of malfeasance in office); *Bromley v. State*, 136 Ark. 270, 206 S. W. 436 (1918) (statutory crime of willfully violating any provisions of law prescribing duties); *State v. Young*, 504 S. W.2d 672 (Mo. App. 1974) (statutory crime of willfully neglecting any duty enjoined by law). *Contra: In re Tull*, 2 Boyce 126, 78 Atl. 299, 230 (Del. Super. Ct. 1910) (negligent conduct of inferior court judge violated statutory criminal prohibition although not in bad faith).

70. E. g., *State of Arkansas v. Prescott*, 31 Ark. 39 (1876) (offense of willfully violating statute giving judge licensing powers); *Bromley*, *supra* note 69.

71. *State v. Grassie*, 74 Mo. App. 313 (1898) (coercive prevention, by nonlawyer judge of inferior court, of cross examination by counsel of witness by threatening contempt charges held not "willful and malicious oppression by office," since due to ignorance rather than bad faith).

72. E. g., *See McFarland v. State*, 172 Nebr. 251, 109 N. W.2d 397, 403 (1961).

NOTES TO §8.2(b)

73. E. g., *State v. Anderson*, 139 S. W.2d 682 (Ark. 1940) (criminal statute prohibiting county judges from being interested in public construction or repair projects); *Sams v. State*, 356 S. W.2d 273 (Tenn. 1962) (criminal statute prohibiting return of weapon to a defendant convicted of having weapon about him in an unlawful manner).

74. *Price v. Commonwealth*, 132 Va. 582, 110 S. E. 349 (1922) (justice of peace held not guilty of giving away ardent spirits seized under writs issued by him when he merely requested persons in his office to taste the same to see if it constituted ardent spirits)

75. *In re Ex Parte Virginia*, *supra* note 25, 100 U. S. at 348 (1879) (federal civil

rights criminal statute prohibiting exclusion of any person from jury on account of race or color).

76. E. g., *Anderson, supra* note 74; and *Sams, supra* note 74.

77. E. g., *United States v. Manton*, 107 F.2d 834 (2d Cir. 1939); *Braatelien v. United States*, 147 F.2d 888 (8th Cir. 1945); *McDonald v. State*, 329 So.2d 583 (Ala. Crim. Apps. 1975).

78. *See supra* note §8.2(a).

79. E. g.: *Hastings, supra* note 44 (Chapter 6), 681 F.2d at 711, n.17.

NOTE TO §8.2(c)

80. E. g., *Commonwealth v. Cauffel*, 79 Pa. Super. 596 (1922) (*ultra vires* judicial order directing compulsory physical examination of complaining witness in criminal prosecution for alleged sexual violations held not criminal assault and battery of witness by judge when he honestly believed he had right to issue order). *Hastings, supra* note 44 (Chapter 6), 681 F.2d 706, 711, n.17. *See also infra* notes 82–83 and 86–87, and the accompanying text.

NOTES TO §8.2(d)

81. *Ex Parte Virginia, supra* note 23.

82. Act of March 1, 1875, 18 Stat., pt. 3, at 336, which made racial discrimination in jury selection a misdemeanor and prescribed criminal penalties for violations.

83. *Chaplin, supra* note 38.

84. 414 U. S. 488 (1974).

85. *Id.* at 503.

86. *Hastings, supra,* note 44 (Chapter 6).

87. *Id.*, 681 F.2d at 711, n. 17.

88. *Id.*, 681 F.2d at 711, n. 17.

89. E. g., *United States v. Claiborne*, 727 F.2d 842 (9th Cir. 1984); *Hastings, supra* note 44 (Chapter 6), *Isaacs, supra* note 44 (Chapter 6), 493 F.2d at 1140–1144.

NOTES TO §8.3(a)(i)

90. E. g., *O'Bryan v. Chandler*, 496 F.2d 403, 414–415 (10th Cir. 1974); *O'Bryan v. Chandler*, 352 F.2d 987 (10th Cir. 1965); *Blum v. Campbell*, 355 F.Supp. 1226 (D. Md. 1972); *Garfield, supra* note 26; *McKinley v. Simmons*, 274 Ala. 355, 148 So.2d 648 (1963); *Young v. Moore*, 29 Ga. App. 73 (1922); *Ginger v. Bowles*, 369 Mich. 680, 120 N. W.2d 842 (1963); *Mundy v. McDonald*, 216 Mich. 44, 185 N. W. 877 (1921); *Nadeau v. Texas Co.*, 104 Mont. 558, 69 P.2d 593, 594, 111 A. L. R. 874 (1937); *Reller v. Ankeny*, 160 Neb. 47, 68 N. W.2d 686 (1955); *Salomon v. Mahoney*, 271 A. D. 478, 66 N. Y. S.2d 598 (1st Dept. 1946); *Karelas v. Baldwin*, 237 A. D. 265, 261 N. Y. Supp. 518 (2d Dept. 1932); *Childs v. Voris*, 6 Ohio Decis. 75 (Summit Co. C. P. Ct. 1897); *Brodie v. Rutledge*, 1 S. C. (2 S. C. L. 69) 67 (S. C. Apps. 1796); *Brech v. Seacat*, 84 S. D. 264, 170 N. W.2d 348 (1969) (communication to prison warden concerning convict just sentenced by judge); *Houghton v. Humphries*, 85 Wash. 50, 147 Pac. 641 (1915); *Bottomley v. Brougham* (1908) 1

K. B. 584; *Law v. Llewellyn* (1906) 1 K. B. Div. 487; *Scott v. Stansfield* (1868) L. R. 3 Exch. 220. *See* Restatement, Torts, 2d, 585; Comment, Absolute Immunity in Defamation: Judicial Proceedings, 9 Col. L. Rev. 463, 474–475 (1909); Annot., 42 A. L. R.2d 825–832 (1955).

91. E. g., *see Albertson v. Raboff*, 295 P.2d 405, 409 (Cal. In Bank 1956); *Glasson v. Bowen*, 267 Pac. 1066, 1067 (Colo. 1928); *Richeson v. Kessler*, 255 P.2d 707, 709 (Idaho 1953); *Weiler v. Stern*, 67 Ill. App.3d 179, 23 Ill. Dec. 855, 384 N. E.2d 762, 763 (1978); *Wendy's of South Jersey, Inc. v. Blanchard Management Corp. of New Jersey*, 170 N. J. Super. 491, 406 A.2d 1337, 1338–1339 (Ch. 1979); *Devlin v. Greiner*, 147 N. J. Super. 446, 371 A.2d 380, 384 (Law Div. 1977); *Beckenhauer v. Predoehl*, 215 Neb. 347, 338 N. W.2d 618, 620–621 (1983); *Reagan v. Guardian Life Insurance Co.*, 140 Tex. 105, 166 S. W.2d 909, 912–913 (1942); *Krenek v. Abel*, 594 S. W.2d 821, 823 (Tex. Civ. App. 1980); *Bergman v. Hupy*, 64 Wis.2d 747, 221 N. W.2d 898, 900 (1974).

92. *See O'Connell v. Hallinan*, 186 Misc. 997, 64 N. Y. S.2d 198, 199 (Sup. Ct., N. Y. Co. 1946); *Anderson, supra* note 8, 1 Q. B. at 771, per Esher, M. R. *See also* Comment, *supra* note 90, at 475.

NOTES TO §8.3(a)(ii)

93. *See Garfield, supra* note 26, 193 F.Supp. at 142; *Ginger, supra* note 90, 120 N. W.2d at 844; *Murray v. Brancato*, 290 N. Y. 52, 48 N. E.2d 257, 258, 146 A. L. R. 906 (1943) (publication complained of was not in the exercise of a judicial function); *Douglas v. Collins*, 267 N. Y. 557, 196 N. E. 577, 578 (1935); *Salomon, supra* note 90, 66 N. Y. S.2d at 600; *Salomon v. Mahoney*, 64 N. Y. S.2d 300, 303 (Sup. Ct. Bronx Co. 1946); *Brech v. Seacat, supra* note 90, 170 N. W.2d at 349. *See* Restatement, Torts, 2d, §585 and comments (c) and (d).

94. *Bailey v. Dodge*, 28 Kan. 50 (1882).

95. *Brech, supra* note 90.

96. *Douglas v. Collins*, 243 App. Div. 546, 276 N. Y., Supp. 87 (2d Dept. 1934), *rev'g* 152 Misc. 839, 273 N. Y. Supp. 663 (Sup. Ct., Kings Co. 1934), *aff'd.*, 267 N. Y. 557, 196 N. E. 577 (1935). *See also O'Connell, supra* note 92, 64 N. Y. S.2d at 199–200.

97. 290 N. Y. 52, 48 N. E.2d 257, 146 A. L. R. 904, cited *supra* in note 93.

98. 297 F.2d 526 (2d Cir. 1962), *aff'g* 193 F.Supp. 137 (S. D. N. Y. 1961), *cert. denied*, 369 U. S. 871 (1962), cited *supra* in note 26. *Cf. also McGovern v. Martz*, 182 F.Supp. 343, 346–347 (D. D. C. 1960) (dictum stating matter inserted by legislators in Congressional Record is absolutely privileged).

99. *Bradford v. Pette*, 204 Misc. 308 (Sup. Ct., Queens Co. 1953).

100. *Id.*, at 318.

101. *Cf. Kraushaar v. Lavin*, 39 N. Y. S.2d 880 (Sup. Ct., Queens Co. 1943) (examination of documents away from courthouse, pursuant to court order, held a judicial proceeding, making statements of parties absolutely privileged if evoked by counsel, but not if gratuitously interjected).

102. See *Salomon v. Mahoney, supra* note 93, 64 N. Y. S.2d at 303

NOTES TO §8.3(a)(iii)

103. E. g., *Wahler v. Schroeder*, 9 Ill. App.3d 505, 292 N. E.2d 521, 523 (1972) (communication by party need only be relevant to subject of inquiry and need not be relevant to any of the issues); *Thourot v. Hartnett*, 56 N. J. Super. 306, 152 A.2d 858 (App. Div. 1959) (same); *Zarato v. Cortiner*, 553 S. W.2d 652 (Tex. Civ. App. 1977). *See* Restatement, Torts, 2d, §586, and comment (c); *id.*, §587 and comment (c); *id.*, §588 and comment (c). Some cases, however, merely state that any communication made by a party, any witness made in the course of a judicial proceeding is absolutely privileged even if not relevant to any of the issues in the proceedings, without specifying that the communication must be relevant to the proceeding. E. g., *Krenek, supra* note 91, 594 S. W.2d at 823; *Zarato, supra* this note, 553 S. W.2d at 655.

104. E. g., *Wahler, supra* note 103, 292 N. E.2d at 523; *Reller supra* note 90, 68 N. W.2d at 691. *See* Restatement, Torts, 2d, §585, and comment (e) (defamatory matter must have "some reference to the judicial function that the judge is performing").

105. *Karelas, supra* note 90, 261 N. Y. S. at 520–523 (reversing judgment in slander action against judge for intemperate and insulting remarks made during arraignments and found by jury to be irrelevant); *Houghton, supra* note 90, 147 Pac. at 642–643; *Scott, supra* note 90. *See Rice v. Coolidge*, 121 Mass. 393, 395 (1876); *Kraushaar, supra* note 101, 39 N. Y. S.2d at 882.

NOTES TO §8.3(a)(iv)

106. *Wahler, supra* note 103, 292 N. E.2d at 523; *O'Regan v. Schermerhorn*, 50 A.2d 10, 21 (1946). *See* Restatement, Torts, 2d, §585, comment (f).

107. E.g., *O'Regan, supra* note 106 (judicial officers), 50 A. 2d at 21; *Wahler, supra* note 103, 292 N. E. at 523 (parties). *See Runge v. Franklin*, 72 Tex. 585, 105 W. 721, 724 (1889).

108. *Kent v. Connecticut Bank & Trust Co. N. A.*, 386 So.2d 902 (Fla. App., 2d Dist. 1980) (jurisdictional amount lacking); *Hager v. Major*, 186 S. W.2d 564 (Mo. App. 1945) (same). *See* Annot., 158 A. L. R. 592–595 (1945). *But compare* Annot., 42 A. L. R.2d 825, 831 (1955).

109. E. g., *Kent, supra* note 108.

110. *Id.*, 386 So.2d at 903.

NOTES TO §8.3(a)(v)

111. E. g., Cal. Civ. Code §47(2); Idaho Code §6–710(2); Mont. Code §27–1–804(2); N. D. Cent. Code §14–02–05(2); Okla. Stat. Ann. tit. 21, §771; S. D. Comp. Laws Ann. §20–11–5(2); Utah Code Ann. §45–2–3(2); P. R. Laws Ann. §3144.

112. E. g., *Ascherman v. Notenson*, 23 Cal. App.3d 861, 100 Cal. Rptr. 656 (1972) (statements by witness in witness interview); *Hughes v. O'Connor*, 313 N. W.2d 463 (S. D. 1981); *Janklow v. Keller*, 90 S. D. 322, 241 N. W. 2d 364 (1976) The cases cited in this note construed the California and South Dakota statutes

as requiring that, in order to be absolutely privileged, a communication made in a judicial proceeding must not only be pertinent to the proceeding and concerning participants in it, but also it must be made to achieve the objects of the proceeding.

113. E. g., Cal. Civ. Code §47(1); Idaho Code Ann. §6–710; Mont. Code §27–1–804(1); N. D. Cent. Code §14–02–05(1); Okla. Stat. Ann. tit. 21, §771; S. D. Comp. Laws Ann. §20–11–5(1); Utah Code Ann. §45–2–3(1); P. R. Laws Ann. §3144.

114. *See Bradford, supra* notes 99–100, and the accompanying text. *See also* note 98, and the accompanying text. *But compare* note 97, and the accompanying text.

NOTES TO §8.3(b)

115. E. g., *see State v. Dedge*, 101 N. J. L. 131, 127 Atl. 539, 544 (1925).

116. *Id.*

117. E. g., *Rex v. Skinner*, Loft 54, 55, 98 Engl. Repr. 529 (K. B. 1772) (indictment of judge for defamation quashed on ground of absolute immunity); *Gilbert v. People*, 1 Den. (N. Y.) 41 (1845); *Comm. v. Culver*, 1 Clark (Pa.) 361 (1843).

118. E. g., La. Rev. Stat. Ann. §14–50.

119. E. g., Cal. Penal Code §258 (Supp.) (criminal slander provisions exempt "words offered in the proper discharge of an official duty, or in any legislative or judicial proceeding"); Okla. Stat. Ann. tit. 21, §772 (criminal libel provisions exempt any publication made in any judicial proceeding). *But compare* Cal. Penal Code §§248–257 (criminal libel provisions, which omit any express exemption as to judges or judicial proceedings).

120. E. g., Ga. Code §16–11–40 (defining defamation as defamation committed "without a privilege to do so"); Minn. Stat. Ann. §609.675(2) (Supp.) (criminal defamation is justified when "the communication is absolutely privileged"); N. D. Cent. Code §12.1–15–01(2)(b) (defense to prosecution for willful defamation if the allegedly defamatory matter is contained in a privileged communication); Ore. Rev. Stat. §163.605(2)(b) (defense to prosecution for criminal defamation, when "the publication is protected by an absolute or qualified privilege").

121. E. g., Colo. Gen. Stat. §18–13–105; Ill. Stat. Ann. tit. 38, §§27–1 to 27–2; Kan. Stat. Ann. §21–4004; Nev. Rev. Stat. §§200.510–200.560; S. C. Code §16–7–150; Tenn. Code Ann. §39–2–401 to 404; Utah Code Ann. §76–9–404.

122. Statutes conditioning the defense of truth on good motives and justifiable ends include, for example, Ill. Stat. Ann. tit. 38, §27–2; Nev. Rev. Stat. §200.510(3); V. I. Stat. Ann. tit. 14, §1174. Statutes not attaching such conditions to the defense of truth include, for example, Colo. Gen. Stat. §18–13–105; Kan. Stat. Ann. §21–4004(2); S. C. Code §16–7–150.

123. E. g., Ala. Code Ann. §§13A–11–161 to 163; Cal. Penal Code §§248–257 (pertaining to criminal libel); Idaho Code §§18–4801 to 18–4809 (pertaining to criminal libel); Utah Code Ann. §§76–9–501 to 509 (pertaining to criminal libel and slander); V. I. Stat. Ann. tit. 14, §§1171–1183 (pertaining to criminal libel; defense of truth plus certain qualified privileges other than truth).

124. E. g., *see Bearman v. People*, 16 P.2d 425, 426–427 (Colo. 1932) (recognizing qualified common law privilege for communications between persons mutually interested in the subject matter of the communication, although criminal libel statute provided for only one defense, that of truth when published with good motives and

for justifiable ends.); and *People v. Fuller*, 238 Ill. 116, 87 N. E. 336 (1909) (recognizing qualified common law privilege for fair and reasonable criticism of conduct of public officials, although criminal libel statute provided only a single defense, that of truth.). *See also* Colo. L. 1921, §6830 (the Colorado criminal libel statute in effect at the time of *Bearman*); Hurd's Ill. Rev. St. 1908, c. 38 (Ill. Crim. Code §179) (the Illinois criminal libel statute in effect when *Fuller* was decided).

Index

About the Authors

MARVIN COMISKY is the Managing Partner of Blank, Rome, Comisky & McCauley, one of the nation's largest law firms. He received his law degree from the University of Pennsylvania Law School and a Doctor of Law degree from the Dickinson College School of Law. He has served as Chancellor of the Philadelphia Bar Association and President of the Pennsylvania Bar Association. He is a member of the American College of Trial Lawyers and the International Academy of Trial Lawyers.

PHILIP C. PATTERSON is of Counsel to Duryea, Duryea, and Zion in Ardmore, Pennsylvania. He received his LL.B. from Yale Law School. A member of the Pennsylvania and California bars, he is Past Chairman of the Antitrust Committee of the Section on Corporation, Banking, and Business Law of the Philadelphia Bar Association.